The Venice Variations

The Venice Variations

Tracing the Architectural Imagination

Sophia Psarra

UCLPRESS

First published in 2018 by
UCL Press
University College London
Gower Street
London WC1E 6BT

Available to download free: www.ucl.ac.uk/ucl-press

A CIP catalogue record for this book is available from The British Library.

ISBN: 978-1-78735-241-4 (Hbk.)
ISBN: 978-1-78735-240-7 (Pbk.)
ISBN: 978-1-78735-239-1 (PDF)
ISBN: 978-1-78735-242-1 (epub)
ISBN: 978-1-78735-243-8 (mobi)
ISBN: 978-1-78735-244-5 (html)
DOI: https://doi.org/10.14324/111.9781787352391

To Tony
for 'not suffering from his imagination'

Preface

The need to imagine an ideal place for living in defines a basic human condition deeply embedded in our cultural memory. From Paradise and the myth of Arcadia through to the twentieth-century Modernist utopias and contemporary ideas about sustainability, imagining better urban environments remains persistently and remarkably relevant, raising recurring questions. How do cities evolve as complex spaces nurturing both urban creativity and the fortuitous art of discovery? By which mechanisms do they foster imagination and innovation? How do they adapt and sustain themselves over time? For architects, planners or simply anyone interested in better buildings and cities, these questions concern the interaction of the urban places created collectively with the power of conscious design and the individual imagination. But while past utopias were conceived in terms of an ideal geometry, contemporary definitions of exemplary models of urban design seek technological solutions and paradigms of optimal organisation. *The Venice Variations* explores Venice as a prototypical city that may hold unique and holistic answers to the ancient narrative of utopia. Venice was not the result of a preconceived ideal, but the pragmatic outcome of informal social and economic networks of communication. Its urban creativity, though, came to represent the quintessential combination of place, buildings and institutions of its time.

Through a discussion of Venice and two works owing their inspiration to this city – Italo Calvino's *Invisible Cities* and Le Corbusier's Venice Hospital – the book describes Venice as a system that emerges like the outcome of a highly probabilistic algorithm, that is, a structure with a small number of rules capable of producing a large number of variations. In *The Venice Variations* I pursue an uncompromising argument suggesting that, deep down, the rapidly escalating processes of urban development in train around our big cities share many of the motivations for survival, shelter and trade that brought Venice into existence. Rather than seeing these places as problems to be solved, we should regard them as complex systems with the capacity to evolve, as Venice did from its unprepossessing origins in the marshes of the Venetian lagoon to the 'model city' that endured a thousand years. The book thus attempts to free Venice from stereotypical representations, to reveal its generative capacity to inform potential other 'Venices' in the future.

Acknowledgements

I remember the *Theofania* well, the Feast of Epiphany or the Feast of Lights, the quayside liturgical ceremony incorporating the Blessing of the Waters. Resplendent in his gold embroidered vestments, the priest would hurl the sacred cross into the sea. Peals of church bells rang out as teenage divers plunged eagerly into the freezing water in a race to recover it. On summer mornings, the market vendors' voices were drowned out by the ships' horns echoing ashore from the sea. On bank holidays, the crowds cheered at students and scouts marching with flags fluttering in the wind. In the evenings, the places of worship and the fishermen's boats turned on their lights, like seafaring vessels of souls starring the dark sea. This was a city nurtured by an intimate and time-honoured relationship with the water, ritual and trade.

The Venice Variations is inspired by two things: Italo Calvino's *Invisible Cities*, a prose poem for cities, and my fascination with living, working cities. I grew up in a coastal town bordering the southern Ionian Sea amidst the remnants of the Mycenaean, Spartan, Roman, Byzantine, Frankish, Venetian and Ottoman empires. Of all empires, Venice was the most immanent, from everyday customs to winged lions on fortifications and a local dialect resonant with a legacy of 'winged words'. We had, of course, forgotten, but language 'remembered', as we took strolls on the *Molo* and ate fresh *dolci* and delicious preserved *naranza*. Venice lay veiled from consciousness, until the day I scrutinised a map of the city, floating in its distant lagoon. Some instinct told me to start work from the squares of the *Serenissima*; from the *campi* (squares), where the spectacle of the water meets the façade of the church; where the stroller encounters the grocery boat, and the gondolier picks up his passengers at the steps by the bridge. My interest in Venice ignited at that moment, from that intuition derived from four thousand years of Greco-Roman tradition, from the patios with the deep wells, the feast days and the processions. Other places – the grand mansions with their waterfront loggias, and their Venetian shutters scoured by sea salt, the walled gardens, the citrus trees, the anachronous train station, the warehouses harbouring raisins and figs, the textile workshops, the cigarette factories, the sandy marshlands, the mills, the river with its mud flats and reeds – were filling the memory gaps, bridging the spaces in between.

The place I set out to explore in the book is not tourist Venice, historic Venice or today's Venice as a museum, but Venice as a cosmopolitan working city, built on water by the forces of travel, ritual, immigration and commerce. The book interrogates the imagination in Venice, seeing this city as the prototype for other cities. Venice is one of the most intense manifestations of how urban places are founded and evolve, revealing, to those prepared to enquire, the operations and the creativity that bring them into being. What I pursue here is the integration of the imagination with analytical explication, the synthesis of architecture, urbanism, literature and the extension of Calvino's literary ideas into an architectural and urban discourse. In the realm of architecture there is no provincial separation, no adversarial loyalties to either buildings or cities, creative practice or analytical work, imaginative or rational thought. There is only the vital drive to create and illuminate, by whatever means, memory and drawing, history and analysis, numbers and words, reflection combined with speculation and the imaginative synthesis of all these complementary modes of thought.

In recent years, I have become increasingly concerned about the regeneration of de-industrialised areas, the economic adversities and land privatisation that threaten our urban civilisation with cultural amnesia. It is not nostalgia for the pre-modern or modern industrial past that motivates this book, but a desire to rethink cities so that their generative activities once more bestow a diversity of economic opportunities, products and people; to revisit and rethink the history of their evolution; to unlock our cities from the sterility of being frozen in time; to restore their natural ability to continuously adapt their productiveness, their public spaces and civic democracy, without the artificial imposition of iconic architecture, corporate offices and postmodern museums; to defy the exclusive, and obsessive, celebration of economic performance, stripping architecture bare of political and social significance and the potential for imaginative cultural innovation. The result, paradoxically, is that the actuality of Venice, the city in a gradual process of political and economic decline since the fifteenth century, is replaced by something even more potent and more universal – the idea of Venice. I hope that Venice and the idea of Venice live long, for the benefit of all cities, and for all of us.

The Venice Variations advances an argument that cities, buildings and books are all results of individual and collective effort. Many hands and minds have helped me to negotiate Venice's tangled paths. I am grateful to Chris Penfold and his colleagues at UCL Press for their continuous support for this project and more broadly the general project of open access publishing. I would like to thank the Bartlett School of Architecture for funding a sabbatical dedicated to producing my manuscript and to colleagues who generously covered for me in my absence. I am indebted to the two anonymous reviewers of the manuscript for their encouragement and critical evaluation. I also want to thank in particular Alan Penn, Jane Rendell and John Peponis, each of whom has provided me in their own way with inspiration and support; and Margarita Greene, Murray Fraser, Sam Griffiths, Daniel Koch, Marina Lathouri and Patricia Austin, who invited me to lecture about Venice, providing opportunities to test out the rigour of these propositions and their appeal to students.

I would like to thank Jonathan Smith for his helpful edits, while secluded on 'vacation' on the Greek island of Samothraki, enhancing the manuscript with his powerful grasp of language and sense for 'winged words'. Likewise, I am thankful to Stefania Maggiato at the Cartoteca of IUAV, the SAND North GIS Lab at the Taubman College of Architecture and Urban Planning, University of Michigan, and the librarians of UCL. My appreciation and gratitude go to all those who have given me permission to reproduce their images in this book.

I was fortunate to have the warm friendship and unquestioned support of Tania Oramas Dorta and Conrad Kickert, who, at various times, carried out analyses of Venice and GIS mapping; Athina Lazaridou, who constructed the three-dimensional illustrations of Venice and the buildings of Palladio and Le Corbusier; Kirsty McMullan, who made many of the maps and drawings in this book more attractive and legible; Tasos Varoudis, who helped with the analysis of the Piazza San Marco; Olimpia Cermasi, who secured many of the image permissions; and Garyfallia Palaiologou, who provided me with the first drawings of the Venice Hospital. My PhD students Mariana Pestana, Nazila Maghzian, Marcela Aragüez and Pinar Aycaç provided me with intellectual nourishment throughout, an invaluable support. Kimon Krenz, Fani Kostourou and Caue Capillè inspired me with their adventurous spirit and dedication to the integration of the design studio with analysis and research.

Special thanks go to my first teachers and mentors at UCL, Bill Hillier and Julienne Hanson, whose ideas provided me with intellectual inspiration throughout. The colleagues who have offered various kinds of support and intellectual stimulation deserve my gratitude: Sonit Bafna, Michael Benedikt, Meta Berghauser Pont, John Bingham-Hall, Ben

Campkin, Caroline Constant, Ava Fatah, Sean Hanna, Penelope Haralambidou, Teresa Heitor, Nick Helm, Jonathan Hill, Frederico de Holanda, Deborah Howard, Roger Hubeli, Aarati Kanekar, Kayvan Karimi, Jian Kattein, Joss Kiely, Daniel Koch, Perry Kulper, Julie Larsen, Ann Legeby, Iris Likourioti, Yeoryia Manolopoulou, Lars Marcus, Vinicius Netto, Alan Penn, Barbara Penner, John Peponis, Peg Rawes, Kerstin Sailer, David Seamon, Tania Sengupta, Richard Sennett, Adam Sharr, Bob Sheil, Ermal Shpuza, Lydia Soo, Phil Steadman, Vaso Trova, Brian Trump, Laura Vaughan, Reem Zako, and all colleagues and students at the Bartlett School of Architecture.

Finally, I thank my husband Tony for rescuing me from the 'stones of Venice' with his sense of humanity, patience and unstinting support. *The Venice Variations* is for him.

Sophia Psarra
London, 2018

Contents

Illustrations

Introduction

Chapter 1

Chapter 2

Chapter 3

Chapter 4

Chapter 5

Figure 0.0 Venice. View of the city and San Marco Basin (Bacino). Drawing by Athina Lazaridou

Introduction: Between authored architecture and the non-authored city

> To distinguish the other cities' qualities, I must speak of a first city that remains implicit. For me it is Venice.
>
> Italo Calvino, *Invisible Cities*

Three artefacts

In 1972 the Italian writer Italo Calvino published his most acclaimed work of fiction, a novel about cities that made a seminal impression on architects and the architectural imagination (Figure 0.1a).[1] Written as a prose poem about cities, *Invisible Cities* recounts how Marco Polo describes to Kublai Khan, the emperor of Mongolia, the cities of the great Khan's own empire. These are not cities Polo has visited, but places he invents in his mind. Kublai soon realises that every time Polo speaks of a city he is saying something about Venice, and that all the cities he describes are merely variations, achieved by an interchange of elements from his native city. Calvino wrote this fictional tale at a time of urban crisis, when architects, urban thinkers and planners were envisioning bold alternatives, drawing attention to imaginative projection as a key resource in constructing better places for social habitation.[2] The significance of Venice in this fiction lies less with Marco Polo as a Venetian explorer, and more with Venice as an archetypal model for the creative imagination (Figure 0.1b). Having evolved from a conglomeration of islands, Venice opened up to classical architecture in the Renaissance, acting as an interface between the conscious creativity of artists and architects and the unconscious collective creativity that combined to produce an extraordinary urban setting. Centuries later, it would again challenge its own orthodoxy by inviting Le Corbusier, in

Figure 0.1 (a) The Invisible Cities Project, an illustration project inspired by Italo Calvino's *Invisible Cities*. Illustration by Karina Puente

Figure 0.1 (b) Aerial view of Venice. Image by Robert Simmon, NASA's Earth Observatory (public domain), via Wikimedia Commons

Figure 0.1 (c) Le Corbusier. Model of the Venice Hospital. © FLC/ADAGP, Paris and DACS, London 2017

the post-war period, to propose a design for a modern hospital. Inspired by Venice – and in striking contrast to his early-twentieth-century visions of a clean slate approach – the archetypical Modernist proposed a radical design, re-thinking architecture and the city as adaptable urban environments (Figure 0.1c).

Not only have urban conditions changed since Calvino's text and Le Corbusier's projects, but so too have the forces shaping cities and architecture. The upsurge in urbanisation and globalisation, the effects of climate change and the rise in social inequality call into question where we live and how we build, demanding new models for urban development. Yet, our confidence in addressing these questions through conventional design is increasingly waning. With the aid of digital technology new approaches have emerged, adopting direct analogies with natural systems through scientific theories of complexity. Trapped between Modernistic utopias of the twentieth century and twenty-first-century technocratic utopias, our everyday urban realities languish, in pressing need of imagination and innovation. More importantly, they require models that link the creative ideas of designers and experimental scientists with the richly woven tapestry of collective human creations, conventions, customs, culture, social relationships, behaviour, artefacts and artistry that produced our urban environments in the past and has the potential to enhance them in the future. However promising the new technologies may be, they will be more effective in improving wellbeing if they engage with the imagination of architects, the rich cultural evolution of urban societies and the lived lives of people.

Rather than providing a new manifesto for the age-old concept of utopia, *The Venice Variations* sees in the three artefacts – Venice the city, *Invisible Cities* and the Venice Hospital – an opportunity to explore architecture and cities as a matter of authorship, asking how they are generated, how they function, who makes them and for what purpose. By contrasting the creative authorship of a work of architecture and a work of literature, both drawing on Venice as their inspirational source, the book explores the creative potential existing in this city, and the deeper insights it holds for other cities and architecture. This subject requires looking deeper, beyond conventional, superficial impressions, at Venice itself and the two other artefacts. What is it, apparently implicit in Venice, that has the generative power to inspire such a wide range of imaginative variations? If Venice provided inspiration for two of the twentieth century's most creative minds, what are the mechanisms by which this was accomplished, and how do *Invisible Cities* and the Hospital inspire the imagination? Beyond its being a unique city in an unimaginable setting, and over and above having an extraordinary outward appearance, what in this city so powerfully stimulates creative invention?

Why Venice?

It may be that the creative potency of Venice emanates from its exceptional capacity to contain a multiplicity of visions and systems of reality, provoking imaginative engagement. This idea invokes the concepts of actual, imaginary and alternative possible worlds, extensively explored by Calvino in his literary text and Le Corbusier in his Hospital building. Calvino described *Invisible Cities* as 'a many-faceted structure in which every brief text is close to the others', as in 'a network in which one can follow multiple routes and draw multiple, ramified conclusions'.[3] There are many instances of mesh-like images and branching routes in his cities, expressing the reality of Venice's urban networks as a model for the fiction. However, Venice is mentioned only once in the text, while the role that the city plays in *Invisible Cities* remains curiously enigmatic.

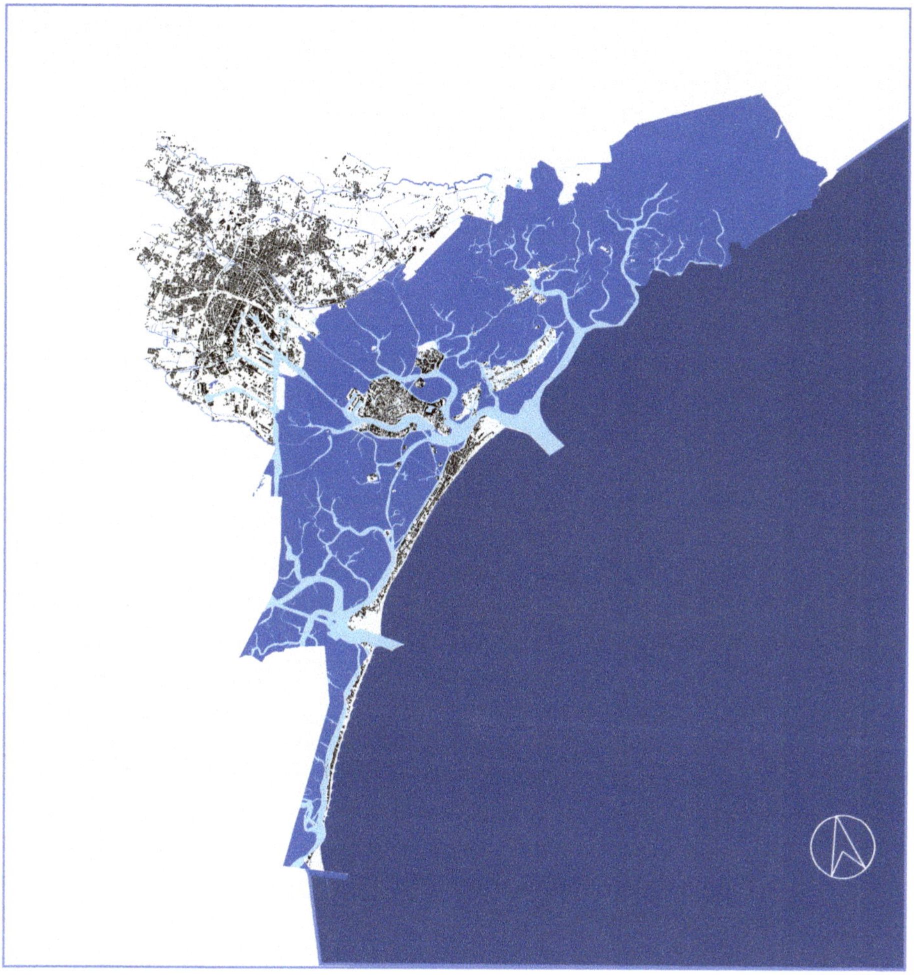

Figure 0.2 Venice in the Lagoon. Drawing by the author. GIS data provided by Università IUAV di Venezia – Laboratorio di Cartographia e GIS

Venice is a non-typical yet paradigmatic city. Its urban development is a story of the conquering of space where once there were only mud flats and shifting sands. In contrast to the instability of its boundaries and its foundations, as a human institution it has a long and stable history. It is a self-made city on the margins of territorial borders and a fragile ecosystem (Figure 0.2). In the annals of the evolution of urban creativity, in the fourteenth and fifteenth centuries it is Florence rather than Venice that is considered as one of the world's most creative places.[4] The fifteenth century was the time when Venice began to fall into decline, and it thereafter continued to diminish in power, relegated to serving Romantic fantasy in the industrial revolution and mass tourism at the time of intense globalisation. To many people, today's Venice is about a maze of alleys, spaces crowded with people, cruise ships dwarfing dilapidated palaces, looming environmental threats, an egregious lack of modern conveniences and inhabitants in defence against tourist invasion.

Yet, Venice in its heyday had formed a network of trading contacts halfway across the world and remained inviolate for a thousand years as the 'richest, safest, best-ordered and most beautiful city'.[5] Just as Venice defied its geographic location by flourishing in the precarious conditions of the lagoon, so it has commanded astonishment disproportionate to its faded significance and multiplicity of problems. As John Julius Norwich explains, it has unchanging qualities, retaining 'the same appearance it had not only in the days of Canaletto, but even in those of Carpaccio and Gentile Bellini'.[6] For Norwich, this triumph over time is an extraordinary phenomenon for any city, and in the context of the most beautiful city in the world, a miracle. Despite the enduring uncertainty about its physical survival and the challenges in regenerating itself, Venice has never ceased to inspire architects, artists and writers. Five hundred years after its zenith, it still contains lessons for other cities as a resilient urban environment. Scholars, artists and practitioners alike identify something within Venice that is capable of nurturing human ingenuity. Lewis Mumford saw its urban structure as involving a series of bold adaptations, which had universal application.[7] Le Corbusier admired its functional efficiency in intersecting and separating the aquatic realm and terrestrial routes and attributed the inspiration for his Venice Hospital to the Venetian typologies of *calle* (street) and *campiello* (square).[8] Kevin Lynch described Venice as the 'imageable' city par excellence.[9] For Calvino, Venice was a prototype for the future. Having bypassed the phase in human history where most people believed the future belonged to the car, Venice was for him in a better position to overcome the urban crisis and form a model for new developments out of its own experience.[10]

It is not only the questionable future of Venice that affects us, but also the timeless contribution it makes to architecture and cities, two of the leading expressions of culture in modern society. Venice belongs to a historical period of intense cultural creativity that still influences our own contemporary culture and its attitude towards innovation. If the civilisation of the Renaissance, as Jacob Burckhardt wrote, 'is the mother of our own, and [its] influence is still at work with us', Venice is an unprecedented example of urban innovation and collective imagination.[11] Like the ancient artefacts of epic and myth, it sustains its universal relevance over and above its transient conditions. *The Venice Variations* neither idealises this city nor seeks to provide solutions to its contemporary problems. It rather sets out from a different premise. If, as humans, we are wired to instinctively seek out ideal places and patterns through architecture, literature, art, science, technology and mythology, Venice is one of those artefacts, which even when we remain in relative ignorance about how they evolved and where they come from, provide us with models and constructs, paradigms of experience and terms of comparison, revitalising the imagination. Taken in its totality, as an artefact across space and time, Venice is like great architecture and great literature, locally communal and eternally global. It belongs to everyone and affects us all. We can begin to address the question of how Venice stimulates invention by looking at the ways in which architects in the past responded to the creative potency of the city in the quest for developing new thinking.

Organic, Classical, Modern

Just as the contemporary explosion of digital technologies has changed the ways in which architecture is produced, the invention of architectural notation in the fifteenth century brought about major cultural shifts and architectural innovations. If today's architects – aided by computational tools – create infinite varieties of forms and workflows of seamless integration, architects in the Renaissance were rediscovering a treasure trove of ancient structures and antique ruins, including the work of Vitruvius, the Roman author whose *Ten Books on Architecture* (*De architectura*) were the only comprehensive treatise from ancient times to survive.[12] The need to record and re-imagine classical fragments through drawings and language led to a clear distinction between the practice of design and the craft of building. Ultimately, this brought about the emergence of architectural design distinct from the artisanal building traditions. The new architecture appeared in the traditional context of the medieval cities and landscapes of Italy. As with the advent of the printed books that started to replace manuscripts, architectural drawings and texts began replacing the formerly integrated process of design and building. This process continued uninterrupted until the arrival of computer aided design (CAD) and digital technology. At that time, Venice and the Veneto were home to more than 450 printers, publishers and booksellers, who fuelled with books, woodcuts and engravings the interest in the ancient world shown by architects and scholars. Before the Renaissance it is rarely possible to identify the creative personalities of individual architects in Venice. As Deborah Howard explains, 'the fact that the title *architectus* was not used in Venice until as late as the 1470s, apart from one known isolated example in 1455, is symbolic of the change in attitude that came about at this time'.[13]

But it was Venice and not the ancient capital of Rome or the creative city of Florence that became in the Renaissance the centre of Vitruvian studies. Vitruvius's *Ten Books* was first printed in Venice. Two distinguished architects, Sebastiano Serlio (1475–1553) and Andrea Palladio (1508–1580), who developed the most important of the architectural theories based on Vitruvius in the sixteenth century, lived in Venice for a time, and had their books on architecture printed there.[14] However, it took Venice longer than other Italian cities to accept the new architectural style, as the city was strongly mindful of its inherited building traditions.[15] But the innovations eventually took root, from Tullio Lombardo's miniature of a temple front in the Basilica of San Marco to the public buildings of Mauro Codussi, Jacopo Sansovino and Palladio, including the last's villas for the Venetian elite in the Veneto, the agricultural hinterland of Venice.[16] It is from Venice and the Veneto that Palladio's architecture spread throughout the world, resulting in what is now known as Palladianism, or Palladio-inspired Classicism.

Venice has never ceased to be a centre of attention, with its colourful mix of buildings and diverse architectural styles. But nowhere does the city express the contradictory trends between the vernacular and innovation more powerfully than in the striking contrast of Baldassare Longhena's and Andrea Palladio's white churches in Dorsoduro and the islands of San Giorgio Maggiore and the Giudecca with the medieval urban fabric (Figure 0.3). No other city can more characteristically exhibit the break that architecture made with the past and its capacity to imagine bold alternatives. Clearly recognising this contrast and Palladio's place in architectural history, Le Corbusier inscribed his project for the Venice Hospital on a map together with Palladio's church of San Giorgio Maggiore, showing that he was measuring himself against a lineage that stretched from Vitruvius to the classical architect (Figure 0.4). Le Corbusier's map documents three significant instances in the history of the urban formation of Venice: first, Venice's organic collection of islands and buildings embedded in the medieval fabric; second, Palladian Classicism framed by the lagoon, pointing through subtle alignments of monuments and their frontages to a coordinated scenography of the major civic spaces of the city; and third, his post-war concern with evolutionary urban growth, through his Hospital project, which, unlike early Modernism, saw the city as a single project of continuous adaptation.

Through this map, Le Corbusier offered a condensation of three major paradigms that influenced not just Venice, but also the canon of Western cities and architecture in general: the Organic (Venice's

Figure 0.3 Baldassare Longhena's Santa Maria della Salute with Giuseppe Benoni's Punta della Dogana (the Sea Customs House) in the foreground and Andrea Palladio's Redentore in the background. Image by Supechilum, CC BY-SA 4.0 via Wikimedia Commons

Figure 0.4 Le Corbusier. Site map of the Venice Hospital project. © FLC/ADAGP, Paris and DACS, London 2017

urban fabric), the Classical (Palladio's San Giorgio Maggiore) and the Modern (the Venice Hospital). Venice combines these three key practices through which architecture as a liberal art meets the evolutionary processes of the medieval urban fabric.[17] Is there something in the physical structure of Venice that inspires new models, unconsciously through the city's pattern of urban growth, and consciously through urban design and architecture? The following sections trace how Venice stimulates creative invention by looking at *Invisible Cities* and Le Corbusier's Hospital.

The city and the imagination as networks

This question of the architectural imagination is at the core of all inquiry about cities and architecture, from ideal cities in the past to contemporary ideas about sustainable buildings and settlements. It presupposes models of the city as dynamic configurations. This is because cities like Venice are transformed gradually from within, by the collective actions of people, rather than being generated by a single mind, or centralised as a single representation. If ideal cities were demonstrations of an ideal geometry, Venice's creativity flourished in its everyday spaces and irregular urban fabric.[18] Fundamental to this conception of the city are its urban networks, establishing systems of connectivity and performance as the products of many hands over an extended period. The idea of approaching buildings and cities as networks is increasingly relevant with the rise of digital technology, which strengthens communication, interactivity, variability of form and a public participatory approach to design. But rather than being a new concept, the notion of networks has been many years in the making. Ever since writer and activist Jane Jacobs studied the city as organised complexity, many architects, urban designers, critics and scientists have described it as a network – or a system of networks – and studied its properties of self-organisation.[19] Issuing an attack on contemporary urban policy, Jacobs in her seminal book *The Death and Life of Great American Cities* presented the term 'organised complexity' as an answer to the question posed by the chapter 'The Kind of Problem a City Is'. She argued that cities present situations where many parameters vary simultaneously in interconnected ways, a stance that draws influences from complexity theory, cybernetics and systems thinking.

It was this perception of the city that influenced Calvino in *Invisible Cities*. Calvino wrote this fiction during a period in which architects were experimenting with networks, addressing the absence of imaginative models in the speculative processes of urbanisation. He had also absorbed influences from the Oulipo literary group (*Ouvroir de Littérature Potentielle*), which used mathematical constraints to invent new poems and fiction. Calvino discussed the combinatorial algorithmic potential of *Invisible Cities* in *Six Memos for the Next Millennium* and in *Cybernetics and Ghosts*.[20] The imagination, he wrote, 'is a kind of electronic machine that takes account of all possible combinations and chooses the ones that are appropriate to a particular purpose'.[21] Calvino's interest in the visionary charge as combinatorial network included 'a repertory of what is potential, and what is hypothetical, of what does not exist and has never existed, and perhaps will never exist but might have existed'.[22] Inspired as much by folk tales as by canonical literary texts, he situated the imagination within three frameworks: first, a conceptual system of interconnections among elements capable of imaginative stimulation; second, a project that includes actual and possible works; and third, works that are authored or collectively produced by word of mouth. His understanding of literature as a combinatorial game meant that he saw it as an open system, echoing with sounds and words from all of history, culture and experience.

Calvino's definition of the imagination calls attention to the fact that while artists, critics and writers have widely engaged the relationship between high art and everyday culture, from the outset architectural design has been – with few exceptions – distinct from the anonymous processes by which buildings and cities are produced at a large scale. In spite of the significant influence of modern architectural practices on ordinary dwellings, contemporary cities and vice versa, there is a clear separation between commonplace, vernacular, speculative buildings and architecture as the outcome of conscious design intention. Although architecture depends upon the imaginative charge, the source of which is both high architecture and the everyday, we know precious little about the relationship between ordinary spaces in human settlement and the spaces of architectural invention. How can we theorise the relationship between the authored architectural work and the non-authored production of cities and buildings? Before looking at Venice, *Invisible Cities* and the Venice Hospital, I will explore the diverse ways in which Venice has been described and imagined. This is not intended to provide a comprehensive overview of these perspectives, but to help place Venice and the imagination within an expanded form of understanding.

Material and immaterial: Venice and its representations

> In fact, which Venice? The official one, of 'myth' and apologies, satisfied with the fullness of her own representations, or the Venice increasingly shaken by internal conflicts, marked by anxieties that obliquely cut across classes and groups?
>
> Manfredo Tafuri, *Venice and the Renaissance*

Every time Venice is described, it is described differently according to viewpoint or purpose. The casual visitor finds in Venice a fantastic array of alleys, canals and palaces. Historiographers discover an empire of coasts and islands, 'of fishermen who grew rich in trade [...] and enriched the West with a splendid cultural heritage'.[23] Economists describe a mercantile city-state, which turned to maritime adventures far from its native islands.[24] Archaeologists see Venice as a place of ingenuity, rooted in wooden pile foundations. For architectural historians, it encompasses a heterogeneous fabric of Byzantine, Gothic and Renaissance architecture.[25] For artists and writers, Venice reveals itself as a water-city of mirroring and inversions. Charles Dickens entered Venice in a dream, and found a 'ghostly city' floating in the 'exotic, fabled lonely sea'.[26] John Ruskin came to it replete with English notions of the Romantic, to produce not art history but fiction.[27] Marcel Proust was taken to Venice, where he received impressions analogous to those he had felt at Combray.[28] Thomas Mann charged Venice with Friedrich Nietzsche's impulse of 'Dionysos' overwhelming rational explication.[29] Canaletto distorted Venice to his own ideal perspectival conception.[30] William Turner came to Venice to paint not Venice, but an atmospheric city of light effects reflected on water.[31] Light, surface and atmosphere epitomised Henry James's Venetian visions through the aesthetic epiphany of 'the sun on the stirred sea-water, flickering up through open windows, played over the painted "subjects" in the splendid ceilings' of Tiepolo in the Palazzo Leporelli.[32]

Aside from externally imposed representations, Venice has also engaged in inventing its own mythology. Often called 'the Myth of Venice', a republican ideology was created within historical discourse in the Renaissance by the Venetians themselves regarding their social and political world.[33] Tracing the civic rituals in late medieval and Renaissance Venice, Edward Muir reveals an intense community life wherein lies a clue to the emergence of this ideology, Venice's lasting contribution to the political ideals of the Western world. The Venetians increasingly saw

Figure 0.5 Gentile Bellini. *Procession in Piazza San Marco* (1496). Image courtesy of Museo Nazionale Gallerie dell'Accademia di Venezia

the city as 'the site of realised utopia'.[34] Going through successive political and urban transformations in that period, they reached back to redefine 'a perfect origin' for their city.[35] This idea is powerfully expressed in works of art such as Gentile Bellini's *Procession* and Jacopo de' Barbari's bird's eye view of Venice, and had significant effects on the urban renovations that took place in St Mark's Basin and the Piazza San Marco in the fifteenth and sixteenth centuries (Figures 0.5, 0.6).

Venice projected itself as the most stable republic in the world for a thousand years, a quality often attributed to its enduring independence from foreign powers. At the trading crossroads between the Middle East and Western Europe, it played a key role in the development of Western political values, until Napoleon put an end to the Most Serene Republic, or *La Serenissima*, as often described by its political elite (1797).[36] As it happens, at the very moment of the end of this era a second cycle of intense influences began as the railway brought the artists and writers of the Grand Tour to Italy, reviving the ancient and Renaissance worlds and interest in them. Tony Tanner describes Venice as

> spectacle – the beautiful city *par excellence*, the city of art, the city *as* art – and as spectacular example, as the greatest and richest and most splendid republic in the history of the world, now declined and fallen, Venice became an important, I would say central site [...] for the European imagination.[37]

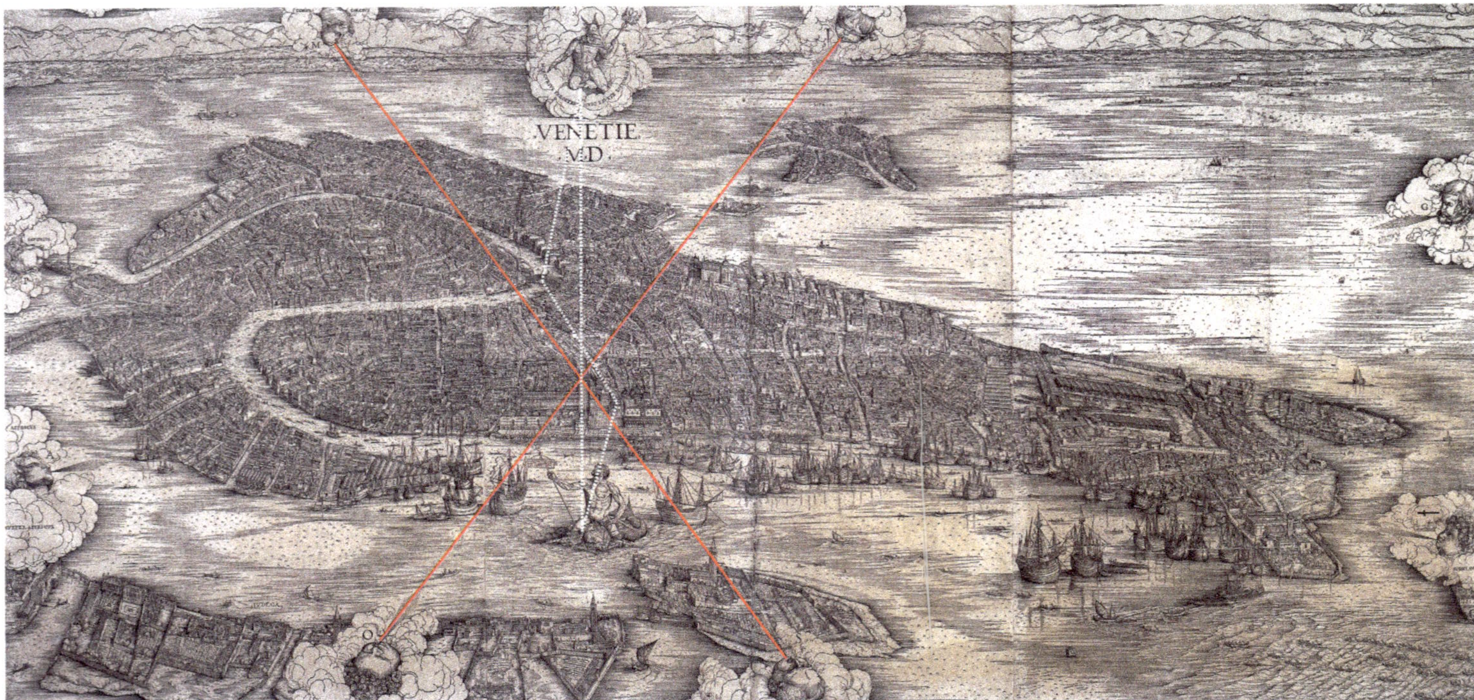

Figure 0.6 Jacopo de' Barbari. *Venetie MD*. Bird's eye view of Venice, *c*. 1500. The superimposed lines (by the author) reveal the geometrical coordination of the Rialto, Piazza San Marco and the mythical figures. Museo Correr, Venice

The early-nineteenth-century Romantic travellers were aware of the Venetian Republic and its end. Venice for them was not only a beautiful city, but also a symbol of loss and labyrinthine decay, central to the taste for the picturesque.[38] Though somewhat obscured behind the distressed image of decadence and decrepitude, the Myth of Venice continued to exercise influence over urban design and politics. It was this myth that supported Ruskin's theories in the nineteenth century and his critique of the social and environmental conditions in the industrialising world.[39]

The proliferation of myths about the aquatic city demonstrates the difficulties in disentangling Venice from its representations.[40] Any effort to describe Venice runs the risk of confusing the city 'with the words and the images that describe it'.[41] At the same time, attempting to avoid Venice's *mise-en-scène* runs the danger of removing the perceptual and representational realms it has generated.[42] Separating Venice *the space*, with its disposition of urban elements, from Venice *the place* and from how it features in human understanding can impoverish both the physical space it occupies and Venice as perception and imagination.[43] The multiple representations of Venice seem to suggest that cities have many modes of existence. They are lived spaces of everyday life with an innate configurational and functional order. But they also provide places where values and meanings are created and celebrated. As Tanner explains, 'Venice was Ruskinised', and that provided a crucial space and place for Proust's imagination.[44] Cities consist of collective 'imaginaries', which are often ceremonially enacted in rituals, festivals and commemorations. For Lefebvre cities are produced by and consist of representations, symbols and spatial practice.[45] The designed, written and pictured city influences the lived city and vice versa. Through a gradual process of accretion, cities become as much the world of streets and social actions from the inside as the perception of minds from the outside. They are at once material and immaterial, shaped by a few as well as many minds, by manifold instances of activity, memory and desire.

Authored and authorless – actual and possible

I have by now disentangled two pairs of crucial ideas: first, the city as a physical entity of everyday life and a conceptual entity formed in the mind; and second, Venice in the architectural imagination and Venice in the collective imagination. Often expressed as dualities, both pairs of ideas relate to one key question: what is the relationship between architecture as the authored product of design, and cities and buildings as the authorless collaborative products of society? Architecture has always been present in human settlement, but the conscious engagement with it is one of the pivotal practices of modernity. It developed during the Renaissance from the separation of design from building craft, through which architects were able to converse with learned men, scholars, philosophers, poets and literati.[46] This transformation is well documented as part of the processes that drove the architectural and urban development of early capitalism.[47] What is less discussed is the process by which architecture broke away not only from building craft, but also from *city-craft*, the evolutionary processes through which buildings and cities were produced, where previously these three were unified. The faculty of architecture as liberal humanist art came about by removing itself from this continuum, manifesting the design of objects as its main ontological purpose.

The fact that architecture is intellectually defined through intentional design, while cities usually come into being out of multiple actions over long periods of time, positions us between aesthetically authored objects and the view of the city as an authorless socio-economic process. As a consequence, architecture is confined in exceptional cases to the status of iconic buildings, or more generally to the status of buildings as instruments of economic production. Currently, buildings and cities are being appropriated by digital technology as a way of managing the city's assets.[48] There is a strong call for collective governance based on social media and mobile devices, where technology is – often naively – cast as the democratic medium able to side-step institutional control in urban and building management. This is largely part of contemporary economic restructuring, promulgating buildings and urban areas as entities that are technologically defined. A characteristic of this regime is the reconstitution of professions and human subjects to serve the knowledge economy and competitive market economies.[49] At the same time, new methods of computational design are taking on the semblance of the self-organising processes which underpin the adaptive growth of natural organisms. These designs are often somewhat presumptuously compared with the evolution of cities and human systems. Buildings and settlements are social artefacts resulting from the interaction of human laws, ideologies, statutory rights, systems of control and political structures. The consequence of these digital cultures is that they take place without adequate governance frameworks or in-depth understanding of those systems involving human factors. Traditionally engaged with the design of objects rather than networks or systems of regulation and control, architecture is left dispossessed of relevance in shaping social capital, politically and intellectually sidelined – almost to irrelevance.

If in *The Death and Life of Great American Cities* Jane Jacobs engaged with how cities satisfy the test of common sense, in *Delirious New York*, published at the end of the 1970s, Rem Koolhaas rejoiced in the pragmatic effects of real estate on the skyscraper island, with its particlar goals that influenced the metropolitan lifestyle of 'Manhattanism' and its irrational culture of congestion.[50] Studying the horizontal (the urban grid) and vertical (skyscrapers) conditions of Manhattan, he prefigured the early-twenty-first-century enthusiasm for the 'cybernetically oriented entrepreneurial culture'.[51] Koolhaas's intellectual embrace of market forces paved the way for other architects, such as Greg Lynn and Zaha Hadid, to engage with the analogy of complex models in their architecture. From the mid-1990s these architects ascribed to architecture the role 'of producing endlessly flexible environments for infinitely adaptable subjects'.[52] Lately, Koolhaas's *Elements of Architecture* (in the 2014 Venice Biennale exhibition) turned to commercial processes using prefabricated building elements and standard methods of construction for assembling buildings, shifting attention away from individual authored projects towards the speculative neo-vernacular and authorless mass production.[53]

While adopting the structures of deregulation, implying the absence of the architect-author, these architects are meanwhile themselves producing individual signature buildings. In this way, they manifest the contradictions in the division between architecture's autonomy and editing out the creative authorship of the designer.[54] A separate, countervailing viewpoint is provided by socially engaged architecture, an intellectual trend recognising the multiple actors participating in the production of everyday spaces, as opposed to singly authored architecture by famous architects or dominant ideologies in architectural design.[55] This viewpoint emphasises the need to redefine the figure of the architect, debunking the myth of the necessity of architectural authorship or expanding it to include the agency of the user. Yet, the ways in which the authored architectural project interacts with the authorless buildings and cities still elude us. Any attempt to reclaim social agency for architecture should proceed beyond the individual episodes of socially engaged projects into a more principled understanding.

This debate exposes a key question deep at the heart of architectural practice. Tasked with conceiving a building or urban plan, should architects think of the aspects that systemically condition design, such as social rules, function, economics and ideology, or give expression to their individual intuitive impulses regarding form and space? Are inspiration and creativity self-contained, or do they largely emanate from the physical world? Is architecture (and the city) immaterial, envisioned by designers and populated by human minds, or is it about material things?

Known as the 'autonomous–contingent' question, this division manifests itself along two conceptual axes, which underlie the discussion of the imagination in this book as a broader conception of knowledge. On the opposite ends of one axis lie the authored architectural work and the unconscious processes that drive authorless buildings and cities; on either pole of the other axis, one finds the actual world of built forms as opposed to forms confined to the domain of the imaginary, the probable, the thought-of or the potential-but-not-yet-realised. Analysing Venice and the two other artefacts, I will argue that if we think of the autonomous–contingent question as a diametrical opposition we are led to accept only one of the two sides in a way which precludes us from logically entertaining the other. In order to surmount the paradox and gain new insights we need to reframe the autonomous–contingent question. This is possible by revisiting the historical moment at which the split between architecture and artisanal traditions achieved its early-modern state of realisation. This is also the moment when Venice achieved its state of dense urbanisation, also shifting in ideology from the community values of the fourteenth century towards hierarchical social structures.[56] Revisiting the beginnings of the emergence of architecture as a distinct discipline can reveal the origin and lineage of our ideas about architectural authorship: if the notion of self-organisation is refashioning architectural thinking, which tradition is being revolutionised? How can one resolve the paradox between intentional design and the authorless city, reclaiming agency for the discipline?

Method

Fundamental as these questions are, they are rarely addressed within a single theoretical and analytical framework. Instead, they are fragmented into separate paradigms. Descriptions of cities as collective creations, for example, often have their roots in planning, urban history, political economy or anthropology. As a result, within these disciplines rarely have the architectural, social, economic and political dimensions of the city been understood as spatial phenomena. Descriptions within the history and theory of architecture, on the other hand, have traditionally tended – with a few exceptions – to privilege the products and discourse of architectural design. In contrast to these two frameworks, the field of spatial morphology (for example, space syntax and typo-morphology) focuses on cities as authorless places of the everyday.[57] Focusing on individual projects, periods or styles, approaches within the history and theory of architecture eschew the opportunity for more systemic modes of understanding. On the other hand, spatial morphologists often reveal, through mapping and analysis, generic properties, recognising shared patterns across a large sample. What they leave out of consideration are the processes by which the conscious imagination combines precedents and invents new designs.

Typological and morphological studies enhance our understanding, but often treat the built environment as though it were free of individual agency. They frequently trace the ways in which historical changes, not directly physical in nature, affect physical structures.[58] Not every social event has spatial correlates in forms that are retrievable in the absence of historical information. Yet, social, economic or technological shifts often bring about radical changes and discontinuities in the physical fabric. Examples are the social and economic innovations that led to the revival of Classicism in the Renaissance and the invention of architectural design; the rise of the mercantile class, the industrial revolution and the advent of large-scale mechanical reproduction in the last two centuries, changing life in cities and altering their physical fabric. Such changes are not detectable by simply studying spatial morphology over successive periods without having a historical-contextual understanding of the processes involved. In addition, buildings and areas can be occupied by diverse uses responding to a restructuring of the urban economy, when, for example, we have large nineteenth-century industrial warehouses re-inhabited by digital start-up companies. The physical fabric of buildings and cities outlives its original intended purpose. At the same time, old types disappear or are replaced by new designs. The sudden breaks that architecture and cities make with their past, or the adaptability of physical structures to different socio-economic conditions, cannot be always understood by simple analysis of their physical design. Without the historical processes that bring about new configurations, new living patterns or adaptations, morphological analysis alone fails to capture the dynamic interrelationship between space and society over time.

In terms of conceptual foundations, the two different routes to knowledge – history/theory and spatial morphology – are both affected by the autonomous–contingent question. If we define artefacts simply as objects of autonomous morphological study, we can learn about their form, but we cannot reawaken events of the past or explain how historical change affected their shape and function. Similarly, if we explore artefacts as entities that are solely contingent upon historical facts, we cannot gain access to properties that can be autonomously understood through their morphological study. By focusing on historical trajectories in architecture, history and theory have been providing conceptual support to design-oriented approaches in academia and practice. In contrast, spatial morphology is conceptually empowered by the 'scientific' paradigm of knowledge: describing the world as it 'exists' rather than changing the world through creative design. Among the proponents of the design-oriented pathway to knowledge, there is the conviction that the analytical pathway deprives architecture of its creative charge, including a critical, imaginative and ethical stance towards the forces enjoying power. Supporters of the morphological paradigm, on the other hand, maintain that, in contrast to conceiving the built environment as a systemic outcome of society, the designed products of architecture are unique examples, subject to individual intuition, associative thinking and artistry. Seen together, these approaches split the city and architecture into analytical-empirical and experimental-design practice. They also divorce the histories of cities and buildings from morphological description, and spatial morphologies from historical understanding.

Rather than speculating without proper verification through design or alternatively generating empirical evidence without making new propositions for a better environment through analytical knowledge, *The Venice Variations* uses historical and morphological analysis (spatial network analysis and Geographical Information Systems) to access the intersection of history with the properties of the physical world and its materiality. It overcomes the autonomous–contingent question, raising queries about how cities like Venice are formed and how they interface the collective production that led to their urban form with the individual production of creative designs. Instead of describing Venice as an autonomous physical entity, the investigation in this book focuses on the practices that create cities, as people congregate to exchange ideas, products and trade. These processes materialise through the network of streets, including both everyday activities and socio-economic and political interactions over time. There is an additional thread, which this study posits as a seminal factor in the shaping of cities and ideology: their representation in myth and fictional creation, addressing the city in the individual and collective imagination. This approach does not involve discarding the existing ways in which the creativity of the city is understood through works of art and architecture, but instead explores the manifold definitions of creativity in both individual works and the spatial processes that make up the city and architecture.

The structure of *The Venice Variations*

Chapter 1 concerns the evolutionary processes of *city-craft* (the Organic paradigm) manifested in the spatial structure of urban form, which stem from the accumulation of human actions over long periods. In this chapter, I investigate Venice together with its major buildings and spaces as systems of urban networks. The purpose is to understand the forces behind the development of the metropolis prior to the split between authored architecture and the authorless city in the fourteenth, fifteenth and sixteenth centuries. This period has particular significance in the book as the time of socio-economic and intellectual changes that led to the physical reconfigurations of cities, buildings and works of art in Western Europe. It is also the period during which Venice reached its mature phase of urbanisation, through both organic operations and deliberate urban interventions. Furthermore, during these centuries there was an ideological shift as the communitarian values of the fourteenth century gave way to a new emphasis on social hierarchy, associating the emergence of architecture as a discipline with the emergence of elite spheres of society.

In Chapter 2 I discuss Venice in the Renaissance, a significant moment when architects and their influential patrons sought, through elaborate processes of *statecraft*, to redefine the city as a representation of enduring stability for which purpose they used the classical style of building (the Classical paradigm). This chapter explores the reconfiguration of the Piazza San Marco and the San Marco Basin in the sixteenth century, a development concurrent with the processes of centralising governance and the aggrandisement of the Venetian Republic. The transformations that took place in the Piazza should be understood in the context of the intellectual and socio-technical changes that had begun a century earlier. The advent of the printing press in the Renaissance encouraged and facilitated encounters between architecture, the liberal arts – literature, philosophy, poetry, art, geometry, mathematics – and nascent scientific thought. Using the newly developed technology of printing, humanist scholars formalised a series of traditional rituals strongly related to the city's spatial and social geography, and crystallised its popular myths into a formal Republican ideology.[59] This chapter is the ideal place to explore the intersection of authorial intent in the design of the Piazza with city-craft and collective mythology, a body of work by builders, priests, rulers and artisans embodying associations between the oral traditions of the city and its building fabric.

This is also the context in which the book articulates the transition to Chapter 3, from the creative imagination in the city to the individual imagination of a creative writer. This third chapter explores the relationship between architecture and *story-craft* in *Invisible Cities*, as Calvino does in the tradition of humanism in his fiction. It considers this subject through the interdisciplinary perspective of generative architecture and generative literature. The discussion goes beyond the acknowledged poetic strength of Calvino's work, attempting to reveal the work's power in its analogic relationship with Venice's urban networks and combinatorial structure of urban elements. It falls within the mnemonic traditions in the Renaissance *teatrum mundi*, and the rotating discs of Raymond Lull, a thirteenth-century Majorcan philosopher, which aimed at achieving universal knowledge, and the reading machines of medieval practice.[60]

Calvino's *Invisible Cities* and Le Corbusier's Hospital were influenced by the post-war explorations of architects, formulated as critiques of early-modern visions, which, employing zoning and geometry, transformed the city into a designed object. Architects in the 1960s defined architecture in urban terms, seeking open-ended processes in architectural form that involved the uncertainty implicit in human interactions. By questioning the disciplinary boundaries of architecture and cities in the context of dominant institutional structures, the visionary projects of the post-war period emphasised performance over appearance and dynamic processes versus static outcomes. Seeking to connect with the anonymous collective production of human settlement, they reformulated architecture and the city as evolutionary networks. Chapter 4 analyses the Venice Hospital in the broader context of Palladio, Le Corbusier and a selection of works by contemporary architects (the Modern paradigm). Without aspiring to being all-inclusive, the chapter seeks to encompass wider horizons than those restricted to the specific cases of a city, a building or a literary text, with the aim of expanding our understanding of the three paradigms and the threads that bind together architecture, cities and design.

Finally, Chapter 5 attempts to restructure the questions raised in the book to provide a synthesis of its main ideas and arguments.

Contributions and significance

It is with these theoretical and methodological considerations that the book begins, seeking to understand first the analogic relationship between Venice and the other two artefacts, and second what factors in

Venice contributed to urban creativity and still continue to motivate the body, excite the mind and inspire the imagination. The first and main ambition is to challenge the definition of architecture as entirely distinct from the evolutionary processes of the city, and the city as distinct from the spatial craftsmanship of the kind we see in architecture. Although strong differences exist, the relationship between these two fields needs to be re-assessed, reframed and theorised. The second intention of the book is to question the generally accepted distinction between authored and non-authored artefacts – the former residing in the imagination of the individual, the latter in the collective imagination – which ignores the interwoven nature of these two spheres.

The first contribution of the book is in highlighting the importance of the connection between architecture and the city, making the link between the spatial, the social and the politically possible; in occupying the void between spatial practices and their representations; and in releasing the creative potential that inherently exists in their paradoxical difference and association. The second contribution is in placing these ideas in the context of the three key paradigms that influenced Western architecture as a way to bring the current, fourth paradigm – the Digital – into the historical tradition. Although it may be a little early to provide a critical assessment, the paradigm of the Digital is briefly discussed in Chapter 4. If architecture parted ways from the artisanal traditions of city-craft in the Renaissance, today's digital technologies integrate informational models of buildings with digital mapping of cities, combining designing with making in continuous seamless process.[61] The Digital paradigm seeks through computation to unite architecture and the city – form generation and evolutionary adaptation – into a single category, described as generative design, evolutionary design or autopoiesis, a total system capable of producing, reproducing and sustaining itself.[62] The conjunction of the digital and the rapid processes of urbanisation means that evolutionary practices of designing and making are becoming not only relevant once more but also necessary. Students of architecture will increasingly find it important to pursue an investigation of both emergent and traditional design processes that also include realised and imagined alternatives. They should try to discover where design thinking and popular thought meet, integrating architecture of the unconscious mind with spatial manifestations of the conscious, while also acknowledging the independence and life of each.

The book also makes a number of important contributions in its individual sections. While the first two chapters approach the imagination and creativity by looking at Venice, the third and fourth chapters examine these notions from the perspective of literature and architecture.

The significance of the former is in revealing the organisation of space and power in Venice, as a self-governing city-state, so that other cities can avoid becoming historical ruins of once proud civic democracies.[63] The last chapter provides an opportunity to study the analogy between the algorithmic potential in the network structure of Venice, and that in *Invisible Cities* and the Venice Hospital. By understanding the combinatorial memory remaining encoded in Venice, the Hospital and other works of architecture, the work can yield the parameters comprising the generative potential in the analytic retrieval of information. The larger benefit of this task lies in finding a bridge between analytical explanation and experimental generation in design.

Every work of research should be conceived without reference to the limitations of its author, bringing to light that which has not yet been discovered or uttered. Yet, no work can easily escape from the viewfinder of its writer. The constraints of the thought system and the rules generated by the author should, rather than being seen as a constraint to interpretation, form a stimulus to exploring other disciplines and points of view in order to spur further discovery. *The Venice Variations* is a work framed by an architect-scholar, not an analyst accustomed to modelling networks and assuming their transferability into architectural knowledge, ahistorically or apolitically, in a single logical leap. This means that, although the work is enriched by the science of networks, as well as historical and sociological understanding, it cannot be divorced from the discipline of architecture and the history and modes of thought that have structured architectural knowledge.

In addition, the book is not concerned with the hyper-determinism of data and computational processes of self-organisation in cities or simulated environments. As Phil Steadman explains, when these processes are used in attempts to make the design process 'scientific', they are problematic, deriving from the technological paradigms and ideological dogmas of the early twentieth century.[64] On the other hand, my focus on the imagination in this book has no relation with contemporary currents of anti-scientific prejudice either. More than at any other time, we need to transcend conventionally conceived barriers between the artistic dimensions of design and rational analysis. In contrast to the traditional idea that the imagination is some inexplicable brainstorm caused by a random meeting of circumstances, introducing into architecture a fuzzy and deeply private experience of the world, this work sees the imagination as the 'possibility space' of permutations, the output of definable processes and relationships. On the one hand, it draws on the early Renaissance idea of *ars combinatoria* – the art of combination.[65] On the other, it is associated with late-twentieth- and early-twenty-first-century developments in the area of information systems and computers. By re-theorising architecture and the city within the canonical narratives that influence their development, the work aims to reclaim the city and architecture from the non-reflexive application of analytical models, or the mindless forces of urbanisation, and describe them 'architecturally'. *The Venice Variations* is an effort to reframe architecture and the city as imaginative and ethical agencies of social capital and make the latter widely available to others.

Figure 1.0 Venice. View of the city and San Marco Basin (Bacino) from the southeast. Drawing by Athina Lazaridou

1
City-craft: Assembling the city

> For the rest of the time wandering on foot or drifting gently in a gondola, I subconsciously absorbed the first Venetian lesson – a lesson, incidentally, that poor Ruskin, beavering away at his crockets and cusps round the Doge's Palace, never learnt: that in Venice, more than anywhere else, the whole is greater than the sum of the parts. However majestic the churches, however magnificent the palazzi, however dazzling the pictures, the ultimate masterpiece remains Venice itself.
>
> John Julius Norwich, *A History of Venice*

Introduction

Unlike Charles Dickens[1] and Gustav Aschenbach,[2] who made their passage by sea, today most visitors arrive in Venice by the causeway connecting the mainland with the island city, one of the most important nineteenth-century modernisations. Even from this way of entering, from the terminus of Santa Lucia and the streets of Cannaregio bustling with tourists and the daily routines of the city, Venice strikes the visitor at once with its singularity. For James Grubb, 'the world of the lagoon defies conventional strategies of description'.[3] Two centuries earlier Goethe made a similar observation: 'Venice can only be compared to itself.'[4] Most accounts of the floating city converge on the fact that it is too extraordinary to be compared with other places, too complex and rich to be easily encapsulated.[5] Yet, as a city that has re-invented itself so many times in the past and is currently facing an uncertain future, Venice continues to raise questions about urban renewal that also concern other historic urban environments. A paradigmatic city that continues to inspire the ordinary visitor as well as architects and urban designers, Venice invites scrutiny about the forces that stimulated its urban creativity in the past and continue to excite the imagination today.

Unlike cities that developed on *terra firma* (solid land), Venice had no previous site, no previous settlement, nor a history of urban planning.[6] Its foundation dates back to the Dark Ages, when, fleeing the Lombards in the sixth century, refugees from the Paduan plains settled in the relative safety of the lagoon and its marshes. The lagoon was dotted with sandbanks and low islands emerging at low tide. Between them lay natural channels scoured out by the action of tidal and river currents. Separated from the Adriatic Sea by a chain of littoral islands (the *lidi*), the city gradually emerged from this archipelago, century after century conquering new territory by dredging, annexing pieces of land and linking isolated islands.[7] In the seventh century the first settlements in the lagoon were already thickly populated.[8] As they grew, their shores were extended and mud flats were made habitable by filling with material dredged from the canal bottoms.[9] By the late fifteenth century Venice had been transformed from a collection of islands to a compact city, criss-crossed by canals, an extensive pedestrian network of alleys and a dense urban fabric.

Few visible changes have occurred in Venice since the mature phase of urbanisation in the fifteenth and sixteenth centuries, to the extent that historians often use the current urban grain as a way of accessing the urban form of Venice in previous periods. Yet, from the large infrastructural projects that linked the city with the mainland to the current hydrological project commissioned to protect the city from flooding, transformations have been continually occurring in Venice, affecting the city and the lagoon's wider environment.[10] As in all ages prior to infrastructural modernisation, visitors continue flocking to the Piazza San Marco, the most theatrical square in any Western city, framed by spectacular buildings, the Bacino (the Basin of San Marco) and Venice's offshore islands. Some idea of how this area looked in the past can be obtained from Gentile Bellini's *Procession* (1496) (Figure 0.5) and Jacopo de' Barbari's bird's eye view of the city published four years later than Bellini's painting (c. 1500, Figure 0.6). These two views are powerful demonstrations of what Venice had come to express to its fifteenth-century visitors and its own inhabitants: a remarkable urban environment of ideal government and perfect political institutions.[11] Between the early stages of Venice in the sand bars and the physical, social and political practices of the Venetian Republic lies a protracted, anonymous and intricate process.

This brings us to Venice not only as urban network and physical fabric, but also as a major economic, social, cultural and political force in its own right. Venice's spatial transformations from an archipelago to a fully formed metropolis were coincident with social and political shifts from an island commune to a state, then a republic and an imperial power. Parallel to these transformations was the creation of an ideal image of the city as a cohesive and stable community, in the process of achieving prosperity through the political virtues of republican governance and communal action. Known as the Myth of Venice, this view of the city coalesced from a loose collection of popular beliefs, which in the fifteenth and sixteenth centuries became formalised through works of art, civic ritual and official historiography.[12] Bellini's painting and de' Barbari's map were both expressions of the Myth: idealising the city's outward appearance and traditions.

Many explanations of Venice's Myth exist, most of which fall into one of three main categories: the geographical explanation, that the lagoon discouraged internal frictions and secured the city's position as a stable, prosperous port; the economic explanation, that a dominant class of rich entrepreneurs relieved the pressure for upward mobility experienced by other Renaissance cities in Italy; and the social explanation, that institutions such as confraternities (*scuole*) and guilds (the *arte*) provided an outlet for the political ambitions of the middle class and feelings of general satisfaction among the lower classes (*popolani*), while socially heterogeneous neighbourhoods mitigated class tensions, and government-enforced institutions such as civic rituals enervated potentially disruptive popular rituals.[13] In the picture of Venice provided by these approaches, socio-economic factors and myth-making practices assume primacy, obscuring how these practices are embedded in the urban complex. If Venice reveals itself as a physical, social and mythical city, what is missing from these explanations is the factor of space: how the matrix of social and myth-making structures was inscribed or even generated through spatial practice. The second crucial aspect that remains obscured in most studies is the relationship between Venice's long history of stability and its history of urban creativity. This concerns the balance struck between the desire for potential continuity and the need for change in a dynamic urban environment.

Venice's potent synthesis of stability and creativity provokes questions about how and why it became a city, about the kind of city it is, and about urban development in general. What were the spatial mechanisms through which the city was generated? If Venice and its Myth have been described as socio-economic structures, can they also be defined as spatial phenomena? Analysing the structure of urban space and the prevailing institutions of Venetian life, the present work seeks not a space-first or society-first approach to Venice, but one that relates urban form, governance and social fabric to resilience and creative invention. Answers to these questions can help to explain the more general characteristics of adaptability and longevity in urban environments as well as the ways in which these phenomena relate to cities as centres of innovation. This chapter traces the story of how Venetian space was created; how Venice evolved; how it was shaped, extended and commercially exploited; finally, how it was culturally and socially delineated and how space helped to define the dominant forces of Venetian society.

Conquering space: from an archipelago to interconnected communities

Of the early days in the lagoon very little is known. What is established, though, is that the churches were the earliest permanent structures to be built on land laboriously reclaimed little by little, as areas were drained and navigation channels excavated.[14] The earliest map of Venice shows the city as a compact 'landmass' perforated by canals (Figure 1.1). Some 90 churches are shown on this map, most of which are still standing in the same places today. Removing all information but the churches and squares from the plan of Venice reveals an archipelago of monuments and open spaces (Figure 1.2a–b). However, what appears as a random distribution of elements has, on closer inspection, a clear logic.[15] The analysis of streets using a property that in network theory is called 'betweenness centrality' (and, in space syntax theory, 'choice') reveals that the squares and churches are joined in a pervasive network of open spaces and alleys at all scales of the analysis (Figure 1.3).[16] Choice accounts for through-movement, or the simplest paths that are most frequently used in order to move between any pair of streets in an urban complex.[17]

This property captures a pattern of evolution based on social and economic activity since early times. The *campi*, the churches and the houses built around them were the urban and social nuclei of parish islands that dotted the archipelago (Figure 1.4a–b):[18] 'Each parish was built up street by street around its own church and *campo*.'[19] Parish squares formed semi-autonomous community centres that contained the houses of leading families, a place of worship, markets, stalls and artisans' shops,

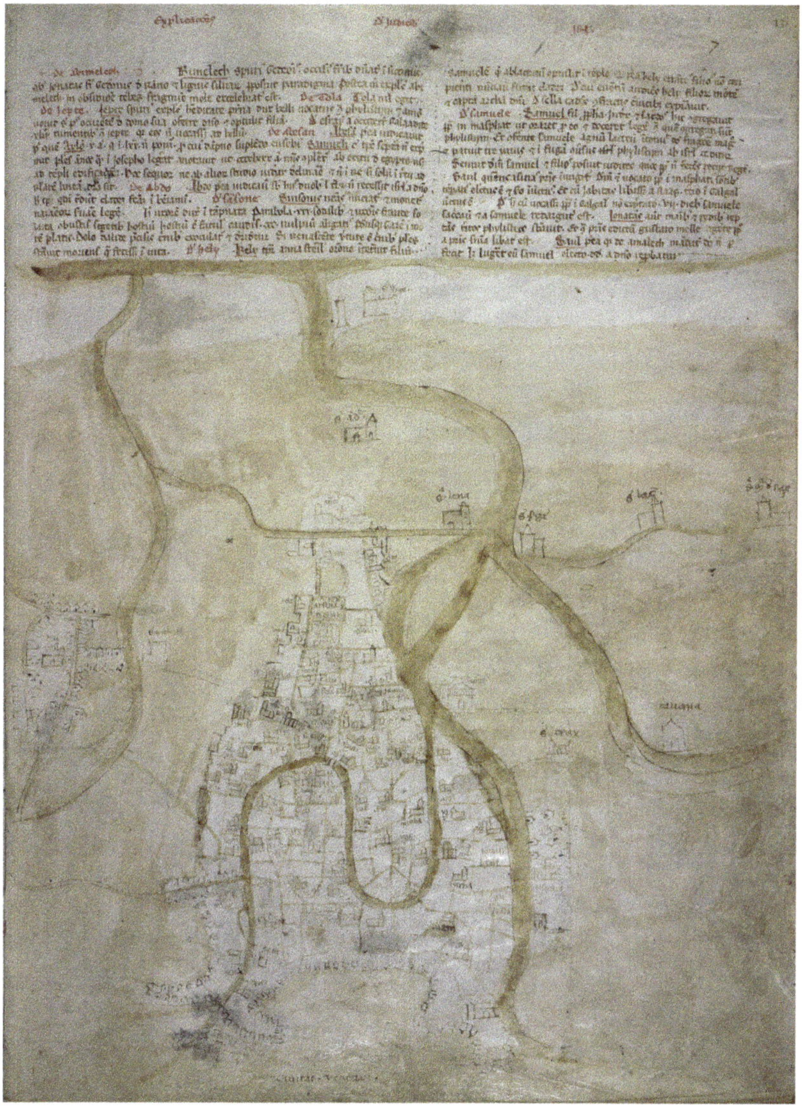

Figure 1.1 Fra Paolino. Map of Venice, fourteenth century. From *Cronica a mundi initio*… Biblioteca Nazionale Marciana, Venice (Ms. Lat. Z, 399 (=1610))

and were serviced by their proximity to a canal (Figure 1.5). Squares also facilitated the collection of fresh water through underground cisterns and channels.[20] This is evident through the *vera da pozzi* – the wellheads – hundreds of which are still present in Venice today. Located at the centre of each square, they collected water from the channels on

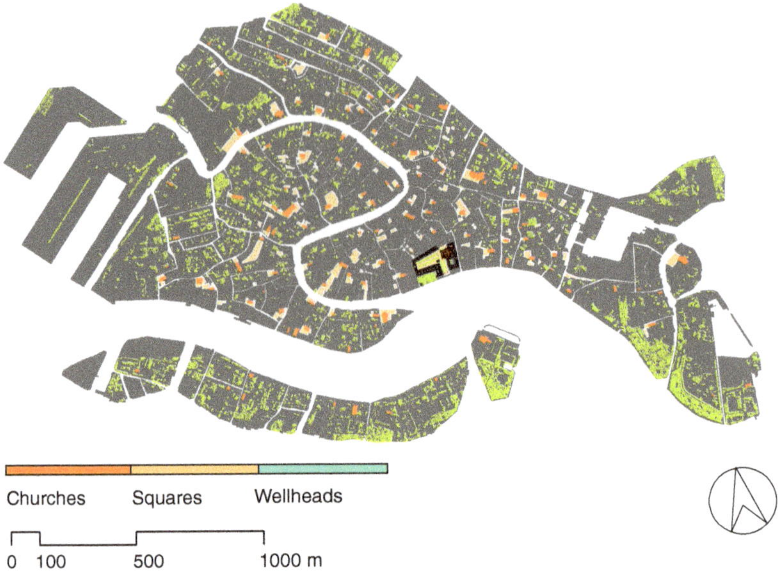

Figure 1.2 (a) Map of contemporary Venice showing churches, *campi* and the Piazza San Marco. Drawing by the author

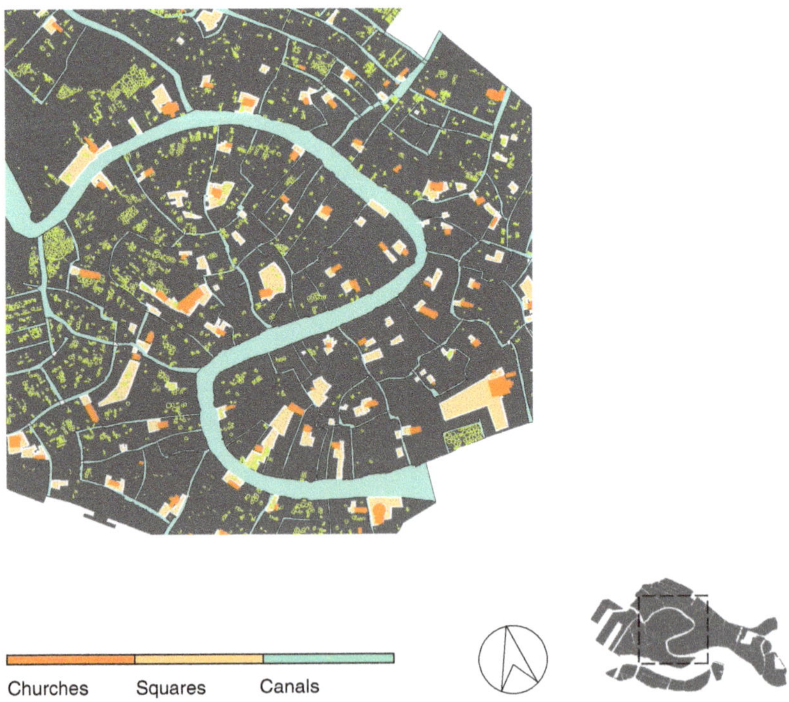

Figure 1.2 (b) *Campi* and churches in Venice. Removing all other information from the map of Venice reveals an 'archipelago' of *campi* and monuments. Drawing by the author

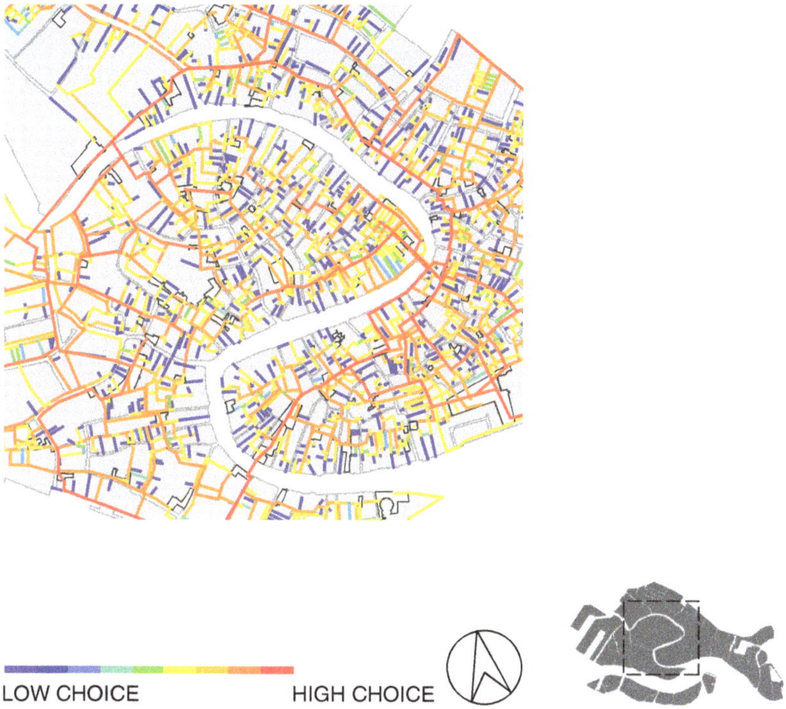

Figure 1.3 Pedestrian network of Venice. Measure of normalised angular choice at radius 3000 metres. The measure of choice accounts for through-movement, or the simplest paths that are more frequently used in order to move between each pair of origins and destinations. Drawing by the author

the *campo*'s surface and filtered it through sand for domestic consumption (Figures 1.6a–b).[21]

The city had nearly achieved its current form by the early fifteenth century, with almost all of its 70 parishes, each with its church and square, firmly established.[22] Until the last centuries of the Middle Ages, though, its form had been entirely different. Parish islands resembled small feudal estates. There were no streets and there was no network of *campi*. The wealthy families reigning over individual islands 'competed with one another for control of the dogeship', an all-powerful position in the early stages of Venice's development.[23] As domestic politics in the twelfth century evolved, the role of the Doge was restricted to being, in effect, the first among equals in the Venetian commune. The island communities began to lose their autonomous character.[24] At the same time, the gradual development of the mercantile society generated the need for more rapid

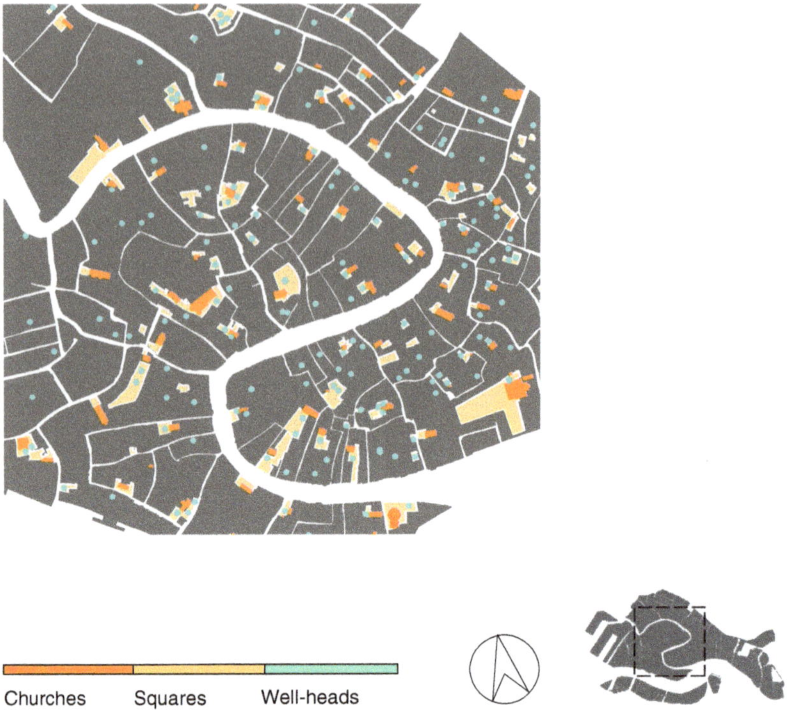

Figure 1.4 (a) Squares, churches and wellheads in Venice. Drawing by the author

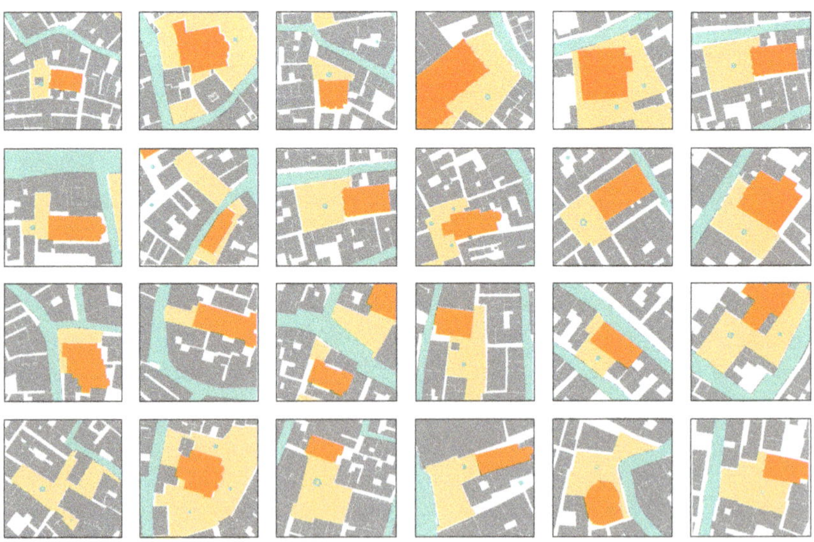

Figure 1.4 (b) A selection of squares in Venice. The squares are irregularly shaped spaces, situated close to one (or more) canals, fronted by a church and comprising one or more wellheads (*vera da pozzi*). Drawing by the author

Figure 1.5 Churches in Venice. 1. San Giacomo di Rialto, sestiere (s.) of San Polo. 2. San Marcuola, s. Cannaregio. 3. Santa Maria Gloriosa dei Frari, s. San Polo. 4. Sant' Aponal, s. San Polo. 5. Eastern facade of San Trovaso, s. Dorsoduro. 6. San Martino, s. Castello. 7. San Zaccaria, s. Castello. 8. Santa Maria del Giglio, s. San Marco. 9. Madonna dell' Orto, s. Cannaregio. 10. San Rocco, s. San Polo. 11. San Sebastiano, s. Dorsoduro. 12. San Pantalon, s. Dorsoduro. 13. I Carmini, Santa Maria del Carmelo, s. Dorsoduro. 14. Southern facade of San Trovaso, s. Dorsoduro. 15. San Gregorio, s. Dorsoduro. 16. I Tolentini, San Nicolò da Tolentino, s. Santa Croce. 17. Miracoli, Santa Maria dei Miracoli, s. Cannaregio. 18. San Marcuola, view from Salita Fontego, s. Cannaregio. 19. Madona dell' Orto with canal, s. Cannaregio. 20. San Moisè, s. San Marco. 21. San Barnaba, s. Dorsoduro. 22. Sant' Alvise, s. Cannaregio. 23. Santa Fosca, s. Dorsoduro. 24. Santa Maria della Fava, s. Castello. Photos by the author

Figure 1.6 Wellheads are the centrepieces of many public squares in Venice. Photos by the author

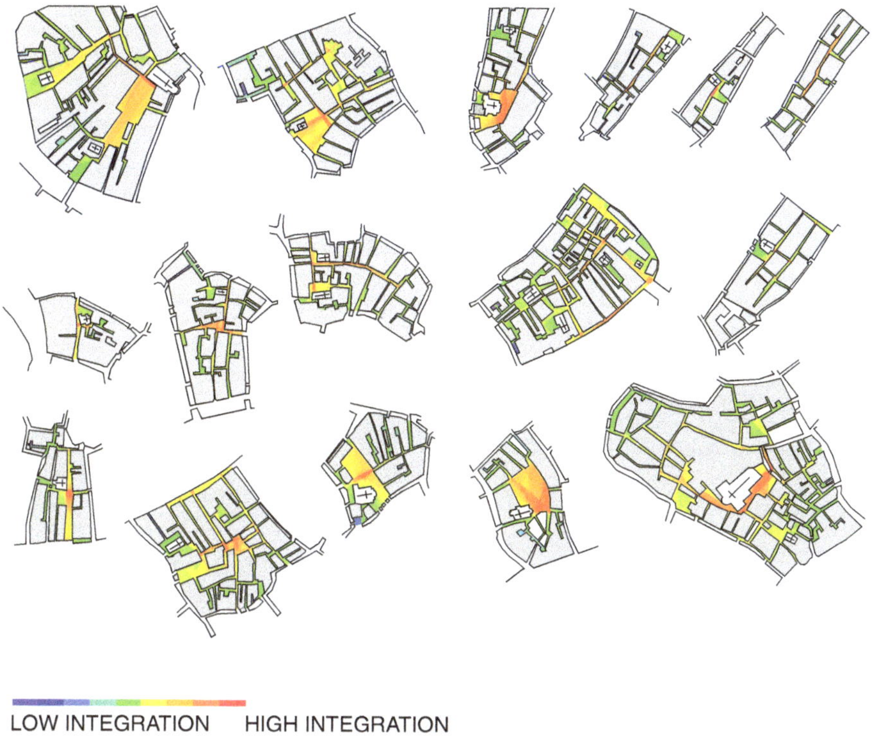

Figure 1.7 Analysis of visual integration within islands in Venice. Integration accounts for how 'close' every element in the map is to every other element in terms of topological turns (or changes of direction). Adapted from Franco Mancuso, *Venezia è una città: Come è esta construira e come vive* (Venezia: Corte del Fontego, 2009)

transportation over land and water, until, through an extended process of land reclamation, the islands were eventually joined up.[25] The city stopped expanding its periphery, 'canals and fish ponds were filled, the course of older canals was regularised, and the building of the bridges began'.[26] Main routes were established through the various parishes, adding to the network of canals a second network of land communications. The continuous network of 'through' routes seen in Figure 1.3 indicates that, in the process of land reclamation, the bridges that joined the islands were built so as to link the *campi* and parishes with each other, producing a network of interconnected centralities (Figure 1.7).

Studying cities as configurational systems, Bill Hillier has uncovered the fact that cities seem to evolve into a 'foreground' network of linked centres at all scales, from a couple of shops through to

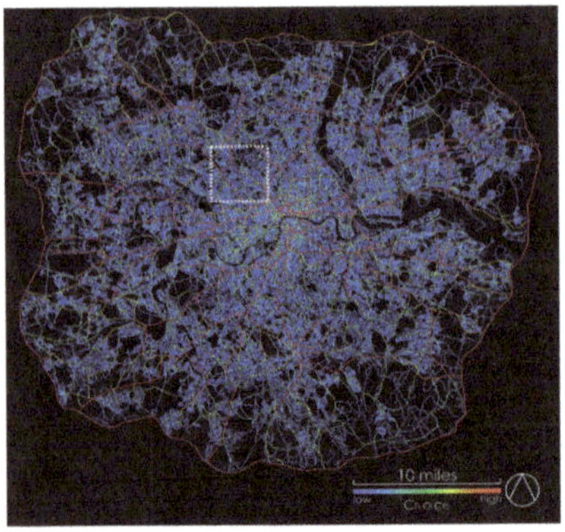

Figure 1.8 (a) Analysis of London. Measure of choice at radius n. Image by Bill Hillier

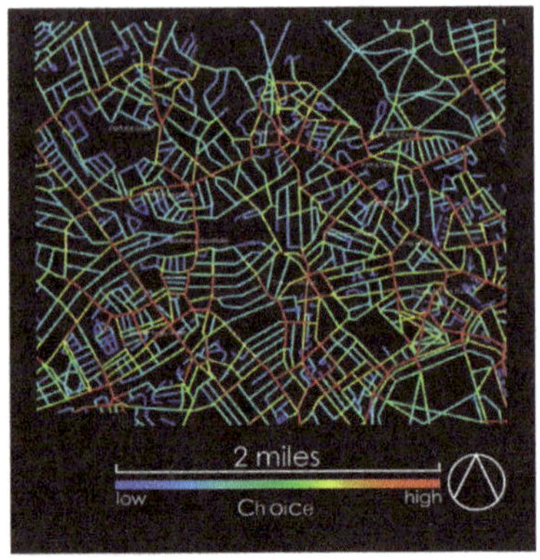

Figure 1.8 (b) Analysis of London. Measure of choice at radius 700 metres. Image by Bill Hillier

whole sub-cities, set into the 'background' network of largely residential space (Figure 1.8a–b).[27] The former consists of a few mainly continuous street elements with high choice values, which attract microeconomic activity. This is because its high potential for through-movement attracts movement-seeking activities such as retail shops and markets.[28] The background network, on the other hand, primarily consists of residential space, tending to restrict large-scale movement. The two networks have universal, as well as culturally determined, spatial features, which play a strong role in embodying and reproducing the underlying social order.[29]

Historical and anthropological studies of Venice reveal that island communities had strong local identities. In spite of the welding of parishes into a pattern that spread throughout the city's quarters, the spirit, customs and social institutions reflected the origins of the city on the many islands.[30] In his study of civic rituals in the Renaissance, Muir explains that the parishes retained their own rituals, while rivalries between them were common. They had their own 'rich and influential families, patron saint, special feasts, customs and defined border', enjoying considerable autonomy over local affairs.[31] The parish (*contrata* or *contrada*) was the essential and fundamental unit of Venetian society, many parishes nurturing their own social and economic identity and allegiance to particular saints. The foreground network of square-centres therefore embodies the origins of the social structure of Venice in semi-autonomous communities, each serving as a 'microcosm of the city as a whole'.[32]

It is important to insert a parenthesis noting that studies of the city network since the sixteenth century reveal a similar pattern of interconnections among the parish squares (Figures 1.26–1.27). Changes in the urban fabric since then have added infrastructural spaces in the north-western area of the city, a small set of canals which were transformed into alleys, three new bridges over the Grand Canal, and some additional links that improved the continuity of the routes that connect Cannaregio with the Rialto and San Marco. A more detailed description of these changes is provided in the Postscript to this chapter on page 74.

The amphibious city – the water and pedestrian networks

> The various parts of the complex system – the rivers, the chain of offshore islands, the porti, the marshlands, and the urban complex – slowly came to be seen as a unit. This chronicle of work projects, ordinary and exceptional, describes the slow emergence of a city and of an urban order. It also shows how, as the group asserted its mastery over an unstable environment, a political and social organisation came to be built, as least in part in response to the challenge of the waters.
>
> Elisabeth Crouzet-Pavan, *Venice Triumphant: The Horizons of a Myth*

Crucial for Venice's many centralities is communication through water. Seawater runs through the compact body of the city, penetrating the ground floor of many buildings in the form of internal quays, which can be accessed on foot as well as by boat. To go from one place to another you have the choice between land and water, as well as a combination of the two.[33] Water travel and pedestrian routes intersect at specific locations through the *traghetti* and loading steps, which are always adjacent to bridges and squares (Figures 1.9a–b).[34] Analysing the canal structure on its own shows that the most 'central' route is the Grand Canal, capturing its key role as the broadest and most navigable waterway, which structures the general form of the city and global movement.[35] The next most significant waterways are the canals of Cannaregio, San Marco and Fondamente Nove, connecting the Grand Canal with the peripheral navigational channels (Figure 1.10).[36] Comparing the canal routes and the pedestrian networks, we see that the former consist of fewer elements, extending over longer distances than the elements of the street network (Figures 1.3–1.10).[37] This difference expresses the origin of Venice in the archipelago. In a city made of island communities, large-scale

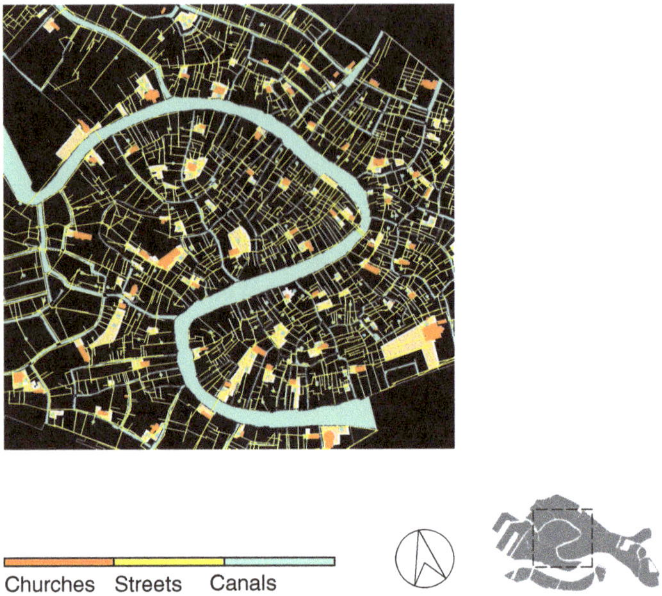

Figure 1.9 (a) The networks of canals and alleys in Venice. Drawing by the author

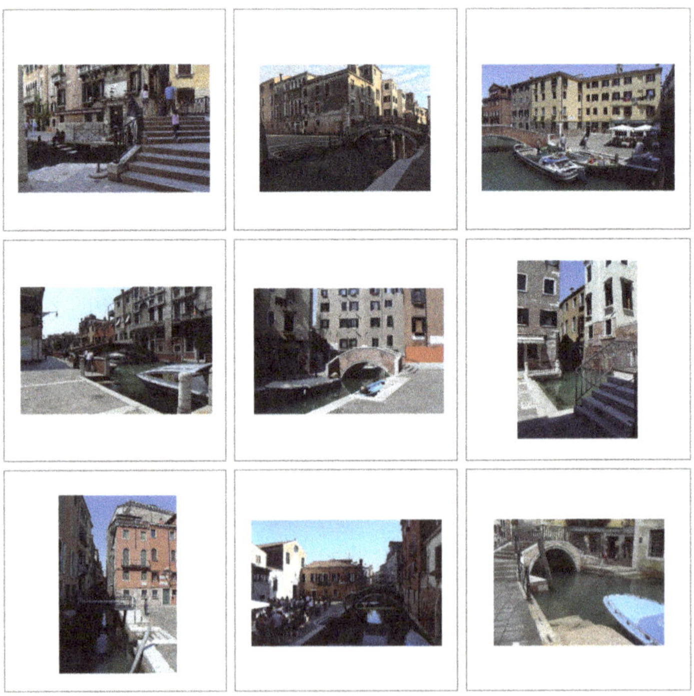

Figure 1.9 (b) Flights of steps linking land with the water in Venice. Photos by the author

Figure 1.10 Canal network of Venice. Measure of normalised angular choice at radius 3000 metres. Drawing by the author

communication primarily took place by water. The canals still serve as the dominant mode of transportation for various types of resources, from building materials to people, working as the main infrastructural system (Figure 1.11).[38]

It is essential in studying the canal and pedestrian networks to join them at the points where they overlap, looking at Venice as an amphibious terrain.[39] The analysis of this combined system (Figure 1.12) shows that, like the street network (Figure 1.3), the dual network comprises interconnections of *campi* in a matrix. This characteristic suggests that, although the canals formed the overall connective force, streets and squares were laid out and adjusted in conjunction with the aquatic infrastructure. The interconnected centralities of the combined types of route show that the squares are located at the intersection of the pedestrian and water networks, forming common nodes in the two systems. This makes sense, as many squares have direct access to canals by mooring docks, or are close to water.

The nodal position of the squares can be further illustrated by measuring their distance from canals. We find that the majority of squares

Figure 1.11 The canals as major elements for the distribution of various types of resources and people. Photos by the author

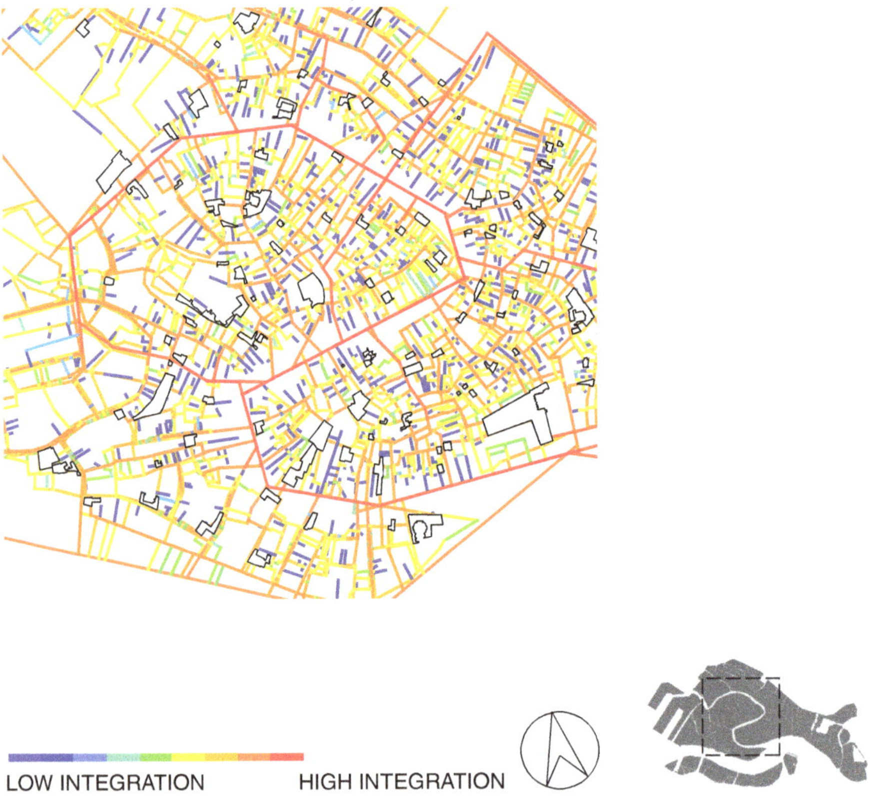

Figure 1.12 Combined pedestrian and canal networks in Venice (joined through steps). Measure of normalised angular choice at radius 3000 metres. Drawing by the author

Figure 1.13 Venice. Topological step-depth from all canals. The red lines indicate one step, or one change of direction from a canal. Progressive difference of colour, from orange to green, signifies one or two turns away from a canal and a square. Drawing by the author

(94 per cent) are within 50 metres of a canal. We can also look at the morphology of the route or the changes of direction one needs to make in order to move between water and land.[40] The red lines in Figure 1.13 indicate straight paths, while progressive changes in colour from orange to green signifies one to two turns required in moving between a canal and a *campo*. *Campi* and canals are linked by simple and straight connections (red lines). This shows an ability to move between water and land without deviating or changing direction. Figure 1.13 shows another key property: traversing bridges, these straight routes (shown in red) reveal a pattern of 'cross-stitching' of squares and islands, or the bonding of parish communities with each other.

Whether at the heart or at the fringes of the city, ceremonially engaging a canal (such as the *campi* of San Giovanni e Paolo and

Carmini) or bordering one obliquely, religious buildings and *campi* have always been close to water and loading bays since the city's inception. Their nodal position in the two networks can be traced to the times when parishes were initially separated, and *campi* were directly serviced by boat. As Venice expanded and islands were joined, squares became interconnected by both water and land, facilitating the unloading of merchandise and people. Evidence of this evolution survives in the names of canals, taking their appellation from the churches they pass along their course. One example is the Rio Di San Giovanni Degolà, which intersects the Grand Canal on the southern side of San Polo (Figure 1.10). Weaving in a sinuous curve through the city, the canal connects San Giovanni Degolà with San Giacomo Dall' Orio, Sant Agostin and San Polo. In the early days these churches would have been approached by and seen from the water. The pedestrian and canal infrastructure therefore explains the evolution from the archipelago to the urban complex. Time in Venice was embedded in space: space was history; it was time.[41]

A multitude of solitudes: from parochial communities to the urban complex

> A hundred profound solitudes together constitute the city of Venice. That is its charm. A model for the men of the future.
>
> Friedrich Nietzsche, *Daybreak: Thoughts on the Prejudices of Morality*

Venice was an intense maritime emporium, where trading routes from east and west converged, exchanging goods and services, 'sugar and cotton, silk and rugs, fruits and perfumes, gums and spices'.[42] Boats, rich wares and products were omnipresent, shaping the socio-economic practices of the Venetians and their customs. The port facing the lagoon was an indispensable part of economic activity, the meeting point of ships arriving from or departing through the Adriatic. However, multiple other sites served as small-scale mooring points and dock infrastructures. Palaces, warehouses, markets and charitable institutions were close to a mooring dock or themselves served as docks to facilitate water access.[43] The dispersed distribution of these parts points to a multitude of elements that congregated like 'building blocks' to form Venice. Just as the *campi* had a spatial and social identity, so too palaces, religious buildings, charitable institutions, trading posts and markets were all distinct formal and social types. They also acted as nodes in the dual infrastructure. Permeated by water and closely linked to the two networks, these sites coalesced to form a porous, sponge-like urban fabric. The islands and canals therefore have a repetitive pattern of typologically similar structures: squares, streets, churches, palaces, public buildings and, in many cases, houses. These typologies comprise, in turn, a collection of micro-elements that recur throughout Venice's urban fabric: steps, loading bays, bridges, wellheads, underground cisterns, bell towers (Figure 1.14). With a clear focus on the evolutionary way in which all these microcosms arose from the marshes, a key question is posed: what makes a whole out of the repetition of parts, a civic identity out of island communities, a polis out of these 'islands' and individual parties?

This question can be first addressed by looking at how the evolution of the city led to recognisable macro structures. A first look at Venice's map, for example, picks up a number of continuous routes, such as the two

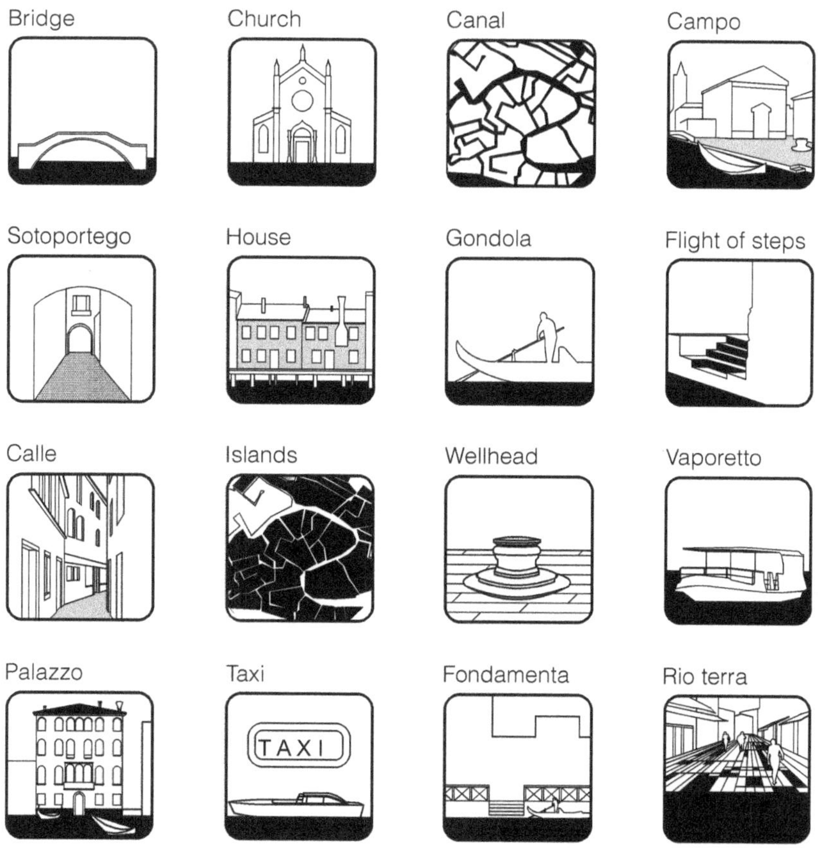

Figure 1.14 Venice. A taxonomy of element-types. Drawing by Tania Oramas Dorta

arteries behind the Grand Canal (Figure 1.3). Extending from Cannaregio to San Marco, and from San Polo to Dorsoduro, the two thoroughfares connect a number of *campi* in sequence, roughly paralleling the U-shaped bends of the canal. The thoroughfares, and the parishes on either side of the Rialto Bridge (San Giacomo di Rialto and San Bartolomeo), are joined by this bridge, capturing the historical importance of Rialto and these two hubs in the development of the city. The thoroughfare on the right-hand side borders the Fondaco dei Tedeschi and opens into the mercantile centre of San Bartolomeo.[44] The one on the left connects the markets in the neighbourhood of San Giacomo with Dorsoduro and the Punta della Dogana (the Sea Customs House). By facilitating pedestrian access to both squares and palazzi, these thoroughfares also enable the large-scale flow of people between the smaller domestic places and the major trading sites.

It is precisely in the process through which macro structures emerge from micro patterns, over and above the purposes the latter serve, that we recognise the city in its generative process. The synergistic relationship between all these elements – canal, street, palazzo and *campo* – creates the need to explore the relationship between these individual parts and the highest values of the foreground structures (of the street, canal and combined street–canal system; Figures 1.3, 1.10, 1.12). This is important if we are to arrive at a better understanding of whether distinctive differences exist in terms of the position of these elements in the system as a whole. A classification of *campi* based on their distance from elements of the highest value of choice (set above 1.3) can help us understand how they relate to the structure of the system.[45] This examination shows that 20 per cent of the *campi* are within 50 metres of the foreground network of the canals (or the canals that have the highest values of choice). In relation to the street network and the combined street-canal network, this figure rises to 40 per cent and 54 per cent, respectively, revealing a direct association of half of the squares of Venice with large-scale movement (Figure 1.15a–c).

We can better understand the significance of this association by considering how networks developed in the evolution of the city. Although canals and streets were shaped together, forming the combined system, the canals preceded the system of pedestrian alleys. The interconnections between the two networks were the last stage in the development of the urban system. The higher number of *campi* directly connected to the foreground of the combined network (compared with the number of *campi* associated with each of the other two networks) suggests that, with the elaboration of water and land interconnections, strong associations were formed between 54 per cent of the squares of Venice and the city as a

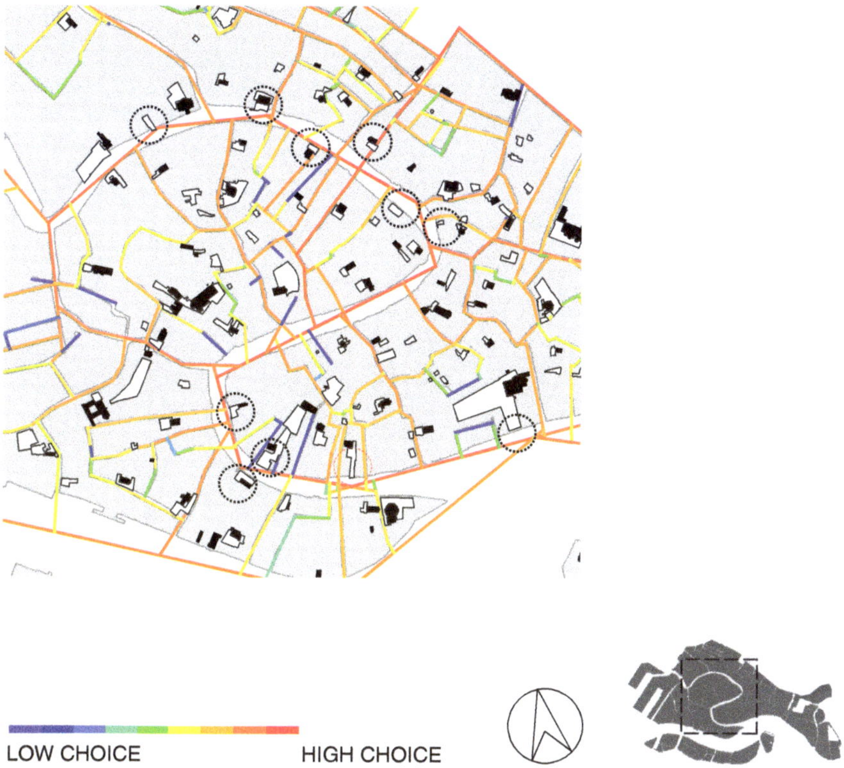

Figure 1.15 (a) Venice. Canal network and squares located within 50 metres from the highest values of normalised angular choice (1.3 and above). Drawing by the author

whole. Therefore, in the long process of transformation, in the successive stages of urban formation, from an archipelago of water-based transportation to water- and land-based interconnections, half of the parish islands were elevated from a local to a global orientation.

Originally serving as mooring quays away from the busiest canals, squares increasingly mediated global movement through ever larger-scale networks, from the boat journey between neighbouring islands to multiple overlapping journeys on both water and land between distant districts. The shift in the number of *campi* bordering the foreground henceforth exposes the transition of parishes from isolated islands to areas well embedded into the city-wide context. The differences in the position of squares in these networks capture the transformation of disaggregated islands into a city and their integration into an urban complex. This begins to demonstrate that the development of large-scale

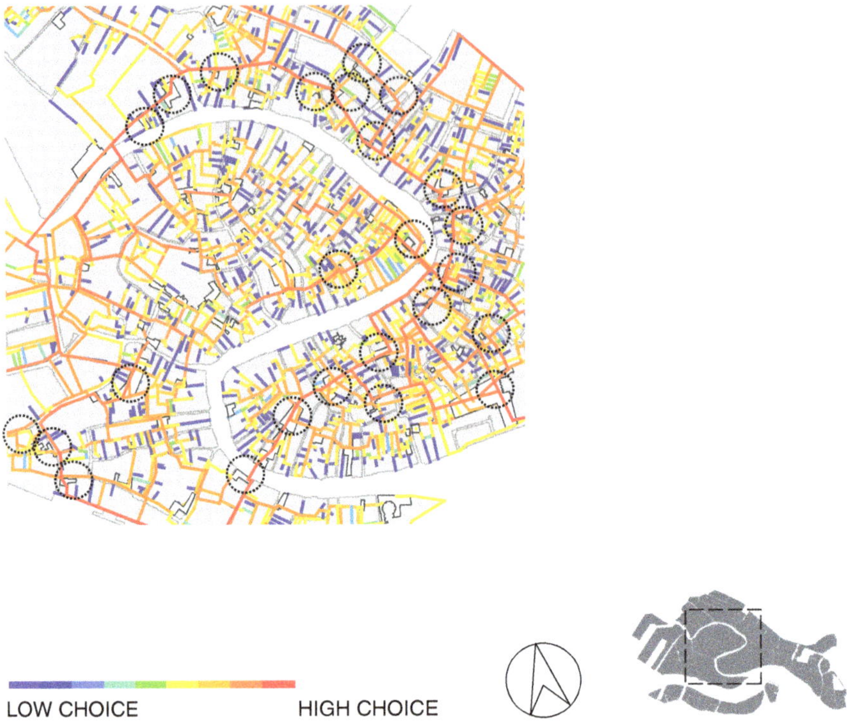

Figure 1.15 (b) Venice. Pedestrian network and squares located within 50 metres from the highest values of normalised angular choice (1.3 and above). Drawing by the author

through-movement is an essential characteristic in the generative process of a city.

If half the individual parish communities shifted towards deeper engagement with the city as a whole, it is important to keep in mind that communities were also organised around micro-level loyalties and customs. Bill Hillier and Julienne Hanson explain that channelling global flows through a space requires strong relationships between global movement and the specific location.[46] Control over a space or territory, on the other hand, requires relative separation of an area from the global system of communication. This stems from the power of such systems to generate un-programmed encounters, putting local customs at risk and weakening cultural boundaries. For the authors, spatial relations embody cultural patterns; the more spaces are interconnected, enabling movement flows, the more social groups occupying them will tend to be susceptible to the generative potential

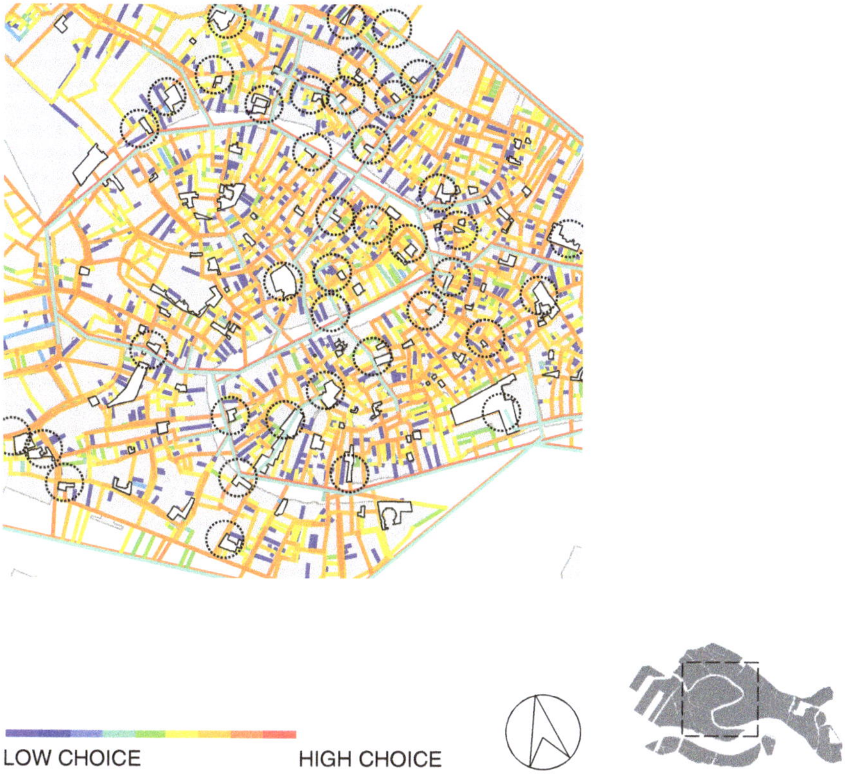

Figure 1.15 (c) Venice. Combined canal and pedestrian network and squares located within 50 metres from the highest values of normalised angular choice (1.3 and above). Drawing by the author

arising from multiple interconnections. In contrast, the lower the number of spaces connecting with each other, the more they reduce the flow of movement and information, protecting social identities and categorisations.[47]

As Venice reached a mature stage of expansion, half its squares made the transition from the strictly parochial to the public, civic domain. The differential relationship of *campi* with the foreground network demonstrates that the urban transformation instigated tensions between control over neighbourhood affairs and a share of the resources passing through the foreground network of the city. The squares in less prominent locations nurtured a more private identity under the patronage of the parish. The almost equal split of public spaces into globally oriented and locally oriented *campi* seems to express two kinds of patronage, one secular and city-wide, the other anchored in the parish at neighbourhood scale.

Between parish communities and the state

> Venetians of the early Renaissance were not the demigods of myth with the answers to successful civic life; instead they were ordinary mortals who struggled constantly with the tension between the caritative act, which would promote harmony, and the selfish act, which would lead to conflict.
>
> Dennis Romano, *Patricians and Popolani*

Apart from parish centres, Venice had two major hubs: the Piazza San Marco and the Rialto. Products arriving from all parts of the trading world brought merchants and foreigners to the mercantile centre of the Rialto with its concentration of banks, workshops and markets. The Rialto was also a place of civic administration, where 'bulk commodities – iron, flour, wine, coal, oil – had to be weighed and assessed for tax'.[48] The Piazza San Marco and the Piazzetta also served as market places, but mainly constituted the spiritual and ceremonial centre of the Republic.[49] They contained the Basilica of San Marco and the highest strata of government, that is, the Ducal Palace and the Procurators of the Basilica, who were responsible for its maintenance and administration. The two centres of the Rialto and San Marco were strongly connected through the Merceria, an area with shops selling a diversity of wares, from weapons to books, silk, leather and fabrics.

Linked with other squares by through-routes, the twin hubs are integral parts of the foreground movement (Figure 1.3). However, their strength can be better revealed through the measure of 'integration' or 'closeness centrality'.[50] While choice ('betweenness centrality') expresses the through-movement potential of a street, integration describes its to-movement potential as a destination, or the ease of getting to this street from all others.[51] Figure 1.16 shows a dense cluster of integrated streets connecting the Rialto with San Marco, reflecting their strong position as destinations in the urban fabric. More importantly, the figure highlights the link uniting commercial interests and state governance through the twin centres and the patrician class, who were both merchants and council members of the Republic. The two measures – choice and integration – express another duality of forces: the collective power of parish communities in forming the

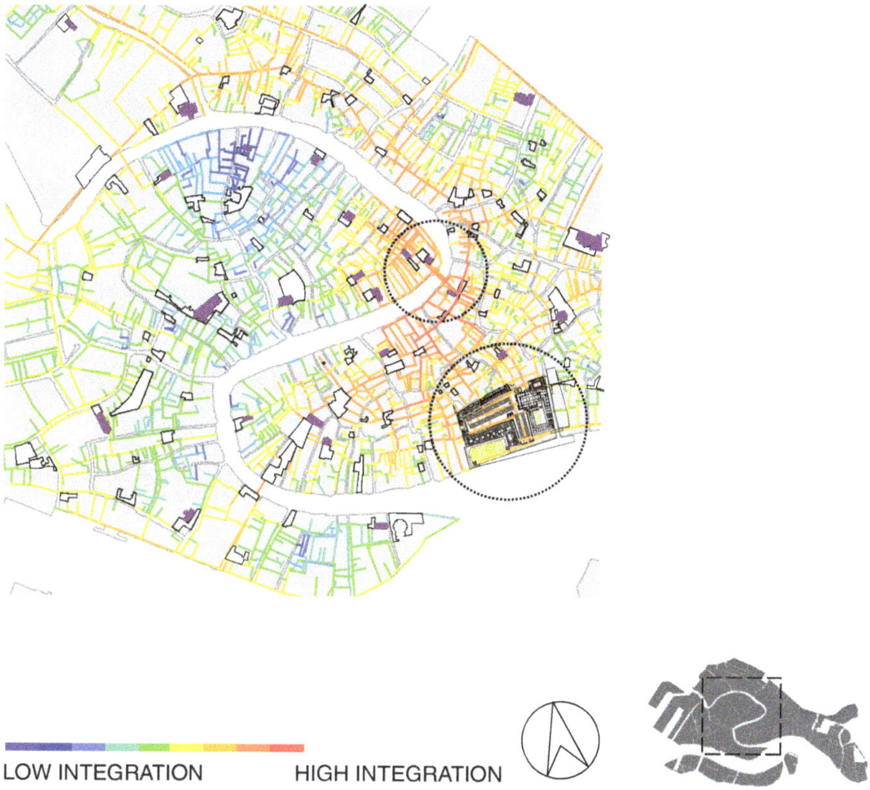

Figure 1.16 Venice. Measure of 'normalised angular integration' at radius 3000 metres. Drawing by the author

city, and the civic community as a whole exerting primacy over and above the parochial centres.

The interplay between civic and parochial patronage was an integral part of Venetian identity, where remnants of shared loyalties in the urban landscape remained endemic. Even as late as the 1980s the parishes still provided a sense of belonging, related to the affective identification of the self with a particular geographically defined place.[52] In parallel to this parochial allegiance, there was an attitude of republican expression at the higher levels of political and civic life. As Muir explains, 'two theatres, the local parish directed by its own saint-protector, and the central city protected by Saint Mark, competed for the attention of the populace'.[53]

We see through this analysis that the properties of Venice's spatial networks lead to an understanding of social relations. But if the examination of the urban form has taught us anything, it is to question reducing the complexity of the city to spatial networks alone. Social factors have to be studied simultaneously with spatial ones, since each of the two layers of relationships can reinforce or modify the other. More importantly, we need to understand not only that an association exists, but also the *nature of the association* between spatial organisation and social interactions. What kinds of social networks were formed, and how did their distribution patterns in the city relate to its spatial structure? The aim in this exploration is not to construct a comprehensive picture of the social anthropology of Venice, but to understand the relationship between the physical realm people lived in and the social and political world they occupied.

Social networks

> In the words of Nicias to the Athenian soldiers on the beach of Syracuse: 'you are yourselves the town, wherever you choose to settle [...] it is men that make the city, not the walls and ships without them'.
>
> Thucydides, *History of the Peloponnesian War*, vii

Venetian society had three major classes: patricians, well-to-do commoners (the *popolano grande*) and commoners (*popolano minuto*).[54] A fourth group was made up of the clergy and sacred communities, while a fifth category consisted of the various ethnic communities in the city.[55] None of these groups was entirely homogeneous in terms of ancestry, social origin, wealth, status or family size. The patrician society was intermeshed in 'large interlocking family complexes' through familial, economic and administrative activity.[56] In certain cases, innovative financial institutions and marriage between nobles and *popolano grande* in the early days of the Republic enabled open associations and institutional dynamics.[57] Work relations, the large family networks and the dispersed locational patterns of the noble class necessitated that patricians and *popolano grande* live in worlds transcending space (dispersed) and time (extending through generations). The *popolano minuto* formed community relations on the basis of the nuclear family or participation in guilds and charitable societies (*scuole*).[58] With the exception of some areas of residential and professional homogeneity, and streets especially dedicated to some guilds or crafts, the residential and work locations of *popolani* were also widely dispersed rather than clustered in particular streets or parishes.[59]

The clergy, monasteries, convents and religious orders had diverse social origins, and like the other groups were geographically distributed across different parishes.[60] Membership in charities (*scuole*) and guilds was socially and professionally highly mixed through the principle of brotherhood, which acted as a binding force in Venetian society.[61] *Scuole* were corporate, charitable and religious institutions that became prominent organisations in the fabric of the city.[62] Confraternities of the guilds usually fulfilled a financial function, receiving one-third of the fines imposed on tradesmen and fees on their qualification. The distinctiveness of Venice's *scuole* and guilds in the late Middle Ages was determined by the city's most distinctive features: a commercialised economy and secular statehood.[63] Exalting poverty and devoted to philanthropy, they stood on the confluence between religious and economic life and between different sorts of people and institutions. More significantly, the members of *scuole* had no interaction with the life of the local community within which they were located. *Scuole* and confraternities were *supra-parochial* institutions attended by their members at some distance from home, potentially easing the political and social tensions deriving from family relations.[64]

Denis Romano explains that for centuries, patricians and *popolani* had no rigid social ties or fixed locations, moving instead in a variety of intersecting social networks and patterns of spatial dispersion.[65] 'Economic specialisation and functional diversification did not transform the city of Venice into a series of closed, occupationally defined neighbourhoods' and spatially defined social groups.[66] Social ties were complex, calling into question any easy division before the early Renaissance into nobles and commoners. As Romano observes, 'On the one hand, residential clusters and a common street at Rialto may have promoted a sense of community among craftsmen.'[67] Furthermore, attachment to the parish or residence was a common factor, neighbourhood relations were strong and the Venetians identified with their parish localities. But, on the other hand, the rhythms of work and social activities took people beyond professional and parochial spheres and into larger orbits.[68] This dual nature of social networks – one operating at the level of the entire city, and one based on the parish – determined notions of physical space (the parish squares, the Piazza, the Rialto and the areas between the two centres). More importantly, this property points to a structural similarity between the duality of foreground–background in the spatial networks and the duality of social relations. The next step in the analysis is to identify how the dual spatial networks and the dual social orientation intersected in space and time through specific buildings, institutions and the activities of everyday life. To this end, we turn our attention to the patrician palaces, the *scuole*, the guilds and the *campi*.

Palaces, confraternities, guilds

More or less identical in form and size, Venice's palace-houses (*palazzo fontego* or *casa fondaco*) served two distinct though complementary functions: as family residences and as trading headquarters for the ruling class of the Republic.[69] A courtyard with an external staircase led to the *piano nobile* of the family quarters on the first floor.[70] A waterfront quay and gate on the ground floor led to a central hall flanked by offices and storerooms (Figure 1.17).[71] As commercial premises and the dominant typology in the city, the palace-houses were an instance of collectively produced port infrastructure. This meant a water gate on a canal and a secondary entrance from a *calle* or a *campo*: 'A canal mooring was needed to bring in supplies of food and fuel, and for loading and unloading merchandise when the owner was involved in trade.'[72] The people who lived in these houses and over these warehouses had the dual role of merchant-nobles, engaging in trading activities and the governance of the city through their membership in the Great Council.[73]

Figure 1.17 Palazzo Franchetti Cavalli, Venice. Photo by the author

If the *campo*, with its church and wellhead, was the centre of the *contrata*, the palace with its dual access from a street (or from the *campo*) and a canal combined the trading and domestic world of the nobility, that is, their dual association with the government and the local parish.[74] With the exception of the Grand Canal, where the prestige of patrician families was put on public display, over two thirds (70 per cent) of the palazzi were distributed throughout the city fabric.[75] At the same time, the palaces retained a close connection to *campi* and the pedestrian–canal system. More particularly, 90 per cent of palaces are less than 50 metres from a square (Figure 1.18a), while 70 per cent of palaces are within 50 metres of a *campo* and the elements that have the highest values of choice of the combined network (≥1.3, Figure 1.18b). The strategic position of these buildings meant that they mediated the relationship of the patrician class with the parochial locales, bridging between trading, state administration and the *contrate*.

Like the squares, the palaces formed the points of overlap between the foreground and background spatial networks. This meant that they were also the nodes in the social networks that were citywide, and the networks oriented towards the parish. Finally, they articulated class and gender divisions in society. Patrician males were involved in commercial and government affairs that took them beyond the confines of the parish. Their preoccupations and prestige depended on the number of offices they held and success in securing state-sponsored favours (*grazie*) for their clients.[76] Their orientation was the economic and political apparatus, leading to the Rialto, San Marco and the *scuole* rather than neighbourhood orbits. Females, on the other hand, largely remained within the limits of the parish. They had social contacts which were based on physical proximity, more personal and more likely to cross class lines. As Romano explains, palaces were 'sprawling edifices with courtyards and covered passageways [and] *popolani* rented space in mezzanines and attics'.[77] The solidarities formed in these building complexes concerned economies and social relations between patrician females and the community of workers, tenants, servants and *popolani minuti*. The association of patrician males with civic space and leadership in the government, and that of females with the parochial space of the *campo* are expressed in paintings, such as Leandro Bassano's portraits of Marin Grimani and of his wife Morosina Morosini. The two portraits are clear demonstrations of gendered conceptions of space, based on male participation in activities, social and spatial networks that were geographically dispersed, and contrasted with the more localised ties of females to the parish.

The difference between males and females in terms of social worlds and spatial locations extended to all sectors in society. Male servants

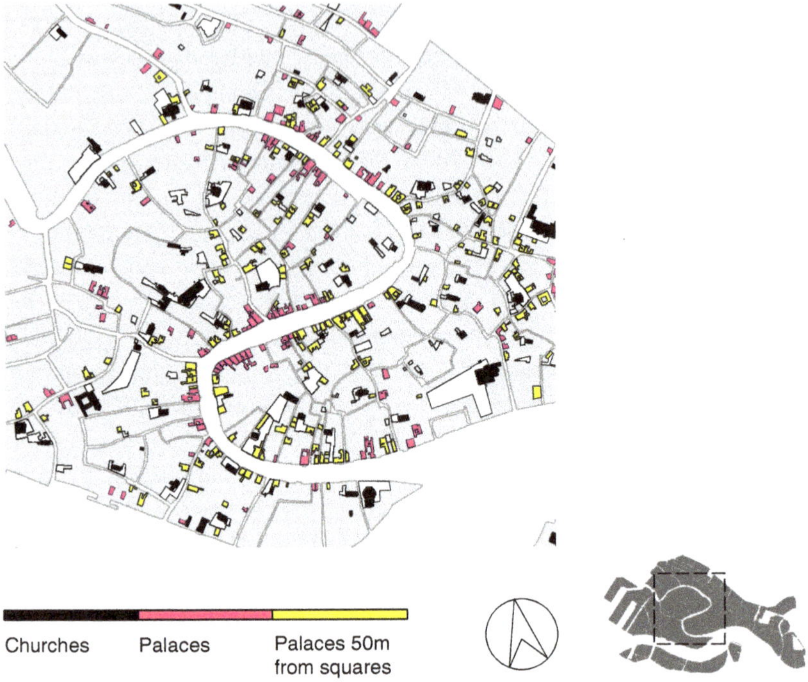

Figure 1.18 (a) Venice. Palaces located within 50 metres distance from a square. Drawing by the author

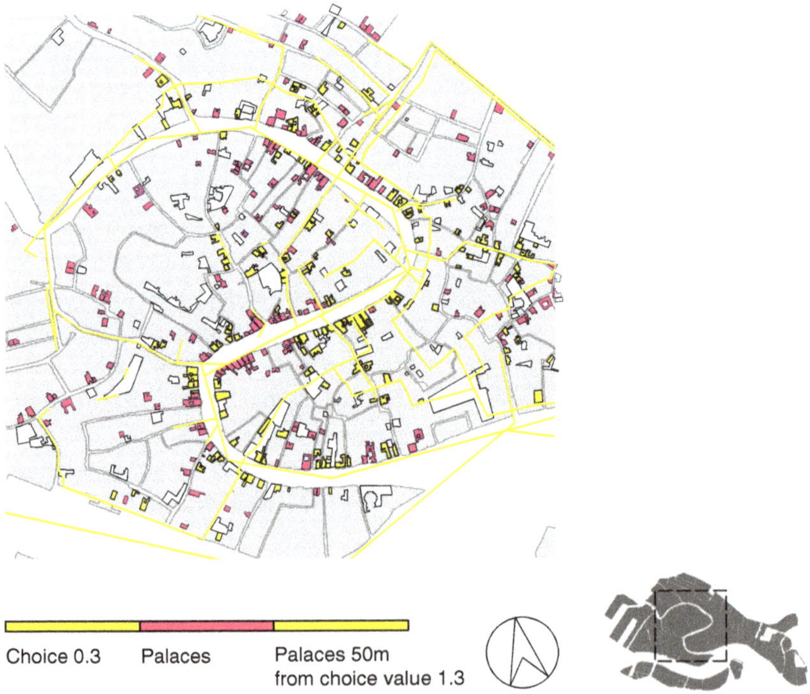

Figure 1.18 (b) Venice. Palaces located within 50 metres distance from a square and the highest values of normalised angular choice in the combined pedestrian and canal network (1.3 and above). Drawing by the author

and *popolani minuti* accompanied patrician males about the city. They collected bills, received goods and transported noble citizens between their home and their business, often making their way through crowded streets, travelling throughout the network of canals that linked the islands of the lagoon and the mainland. The social contacts of female servants, on the other hand, were much more geographically circumscribed, centred on the household, its courtyard and the immediate neighbourhood.[78]

Like the palaces that constituted bridges between the noble group, the parishioners and the *popolani*, the *Scuole Grandi, Scuole Piccole* and *Scuole Dell'Arti* were institutions that channelled the aspirations of the middle class and mediated between the wealthy and the poorer classes. With the exception of the *Scuole Grandi* with their own impressive premises in different parts of the city, brotherhoods were located in parish churches, where they maintained many altars (Figure 1.19a–b).[79] There were many cases where more than one *scuola* was situated in the same church or *campo*, reaching wider spheres than the *contrate*. Their geographical location was associated with a patron saint and played a crucial role in the creation and maintenance of identity.[80] But at the same time, through the orientation and location of certain *scuole* close to major arteries, the brotherhoods established associations with large-scale movement, diverse social groups and spatial practice. If the palaces unravelled complex associations between large-scale commerce, central administration and the locality, the *scuole* added to the interlocking of scales and solidarities. They strengthened the dual orientation of parishes towards the particular locale and towards the institutional super-structures of society.

The generic city

As an anatomy of Venice's urban networks and social interactions, this study highlights two main factors. First, the urban expansion of Venice was a story of the creation of space. As large-scale mercantile activity generated wealth, it also gave rise to the need for further land reclamation. This brought about an evolutionary shift from a *centralised* network – in which the links between islands were through the body of water – to a *distributed network* based on multiple land and water interconnections. This process of adaptation of the network led to the de-territorialisation of parishes from feudal enclaves to a dense urban fabric of expanding flows of movement and access. Simultaneously with

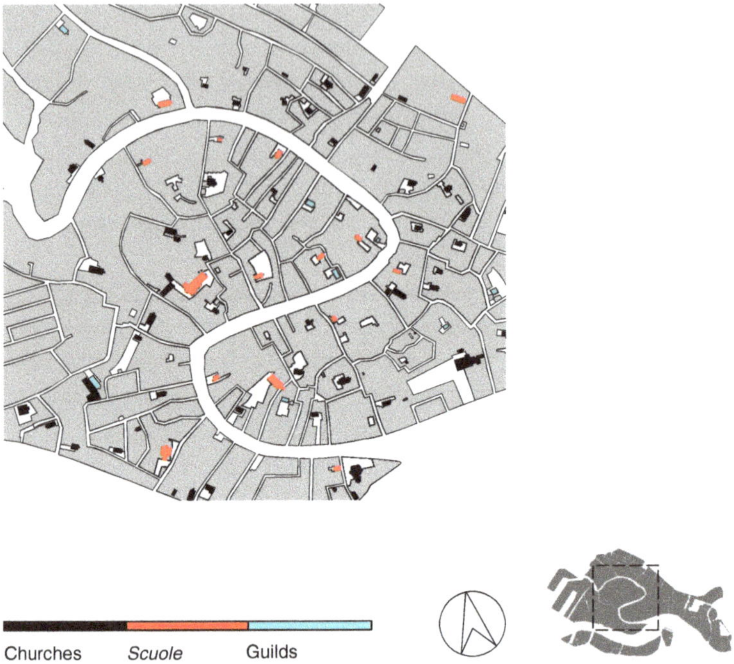

Figure 1.19 (a) Venice (1829). *Scuole* and guilds. Drawing by the author

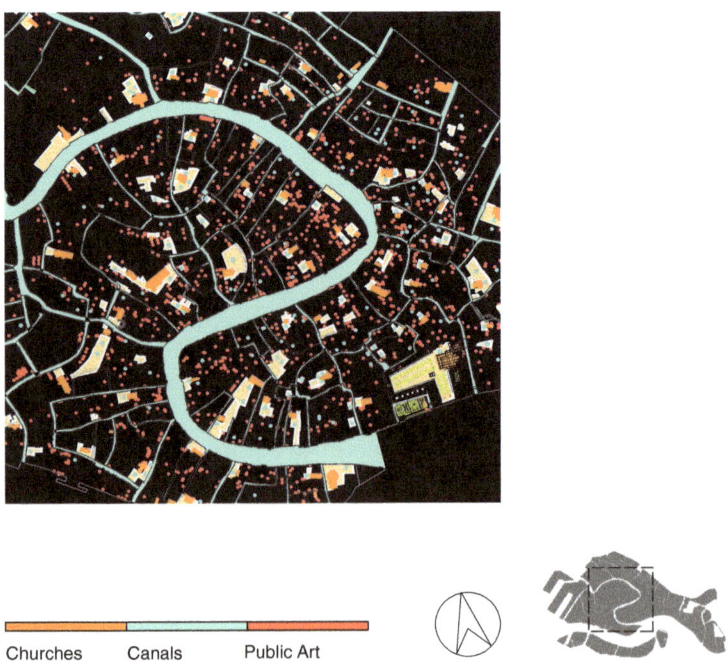

Figure 1.19 (b) Venice (contemporary). Small pieces of public art that decorate the city. Drawing by the author

this transformation, a geographical dispersion of family, work and religious and secular associations occurred so that they spread throughout the city quarters. This means that the spatial interconnections of islands and the geographical dispersion of people were coupled with social network bifurcation and diversification, enabling inter-group relationships and cross-scale encounters. In this way, the social system shaped, with its activities and interactions, the spatial system, and vice versa.

The second factor emerging from the analysis concerns the ways in which small-scale spatial changes affected the urban network as a whole. The effort invested into shaping economic and social requirements and their spatial counterparts at the micro-level produced global-scale effects. With time, an emerging perception of the whole arising from this process must have played its part, making the foreground networks more accentuated. This is seen in the increase in the number of squares that are closer to the elements of the highest choice values in the street network and the combined pedestrian–canal infrastructure, compared with the canal network. Global patterns emerged as recognisable stable structures, causing squares to shift their orientation from a local to a global position in the city complex. Another powerful instance of the emergence of global-scale relationships is the twin centrality of the Rialto and the Piazza San Marco, linking the edges of the city with the two urban hubs and structuring accessibility relations at the level of the city as a whole. The more the city itineraries brought commerce to the Rialto and officials and dignitaries to the Piazza, the more they attracted, respectively, additional business and ceremonial practice.[81] At the same time, half of the total number of parishes became strong in terms of distributing and controlling movement through their spaces, interweaving global flows through the Piazza and the Rialto with the localised activities of the parish.

Venice's spatial properties and the transformations that drove the urban process support Hillier's definition of the 'generic city'. Studies of a large number of cities by Hillier and his colleagues led to the discovery that, at the spatial deep level, 'there is a generic city, that is, a structure that makes a city a city in the first place'.[82] The generic city consists of a foreground network structuring micro-economic activity, and a closely related background network organising residential culture. The shift of half of Venice's *campi* towards the highest values of the foreground network illuminates this system as the quintessential force driving the generic city and making the particular city possible. Hillier explains that the foreground and background networks generate and reflect two kinds of knowledge: practical knowledge, which drives the economic aspects of human existence, and social knowledge, assigning a 'label' to individuals and groups, which, although possibly spatially defined, is fundamentally a-spatial, arising from clan, family, kinship or profession.[83] In urban societies the foreground is a sparse network that is geographically distributed, while the background forms a dense, more locally spatialised, network. Sparse network relations in Venice were formed through family, class, profession and organisation (patricians, commoners, *popolani*, officials, professionals and confraternities), operating across the entire urban orbit, while dense network relations worked at neighbourhood level and in the domestic sphere. Sparse network relations were about commercial and institutional interactions manifested in civic or domestic buildings, public spaces, *scuole* and market places. Drawing their members from different parts of the city, they functioned across territorial boundaries. Dense network relations, on the other hand, were formed within the household and the parish, reinforcing associations among the people that lived on each island and met in its streets and *campi*.

All social formations appear to exhibit dense and sparse networks, operating jointly and having emergent morphological consequences for society. The dense network tends to build ties that reinforce the same local group at the expense of the global system, comprising many sparse networks. The sparse model, on the other hand, creates social networks that reinforce both the dense network and the relationships of members across networks.[84] The former emphasises formality, hierarchy and exclusiveness, the latter informality, equality and inclusiveness, marking differences over individuals rather than social categorisations. In the generic city, this knowledge duality and the social networks it involves are reflected in the duality of the spatial network. In Venice, the system of the canals, the combined canal–street infrastructure and institutions such as palaces, guilds and *scuole* interfaced the two kinds of social networks, reinforcing global-scale relations (sparse) while also strengthening local affiliations (dense).

Coupling, interlocking, decentralising – Venice as a particular city

The concept of the generic city helps understand the spatial and social interactions that made Venice possible. It is important, though, to consider the specific spatial and social properties responsible for making Venice a particular city. Three factors were crucial in this process: first, Venice's propensity for wide heterogeneity of social categories, coupled identities and social structures; second, the wide geographical distribution of these structures; and third, their interlocking relationship across scales. In terms of coupling, until the sixteenth century, the patrician group was effectively the governing and merchant class associated with the institutional and commercial structures of Venice. Because of the convergence between political and economic forces in this group, what constituted the top tier of power (the prince) in other Italian cities was in Venice distributed among the Great Council members and spatially dispersed across the city's many islands.[85] Stanley Chojnacki writes:

> the households of the patrician families were spread out in every corner of the city. Of the 156 patrician families in the *estimo*, 110 had members living in at least two of Venice's six *sestieri*; of these 68 were represented in three or more *sestieri*. ... and altogether, 76.9 per cent of all the patrician families in the fiscal census were represented in more than one *sestiere*. This is remarkably different from the situation apparently prevailing in contemporary Florence.[86]

Thus, the ties between the nobility and the other members of society linked Venetians in diverse socio-economic relationships which had localised as well as dispersed spatial orbits.

In terms of heterogeneous formations and interlocked identities, social institutions, such as the confraternities and trading, brought together participants from all sectors of society, and spread them geographically throughout the many palaces, churches and altars that dotted the islands. Charged with professional, institutional and charitable work, the headquarters of these institutions interlaced secular and religious activity in locations that brought together global and local spatial networks in their own right. Another instance of interlocking was through gender relations in the palace, mixing family and neighbourhood affairs with global commerce and the politics of the Republic. This pervasive process of *coupling*, *interlocking* and *decentralising* meant that the economic, political, social, religious and family relations interacted at all scales, based on a distributed apparatus of power (palaces–squares–churches–*scuole*), mixing patricians and *popolani*, the parish and the state, and diverse social classes across residential sectors and the spatial fabric. These processes took place in all islands, and in strategic locations in relation to the combined network of water and land, especially the foreground network. In social network terms, a *popolano* with their family and personal connections in Venice was never too far away from members of city-wide social networks that brought products from distant markets to the city and also governed in the council.

This property of multiple, distributed, one-step relationships between social networks is reflected in one-step relationships in the spatial networks of Venice. From the most unique to the most ordinary, from the most private to the most public, buildings and open spaces mediated between the local scale of the neighbourhood and the global networks of socio-economic relations that took people into larger spatial ambits. The squares, private and public buildings, palaces, churches, bridges, loading steps, cisterns, wellheads and bell towers were 'switches', facilitating the flow of activities between the spatial, the social and the political fabric. They had powerful monopolies, performing as multiple distributed stations of control between local and global practice. Their role across scales indicates that they modulated cross-scale movement and interaction in both dual networks of space and society.

The Most Serene Republic: interpretations of Venice's Myth

For centuries Venice celebrated the fact that it had endured, intertwining the threads of parochialism and patriotism with the ideals of civic life. More than a millennium of unbroken self-government led to Venice's Myth, an inchoate system of beliefs that in the fifteenth and sixteenth centuries became formalised as an ideology, posing Venice as the exemplary Republic. From the mosaics of the Basilica of San Marco to de' Barbari's bird's eye view, and from public laws and private acts to humanistic discourse, 'Venetians celebrated their social harmony and the universal virtues of social concord and justice'.[87] The central elements of the Myth were the beauty of the city, the greatness of its empire, the stability of its institutions, the piety of its society and its preservation of independence from foreign powers. The situation in reality was more complex than this, as tensions indicated that Venetian society was also 'rife with conflict'.[88] However, these tensions were not severe enough to undermine a remarkable degree of internal cohesion based on the continued domination by an elite society.

Around the eleventh century, the government designated each of the parish churches as a *contrata*, superimposing 'a regularised system of secular administration on the pre-existing ecclesiastically-based parochial system'.[89] The political power of the *contrate* was further restricted by the growing employment of men in business and government, while local festivals were gradually suppressed and replaced by state rituals in the name of the Republic.[90] In the fifteenth and sixteenth centuries, civic initiatives and the emergence of the sovereign city were buttressed by administrative centralisation. These forces make Venice appear 'less serene and more real', and its Myth an enterprise of propaganda and promotion.[91] They also point at the difficulties in separating reality from the representation of Venice in popular beliefs, historiography and culture at the time, including subsequent accentuations of Venice's expression as an ideal society by scholars of the Myth in the nineteenth and twentieth centuries. As Martin and Romano explain, republican traditions born in the West – preoccupied with building their own strong democratic states – have put Venice to ideological use, serving particular interests and purposes.[92]

Of the many explanations of the Myth – ranging from the city's location and topography to its government, its policy and its political, commercial and social organisation – a few interpretations stand out. The first of these is Romano's analysis of social networks from 1297 to 1423.[93] For Romano, social stability was based on the fluidity of social ties necessary to develop and maintain trading networks, maritime activity and an ideal of community life: 'Even the patricians, the most status-conscious members of society, associated freely with the subordinate classes.'[94] These observations suggest that Venetians moved in a variety of intersecting social networks that were shaped and influenced by an overriding sense of civic community.[95] This fluidity prevented Venetian society from becoming 'overly polarised either along factional or [along] class lines'.[96] Yet, by the second quarter of the fifteenth century a new political and social order had emerged, intent on suppressing loosely formed associations across classes and reinforcing the hierarchical structure of society.

A second key interpretation of the Myth is Muir's study of rituals in the sixteenth century, suggesting that the competing 'theatres' of the parish and the state were the major force behind Venice's social concord. The resolution of this conflict was ensured by the supremacy of the centralised city-Republic, expressed in the form of a closed patrician class. Muir argues that in the sixteenth century, the patriciate created social institutions and a historical discourse in which the interests of the people were bound to the interests of the government. An intense community life through civic rituals developed in that period, giving rise to a Republican ideology. This class engendered the transformation of the Myth into official historiography, and 'created a new dramatic form, civic ritual, out of the struggle between parish and the city'. It henceforth adapted popular rituals – formerly organised by the *contrate* – 'into formal civic rituals, thereby rendering them inoffensive'.[97]

A third influential interpretation of the Myth comes from Richard Mackenney's study of guilds and charitable institutions, arguing that social diversity in these organisations and their participation in rituals created a demonstration of support for the body politic of the

Republic.[98] Finally, Elisabeth Crouzet-Pavan offers an explanation of the Myth as an ecological phenomenon, suggesting that the city's efforts to wrest land out of the waters of the lagoon forged solidarity through the natural environment, ideology and communal action.

These historians adopt different definitions of the Myth, examine it in different periods and use different methods. Romano lets Venetians 'speak for themselves', through political, social and work connections in everyday life, assembling knowledge about social networks bottom up from social deeds and actions.[99] Muir, instead, focuses on the ceremonial events of the sixteenth century, organising superordinate ideological structures. Mackenney links participation in *scuole*, *arte* and guilds with the ritualistic aspects of Venetian life. Finally, Crouzet-Pavan explores the collective, administrative, technical and ideological efforts to maintain the crucial relationship between land and water.

In spite of crucial differences, all the authors offer their various interpretations of the Myth in the form of dynamic interactions between historical, social, political, economic and ideological factors. More importantly, as John Martin and Denis Romano explain, scholars have more recently further diversified the Myth as 'discourse', rooted in the rich cultural life of the city's churches, monasteries, guilds and confraternities, its art, music, literature, ritual and theatre.[100] But if the Myth was, in effect, an expression of social, political and cultural life, the urban landscape constitutes one of the strongest elements of culture. Implicit in these authors' interpretations is the recognition that social and cultural phenomena had spatial manifestation by virtue of occurring in specific spaces and being dispersed or spatially localised. Yet, the role of space, spatial networks and locational patterns is tenuous in their analysis. The implication is that the urban landscape is devoid of a role in the formation of the Myth or, more generally speaking, in society and culture.[101]

The analysis of Venice's urban structure shows that space actively interfaced with the dynamic potential embedded in spatial networks where socio-political motivations influenced the distribution of benefits. Buildings, open spaces and infrastructural elements were the devices through which the socio-economic and political forces at work in the development of the city were made visible. Lying between the physical means of defining space and the invisible networks of communication and information, architecture and urban form have *active agency* in this process. If the structural coupling of spatial and social networks discussed earlier was the mechanism of city-craft, could they have contributed to Venice's Myth and the formation of *Civitas Venetiarum*? Now that we have identified the structural interdependence of space and society, answers to this question can be explored by focusing on space as discrete from the other factors.

Four-pointed star centrality: spatialising economic potential and institutional dynamics

The pervasive centrality of squares and the global centrality of the Piazza and the Rialto show that island communities shared the formation of both the foreground and the background networks. They also indicate that what the squares were to the islands, the Rialto and San Marco were to the city as a whole. Finally, they reveal the key role of the patrician society, the church and the professional organisations in shaping the city.[102] These institutions collectively constructed through the interrelations of water and land the geography of the parishes (the background) and the major structure of the city as a whole (the foreground).

To explore the variables of the parish and the city seen as a whole, we can represent the spatial values of the urban networks using a four-pointed star model (Figure 1.20).[103] The points on the vertical axis of the star plot the mean choice value (top) and mean integration value (bottom). The left and right points on the figure are the mean and maxima for these measures, respectively. Because the great majority of streets in cities belong to the background residential network, the mean choice value in urban systems represents the through-movement potential of this network. In contrast, the value of maximum choice stands for the potential for through-movement in the foreground system.[104] Figure 1.20a–b shows the plots of values for each of the four networks (street, canal, street–canal collapsed into one layer, combined street–canal linked through steps) in a single four-pointed star figure.[105] In terms of streets, Venice has the lowest mean and the lowest maximum value for both integration and choice that has been found in the analysis of 50 cities.[106] In addition, unlike cities which strongly distinguish between foreground and background (Figure 1.21), in Venice the mean and maxima are equal across a large number of elements.

Looking at the canals, we see that the values generally increase in relation to those of the street system, demonstrating the properties of the generic city and the role of the canal network as the city's main foreground structure. This network has the highest values in terms of mean choice, but is weak in terms of maximum choice. This means that the canal system is strong on movement in its background, but not very

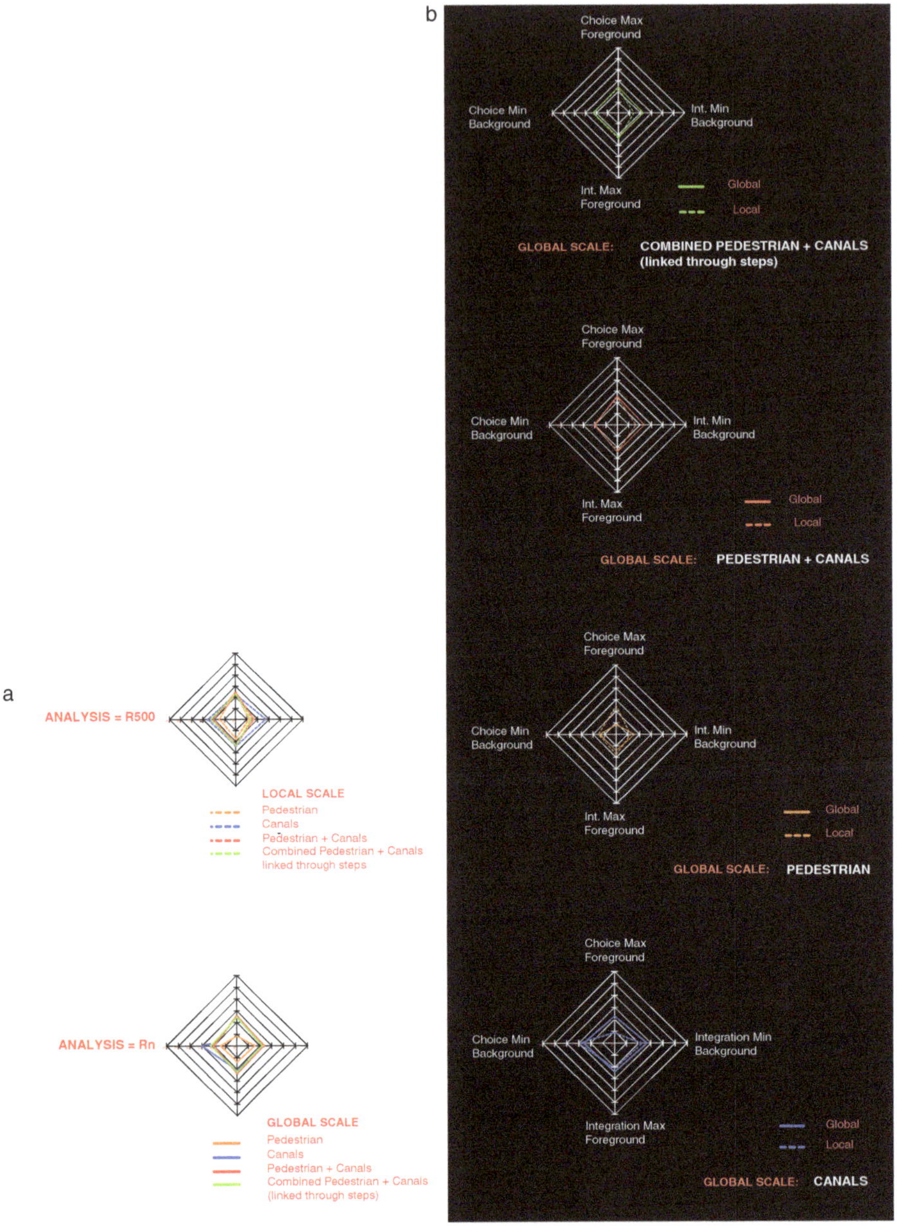

Figure 1.20 (a) Four-pointed star models of Venice of radius 500 metres (top left) and radius n (bottom left) for each of the four networks (1. pedestrian / 2. canal / 3. pedestrian + canal collapsed into one system / 4. pedestrian + canal joint through flights of steps and unlinked at bridges). Drawing by Tania Oramas Dorta
(b) Four-pointed star models of Venice for each of the four networks. Drawing by Tania Oramas Dorta

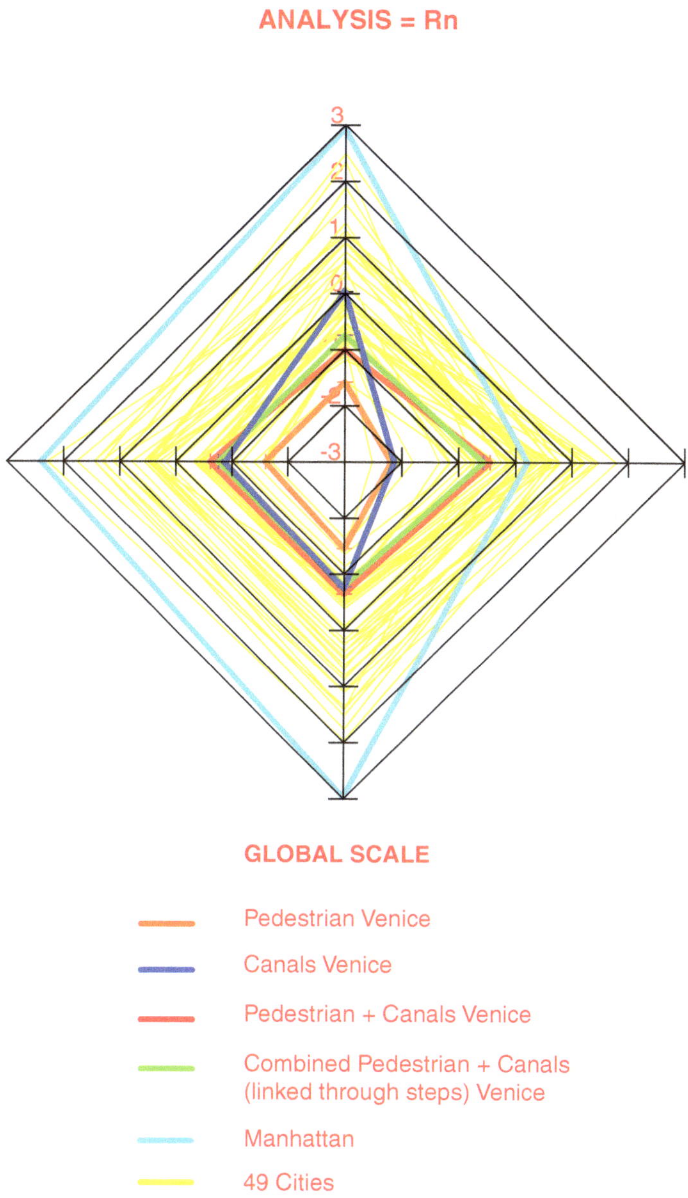

Figure 1.21 Four-pointed star models of 51 cities, including Venice and Manhattan. Drawing by Tania Oramas Dorta. Database of cities: courtesy of Bill Hillier

strongly differentiated, since there is no difference between mean and high values. The canals prioritise the background rather than the foreground; in other words, all canals become almost foreground due to the similarity of their mean values to the highest value. Another way of saying this is that they constitute a spatially equalising system in which the whole network is foreground and background, easing movement throughout its elements alike. Although much weaker in values than the canal system, the street network also has a stronger background than foreground (Figure 1.20a–b). This again illustrates an emphasis on equalising strength along the background of streets and on a similar type of relationship of each element with every other element in the system.

Finally, looking at the diamond shape of the canal–street system, we see that all values have equal strength, forming an almost perfect diamond shape (Figure 1.20a–b). The minimised differences in terms of foreground and background mean spatially equalising the potential of the network to attract movement and structure routes throughout the system. This equalisation of values shows that the residential areas forming the parishes (background) are just as strong as the foreground network that structures global-scale movement. If spatial differentiation of values is what creates structure (distinguishing a few elements of the foreground from the many components of the background), in Venice the background competed everywhere with the processes that were shaping the foreground, giving structure to local areas as well as to the system as a whole.

Assembling the Myth: urban form, urban ideology and the social fabric

The equalisation of movement potential throughout the physical fabric indicates that Venice's spatial networks were decentralised and distributed, the outcome of bottom-up action, where no element or node monopolises control. This spatial characteristic goes hand in hand with the coupling of social identities, the interlocking of solidarities and the geographical dispersion of social classes. Facilitating equal access to streets, canals and various quarters, the urban networks of Venice can both illuminate and be explained by many factors, such as the palaces functioning as dispersed centres of economic activity with strong relationship to foreground and background. The spatial characteristics, the political and commercial interests of the Venetian oligarchy, which invested in equality of power among their peer group, the wide participation of residents in the corporate bodies and, finally, the spatial dispersion of social groups reveal a collaboration between public and private interests, distributing to every canal, street and site equal rights of access.

In the early days of the city, responsibilities for the management of space lay with the leading parochial families and the parish. As the parishes lost their autonomy, officials known as the *capi di contrate* were assigned to each parish, while others (*giudici del piovego*) had the task of maintenance of the city's public facilities.[107] Efforts were made to consolidate public space in the interest of the 'common good', easing the flow of movement through the city quarters. These actions, terms and laws reveal that 'the notion of the common good became increasingly associated with the government'.[108] The numerous responsibilities assigned to parishes and their officials, however, reveal that the government viewed parishes as communities of interest with responsibilities to the city itself. The collaboration of the political and private economic spheres 'blended into collective spaces and infrastructure particularly at times when the city was involved in accelerated commercial expansion'.[109] There was a large demand for modification of the housing stock, while linear plotting in Cannaregio shows that norms were imposed by the commune in areas of recent land reclamation.[110] The high cost of construction, the scarcity of land, and the need for providing housing for all classes favoured groupings of compact residences. Private individuals and charitable societies initiated housing projects for those who could not afford a residence.[111]

> For centuries the people of the city gave unstintingly of their creative energy. Indeed, as the sources make clear, even if improvement did provoke conflict, encourage speculation, and made some people rich, there was nevertheless strong solidarity in the face of a hostile environment. The *vicini* of the parish societies led an effort that, if not always collective, was at least concerted.[112]

The *vicini* were people owning land in the parish where they resided, and who carried most of the burden of urban policy. Whatever the project, widening, repairing or paving an alley, dredging a canal or constructing a bridge, landowners paid for the work, and *estimi* of real estate values determined the share for each property owner. In many cases this meant that only adjacent properties were involved, while for larger projects 'the entire neighbourhood bore the financial burden collectively'.[113] Crouzet-Pavan describes this period as the 'heroic age of progress', during which the city was built through land reclamation. Later, from the fifteenth century on, came 'the age of water', in which the city took active measures to defend itself against dangers arising from the fragile, unstable lagoon environment and the unpredictable behaviour of its water.[114]

This meant increased state intervention in resource management, underwriting the resulting costs of private initiatives, including the establishment of a bureaucratic system of administration and new technical expertise in managing the environment. For Crouzet-Pavan, both 'ages' involved strong bonds of solidarity among the members of the lagoon community, bestowing upon the political authorities of Venice the responsibility for ensuring the city's survival. These factors indicate that the tension between the parishes and the state was resolved through extensive acts of manoeuvre and cooperation, negotiating and distributing movement potential through the city's quarters. As Wilson explains, 'local urban growth, the linked efforts of orderly expansion and public works to assuage the destructive potential of the sea, citywide organisations, and service to the state thereby worked together to reinforce associations between the parts of the city and its geography'.[115]

In spite of social stratification, the processes through which Venice, as a totality, became materialised by individual initiatives, together with its spatial and social networks, reveal a growing civic consciousness: the emergence of an urban ideology that celebrated the city's liberty, stability and achievement. Motivated by the requirements of political efficiency and commercial aims, the alignment of public and private interests and collective construction also enabled the development of communal values. Civic consciousness and a sense of urbanity became common among cities in the later Middle Ages, when civic bodies such as guilds established value systems of 'mutuality, solidarity, exchange and equity'. Anthony Black explains that such values were to be taken up as themes for European urban civic society, which drew on Aristotle's *Politics* but was also inspired by a broader philosophy centred on idealism in the Enlightenment.[116] Yet, due to the characteristics of structural coupling of spatial and social networks, spatial dispersion, dual social identities, loose class associations and interlocking of solidarities, Venice evolved unique and distinct properties in comparison with other cities. This meant that the collaboration between the public and private initiative intervened in a stronger form and with more consistency in the lagoon city than elsewhere.

One particular expression of this civic consciousness was *mediocritas*, a commonly held value that saw moderation and equality as the main principles in expressing the prestige of wealthy families. An outward demonstration of this was the palace façade, expressing equality of power status and prestige through a shared harmony of adjacent structures. It was widely accepted that no one should demonstrate excess in the appearance of their palaces, collectively enforcing norms of aesthetic principles among the powerful members of society. The equalisation of spatial properties and their visual manifestation therefore encode not only the memory of city-craft, but also the transformation from self-governed parishes into a commune of civic participation and a sovereign city, that is, the making of the *polis* as a spatial, social, economic, political and ideological project. These principles mediated the delicate tensions between private interests and public good, between the parishes and the state in urban affairs, as well as between the governing families of the Republic, which were embedded in all aspects of Venetian life.

For centuries, political theorists, historians and anthropologists have attributed Venice's Myth to various sources, from the heterogeneity of its parish communities to charitable institutions, civic ritual and juridico-political and ideological super-structures. What has been missing from this variegated picture, however, is the urban landscape as the collective product of culture. Based on an anatomy of Venice's urban networks and society, this study provides a definition of the Myth as a spatial phenomenon. It argues that in channelling flows between the foreground and background, Venice's parish-islands brought together palaces, churches and *scuole*, interfacing multiple solidarities and preventing society from being polarised. The spatial networks and their structural analogy with social networks were among the very mechanisms of longitudinal harmony and urban creativity that served a double purpose: maintaining class difference by directing attention to global politics and trade, and mitigating status difference through participation in the local politics of the parish. The second contribution the work makes is to describe Venice's Myth as urban ideology gradually emerging in synergy with the generation of urban morphology. It suggests that this ideology was as much an aspect of the super-ordinate structures of society as of the social actions of people, as much an issue of political and social meanings imposed from the top as an issue of the active agency of space rehearsed from the ground.

What relevance does Venice have for urban societies of today? Historians have been comparing Manhattan and Venice as two exceptional island metropolises connected with territories larger than their geographical limits.[117] In spite of having different histories and spatial geometries, the two cities have strong similarities. Like Venice, which was a strategic node in trading networks in late medieval and early Renaissance times (Figure 1.22), New York in the early twentieth century was a crucial hub of global networks of finance. Unlike Venice, which gradually integrated a system of regulations into the evolutionary operations that drove the development of the urban fabric, Manhattan was changed into a regular urban grid through the Commissioners' plan to suit the needs of an emergent capitalist society (Figure 1.23). The Commissioners of the grid sought to maximise economic utility, serving the real estate interests of their day and laying the political and economic foundations of the American empire. This is clearly reflected in the mean values of the background network in Manhattan, demonstrating, as Hillier has argued, equal distribution of economic potential over the territory (Figure 1.21).[118] Like Manhattan's grid, Venice's networks created a spatially 'democratic' system that was economically driven as much through the neighbourhoods as through its foreground. In spite of differences of spatial geometry, and the fact that the

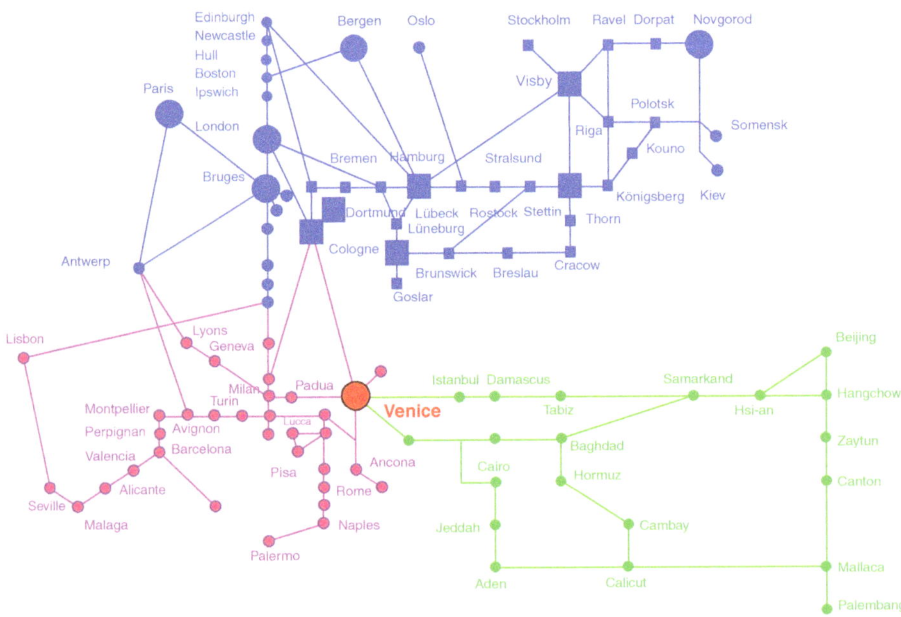

Figure 1.22 Trading networks of cities in late medieval period. Drawing by the author

Figure 1.23 *Plan of the City of New York and of the Island, as laid out by the Commissioners, altered and arranged to the present time*. New York: A.T. Goodrich, 1828. © British Library Board. Maps 73953(9)

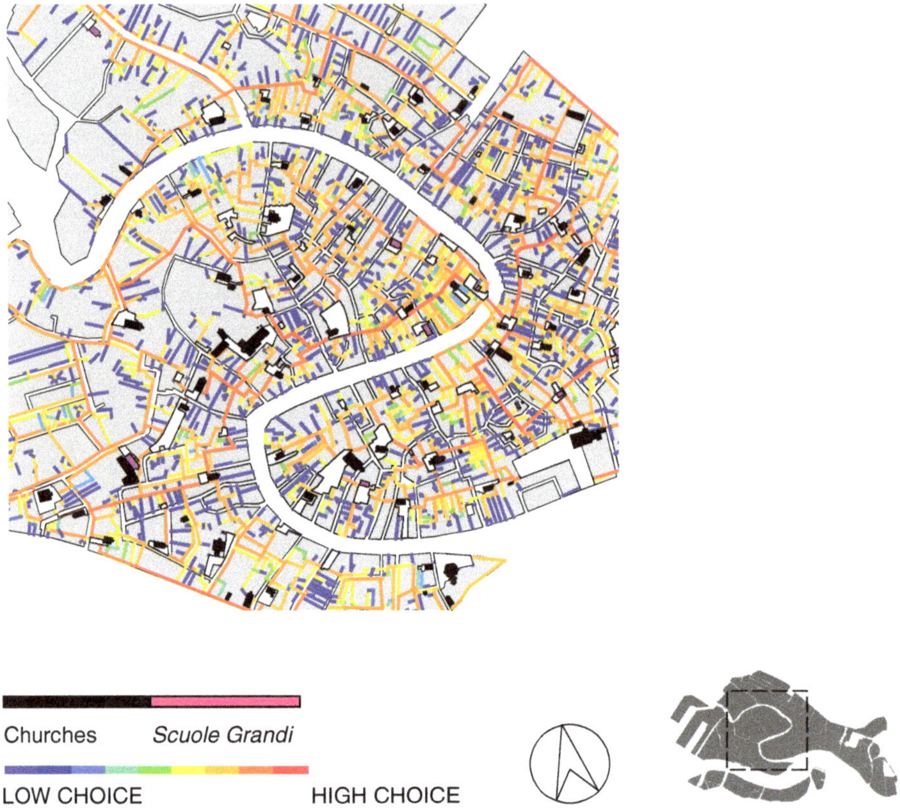

Figure 1.24 (a) Venice 1829. Pedestrian network, measure of normalised angular choice, at radius 3000 metres. Drawing by the author

equalisation of routes in Venice was bottom-up rather than top-down, Manhattan and Venice can be seen as *pragmatic utopias*, equalising economic opportunity in space.

Postscript

If entities are ontologically specific whereas the generic is the more general category they are part of, in Manhattan the generic 'craftsmen' of the city were the Commissioners, while in Venice they were the anonymous members of a society with its multiple artisan-authors. Gradually the imposition of organisation from the top down and the evolution of urban growth from the bottom up converged through a process of adaptation over time. This was the case even when Roman towns were

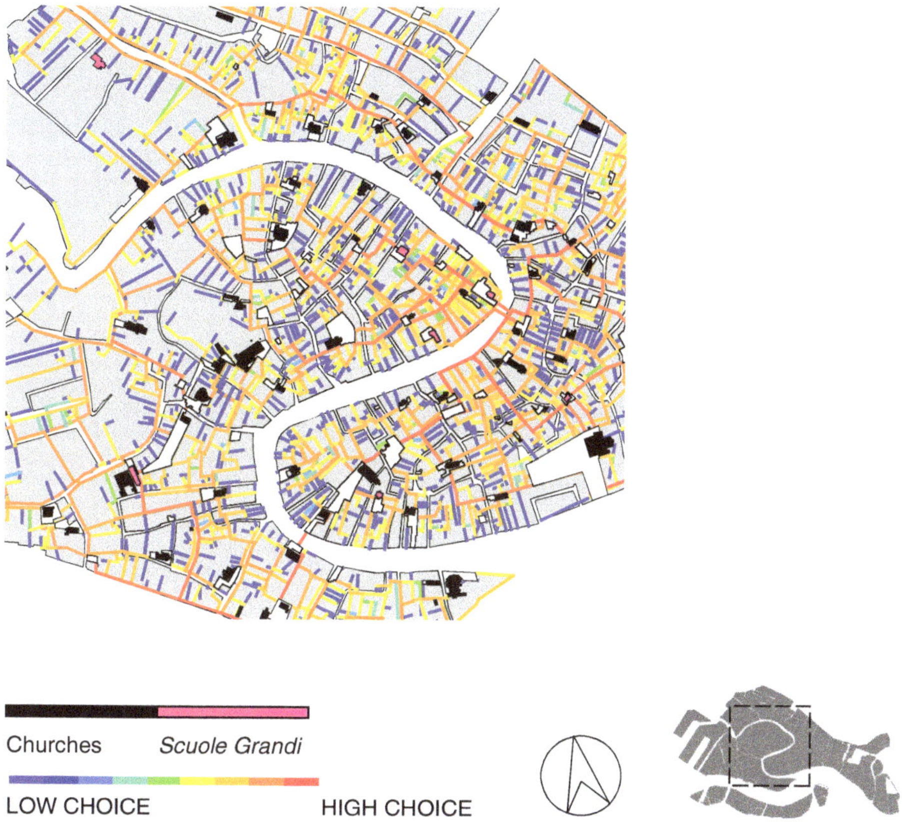

Figure 1.24 (b) Venice 1859. Pedestrian network, measure of normalised angular choice, at radius 3000 metres. Drawing by the author

built from scratch through a generic model that was repeated on every occasion and subsequently evolved as a result of a long-term process. In Venice this process had been taking place for centuries before two interconnected factors took charge: the centralised city with its values of civic government, and the rise of classical architecture. Changes to a new political order in the fifteenth and sixteenth centuries led to social stratification, in which Venetians looked less to personal ties and more to institutionalised forms of association. Along with these transformations came the development of a Republican ideology 'where the analytic rhetoric of the humanists clothed Venetian institutions in neoclassical dress and made them appear as if they were living models of ancient ideas'.[119] For Muir, the ideology of social stability, liberty and the perfect political system was then promoted by the hands of the

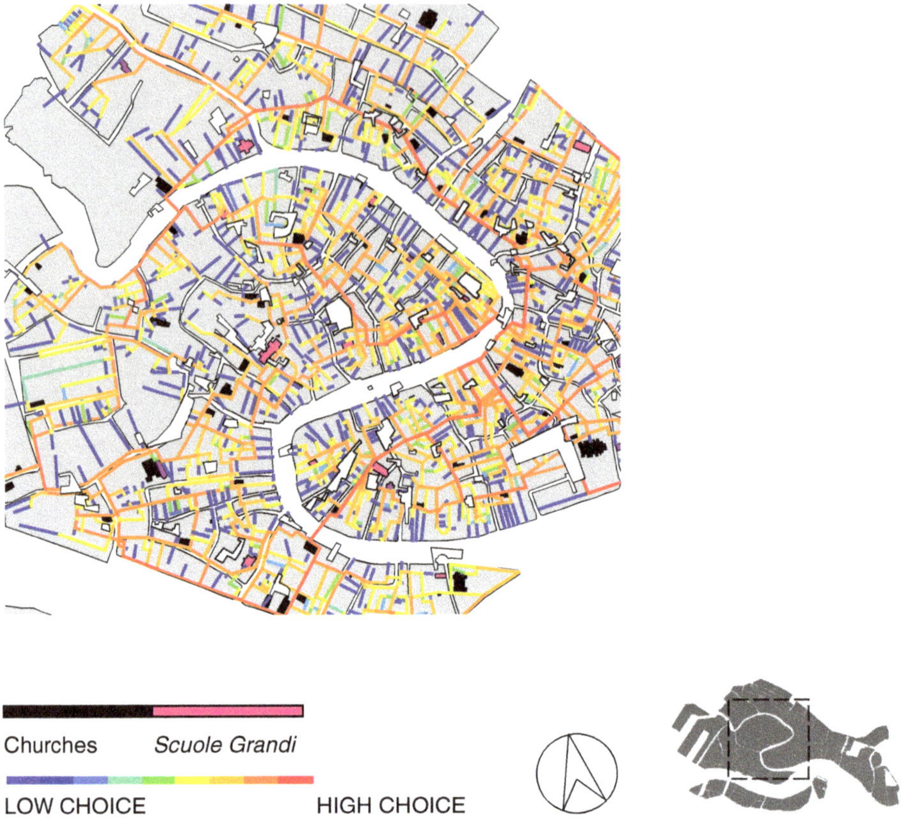

Figure 1.24 (c) Venice 1910. Pedestrian network, measure of normalised angular choice, at radius 3000 metres. Drawing by the author

governing patricians bringing about the civic ritual – a new dramatic form in Venice.[120] Coincident with the emergence of the centralised city of ceremonial processions was the rise of architecture as liberal art with an attributed author. This is the time when Jacopo Sansovino and Andrea Palladio came to Venice.

Before moving to this discussion in the next chapter, it is essential to report on investigation of historical maps of Venice as a way to test the results of the analysis against previous periods. Looking at maps from 1829, 1859 and 1910, one sees that the network of *campi* had been in the making for a long time (Figure 1.24a–c).[121] The second thing we observe through this historical analysis is that from 1829 to 1859 the major through-routes become increasingly continuous along the right side of the Grand Canal. A clear thoroughfare exists, shown

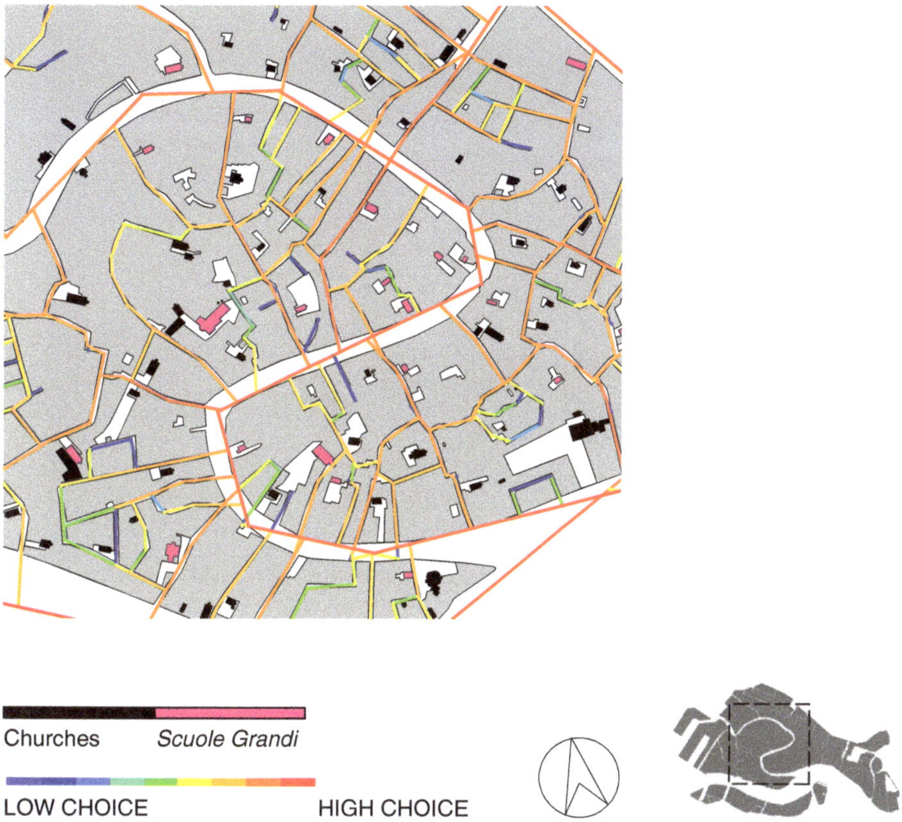

Figure 1.25 (a) Venice 1829. Canal network, measure of normalised angular choice, at radius 3000 metres. Drawing by the author

in red, connecting Cannaregio via the Rialto and the Academia Bridge with Dorsoduro and the southern perimeter of the city at Zatere. From 1859 to 1910 this major through-route extends to the north-east side of Venice, linking with the train station. This change in the pattern of routes reflects the need to ease the flows of people arriving at the railway station and the bus termini. Over time spatial connections in the urban fabric of Venice have been enhanced, facilitating movement from the entrance to the city at the terminal of Santa Lucia and Piazzale Roma to the Rialto and the Piazza, the two major tourist attractions. What this analysis reveals is that the parishes retain their network-like connections and their strength in terms of pervasive centrality, but there is also evidence of the large-scale impact of industrialisation, tourism and migration.

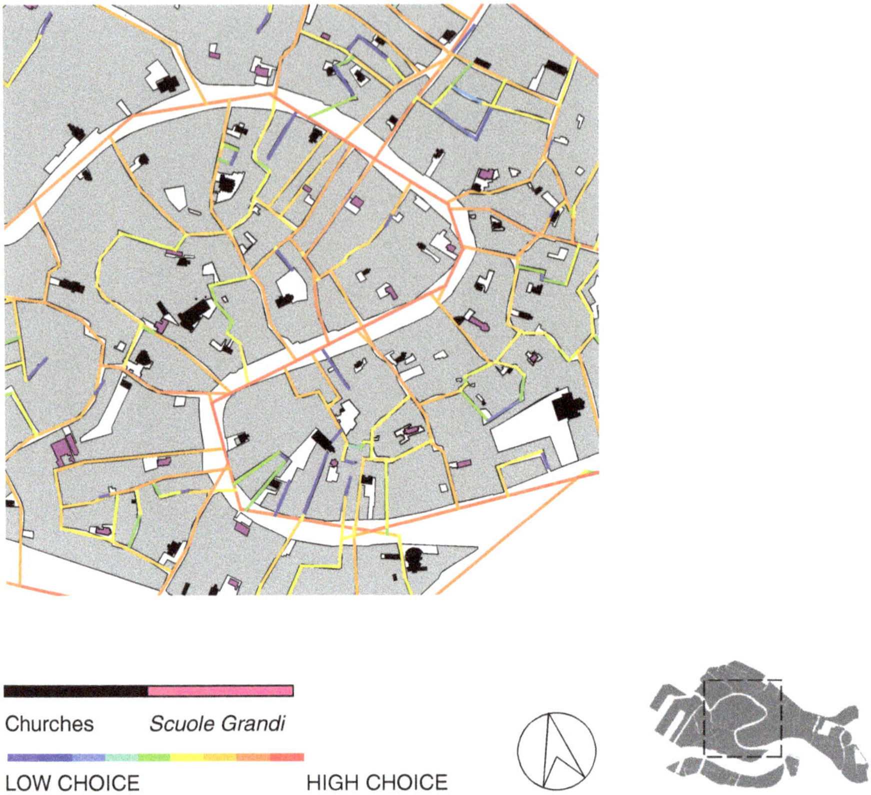

Figure 1.25 (b) Venice 1859. Canal network, measure of normalised angular choice, at radius 3000 metres. Drawing by the author

Over the centuries, many old canals have been filled in (*rii terra*), while new ones have been dug in newly reclaimed areas. However, on the whole, these changes have not influenced the configurational logic of the canal system, as the analysis of historical maps suggests, showing that the structure of waterways has changed little over time (Figure 1.25a–c). The nodal function of the *campi* between water and land is a constant characteristic in the 1829, 1859 and 1910 maps of Venice. But it must have been fundamental since the early days, as we see in the 1500s map of Jacopo de' Barbari (Figure 0.6), showing that many *campi* were always directly connected with the water. Looking at the 1859 combined canal–street map, we see that 52 per cent of *campi* are located close to the foreground structure of the water–land system (Figure 1.26). Based on the very few changes that took place in

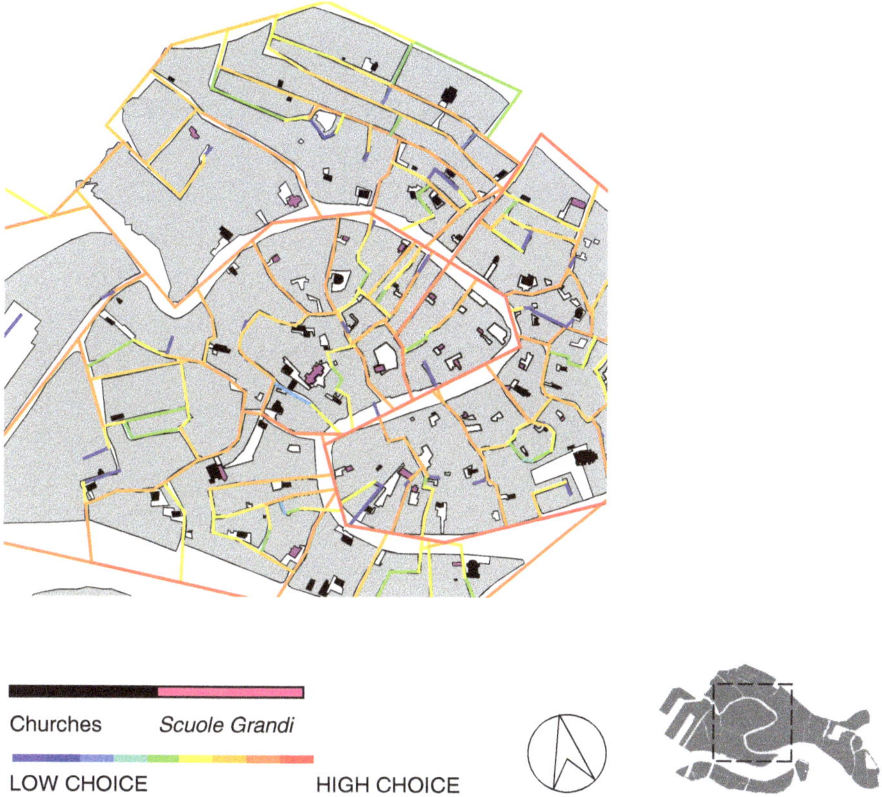

Figure 1.25 (c) Venice 1910. Canal network, measure of normalised angular choice, at radius 3000 metres. Drawing by the author

Venice after the sixteenth century, we may suggest that the majority of squares have been close to this network since the beginning.

The analysis of integration shows that the twin hubs are constantly well interconnected and integrated over time (Figure 1.27). Yet, from 1859 to today, a gradual shift of 'integration' values has occurred, linking the north-western and south-eastern parts of Venice, spreading integration from Cannaregio to the Rialto, San Marco and, through the Academia bridge, to Dorsoduro. As previously observed when looking at choice, these shifts reveal the need to link the train station in Cannaregio with the most popular locations in the city, such as the Rialto, San Marco, Academia and Santa Maria della Salute. Before the railway, when arrival at the city would have been by boat from the south-east, the distribution of integration would have made a stronger distinction between the twin hubs and the rest of the city's

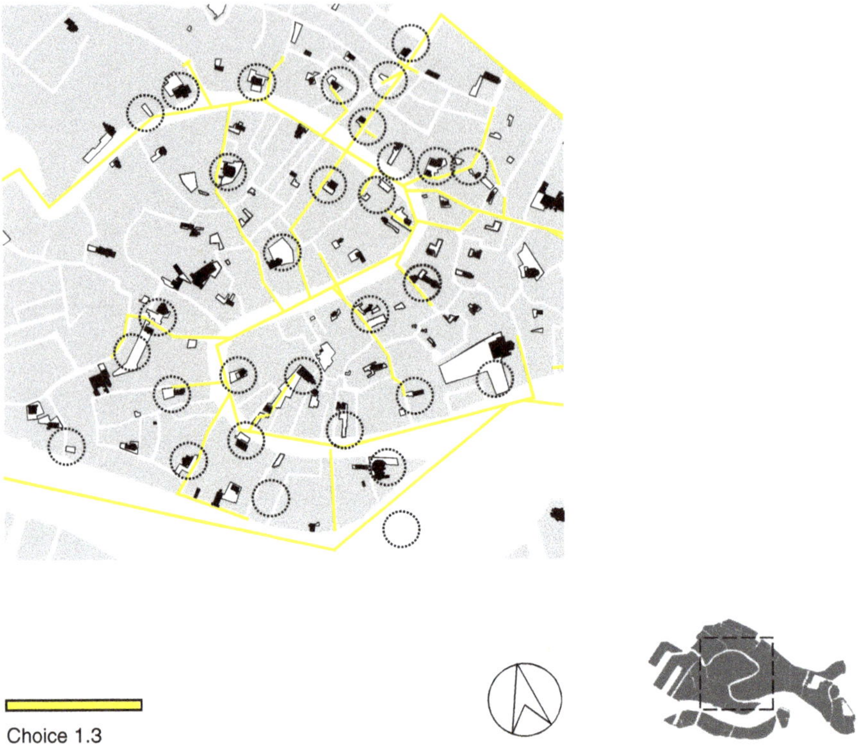

Figure 1.26 Venice 1859. The squares located within 50 metres from the elements of the highest values of normalised angular choice in the combined pedestrian–canal system, radius 3000 metres. Drawing by the author

quarters. In the past, the two centres would have been the busiest spots, with shops, market stalls, boats, envoys, festivities and traffic. In contrast, the rest of the areas would have been less prominent destinations located between the canals and the capillaries of alleyways. Arriving from the mainland or from the sea, visitors would have disembarked at the Piazzetta or further along the Grand Canal at the Rialto. Travellers entering the city would have been greeted by the extraordinary spectacle of the Basilica of San Marco, the Campanile, the Doge's palace and the palaces lining the Grand Canal perforated by loggias and windows and crowned by chimneys and *altanas* (wooden terraces). As Venice has become the focus of mass tourism, the changes in the structure of the to- and through-movement routes have reflected the practical need to facilitate large flows through the city. Arriving at the opposite end of the ceremonial entrance to Venice, today's visitors have to negotiate

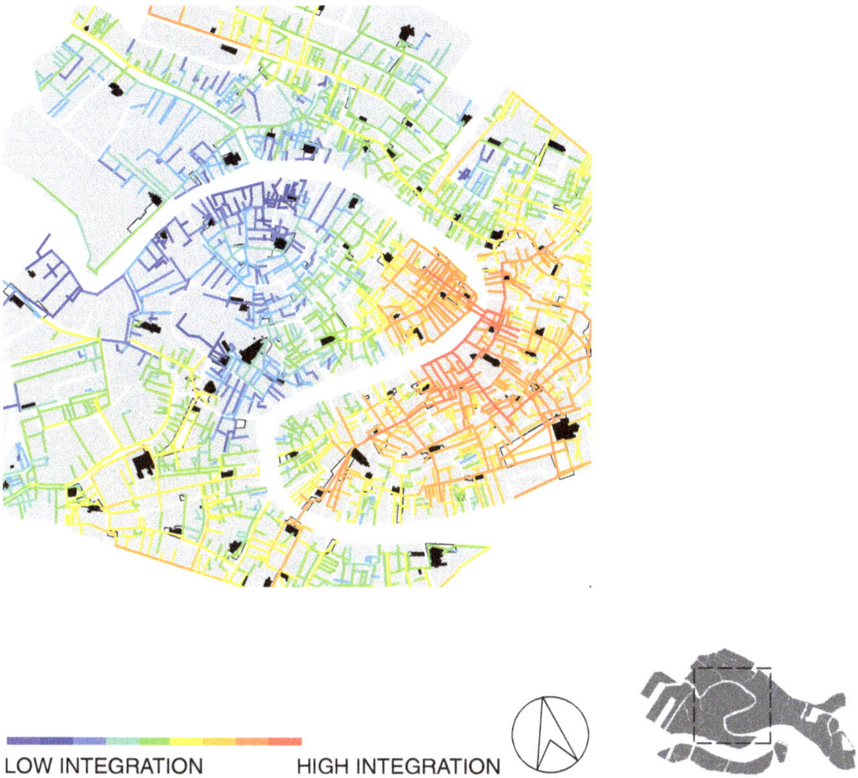

Figure 1.27 Venice 1859. Canal network, measure of normalised angular integration, at radius 3000 metres. Drawing by the author

the labyrinth of streets before marvelling at the Palazzo Ducale, the Piazza and Palladio's churches on the opposite islands.

The Piazza, the Piazzetta and the Basin of San Marco still form the main civic entrance to the city for those arriving by boat, and have been throughout history the sites of spectacles, particularly on the feast of Santa Maria della Salute on 21 November and the Festa del Redentore on the third weekend of July, when the Venetians cross the Grand Canal and the Giudecca Canal on a temporary bridge of boats.

Figure 2.0 Venice. View of the city and San Marco Basin (Bacino). Drawing by Athina Lazaridou

2 Statecraft: A remarkably well-ordered society

> Hence there is no difficulty in telling these apart from those that date from the time of the Goths, and also from many years after that, because the two are almost what you could call diametrically opposed extremes. Nor is there any difficulty in telling our modern buildings apart from the Gothic ones, if for no other reason than their newness, by which they are recognizable.
>
> Letter to Leo X by Raphael and Baldassare Castiglione (c. 1519), in Vaughan Hart and Peter Hicks (eds/trans), *Palladio's Rome: A Translation of Andrea Palladio's Two Guidebooks to Rome*

Introduction: the interlocking spheres of city-craft and statecraft[1]

Trade was Venice's raison d'être, developed through interconnections of water and land, and constituting the primary force shaping the city's form, establishing its relationship with its wider surroundings in the lagoon and the mainland. This was the driving force drawing the flows of cargo and people, impelling the draining of the marshlands and clearing of the swamps. It led to the creation of landfills and quays, parcelling the land into plots, and the improvement of canals. The requirements of trade threaded the city with streets and enlarged and enhanced the urban fabric.[2] At the same time as the organic form of the city was evolving, there was the gradual development of a parallel 'project' of aggrandisement in the strategic spaces of the Rialto, the Arsenale and the Piazza

San Marco, eventually superimposing a Roman classical style on the original Byzantine and Gothic medieval styles. The collective production driving Venice's urban networks was a response to economic and cultural processes, defining characteristics through which we recognise the anonymous processes of cities and the culture they nurture. The amplification and celebration of major civic spaces, on the other hand, was the outcome of a self-conscious engagement with the image the city presented.

The long series of architectural renovations that progressively took place in the major public spaces of Venice expresses the synthesis of the trading imperatives of a nation whose lifeblood was marine mercantilism with the need of an imperial power to give its aspirations civic expression. The Piazza San Marco in particular, with the Basilica of San Marco, the Ducal Palace, the Campanile and associated structures in the Bacino (the Basin of San Marco), was the epicentre of Venice, the seat of its religious and political power. Theatrically shaped and the host for various rituals, the Piazza became a dramatic stage performance in its own right (Figure 2.1). From the spectacular arrangement of buildings and festivities to its emblematic architecture, it crystalised the values and ideologies of the Venetian Republic. These values were expressed through various representations, collectively forming the Myth of Venice, a system of beliefs

Figure 2.1 Il Volo del Turco. Anonymous woodcut showing the unfinished library and the two-storey Zecca (sixteenth century). Museo Correr, Venice

that saw the city as the embodiment of civic perfection. The appearance of the Piazza and how it manifests Venice's Myth has been widely discussed in architectural literature.[3] What has not been addressed is whether the Myth was a matter not only of the richness of its social and political history, but also of spatial relations. In the previous chapter I described Venice's urban form, arguing that the property of equal access to spaces forms a particular expression of the Myth, which is recorded in its spatial networks. In this chapter, I raise the question of whether the Myth was inscribed in the spatial strategies that shaped the Piazza San Marco, over and above the external appearance of its individual buildings. This chapter explores the Piazza and the Bacino in the fifteenth and sixteenth centuries, since this was the period during which architecture emerged as a liberal art. These were the particular spaces where the Myth of Venice and architecture coalesced into a formal ideology personified by the Roman classical style. Hence, I raise a number of questions. With the benefit of a clear understanding of the ways in which Venice grew out of parish communities, can the Piazza illuminate the encounter between the organic evolution of the city and the conscious strategies of the Republic's elite? How can the relationship between the constituent parishes and the state as a unitary whole be understood through the transformations that took place in the Piazza? What role did architecture and ritual play in the spheres of *city-craft*, the anonymous processes that had built Venice, and *statecraft*, the conscious engagement of the patrician society with architecture and the urban fabric?

Imago urbis

Like the present day's explosion of mobile devices, online mapping and geospatial applications, the advent of the printing press and the discovery of the New World at the end of the fifteenth century revolutionised both mapmaking and the geography it sought to represent. Venice and the Veneto were the birthplace of the business of publishing, home to more than 450 printers, publishers and booksellers. Many of these businesses were located in the Merceria, the commercial streets that linked the Rialto with San Marco, dealing in texts in Latin, Greek, the vernacular and foreign languages.[4] Printers and booksellers not only fuelled interest in the Classics, architecture, geography, mathematics and philosophy, but even inspired wonder in Venice itself with engravings of the city's topography. Condensing the world into an imprint, maps and texts did not just disseminate a factual account of Venice, but also promoted the 'ideal' notion of Venice as the theatre of the world, the perfect union of place and institutions.[5]

By the sixteenth century, Venice had ten theatres and also made use of floating theatrical tableaux (*teatri del mundi*) on the water's edge and in the Basin.[6] More importantly, Venetians practised public theatre in the form of ceremonial occasions and performances in the Piazza San Marco. The whole area of the Piazza and the water beyond became a unified visual space. It had also come to resemble in its form a stage set in itself, celebrated in numerous maps and works of art since early times (Figure 2.1). An idea of how the Piazza looked at the beginning of the sixteenth century can be obtained from the map of de' Barbari, the largest and most detailed plan of Venice prior to modern times, and the earliest aerial perspective of the city that has survived (Figure 0.3).[7] Printed to the scale of a mural, the woodcut depicts Venice, framed by the outlines of the lagoon, as a triumphant metropolis. The centrepiece of this image is the Piazza, marked out by its major buildings. De' Barbari's print inspired a series of maps portraying Venice as a 'walled city', similar to contemporary visualisations of ideal cities and their customs (Figure 0.6). By the end of the sixteenth century, the bird's eye views of Venice with a centre at the Piazza San Marco, a distorted view of the Alps, and the shoreline with the islands in the lagoon encircling the city had become emblematic of the Republic itself (Figure 2.2).[8] Placing Venice and San Marco at the centre of an ideal cosmography, these images promoted the idea that if the Piazza was central to Venice, Venice was central to the world as a realised utopia of prosperity and ideal political institutions.

In contrast to this idealised representation of the state, the actual prominence of *La Serenissima* had begun to fade. The city's economic stability was successively undermined by three main developments: the loss of Byzantium to the Ottomans (1453), reducing the scope for Venice to dominate trade in the eastern Mediterranean; the War of the League of the Cambrai (1508–1516) in which the Pope and the European powers united to stop the expansion of Venice's territories on the mainland; and, finally, the opening up of trading routes in the wake of a surge in oceanic exploration.[9] Confronted with a progressive loss of power, the Venetian elite saw Venice as the successor to the fallen Eastern capital. A process of redefinition was launched, under Doge Andrea Gritti (1455–1538), with the purpose of consolidating the image of an ancient, stable and monolithic state. These transformations involved institutional and intellectual means as well as serial physical reconfigurations. The latter comprised an ambitious and grandiose programme of urban renovation (*Renovatio Urbis*) aimed at improving the urban fabric.[10] This programme officially started in the fifteenth century, but in reality was a continuation of a long, fragmented process to reconfigure the Arsenale, the Rialto and the Piazza

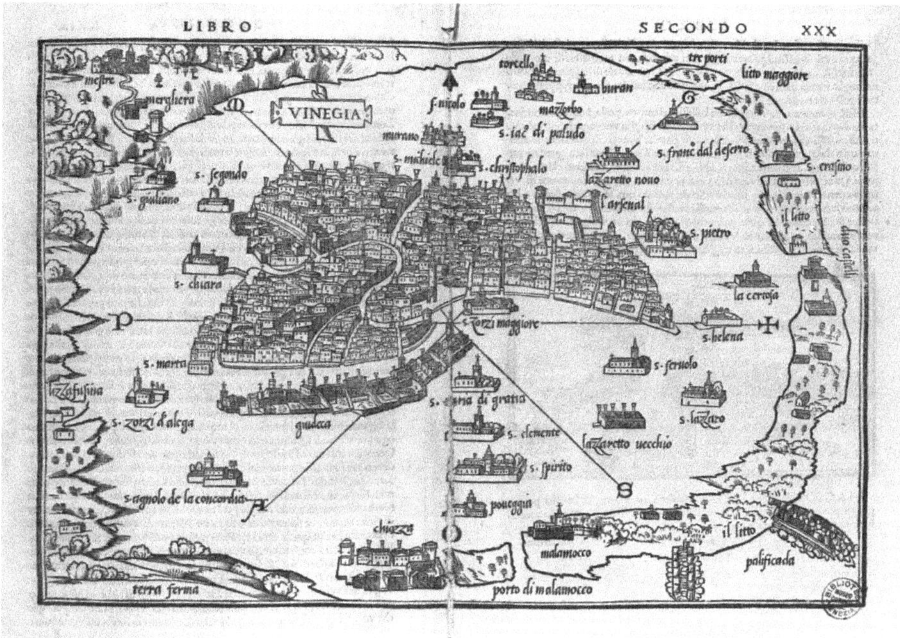

Figure 2.2 *Vinegia*. From Benedetto Bordone's *Isolario* (1528). Museum Correr, Venice

San Marco that had begun a few centuries earlier.[11] The first two sites were central to the military and commercial life of Venice, respectively, and had their own operational and symbolic requirements.[12] The civic and religious space of the Piazza, on the other hand, offered the clearest opportunity for public expression. The transformations at San Marco lined up the Piazza and the Piazzetta with new structures in the emergent classical style, expressing the re-invention of these spaces as an imperial forum.

A reformed discipline

Venice might have lost its maritime supremacy but, by that time, it had become the most dynamic publishing centre in Europe, the union of dissemination of information with artistic, scientific and geographical discovery. The explosion in the publishing and printing of books meant that editions of architecture, theatre, classics, mapping and navigation began to circulate in unprecedented numbers; this sudden surge in the availability of information was instrumental in bringing about the birth of modernity.[13] Printing technology and the discovery of Vitruvius' *Ten Books on Architecture* were reforming the discipline of architecture through the publication of treatises from the early Italian Renaissance onwards.[14] While building practices in the medieval era were transmitted from one generation to the next through direct observation, memory and speech, Renaissance architects developed an expanding repertoire of illustrated media. These media reproduced antique examples from architects' surveys and written descriptions by Vitruvius, often presenting the architects' own work as models in the classical style.[15] Collectively, these treatises document the separation of architecture from the medieval traditions of craftsmanship, marking its transformation from a practical to a liberal art. Prominent in this sea change was the emergence of the figure of the architect, closely resembling the concept of the professional architect today, concerned with authorial control over the finished product of design.[16] Nowhere else in Venice is the break between self-conscious architecture and vernacular architectural more clearly visible than in the urban renovations in the Piazza and Venice's southern islands.

These renovations were the work of many contributors, but among the series of architects, patrons and master builders leaving their mark on the area two main figures stand out: Andrea Palladio (1508–1580) and Jacopo Sansovino (1486–1570). Palladio was born in the Veneto, and practised there before moving to Venice in the early 1550s, having attracted, with his designs for palaces and villas, the patronage of powerful Venetian patricians such as Daniele and Marcantonio Barbaro. In 1554 he accompanied Daniele to Rome to assist in completing work on the first translation of Vitruvius's *De architectura*, edited by Daniele and illustrated mainly by Palladio.[17] Sansovino, originally from Florence, had a thriving professional practice in Venice for 30 years. He was the official state architect of the city (*protomaestro*, abbreviated to *proto*), responsible for the reconfiguration of the Piazza San Marco. While Sansovino operated in the heart of Venice, Palladio's commissions were principally in the urban periphery of Venice and the mainland.[18] The former was a skilful translator of the indigenous building tradition through his own architectural language. The latter was more uncompromising, making few concessions to the existing built legacies of the city.[19]

Architecture and the Myth of Venice

Both architects were supported and controlled by a centralised bureaucracy supervised by officers from the patrician elite, and serviced by local district governors, engineers and surveyors. The central administration of the physical and symbolic landscape of the city constituted a social network located at the heart of learned discourse on the practical and liberal arts among the political elite of the Republic. The wider socio-political context within which the two architects operated was changing with the contemporary foreign challenges facing Venice. However, the most radical shift had already taken place at the turn of the fourteenth century. This concerned the closing of the Major Council to new members (*serrata del Maggior Consiglio*, 1297), a move that defined the political elite as a self-perpetuating hereditary oligarchy.[20] This had resulted in the exclusion from decision-making power of all but a select few families in the patrician circles, by comparison with the thirteenth century, when Venetians had much more fluid and wide-reaching social ties. The defining context of Venice's enduring qualities, or the Myth of Venice, within which architecture rose in the lagoon, intertwined idealised visions of high art with complex definitions of identity, social and civic order. The emergence of architecture was therefore interwoven with *statecraft*, a centralised bureaucracy of patrons and intellectuals, accustomed to pageantry, practised in ritual, and dedicated to exalting the Myth of the Most Serene Republic.

The history of architecture in Venice and the Veneto is characterised by privileged, conscious architectural authorship based on the production of artefacts, synthesising various kinds of human understanding (architecture, optics, cosmology, music, philosophy, engineering, mathematics). Even when historians look at buildings in the social and economic context of the society that created them, they tend to confine their attention to the interactions of architects with patronage, dissociating architecture from the emergent collective processes, continuously creating the city and the spaces of everyday life. This oversight obscures the fact that the benefits germinating from the evolutionary city-making process – the civic and religious places, institutional territories, processional routes, ritual centres and spatial borders – were all the products of shared knowledge among the patricians, architects, craftsmen and ordinary citizens in the Republic. The history of architecture and its patrons has been well rehearsed in terms of how it developed as a reformed art, and the changes it brought to the physical fabric. What is less well known is the encounter between *popular thought* underlying the evolutionary processes of the city, and *elitist thought* in the conscious articulation of architecture and civic space. Focusing on the Piazza complex and the Bacino, this chapter describes the interlocking relationship of conscious architecture, the institutional and intellectual resources mobilised by statecraft, and the networked spaces of everyday action. It argues that the *Renovatio Urbis* provided an architectural opportunity for statecraft. It annexed architecture and city-craft, popular myths and official historiography, parochial rituals and civic rituals to promote the vision of a centralised city arranged for ceremonial processions. The Republican apparatus externalised and schematised the spatial and ritual geography of Venice, previously formed by the practices that had shaped the city since medieval times, to provide an integrative vision of Venice that epitomised and exalted the state. This casts new light on the widespread view of the emergence of architecture as the separation of conscious architectural intent from the unconscious processes responsible for cities and ordinary buildings. I propose that this separation became a political instrument, inciting an intentional divorce of the centralised city from the implicitly democratic processes that had given form to the collective city. Before examining the spatial and ideological means that orchestrated this, it is essential to briefly describe the transformations that took place in the Piazza and the wider urban complex.

A Byzantine chapel and a new Roman forum

The island of San Marco has a strategic position, controlling the entrance to the Grand Canal and the route towards the littoral islands that separate the lagoon from the Adriatic. Its focal point is the Piazza, with the Ducal Palace and Basilica of San Marco, the Doge's residence and private chapel (Figures 2.3a–b). The Piazza is enclosed on three sides by the loggia façade of the Procurators of San Marco, the most prestigious group after the Doge, being elected for life and tasked with looking after the Basilica. The Piazzetta forms an extension of the Piazza to the waterfront, and is flanked by the Palace on the right and Sansovino's Marciana Library (Libreria Marciana) on the left. Until 1846, when the railway line connected Venice with the mainland, the Piazzetta was the formal entrance to the city. When foreign dignitaries and ambassadors arrived from the lagoon, their first view of the city was from the waterfront, looking towards the Piazza through the Piazzetta (Figure 2.4). The two columns at the water's edge (Porta da Mar) would greet them, bearing symbols of the two patron protectors of Venice: one surmounted by a winged lion, the symbol of St Mark the Evangelist, patron saint of Venice, and the other, the Greek soldier St Theodore of Amasea and his dragon, an older Byzantine guardian of the city. The two columns marked the place of execution for criminals and the arena where spectacles would be conducted. The Piazza, the Piazzetta and the entire water expanse of the Bacino were the heart of ceremonial occasions, from processional rituals to festivals, regattas and mock sea battles (Figure 2.5), expressing the ritual structure of society and the social order of justice.

Figure 2.3 (a) Map of contemporary Venice with Piazza San Marco. Drawing by the author

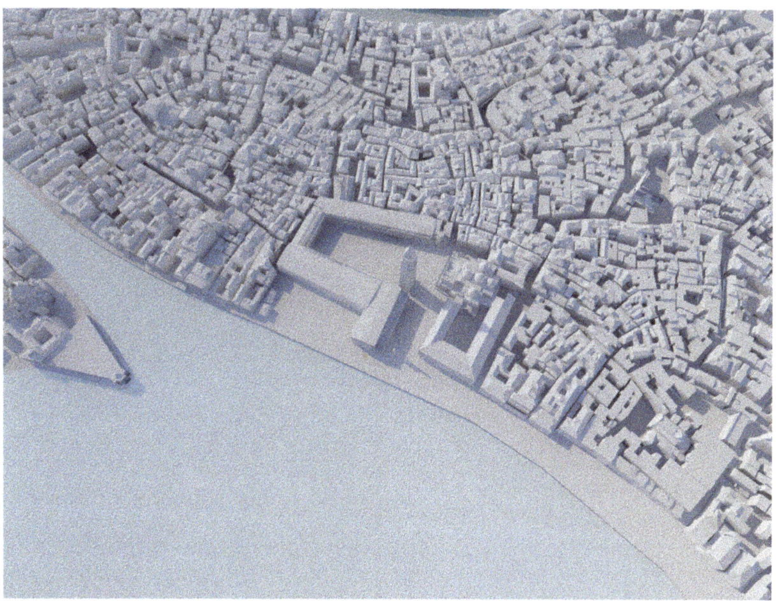

Figure 2.3 (b) Three-dimensional model of Venice with the Piazza San Marco. Having served as the religious and civic centre of Venice in the days of the Venetian Republic, the Piazza is one of the most celebrated urban squares in the world. Drawing by Athina Lazaridou

Figure 2.4 Venice. View of the Piazza and the Piazzetta from the water. Image by Mariordo (Mario Roberto Durán Ortiz) – own work, CC-BY-SA 4.0 via Wikimedia Commons (https://commons.wikimedia.org/w/index.php?curid=61002136)

Figure 2.5 Canaletto. *The Bacino of San Marco on Ascension Day*. Royal Collection Trust / © Her Majesty Queen Elizabeth II 2017

In his letter to Pietro Bolognese in 1364, Petrarch (1304–1374) described a series of celebrations he had witnessed in the Piazza, a space which for him was without equal in the world.[21] The Piazza Petrarch saw was very different from that of previous times, and had yet a long way to go before it reached the form it took in the fifteenth and sixteenth centuries. The entire complex was elaborated over a long, fragmented process. An idea of its appearance in its early days can be obtained from Fra Paolino's map (c. 1346), showing a defensive compound enclosing the palace and the Basilica of San Marco (Figure 1.1). The original castle-palace was on the water's edge, surrounded by a natural moat of canals, while the Basilica faced onto a square just half the length of the present area. At the western end of the square was a canal, on the opposite bank of which stood the old church of San Geminiano.[22]

The first major transformation leading to the present appearance of the Piazza came in the 1170s with Doge Sebastiano Ziani (1172–1178). Ziani's vision was to create a vast space where all Venice's citizens could congregate, in the form of an ancient forum, to legitimise his political choices.[23] He doubled the length of the Piazza and created a continuous line of buildings around it for the Procurators.[24] Ziani also created the Piazzetta, placed the two columns on the Molo and enlarged the Ducal Palace.[25] The next significant changes came in the fourteenth century, with the redevelopment of the Basilica and the Palace (1340, Figure 2.6). The Basilica was modelled on the Apostoleion, a Byzantine temple in Constantinople. A triumphal arch between the Palace and the Basilica (Porta della Carta) was also constructed a century later (construction began in 1438), forming an official entrance to the Palace courtyard for foreign dignitaries (Figure 2.7).[26] Finally, the construction of the Clock Tower (Torre dell' Orologio) began on the north side of the Piazza (1496). The Orologio was the most advanced astronomical clock then in existence, celebrating the entry point to the commercial thoroughfare leading to the Rialto. It set automata in motion, signalling the passage of cosmological and civic time.[27] The state of the Piazza at the turn of the fifteenth century can be seen in the map of de' Barbari (1500), showing the central wing of the Orologio, then under construction (Figure 0.6).

In the first decades of the sixteenth century, the Venetians intensified their efforts to improve the image of the city in inverse proportion to its declining power. The ambitious *Renovatio Urbis* was inaugurated following the appointment of Sansovino as *proto* (1529), in charge of the entire area of the Piazza complex.[28] Sansovino widened the Piazza and the Piazzetta, improving the position of the Basilica in relation to the other structures. He completed Bartolomeo Bon's Procuratie, built the Little Loggia (Loggetta) at the foot of the Campanile and the new government Mint (Zecca) facing the Basin just round the corner from the Piazzetta, and began the Marciana Library. He also proposed a unifying two-storey wing extending from the Library to the church of San Geminiano (Figure 2.8). This had the impact

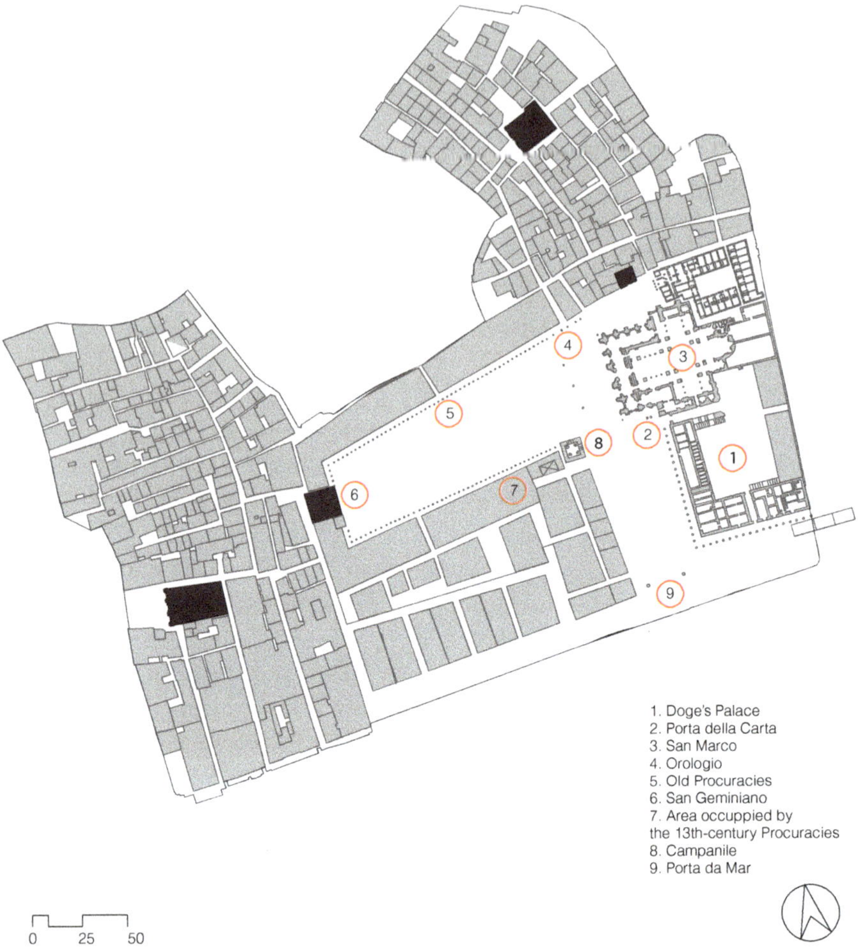

Figure 2.6 Venice. Piazza San Marco, fourteenth and fifteenth centuries – hypothetical reconstruction. Adapted from Giulia Foscari W. R., *Elements of Venice*. Zurich: Lars Müller Publishers, 2014

of turning the Campanile into a free-standing monument and giving the Library a northern façade on the Piazza (Figure 2.9). It was Vicenzo Scamozzi (1548–1616) in the 1580s, and Baldassare Longhena (1596/97–1682) from the 1640s onwards, who completed this part of the project, realising Sansovino's idea of a wider Piazza with a continuous façade surrounding its fabric. The connecting section joining the Procuratie Nuove with San Geminiano was eventually demolished under Napoleonic rule in 1807 and replaced by an imperial ballroom.[29]

Figure 2.7 Venice. Doge's Palace. Porta della Carta. Photo by the author

Figure 2.8 Canaletto. *The Piazza looking west from the Procuratie Nuove*. Royal Collection Trust / © Her Majesty Queen Elizabeth II 2017

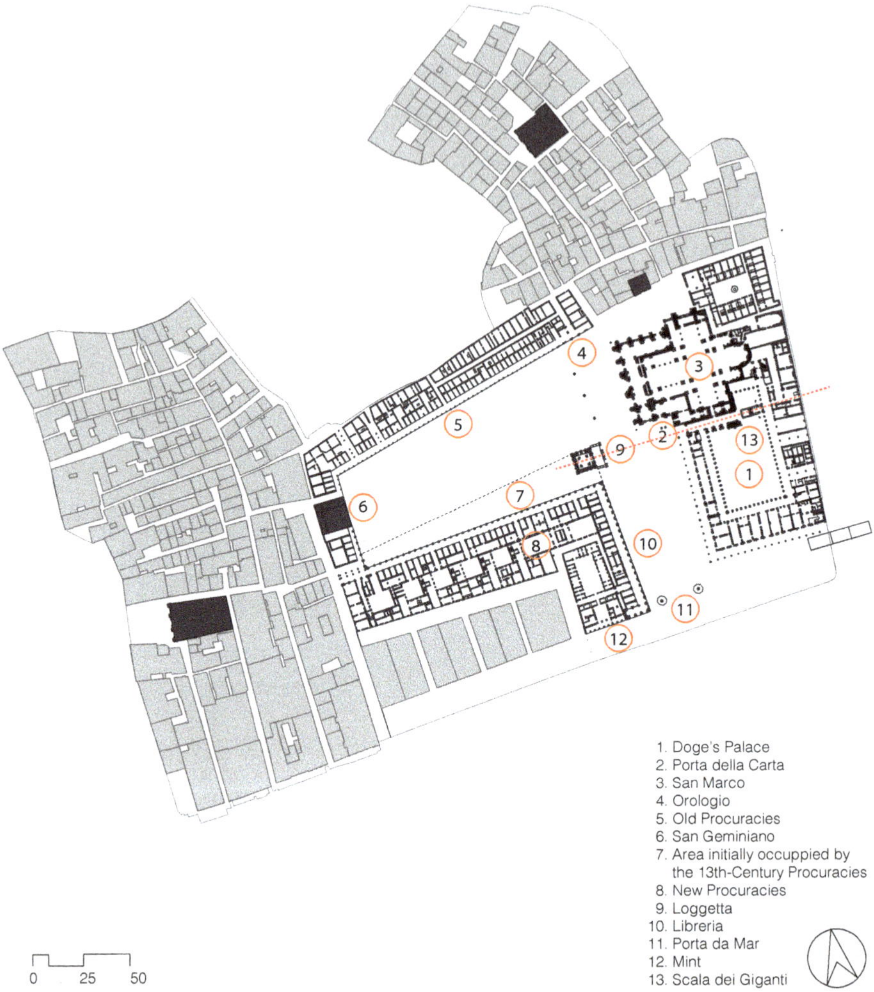

Figure 2.9 Venice. Piazza San Marco, sixteenth and seventeenth centuries – hypothetical reconstruction. Adapted from Giulia Foscari W. R., *Elements of Venice*. Zurich: Lars Müller Publishers, 2014

The Basin also changed over the fourteenth to seventeenth centuries. The Giudecca island was extended eastwards around 1330 to create a narrow canal between it and the island of San Giorgio (Figure 1.2a). Towards the end of the sixteenth century, Palladio's churches – San Giorgio Maggiore (1565–1611) and the Redentore (1577–1592) – changed the aquatic realm, commanding views to the south.[30] Longhena's centralised church of Santa Maria della Salute (1631) was built next, on the strategic site adjoining the Sea Customs House (Dogana) at the mouth of the Grand Canal in Dorsoduro (Figure 0.3). Dominating views in the entrance to the Grand Canal with its towering dome, the church added to the constellation of religious buildings that punctuate the Basin. Before examining the impact of these urban transformations on the spatial structure of the Piazza and the Bacino, it is necessary to explore contemporary perceptions of these spaces and monuments. A vivid representation is given in Jacopo de' Barbari's woodcut, one of the earliest demonstrations of Venice's Myth, synthesising political ideology with the urban fabric.

The map of de' Barbari

Consisting of six large sheets (135 x 282 cm), the famous 1500s woodcut (*Venetie MD*) by de' Barbari was a monumental feat of printmaking (Figure 0.6).[31] It took three years to complete, composing a south-west view of the city from a height of 500 metres, a viewpoint previously unimaginable. Yet, the naturalistic detail of the Venice it depicts also draws viewers towards the particulars of topography.[32] Venice seems to emerge from the water framed by the Giudecca, the mainland and the mythological figures of Neptune, Mercury and the eight wind gods, who waft their winds towards its islands. Viewers enter the scene from the south, gazing over the Giudecca's suburban villas and gardens. Looking further into the distance, the compact mass of the city is revealed. Galleys and smaller boats animate the lagoon, completing the view as it would appear to the human eye from a position over the bell tower of San Giorgio Maggiore. Exaggerations of proportions and the artistic composition give emphasis to a number of features, particularly the Piazza and the Piazzetta with the Ducal Palace, the Campanile, the Basilica of San Marco and the central wing of the Orologio. The Rialto Bridge is also clearly visible, arching over the Grand Canal, while the expansive site of the Arsenale dominates the print on the eastern fringe of the city. Although these buildings are clearly recognisable, the density and detail of the topography give the city a uniform image. The whole presides over the parts, and every building contributes to the compact appearance of the urban whole.

Expressing Venice's imperial and mercantile power, the figures of Neptune and Mercury direct the viewer to the commercial and political centres of the Rialto and San Marco.[33] With title and date stamped at the top – 'At Venice 1500' (VENETI[A]E) – the print declares its own historical significance. The naturalistic urban features and these historical 'facts' are invoked as real 'data' to evidence the spectacular setting and the commonwealth of Venice. The publisher, Anton Kolb, had commissioned the view 'for the glory of this illustrious city'.[34] Yet, the purpose of the typographical image remains unclear. It did not serve a technical cartographical purpose, such as fixing property lines or recording data essential for military, architectural or urban planning.[35] Schultz concludes that it was a map of didactic content that used geographical and topographical facts to construct a moralising portrait of the city, in the tradition of the *Mappae Mundi* (medieval world maps) produced in the fifteenth century by Venetian cartographers.[36] Kolb had commissioned a work of 'high Renaissance art' in the 'astro-mythological vocabulary of the humanists and incarnated in forms of an almost obsessive naturalism'.[37]

Looking closely at the print, we see that Jacopo used a geometric device common to *Mappae Mundi*. The vertical axis connecting the two mythological figures traverses the Orologio and runs between the two columns in the Piazzetta (Figure 0.6). While the columns guarded the entrance from the sea, the Orologio, which had been recently erected, signified entry to the Merceria, the set of streets that led to the Rialto. Two diagonal lines, established by the shafts of wind emanating from the gods that circle the city, also organise the print, intersecting at the top of the Campanile. Between the pairs of vertical and diagonal lines, de' Barbari establishes an *axis mundi* (a world pillar), placing the Piazza, the Rialto and the urban streets that connect them at the 'centre' of the city, and the city at the centre of an ideal cosmology. The Campanile – signalling the cosmological time of rituals – and the Orologio – measuring the time of business and clocks – are metonymically linked with the two Olympian gods and with Venice's two urban centres. Jacopo's image translated the empirical city into a transcendental mythical city of imperial achievement and republican ideology.

Imposing geometric centrality on the Rialto and San Marco, the print externalised their spatial and social significance and manifested them to the viewers as a stable image. The Venetians and visitors familiar with Venice would be able, from the symbolic geometry and the physical facts of the topography, to perceive the pedestrian route between the two hubs as the urban spine of the city. However, the *campi* of various parishes are also clearly shown with their paving, toponyms, wellheads and bell towers. As viewers moved towards the surface of the wall on which the print would be displayed, the detail would encourage them to observe the cityscape as though they could see it from ground level. Due to the previously unimaginable viewing position, Jacopo's Venice would have appeared physically and perceptually unknown, engaging them to identify their own houses. Aids to orientation were provided by the squares, which identified the local domain of every resident in the city.[38] With their accentuated height, the bell towers would direct viewers from *campo* to *campo*, as though they were experiencing the spatial geography through spatial immersion. While situating the viewers simultaneously 'inside' and 'outside' a representation is a characteristic of all maps, Jacopo's view intensively engages viewers in resolving a split between two places: mentally navigating through specific locations and surveying the whole through disembodied observation.[39]

Jacopo's view, Schultz wrote, 'is so astonishingly and brilliantly detailed that one is apt to accept it unquestionably as a record of fact, but such confidence is misplaced'.[40] Yet, the synthesis of naturalism and inaccuracy is not its only contradiction. Like most works of art, it appropriates and distorts facts to articulate 'fiction'.[41] It is a record of topographical information and the fabrication of virtue. In its processes of translation, it synthesises vision from above with the mental projection of embodied vision back to the streets' surface. Like almost every representation, the woodcut superimposes an artificial coherence onto the world, making us forget that the city is different from its image. In this way, it becomes an expression of suppressed tensions and reconciled contradictions: between the organic urban form and the aesthetics of centralised composition, between parochialism and civic glory, politics and commerce, city and nature, facts and fiction. In its centred and closed synoptic form, Jacopo's map turns Venice into a figurative pictorial discourse, expressing the imaginary relationship between ideology and spatial conditions.[42]

This is not to say that the ideal cosmology of Jacopo's Venice was his own construct and not a product of the city and its people. On the contrary, the print attests to the parochialism and patriotism of medieval and Renaissance Venetians, as well as to the fact that Jacopo captured the heartbeat of the city. It is rather to stress that, as with every representation, in Jacopo's print certain things are lost in translation. Being both factual and mythical, it raises the fundamental problem of deconstructing Venice's Myth into its constituents – spatial relationships and ideology – in order to understand its internal conflicts. How did the symbolic instruments of Venetian identity relate to the city's spatial geography, social and cultural institutions? This question can be explored by looking at two filters of information: first, the spatial organisation of the Piazza San Marco and the Bacino in the wider urban context of the city; and second, the social and cultural filter related to civic rituals, popular myths and local traditions.

Enlarging, linking, unifying

The urban transformations in the Piazza, the Piazzetta and the Basin show deliberate intent to use architecture in order to celebrate these spaces and embed them into the city fabric. Figure 1.3 shows the distribution of the measure of choice of the pedestrian system, introduced in the previous chapter, which captures through-movement, or the shortest paths linking all pairs of origins and destinations. Focusing on the canal network alone, one sees that the Piazza complex faces the entrance to the Grand Canal, the most integrated element in the water infrastructure (Figure 2.10). The choice values of the pedestrian structure, seen in Figure 2.11, reveal that the Piazza and the Piazzetta are criss-crossed with lines, connecting them with squares belonging to neighbouring islands. Two strong lines, one travelling through

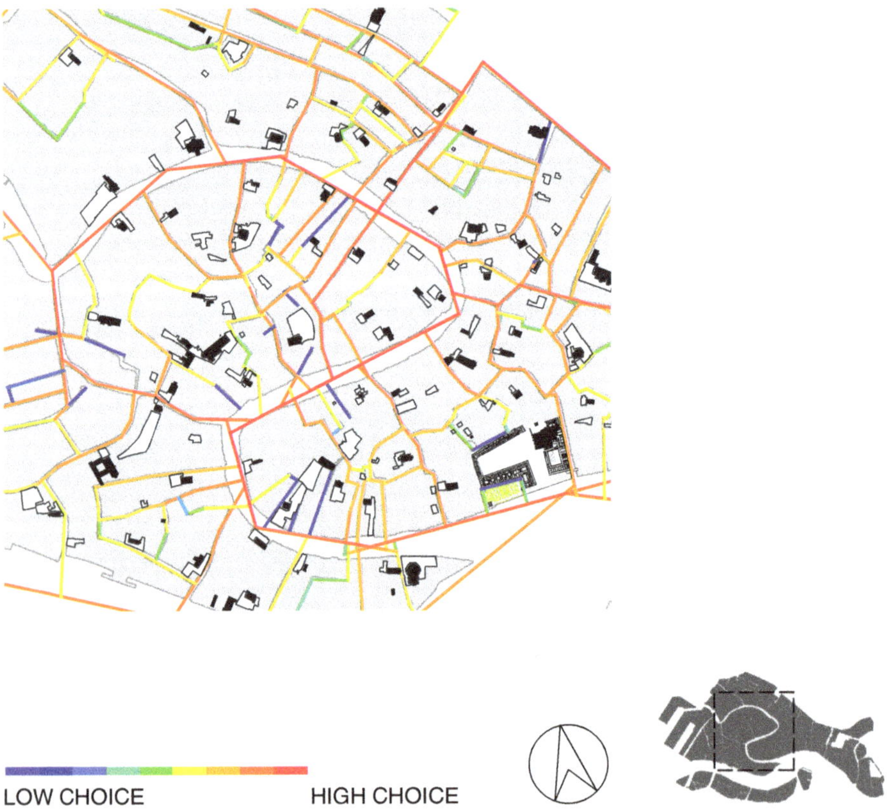

Figure 2.10 Venice. Canal network. Measure of normalised angular choice, at radius 3000 metres. Drawing by the author

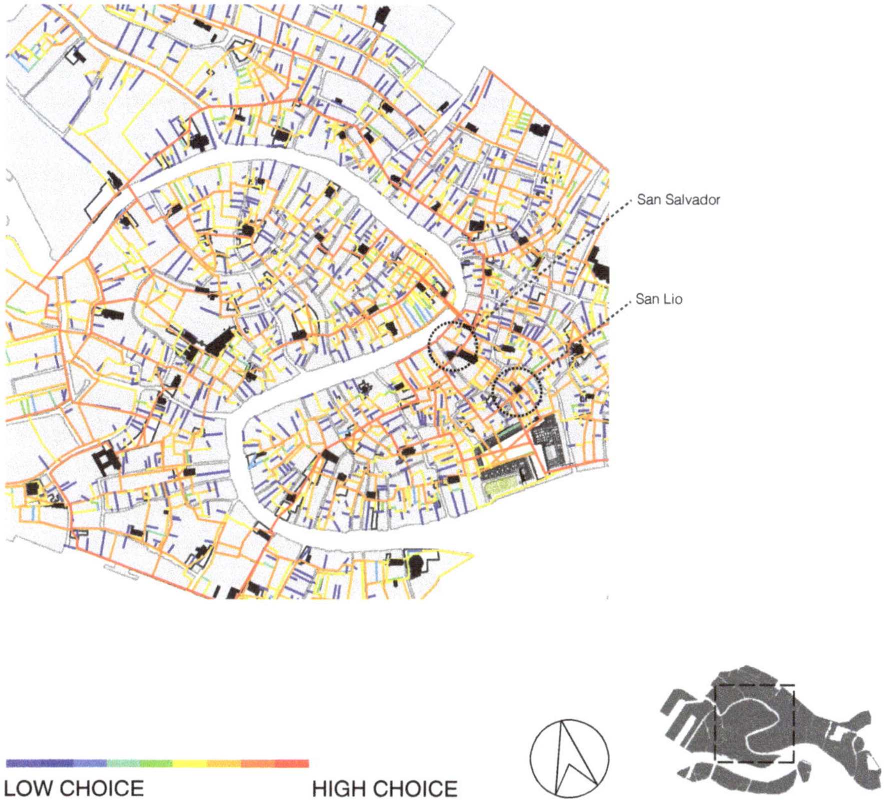

Figure 2.11 Venice. Pedestrian network. Measure of normalised angular choice, at radius 3000 metres. Drawing by the author

the Merceria and the other through the Calle dei Specchieri, connect the complex, through the *campi* of San Salvador and San Lio, with the commercial district of Rialto (Figure 2.11). The combined pedestrian–water structure shows a similar pattern, although the emphasis in terms of choice values shifts from the pedestrian elements to the canal infrastructure (Figure 2.12).

The distribution of the measure of integration in Figure 2.13 – expressing to-movement or the strength of each street as a destination – shows that the Rialto, the Piazza and a group of streets connecting these two hubs define a deformed wheel that links the heart of the city with its periphery extending in opposite directions. This is a common characteristic in cities, easing movement from the outside to the central streets and squares, facilitating trade and large-scale communication.[43] While the property of integration reveals the strength of San Marco and the Rialto

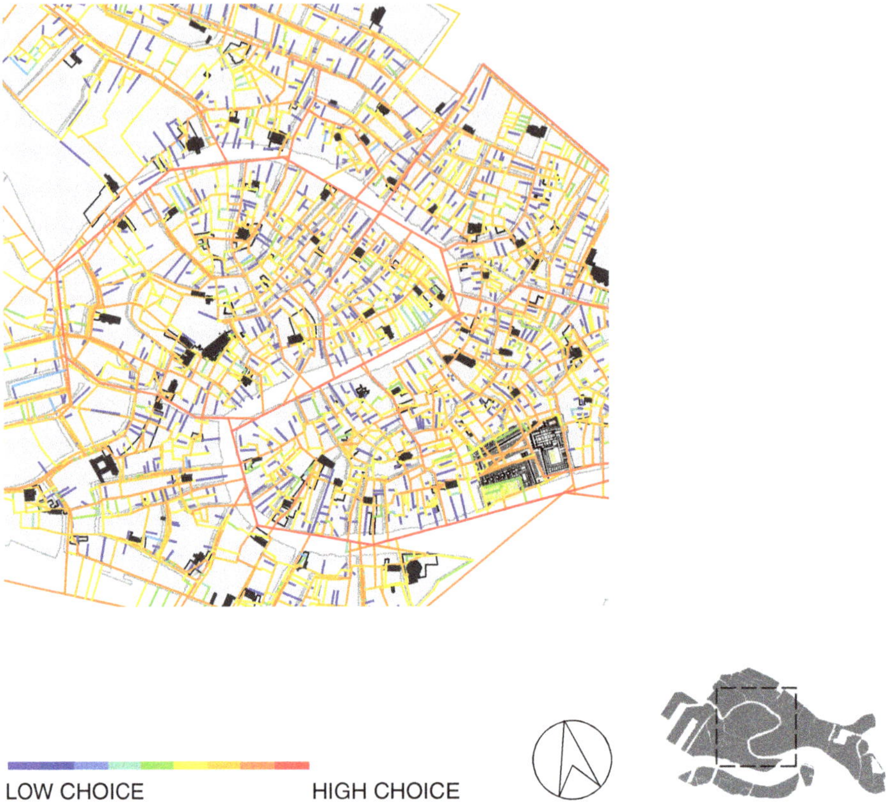

Figure 2.12 Venice. Pedestrian network. Measure of normalised angular choice, at radius 3000 metres. Drawing by the author

in the context of the city as a whole, the measure of choice shows that the Piazza and the two squares on either side of the Rialto Bridge (San Giacomo and San Bartolomeo) have the highest values in comparison with all the other *campi* in the city (Figure 2.13). These spatial properties suggest that the Piazza and the Piazzetta were shaped as highly accessible spaces, channelling movement from anywhere to everywhere else, as well as attracting movement from every place to the heart of the urban complex.

The Venetians, and any visitor familiar with Venice, would intuitively grasp these characteristics by moving around the city. How did Sansovino's scheme respond to spatial properties which were part of the everyday lived experience of Venice? Sansovino was a proponent of the classical style, but constantly adapted it to the specific conditions of each site. Each of the structures he built in Venice had a unique character,

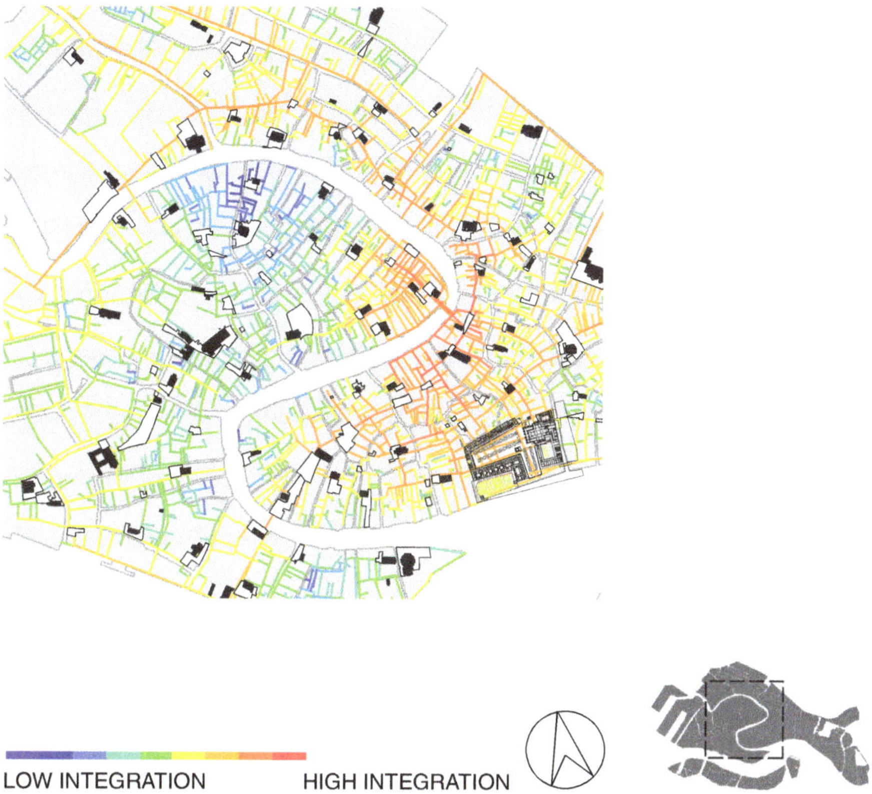

Figure 2.13 Venice. Pedestrian network. Measure of normalised angular integration, at radius 3000 metres. Drawing by the author

while the Piazza complex was translated from its existing structure into his own vocabulary.[44] In addition to using his particular style and local materials, he intensified spatial connections, extending lines, opening new points of entry, mirroring and doubling elements from different periods and styles that had defined the diverse spatial fabric through the ages. This can be seen in the Loggetta, which is in frontal axial relationship with Bon's Porta della Carta. Both structures are shaped as triumphal arches, reflecting Alberti's advice to mark intersections of pathways with arches, arcades or porticos, acting as doorways to urban rooms.[45] At the other end of the Porta is the Scala dei Giganti where the coronation of the Doge took place, and to which Sansovino later added the statues of Mars and Neptune (Figure 2.9). The line connecting the two arches is almost perpendicular to the line that emerges from the Merceria, traversing the Piazza from north to south. It thus reveals to the perceiver the axial relationship between the Orologio and the two Columns of Justice, also built as triumphal entrances in the previous century.

If the Loggetta is a response to the entrance to the Palace courtyard, the Libreria – the most famous of all Sansovino's buildings – is in dialogue with the Gothic loggia of the Palace across the Piazzetta. With their humanistic emphasis clearly established, both structures were meant to glorify the Venetian Republic. Palladio called the Libreria the richest and most ornate building since ancient times.[46] Howard states that few libraries 'were until then open to the public, while the remarkable resemblances between Sansovino's building and the fragmentary evidence from ancient sources, such as Vitruvius and Pausanias, gave an *all' antica* language to the city's political centre'.[47] Richly animated with chiaroscuro effects, the continuous loggia around the library and along the Procuratie provided a unifying force to the entire ensemble, expressing the relations among the Palace, the Basilica and the forecourt of the Procurators. The arrangement of various buildings in a single unified scheme was common in Italian urban centres, such as the new town of Pienza and in Florence.[48] Yet, Sansovino's programme uniquely provided a monumental three-dimensional re-interpretation of the area in classical language through the typology of the ancient Roman forum. By fulfilling the desire of the *Serenissima* to imitate the architecture of ancient civilisations as described by Vitruvius, it supported the Myth of Venice that 'drew from the most advanced theory of political utopia formulated to date by the Renaissance'.[49]

However, architecture is not only a matter of style or appearance. Sansovino's efforts to unify existing elements into the new scheme demonstrate a concern for integration between the aesthetic treatment of buildings and the urban fabric deep down at the level of spatial structure. This can be explored by looking at the visibility relations in the Piazza complex, seen separately from the organisation of the surrounding fabric. Superimposing a fine grid at an appropriate resolution on the plan, we measure the visual integration of each grid unit to all other units based on visual interconnections. The results show that integration spreads throughout the entire layout (Figure 2.14). Yet, the highest values are concentrated in the space in front of the Basilica and around the Campanile. Improving the visual connections between the Piazza and the Piazzetta, Sansovino strengthened the expression of the union of religious and political life. This union is also communicated through two strong diagonal links connecting the Palace and the Basilica with the western part of the Piazza, its more secular side.

Figure 2.14 Piazza San Marco, sixteenth century. Visual integration. Drawing by the author

Gentile Bellini's painting of the *Procession* in the Piazza San Marco, produced before the *Renovatio* (1496), seemingly provides an accurate representation of the Piazza and religious processions at the time (Figure 0.5). Looking closely, one discovers that Bellini deliberately moved the Campanile to the right, allowing a view to the Palace and the Porta della Carta. A large number of paintings in Venice mediated between the viewers' actual experience of the city and its representations. They organised people's relation to the urban streets through perspective and thereby altered their perceptions of it.[50] It is possible that Sansovino's proposal to free the Campanile from the Procuratie was influenced by Bellini's image. Yet, Sansovino's scheme did not simply reveal the entrance to the Palace, but also strengthened its connection with the Piazza and the urban fabric. It was not only that architecture, painting and perspective were changing the city, but also, in a symbiotic way, the city was influencing the work of the architect through its geographical structure. This is strikingly revealed when we look at the Piazza in the context of the neighbouring islands. A powerful axial link, clearly distinguished by its red colour, emerges from the Merceria, thrusting diagonally forward to the Molo and the Columns of Justice. The line asserts the north–south pattern of integration that joins the Piazza and the Rialto in the analysis of the city (Figures 2.13, 2.16, 2.17). The consonance between the properties of the Piazza and the properties of the city as a whole shows the strong role of the Piazza and this particular axial link across all scales of the analysis.

Looking at the complex as it was in the fifteenth century brings Sansovino's programme sharply into focus. The entire area was previously much narrower, a factor having the effect of concentrating integration in two spots, one in front of the Basilica, and the other at the Porta da Mar (Figure 2.16). Comparing this layout with Sansovino's enlargement, it is apparent that the latter enabled visual integration to spread evenly through the Piazza and towards the Piazzetta. A second outcome of his scheme was the line running from the Salizzada San Moise to the Palace parallel to the Procuratie Nuove, detaching the southern elevation of the Piazza from the Campanile (Figure 2.17). The new configuration allowed the continuous loggia to be experienced from the Piazzetta, and the entrance to the Palace courtyard to be seen from the Piazza. Wrapped around the Piazza and the Piazzetta, the continuous loggia provided three-dimensional expression of the integrated structure of visibility spreading throughout the complex.

The line linking the Palace courtyard with the entrance to the Piazza north from San Geminiano was the outcome of opening the previously fortified palace by Ziani, expressing a connection between Venice's citizens and the rulers of the Republic (Figures 2.14–2.17). Finally, the axial link from the Merceria was also present in the previous configuration. The significance of this link in the life of the Venetians is evident in the fact that they felt the need to provide a ceremonial entrance for the commercial thoroughfare by building the Orologio, heightening its relationship with the Columns of Justice. Seen together, the horizontal and linear spread of integration in Figures 2.14–2.17 captures the interrelationship

Figure 2.15 Piazza San Marco, fifteenth century. Visual integration. Drawing by the author

of the Procurators' forecourt with the Palace and the spatial core of the city, which connects the Piazza with the Rialto. Emerging from the collective, unconscious efforts responsible for building Venice over time, the Merceria line helped to articulate the self-conscious relationship between architecture, the city and the viewer. It is this interweaving of the urban structure crafted by many hands with the architectural structure of the Piazza, the creation of few hands, that defines the emergence of humanist architecture in sixteenth-century Venice (Figure 2.18).

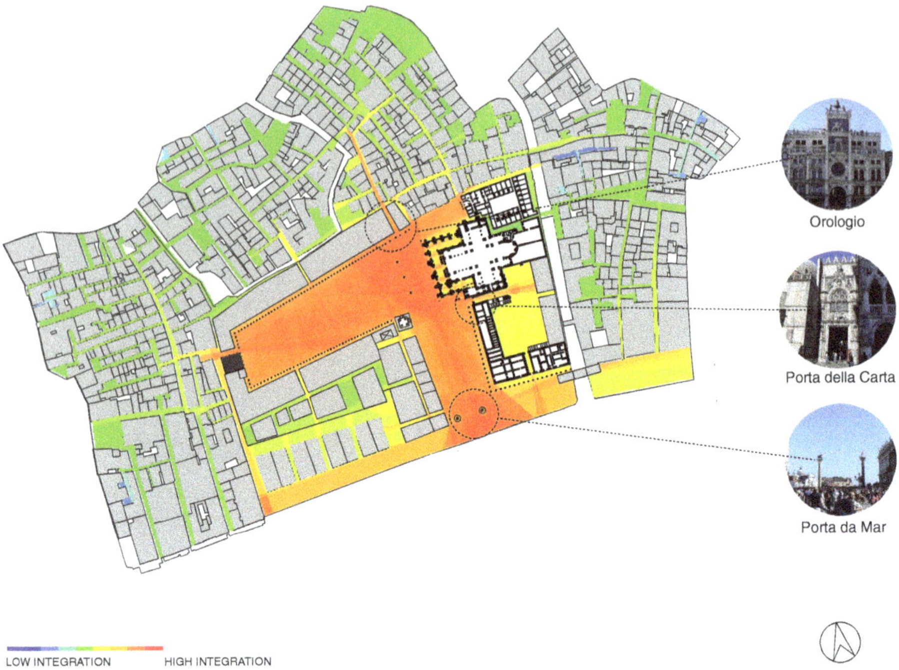

Figure 2.16 Piazza San Marco, fifteenth century. Visual integration in the urban context of the adjoining islands. Drawing and photos by the author

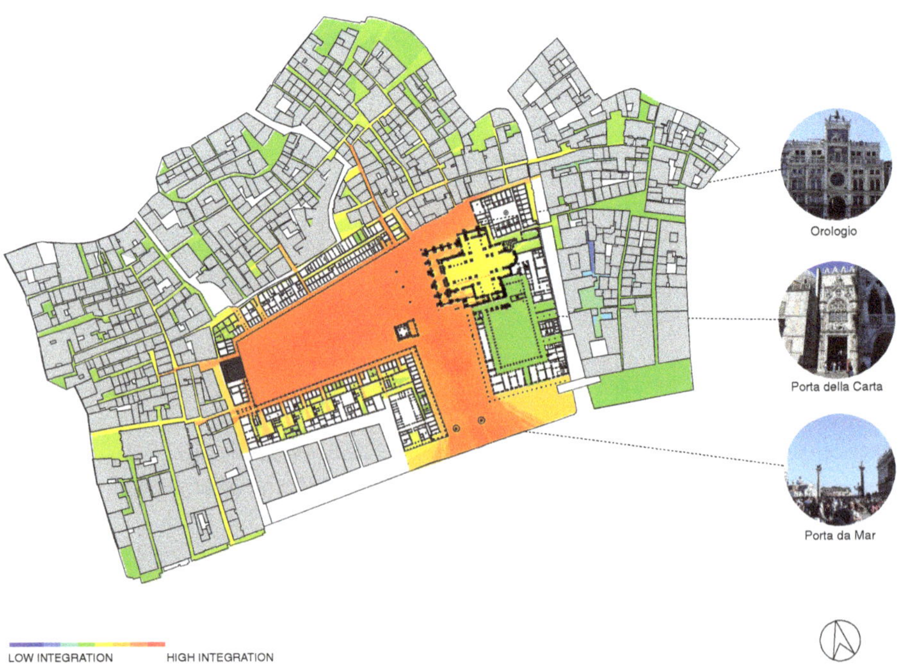

Figure 2.17 Piazza San Marco, sixteenth century. Visual integration in the urban context of adjoining islands. Drawing and photos by the author

Figure 2.18 Piazza San Marco, sixteenth century. Visual integration. Drawing by Athina Lazaridou

Spatial coordination and scenographic progression

The programme of celebrating the ceremonial spaces of the Republic progressively transformed the area, by acknowledging entry points and borders, enlarging, linking and integrating centres of commercial, political and ritual significance. The architects and their patrons collaborating in these transformations employed a method of unification and integration with two primary aspects. The first was a spatial strategy establishing interconnections. The second consisted of an optical approach, using scenic coordination and spatial progression. Having investigated the spatial relationships in the complex, I will focus next on the second approach, looking at the iconographic programme and optical relations as seen by a viewer through movement and observation.

The Piazza and the Bacino have often been described as manifestations of scenographic treatment. Howard explains that from the Bacino 'the Clock Tower acts as the focal point in this prospect, while the Loggetta and the Basilica project forward in front of it on either side like the wings of a stage', enhancing the theatrical allusion.[51] We derive a similar impression

Figure 2.19 (a) San Giorgio Maggiore (Andrea Palladio) framed by the arch of the Orologio. Photo by the author

Figure 2.19 (b) San Giorgio Maggiore (Andrea Palladio). Photo by the author

Figure 2.19 (c) Canaletto. The Piazza and the Piazzetta from the Torre dell'Orologio towards San Giorgio. Royal Collection Trust/ © Her Majesty Queen Elizabeth II 2017

when looking from the Piazza towards the Porta da Mar. The addition of Palladio's San Giorgio Maggiore at the end of the sixteenth century defined the southern point of the axial view extending over the Basin. Advancing from the narrow dark alleyway of the Merceria to the vast open space of the Piazza, the spectator is instantly struck by the brightness of San Giorgio's façade framed by the archway of the Orologio (Figure 2.19a–c). The longitudinal extension of the vista to the church pulls the viewer to the edge of the water. Moving to the Piazzetta, visitors encounter on the left-hand side the richly decorated façade of the Basilica. The mosaics on its lunettes show the *translatio*, the transfer of the relics of St Mark from Egypt in the ninth century (827 or 828). The sequence in the story they depict can be read from right to left in the direction from which the relics had arrived from Alexandria, and from which foreign visitors would enter Venice from the Adriatic. Diagonally opposite the Basilica, the spectator encounters the Loggetta at the foot the Campanile. Bearing sculptures that glorify the Republic, this triumphal arch is in dialogue with the Porta della Carta, symbolically crowned by Venice as the figure of Justice. The Libreria Marciana is seen next on the right, topped with obelisks and statues. To the left side are the Gothic arcades of the Palace, with its lozenge patterns of white and red squares, its crenellations and another figure of Justice. Walking from the Merceria to the Molo, the spectator is led from one marker to the next,

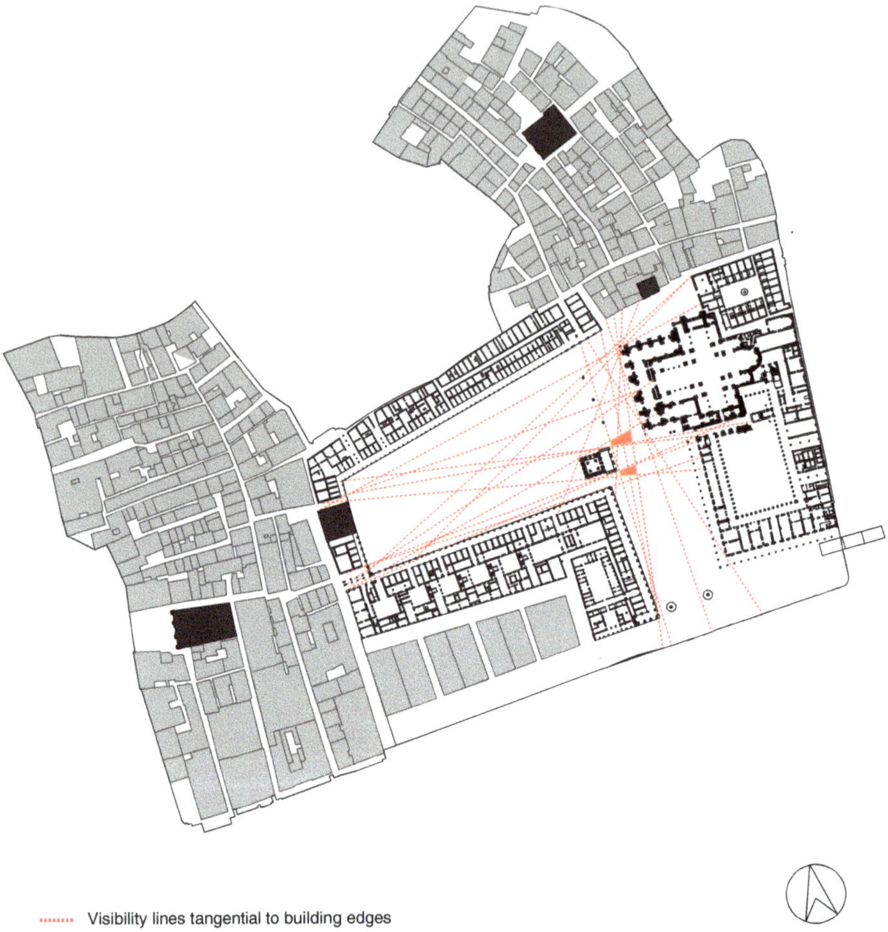

Figure 2.20 Piazza San Marco. Network of visibility lines drawn at a tangent to all entrances and buildings. Drawing by the author

experiencing a series of emblems that expressed the most significant ideals of the Venetian Republic (Figures 2.14, 2.16, 2.17, 2.19c).

If we draw all the lines crossing the Piazza and the Piazzetta so as to be tangential to entrances and surfaces, we construct a network of visibility lines (Figure 2.20). Most of these lines intersect at the space on either side of the Campanile where the Piazza meets the Piazzetta. From the triangular subdivisions defined by the intersections of these lines the spectator has access to maximum visual exposure of building façades and all entrances to the complex; specifically, two triangular areas on

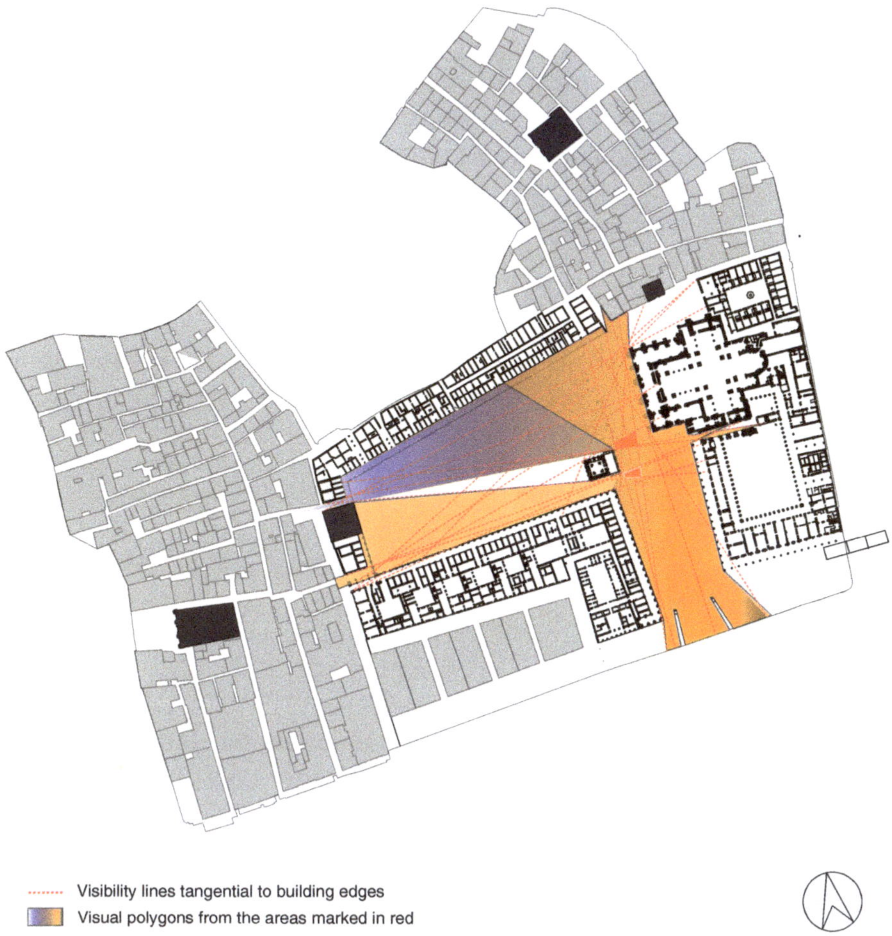

Figure 2.21 Piazza San Marco. Visual polygons representing views from the highlighted areas located on either side of the Loggetta. Drawing by the author

either side of the Loggetta work together to reveal the entire layout (Figure 2.21). This can be seen by drawing the maximum area that is visible from these spaces and superimposing the two visual fields on the plan (Figure 2.21). The space at the foot of the Campanile, where the Loggetta was built, was an informal place of gathering for the nobility during sessions of the Great Council. As well as offering an evocative backdrop through its sculptural treatment, it was the position from which they could visually survey the whole complex. In various records the Porta da Mar was described as the 'eyes' of the Republic.[52] In reality it is on either side of the Loggetta and at the top of the Campanile that those 'eyes' are found. Sansovino's proposal to enlarge the Piazza turned the Campanile with the Loggetta into a three-dimensional hinge, physically and optically unifying the layout.

On reaching the Molo, the spectator has a view of the Giudecca Canal and the Grand Canal framed by Palladio's San Giorgio Maggiore, the Zitelle, the Redentore and the Salute (Figure 2.22a). San Giorgio Maggiore was commissioned by the Benedictine monks on the island of San Giorgio. The Redentore and the Salute, on the other hand, were votive temples, the fulfilment of a public vow taken at the height of terrible outbreaks of plague.[53] Both temples were visited on feast days by the Doge, in honour of the events, by means of a pontoon bridge of boats specially constructed for the occasion. The two votive monuments were designed to be viewed not only from a distance, but also closer up during an approach by water, a custom still enacted in ritual celebrations in Venice.

'Temple fronts', wrote Palladio, 'should be constructed overlooking the most impressive part of the city so that it seems that religion has been placed there like a guard and protector of the citizens.'[54] In his foreword to his Fourth Book (in *The Four Books of Architecture*), he added that 'their front' should be made to overlook public streets or rivers if sited close to them, 'so that the passersby can see them and demonstrate their respect and reverence in front of them'.[55] Obliquely engaging the impressive space of the Piazzetta, and frontally facing the area where the two watercourses intersect at the tip of the triangular complex of the Sea Customs House, the façade of San Giorgio is the embodiment of Palladio's ideas about church frontages (Figure 2.22a). The Senate considered various possible sites for the Redentore and the Salute before settling on their preferred locations next to the water. The church of San Giorgio, on the other hand, was originally hidden by intervening structures, until Doge Leonardo Donà had them demolished in 1609 to make it visible from the Ducal Palace.[56] In this case, San Giorgio's siting was fortuitous, but Donà secured its place in an integrated ensemble, gradually developing over time.

Wittkower has shown that the Salute lies at the centre of a semicircle, with San Giorgio Maggiore and the Redentore being equidistant from the centre (Figure 2.22b).[57] While Palladio's churches demarcate the perimeter of the Bacino, Longhena's votive temple superimposes a radial plan on the aquatic cityscape with an octagonal rotunda at its centre. Crowned by the Immacolata high above its imposing dome, the Salute is a conceptual 'pivot' integrating the religious monuments in the area

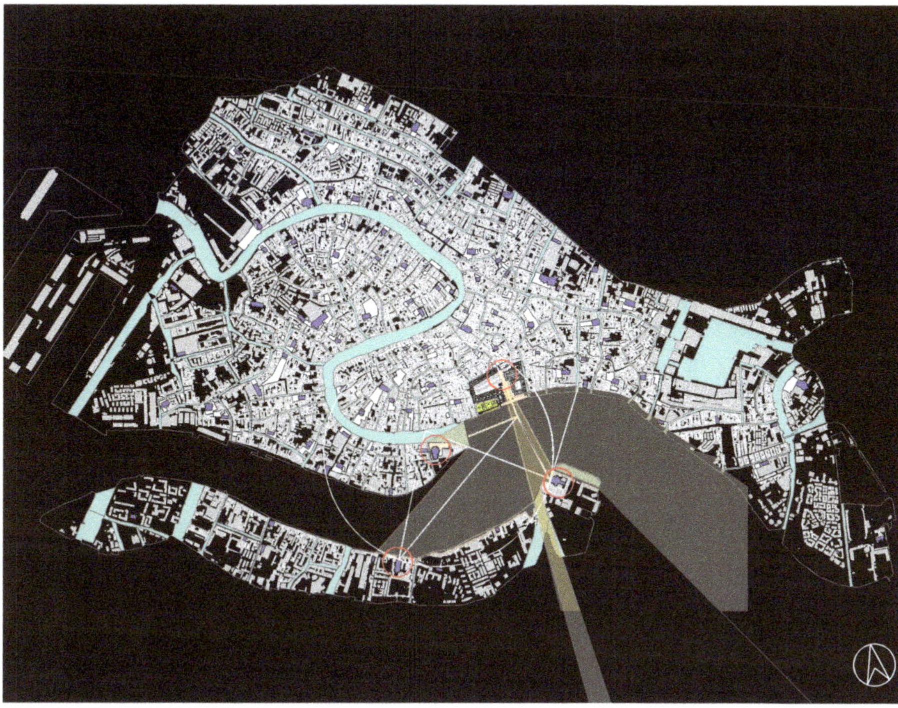

Figure 2.22 (a) Piazza San Marco and Basin. Visual polygons representing views from the Orologio and the Molo and lines drawn frontally to the Redentore and San Giorgio Maggiore. Drawing by the author

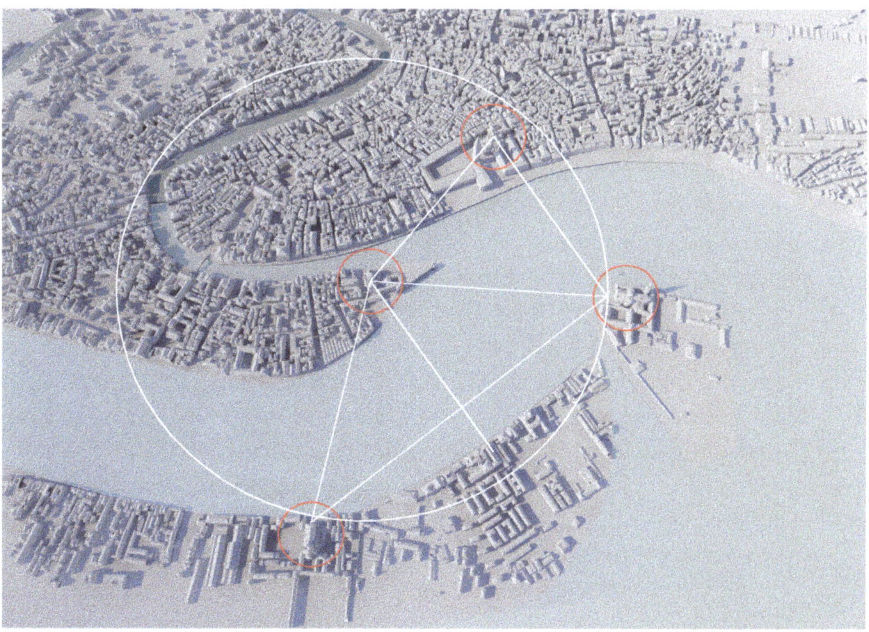

Figure 2.22 (b) Piazza San Marco and the Bacino. Geometrical coordination of monuments. Drawing by Athina Lazaridou

into a geometrical network (as opposed to the optical hinge, which, as previously argued, is the function of the Campanile and the Loggetta). The approach to the Bacino by boat along the Grand Canal reveals these monuments in sequence, from the Salute to San Giorgio, to Zitelle and finally to the Redentore. From the Molo or from a position afloat, on the other hand, all the churches come into view synchronically, articulating the coordinated scenography of waterborne architecture in the bay (Figure 2.22a).

A navigational network and an *axis mundi*

I have unravelled two important properties shaping the Bacino and the Piazza complex: a network of monuments and entry points into the area, and the Merceria–San Giorgio line, demarcated by the symbols of the Republic and deeply anchored in the urban fabric. Carefully structuring the relationship between the city, the monuments and the viewer, the coordinated planning produced by architects and the patriciate was met by an equally powerful force. Rising up from behind the Riva dei Schiavoni, the Grand Canal and the Zattere is a varied skyline, a constellation of bell towers, domes and rooftops, signalling the churches and *campi* that articulate Venice as a mosaic of islands. Venice's churches have presided over the life of their parish communities since the city's early days. They had a historic relationship with waterfronts as they would have initially been approached by and seen from water.

With the exception of the Grand Canal and the outer boundaries of the city, the tight network of streets and canals did not offer plentiful opportunities for frontal viewing. At street level most views are short, sequentially unfolding along the course of movement. Views from the canals are longer, but lack the expanse essential for frontal relations. Even in those *campi* fronting the water, despite their imposing appearance, churches are only accidentally discovered (when viewed from a boat or a street). However, before the city took its compact form, churches were dotted along the waterfronts of islands in the archipelago. Seen across the water from afar, they were landmarks of an assured anchorage for merchants and sailors, under the protection of the parish saint. Founded on maritime enterprise, Venice's island settlements had long-time associations with old navigational practices, guided by churches that blessed its waters through *loci sancti*. Toponymy bears witness to this process, as Venice's *campi* are named after their saints, while the portolan maps linking rose compasses with navigational lines must have expressed, for

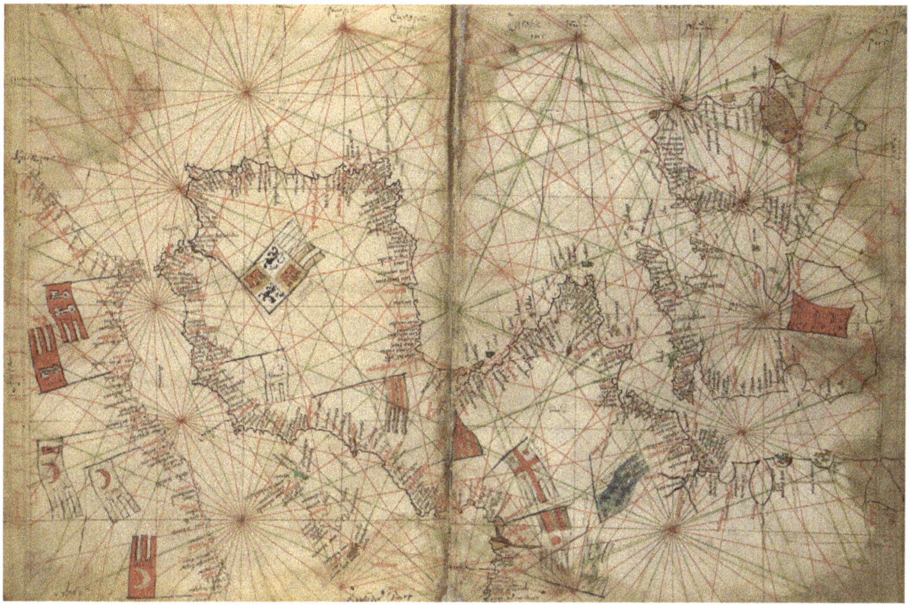

Figure 2.23 Portolan map: these maps were navigational charts based on compass roses, estimated distances and designated lines of bearing. Maps of the Liber Secretorum Fidelium Crucis. Author: Vesconte Pietro. Italy (Venice). Circa 1320–1325 Latin. © The British Library Board. C13671-25/2737

Venetians of previous generations, a waterborne network of sacred sites (Figure 2.23).[58]

If the cult of St Mark in the Piazza guarded sailors' entrance to Venice from the south, Venetian hagiography included a series of other saints protecting significant sites. St Theodore, whose statue gazed down from one of the two columns in the Piazzetta, was a partner of St Mark and the first old patron of Venice. St George, the warrior saint, whose church, San Giorgio Maggiore, was built by Palladio, and St Nicholas, a patron of sailors and Venetian naval exploits, marked two other strategic positions: the island of San Giorgio at the entrance to the Basin, and the Lido, presiding over the gateway to the Adriatic, respectively. When Venice's islands became conjoined to form the compact city, the waterborne network of squares and churches was ritually connected through processions, transforming streets and canals into *viae sacrae*.[59] The constellation of monuments and the waterborne processions to the Redentore and the Salute, therefore, were translations of popular ritual in the lagoon into formalised ritual and unified scenography.

While the network of monuments in the Basin grafted onto the aquatic landscape the old practices of ritual and navigation, the

Merceria–San Giorgio link helped translate the strategic connection between the commercial nucleus and the religious centre of Venice. This link became architecturally expressed over time. By integrating the Piazza along the north–south direction by which people and goods entered the lagoon before moving into the city, the line of the Merceria described the axis of the Venetian economic and imperial world. It thus affirmed that everything entering and leaving Venice was subject to the intersection of forces between the two urban centres of the Rialto and San Marco. The emblems of popular mythology and Republican ideology were superimposed on relations normally understood through movement and embodied perception, expressing the union of architecture with the urban networks in the city. This confirmed the union of the inside with the outside, the space of everyday life with the space of rituals and ceremonial practice. The Merceria–San Marco link defined key perceptual territories and relationships for Venetians in the days of the Republic: empirical time and cosmological time, commerce and civic life, religious order and social justice.

It cannot be coincidental that de' Barbari uses the same link as the compositional device unifying the city in his map. In his appropriation of the urban structure, perceived only through embodied experience over time, Jacopo turned the spatial connection into a geometrical device, making it visible and immediately graspable. For Marin, the genre of utopia exists through representation, a fiction that synthesises and idealises rather than accepts or negotiates empirical tensions.[60] In the *Renovatio Urbis*, this appropriation is achieved through the integration of the urban structure of the city as a whole with the spatial structure of the Piazza, the architectural and iconographic programme. The harmonious totality of the metropolis in de' Barbari's map and the *Renovatio Urbis* belong to the utopian tradition. They integrated instrumental and symbolic elements, spatialising and externalising the Myth of the Republic.

Ordering, classifying, separating

Sansovino's scheme took decades to implement, being completed only some time after his death. Delays were encountered, even in the early days after his appointment, caused by difficulties in banishing the food stalls from around the columns in the Piazzetta.[61] As well as being the centre of formal celebrations, the Piazza was the place of carnival where bulls and pigs were chased and slaughtered, and a market place where vendors, pilgrims and spectators gathered both daily and on ceremonial occasions. Iain Fenlon writes:

> Taverns operated in the square, pilgrims gathered to change money and arrange to travel to [the] Holy Land, charlatans and tooth-pullers plied their trades under the clocktower and bread was baked in the ovens [...] News-sheets and popular prints were hawked in the Piazza by itinerant vendors around the Basilica, and strolling players – the forebears of today's performers of Viennese salon music – stood on benches and improvised staging to entertain the crowds. On occasion the square became the site of more sombre rituals when, under the watchful gaze of the figure of Justice on the façade of the Ducal Palace, criminals were executed between the two columns of the Piazzetta.[62]

These activities were accommodated in a series of shops and booths spread across the Piazza, the Piazzetta and the Molo:

> Money-changing booths stood at the base of the Campanile, and bakers' shops occupied some lean-to huts nearby. Meat and vegetable stalls and even latrines surrounded the great columns, at the very place where the most distinguished visitors were welcomed to the city. Five rather dubious hostelries, as well as the meat market, were housed in the decrepit buildings in the Piazzetta, facing the Doge's Palace. And there was a row of cheese- and salami-shops along the lagoon side of the Mint.[63]

The diversity of these uses indicates that commercial activities and the cacophony and odours of blacksmiths, butchers, bakers and food-sellers were defining not only the Rialto and its surrounding streets but also the vast civic space of the Piazza.

All Italian city centres had spaces where open markets, shops and stalls were concentrated, allowing maximum accessibility and visibility of goods and transactions. In Venice, commerce was clustered in specific areas and streets as well as spread throughout the city's fabric. Yet, a different perception about city centres started developing in the sixteenth century, suggesting that streets and squares should be neatly arranged and labelled according to specific purposes.[64] Alberti argued that the wealthy citizens in an ideal city

> are happier in more spacious surroundings and would readily accept being excluded by an inner wall and would not unwillingly

> leave the stalls and the town-centre workshops to the marketplace traders; and that rabble [...] of poulterers, butchers and cooks, and so on, will be less of a risk and less of a nuisance if they do not mix with the important citizens.[65]

Evelyn Welch explains that the writings of theorists such as Alberti, Francesco di Giorgio and Filarete reflected a common attitude for the period. This thinking sought to isolate the bustle of everyday commerce from the gentry, and order it according to principles of hygiene and beautification imposed by an increasingly 'self-aware' patrician class.[66]

This desire to distinguish between different types of social activities and elevate the civic space of San Marco underpinned the scenographic coordination of the Piazza, the Piazzetta and the Bacino. The Piazzetta was modelled on Serlio's 'tragic scene' for theatre design in his *Five Books of Architecture*, the first Renaissance work on architecture to include a section on theatre. Serlio was Sansovino's friend and had greatly influenced architectural thinking at the time. In his second book, he explained that the dignified tragic stage, with its classical palaces depicted in perspective, was appropriate for patricians and noble deeds.[67] The 'comic scene', by contrast, captured the more chaotic stage set of the typical street. Finally, the 'satyrical scene' was a bucolic vision, populated by shepherds succumbing to the laws of nature (Figure 2.24). Combining theatre, classical architecture and perspective with the writings of Vitruvius, Serlio provided Renaissance architects with a framework to build their own theatres. His influence on the Piazza is made clear in Giacomo Torelli's design for the set of the opera *Bellerofonte*. The opera was premiered in Venice in 1624 with a set portraying a distant view of the Piazzetta from the lagoon.[68] Palladio's Teatro Olimpico in Vicenza, with Vicenzo Scamozzi's three-dimensional interpretations of perspective scenery, constructed after Palladio's death, provides a realisation of Vitruvius's Roman theatre and the conceptual union of theatre and street (Figure 2.25a–b).[69] This combination was made possible by the perspectival vista, with symbols expressing the integrated ideal city enacted through rituals.

Gasparo Contarini referred to the nobility – and by analogy the Piazza – as being the 'eyes of the Republic, seeing all and directing the actions of the body; the plebians were the lower, more menial limbs, following the orders of the eyes. Yet there was reciprocity: the eyes and limbs depended on each other for survival.'[70] Combined with the Christian conception of a divine cosmic order, Vitruvius's notion of architecture as a mirror of the human body provided humanist architects and

Figure 2.24 Sebastiano Serlio. Three types of stage sets, showing different kinds of street scenes. (Top) The 'tragic scene' capturing a street with noble buildings and palaces. (Bottom left) The 'comic scene' comprising a typical street. (Bottom right) The 'satyrical scene', a bucolic vision of the countryside

Figure 2.25 Palladio. Teatro Olimpico, Vicenza. Photo by the author

historiographers with another symbol to frame architecture, the city and the commonwealth. While the Piazza and the Bacino were thought of as the 'eyes' of the Republic, the wider area of the Merceria was the viscera (*viscericus urbis*), adding to the theatrical allegory of the tragic and comic scene the metaphor of the urban body.[71]

Like Alberti and Serlio, Sansovino was eager to establish order in the Piazza. The removal of commercial activities was not a simple matter, since the crowds that gathered in this space needed its money-changing facilities, markets and taverns.[72] In addition, the rent from the stalls and the shops was substantial revenue for the Procurators. Dealing with illegal stallholders meant a series of penalties, while clearing the area of legal tenants required offering accommodation elsewhere. The desire to increase the visibility and splendour of the Piazza raised the need to strengthen its physical connection with the rest of the urban fabric. Yet, the interest in order and solemnity demanded the severance of this space from the spontaneous economic and festive life, the natural outcome of spatial integration. Such contradictions between spatial assimilation and programmatic separation are usually resolved through legislation, rules of behaviour and codes of practice. Initiated by Sansovino, the long process of separation was eventually formalised in 1569 by a decree banning stalls and counters from the columns and the arcades of the Palace. This process paralleled an earlier decree in 1525 from the Council of Ten, at Doge Gritti's encouragement, which suppressed the Rabelaisian entertainments and the slaughtering of animals in the square during carnival.[73]

Sansovino never lived to see the final result, but gave the Piazza a single unified scheme in classical language, while aiding the separation of the political from the spontaneous commercial and social life. During the protracted process by which Venice was formed, city management had worked alongside Venetians, facilitating material and spiritual needs for the peaceful mercantile life of a sovereign maritime nation in conjunction with the dual domain of politics and commerce. This process had ensured that all roads and canals led to and from the Rialto and the Piazza, easing the flow of goods, vessels and people. Developments in the sixteenth and seventeenth centuries, however, projected an idealised view of the intersection of *emporium* and *imperium* in Venice. This view was clearly differentiated from the evolutionary way they had both naturally developed, intermingling with each other.

Sansovino's visions were complemented by the ambitions of the oligarchy, which was, at the same time, restructuring the city's processions. If the ideological requirement of the *Renovatio Urbis* was to aggrandise the spaces of the Republic, the practical requirement was to create larger spaces for state ceremonies. At the architectural level, this requirement necessitated the close coordination of the urban and architectural programme with the mythographic and iconographic discourse. At the ceremonial level, it appropriated popular myths and civic ideology, parochial rituals and state rituals, and reformed them for the frequent symbolical enactment of centralised power. The vision of the centralised city presented through ritual will be discussed in the following sections. At present, I stress the role of architecture in forging the relationship between space and civic ideology. Architecture emerged as a reformed discipline by interfacing statecraft and city-craft, promoting to both visitors and the Venetians a portrait of a remarkably well-ordered society.

Techniques of integration: mythography and historiography

Before considering ritual processions in the Piazza, it is important to discuss the role of myth in Venice. Venetian mythology comprised a web of pseudo-histories organising collective memory and exciting the imagination of people. In contrast to the reality of a city that arose from the marshes, myths in Venice traced the city's ancestry back to Troy or Rome, its origin to the day of the Annunciation, and its divine foundation to possession of the relics of St Mark the Evangelist following their transfer from Alexandria.[74] Modelling their relationship to St Mark on the relationship of the popes to St Peter, the Venetian doges claimed independence from external powers. The Evangelist gradually came to 'personify the divine destiny of the Republic and represent the entire civic corpus'.[75] Earlier Byzantine and Roman influences had supplied a plentiful source of other saints, relics and cult objects, particularly St Theodore, St George and St Nicholas, who assumed religious and civic importance. Combining popular sentiments and elite desires, these legends cut across classes. With time, they defined the popular dimensions of official mythology – the Myth of Venice – educating 'Venetians about the city's noble foundation in freedom, about its divinely ordained military and maritime destiny, [and] about ducal rights to authority over ecclesiastical institutions'.[76]

Venice's mythographical and hagiographical heritage was grounded in ceremonial occasions, calendric rituals, liturgical rhythms and a network of ritual centres scattered across the geography of the lagoon and the city. The Basilica of San Marco presided over this geography, inextricably linked with the Procurators' forecourt and the Doge's Palace. Other churches, monasteries and sacred sites that had dotted the archipelago since its early days were ritually linked through a plethora of processions. The succession of rites structured ritual around feast days and anniversaries of important events in Venetian history. While festivities and processions re-enacted myth according to time, ritual centres organised myth through space. They associated places with religious beliefs, superimposing a web of popular mythology over the landscape. This complex of space, time and ritual knitted together the social fabric with the spatial structure of the city through cyclical communal acts.

Like the polychromatic urban fabric lacking an overall blueprint (or an architectural treatise), myth was essentially local, variant, changing and transmissible by word of mouth. It did not have an official recognition to command belief and secure the continuity of Venetian identity. In addition, other Italian cities were making similar claims to perfection through their mythology and ritual occasions. In order to consolidate myth as immutable and unquestionable, historical facts were amassed and translated into insignia used in ducal processions.

Such symbols, and the annual ritual marriage of the Doge to the sea, helped to organise the inchoate, amorphous collection of collective imaginaries.[77]

With the waning of Venetian power in the sixteenth century, Venetians retreated deeper into the sphere of representations. Combined with the exaltation of Venice through architecture, official historiography and the centrally controlled intensification of ritual helped assuage anxiety over a diminishing dominion by acts of liminality. Liminal acts involve the suspension of identity and of empirical links with space and time, celebrating a mythical past.[78] Turning away from Byzantium, Venetian discourse articulated an extension of the Myth as the antique Rome and formalised it into official historiography. Articulated in the closing years of the fifteenth century by humanist patricians such as Bernardo Giustiniani, Gasparo Contarini and Paolo Paruta, the Myth of Venice envisioned the city as the perfect place and product of mixed government, a living reincarnation of ancient ideals, 'in which the interests of the citizens were almost mystically bound to the ruling system'.[79] Translations of Contarini's *De magistratibus et Republica Venetorum* helped spread the Myth to Western Europe, exciting the imagination of the Enlightenment theorists.[80] As William Bouwsma suggests, Venice presented itself to Europeans as an example of political wisdom.[81] The Renaissance Venetians acknowledged the Myth not only in popular history, historiography and rhetoric, but also in poetry, musical lyrics, humanist works and the visual arts.[82] But above all they mobilised architecture and ritual to exalt the state and the Republic.

Architecture and ritual processions

The appropriation of mythology by official historiography parallels the transformations in the Bacino and the Piazza, presaging an emerging tension between popular and elite institutions in Venice. This is evident not only in the cleansing of the Piazza of certain commercial and festive activities, but also in the adjustments of ritual made during the fourteenth century by the Republic. These shifts reflect a larger restructuring of Venetian society, especially after the curtailment of membership of the Great Council in 1297, which ensured that political power became the exclusive domain of patrician families. A new political and social order had slowly emerged, replacing the overlapping social connections cutting across elite and popular groups with social divisions in society. These changes enervated the previous dynamism in Venetian life and brought about a separation of the population from the oligarchy. This process was part of a general trend towards elitism that swept Italy in the later Renaissance.[83] Yet, while other Italian cities were dominated by specific leading families, in Venice there was an oligarchy of families determined to prevent the assumption of autocratic power by any single individual. Although social stratification replaced dynamism, the political ideology of the patrician class was republicanism, founded on Aristotelian ideals and guaranteeing all patrician citizens the rights to vote and seek elected office. Social divisions and republicanism were not seen as contradictory, but as fused virtues, mitigating tendencies towards power struggles.[84] This fusion was best expressed in the organisation of government practice, based on a hierarchical ordering of numerous committees with rotating office, which reached their decisions by a majority vote.

The new hierarchical conception of Venetian society is best seen in the shifts from Byzantine to Western ritual after the *Serrata*, thus suppressing the medieval parochial feasts previously financed and organised by the *contrate*. Investing parishioners (*contradaioli*) with group identity, these festivals were part of the carnival season, during which social roles were temporarily suspended and parishioners competed with each other on the basis of their strong identification with the parish. Equally important was the ritual link between these festivities and the organisation of alms by the parishes. From the fourteenth century, the *contrate* were sidelined as constituent groups in processions, and ceremonies were organised by the magistrates, becoming more republican rather than ducal, 'to display the centralisation and unity of the Venetian commonwealth'.[85]

By the end of the sixteenth century, a marked increase in the number of processions had become apparent, with the growing employment of men of ancient Venetian ancestry (*cittadini originarii*) in the business of government as notaries, and the transfer of the organisation of alms from the parishes to the *scuole*. Expanding in parallel with these changes was a secular bureaucracy in charge of ceremonies. Civic ritual thus became more institutionalised in accordance with the authoritarian priorities of the oligarchy, displaying growing class distinctions: 'The nobles, *cittadini* and plebians were separated [...] and the first two groups were classified according to an elaborate hierarchy of official precedents.'[86] While in the thirteenth century nobles and citizens in ducal processions had walked as an undifferentiated group behind the

Figure 2.26 Detail, Matteo Pagan, Procession of the Doge on Palm Sunday, c. 1556–1557. Woodcut. Photo © Museo Correr, Venice

Doge, after the *Serrata* there was a separation between the *cittadini*, *scuole* and guilds, which preceded the Doge, and the noble magistrates, who were ranked according to status behind him (Figure 2.26). Attention shifted to the Piazza San Marco, which was expanded and embellished under the influences of architectural humanism and Classicism.

It is important to note a number of other changes taking place in the city and affecting the relationship between ritual processions and the urban fabric. An example is the church of San Salvador, standing in a strategic *campo*, the meeting point of two economically important arteries connecting the Piazza with the Fondaco dei Tedeschi and the Rialto (Figure 2.27). In the early sixteenth century, the church was reconstructed to resemble the Basilica of San Marco, which has the form of the Greek cross with domes. San Salvador and San Marco were connected not only literally through the Merceria and the similarities in their layout, but also through the cult of St Theodore, the original patron of Venice, a Byzantine saint who was later superseded by the cult of St Mark, whose relics were moved to San Salvador from San Marco. The cult of St Theodore was revived around the middle of the fifteenth century with a ducal procession, giving a new conceptual expression to the route that linked the 'eyes' of the Republic (the Piazza) with the

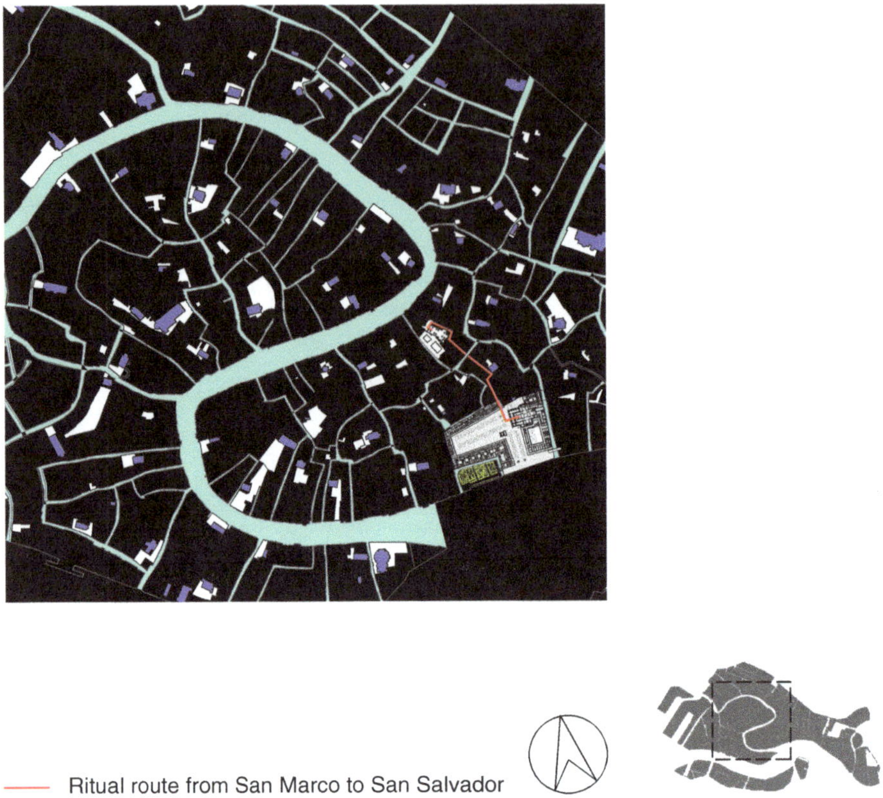

Figure 2.27 Venice. San Marco and San Salvador. Drawing by the author

'viscera' ('*visceribus urbis*') of the city (the Rialto), and the Basilica with this church.[87] Manfredo Tafuri explains:

> The two patron saints represented on the two columns of the Molo, were thus connected by the processional path that runs along the Mercerie and by analogy between the spatial layouts of the two churches. What was in the popular imagination and what was official ideology became part of the same continuum. From San Marco, via the Mercerie, to San Salvador: the explicit message of the porta da mar [...] formed by the two columns in the Molo, was thus projected onto the urban body.[88]

The changes in the church of San Salvador and the revival of an older cult with a ducal procession were examples of a socio-political reform reaching back to redefine the past in order to perfect the present. The 'tragic' scene of the Piazza needed the 'comic' scene of the Merceria and the Rialto, and statecraft depended on city-craft for its survival. From that time, self-conscious architecture and the non-authored city ceased to be part of the same continuum, following paradoxical paths that were both separate and interconnected.

Vecchi and *giovani*: Palladio and the scenography of the lagoon

The changes in the Piazza were part of the larger phenomenon of social reform around conflicting ideologies. These involved the hierarchical structuring of society and republicanism within the elite society; parochial allegiance and the centralised state; and, finally, the social geography of the mercantile city dispersed into many centres and the centralisation of power within the patrician oligarchy. The Piazza complex and the coordinated scenography of the lagoon achieved through Palladio and Longhena's churches were the outcome of a protracted series of tensions emerging between the traditional integration of communal beliefs, the new social order and urban fabric. These tensions are captured by the vigorous debate between the opposing groups of *vecchi* (old) and *giovani* (new). The *vecchi* comprised patrician families occupying places in the Major Council before AD 800 and with close ties to the papacy. The *giovani*, on the other hand, had been elevated to the aristocracy after AD 800 and were staunchly resistant to any control by the Pope over Venetian affairs. The former promoted the new *all' antica* architecture as the carrier of a technical, scientific and ideological renovation. The latter supported traditional aesthetic values in Venetian architecture and the principle of *mediocritas* in public life.[89]

The disagreement between the two factions is revealed in the contentious debate associated with the site and form of Palladio's Redentore. Unlike the architecture of Sansovino, who had incorporated 'many aspects of the Venetian architectural tradition into his own style', Palladio's architecture was 'uncompromisingly modern', and above all 'proudly autonomous'.[90] As a result, he was not commissioned as a state architect (*proto*) by the conservative Venetian establishment, and his works were denied the attention they had received outside the metropolis. The *vecchi* Procurator Paolo di Stefano Tiepolo advocated a prominent location for the Redentore at San Vidal on the Grand Canal and Marcantonio Barbaro argued for a centralised church in a circular form, which 'would make resplendent the dignity of the Republic'.[91] Donà provided the *giovani*'s refutation. He was of a traditional architectural inclination and devotion to *mediocritas*, values which were clearly expressed in his own palazzo on the Fondamente Nove. Located at the northern periphery of Venice, the palace was away from public spectacle, being austere in form and architectural treatment. Donà argued for a longitudinal layout for the Redentore, and gained Doge Alvise Mocenigo's support for the construction of Palladio's church in the Giudecca.[92]

It is not difficult to see why Palladio's churches with their pure classical form proved divisive, reflecting the internal contradictions of the Republic. As Tafuri explains, his innovations attracted suspicion and were marginalised within the establishment.[93] The project of constructing the image of a perfect enduring state was embodied in the tension between re-imagining the city according to the humanist ideals of the antique style, as offered by Palladio, and forces that valued the continuity of *venezianità*.[94] The latter was further endorsed by recurring opposition to humanist projects, such as Palladio's proposal to rebuild the Doge's Palace according to a classical design; Donà's opposition to Palladio's design for the Rialto Bridge; the proposal for a third storey for Sansovino's Library; and Scamozzi's design for the Procuratie Nuove. Yet, the integration of the Piazza area and the Basin triumphed.[95] Donà eventually supported the coordinated scenography in the Basin, by ordering the demolition of the structures in front of San Giorgio to enable them to be viewed from the Doge's Palace.

The transformations in the Basin reflect a change from the late medieval conception of Venice, whose spatial boundaries and connections were guarded by a network of sites associated with a mercantile society that required a clear prospect of the aquatic landscape and a web of images, rituals and sacred objects. Enacted with ritual processions, pedestrian links over causeways, floating theatrical tableaux (*teatri del mondo*) and sea battles, the *Renovatio Urbis* gradually appropriated the ritual geography of the lagoon, transforming it into a humanistic ensemble of monuments and axial alignments. The network of religious buildings captures the grafting together of spatial navigational and ritual networks of medieval Christian origin onto Republican ideology and humanistic cosmology, as exemplified by Renaissance theatres and churches.

Sansovino had simulated ancient amphitheatres in Rome and nearby Pola in his design of the Libreria.[96] In 1565, the year he began San Giorgio, Palladio designed a *teatro del mondo* in the bay for the

Compagnie della Calza degli Accesi, and in 1580 he began the Teatro Olimpico in Vicenza based on Vitruvius's cosmological prescriptions for theatres. In the Teatro Olimpico, Palladio reinterpreted Vitruvius's Roman theatre as a circle formed by four equilateral triangles, expressing a cosmological vision of the world as theatre.[97] As to Longhena, in an accompanying letter he referred to his centralised scheme for the Salute as a *rotonda machina*. Howard explains that the word *machina* meant not only an imposing building, but also the flamboyant, towering festive boats 'shaped like merry-go-rounds, in order to look effective from any viewpoint' in the Venetian regattas.[98] Theatres and churches in the Renaissance integrated the terrestrial and celestial realms and rendered them visible to spectators. In the same way that the Venetian civic ritual displayed the corporate body of society on the waterborne body of the city, the urban stage in the Piazza and the aquatic scenography united political ideology with cosmological belief, and architecture with ritual, through the integrating model of the theatre.

Architecture and representations

> For this is the city of the eye; your other faculties play a faint second fiddle.
>
> Joseph Brodsky, *Watermark: An Essay on Venice*

Two theoretical propositions about theatre must have had a profound influence on Venetian humanists. The first was the theatrical conception of the Bacino by Alvise Cornaro (1484–1566), published around 1560, before the transformation brought about by Palladio's churches.[99] Cornaro was interested in theatre and had expanded his patrimony in the Paduan plains through reclamation projects. His proposal for the Bacino involved a fountain with fresh water in the Piazzetta, a wooded island with a loggia in the middle of the Bacino and a floating theatre in the ancient Roman style for the education and entertainment of all Venetians (Figure 2.28). His project was linked with the proposition he made to divert the rivers from the lagoon, close all the water entrances to it except the one at the Lido, and surround Venice with public walkways through parklands. The second project to exert an influence on the Basin was Guilio Camillo's theatre of memory, published in his *Idea del Teatro* in 1550. In this work, Camillo described a wooden structure constructed as a Vitruvian amphitheatre. The observer stood on the stage and looked

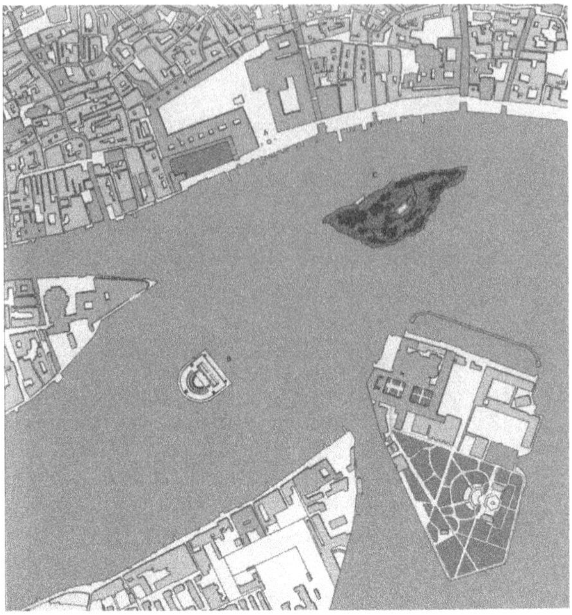

Figure 2.28 Graphic reconstruction of Alvise Cornaro's project for the Bacino of San Marco. Image by Manfredo Tafuri, *Venice in the Renaissance*. Cambridge, Mass: MIT University Press, 1979

out on a semi-circular structure of seven tiers marked with images and boxes. The structure was intended to represent 'the universe, expanding from First Causes through the stages of creation', and enabling a complete recollection of all the knowledge available at the time.[100]

Cornaro's reading of the lagoon as a landscape theatre and Camillo's mapping of geometrical and astronomical order onto architecture came together in the scenographic treatment of the Basin at the end of the sixteenth century. From architectural notations and paintings to astronomical calculations, geometry and mathematics comprised the necessary tools for the unified natural science of the later Renaissance. Geometric and mathematical literacy among the patrician class underpinned the role of architecture, cartography and natural science in cultural life. This was based on a 'broader familiarity with mathematics and geometry of spatial representations, geometrical training in the abacus which involved the recognition of simple spatial and volumetric relations together with mathematic proportions and calculations'.[101]

The invention of architectural drawings produced by specific geometrical conventions, as described by Alberti and Raphael, was, in effect, an invention of 'inscriptions': translations through which entities are refashioned, turning the materiality of the world into sign systems.[102] Perspective was another example, drawing viewers into the scene and making them aware of the effects of looking. Cast as the relationship between perception and the visual field, it captured space, which people were aware of through empirical observation, translating spatial relationships into visual modes of understanding.[103] As Bruno Latour explains, the technology of print turned inscriptions into 'immutable mobiles', devices which made building plans and maps of places transportable, widely distributed and presentable synoptically to the eye, far away in space and time.[104] The permanence and portability of books, maps, drawings and sign systems in a medieval city with unstable boundaries, which was conveying goods from places as far away as the Silk Road, must have been received as an epoch-making change, comparable to the digital revolution of our age.[105]

This raises the question of the intersection of thought and perception with the city's urban networks and buildings as physical systems. Unlike inscriptions that condense the world into ideas, measures or diagrams, the spatial practices of commerce, ritual and everyday life that had configured the city's networks were neither transportable nor synchronic. These were not activities resulting from consciously implemented intentions, mechanisms of calculation, distribution and speculation from which inscriptions could be exacted. The operations affecting the water and land in Venice were performative, pervasive, site-specific and time-bound. Although capable of transforming the course of canals, the direction of streets, the mooring of boats, the exchange of goods and the complexity of infrastructures, they lacked the overall perceptibility of a print, the moralising force of symbolic iconography, the all-seeing visualisation that communicated to the visitors and citizens of Venice the superiority of the city and its customs. In the intersection between thought and spatial conditions lies the tension between spatial practices – determining the evolutionary growth of the city – and the conscious interventions of architects, geometers, planners and mapmakers that constituted the self-conscious mechanisms of the Republic.

City-craft and statecraft

The *Renovatio Urbis* constructed meanings combining political longevity and ancient origin, reaching far into the past in order to surmount the political and economic challenges of the present, planting the seeds of self-perpetuation. Promoting a powerful centralised city was a process of changing relationships between urban spaces and mobilising representations. Just as Sansovino had integrated the existing urban network and the indigenous building conditions with his own Roman vocabulary, and de' Barbari geometrised spatial relationships of urban centrality in the map of Venice, so the Republic merged parochial ritual with civic ritual, popular myths with official historiography, conceptual representational techniques with the empirical realities of the city and its urban fabric.

If statecraft constructed symbols of noble ancestry in the major civic spaces, in the squares, the canals and the alleys of Venice, the Venetians celebrated the mythical origin of their city as the foundation of the world and their society. Simultaneously with its evolutionary construction, the city was producing its history and a mythological structure enacted through rituals. Ritual was dramatising the construction of Venice, uniting myth with architecture and theatre in a coherent development of space and place. The Venetian historiographers provided a political and mythological interpretation of the city, but omitted any description of its ritual processes, obviously knowing that the public, immersed in social customs since their birth, had no need of a coherent and detailed description.[106] People participated in the rituals but no text bothered to describe the ritual use of space. It is evident that they had internalised the spatial and ritual structure of their society, making any verbal description redundant. In contrast to architecture and its emergence as a liberal art, the space of the city was part of everyday practice and memory, rather than public speaking and writing. Public space was associated with movement, spectacular performances and their sequence. Its significance was defined by what happened in it and never by specific instructions such as 'go to this place, follow this route, pass through this space or perform such and such ritualistic actions'.[107]

This is the defined context within which architecture emerged, interweaving practical realities and philosophical concerns in the intensified engagement of the Republic with the city and its representations. For five centuries, the history of architecture is a story of representation and transmission, the technologies used to record it and communicate it through space and time. Since the sixteenth century, the city as spatial ritual and mythological construction arising from collective spontaneous processes has been bypassed in favour of conscious construction that retains the imprimatur of the author. Vernacular urban development has been ignored, privileging architectural design. Space and events do not have a medium of representation and description, as does architecture; they lack words and media to enable description and transmission. As Mario Carpo explains, 'what cannot be recorded will not be transmitted'.[108] The complex logic of the daily practices of movement, activities and rituals, and the building practices of city-craft resist documentation. In contrast, architectural design is pursued and recorded through specific kinds of documents and technologies. Since the city cannot be recorded, we are faced with a void of understanding concerning the relationship between the city, with its events, memory and mythology, and the aesthetic definition of architectural objects. As a result, the interwoven fate of the authored and authorless, of statecraft and city-craft, has been formalised and transmitted only through architecture and urban design, those things admitting of record and communication. Even when the history of architecture is considered in relation to the society creating it, it features the theoretical and practical concerns of buildings as static products of design, formalised through tools of recording and transmission. Tracing the history of urban transformation, this work points to the need to understand the interlocking spheres of city-craft and statecraft, alongside the social logic of their transmission.

Postscript

On 11 August 1508, the mathematician Luca Pacioli gave a lecture in San Bartolomeo at the Rialto on the fifth book of Euclid's *Elements*, dealing with proportion. The lecture was attended by statesmen and humanist scholars such as Bernardo Bembo, sculptors such as Pietro Lombardo, architects such as Giovanni Giocondo, and Aldus Manutius, who had invented the portable book, and whose publishing press in Venice had revolutionised the technology of book printing. De' Barbari's painting of Luca Pacioli (1495) shows the mathematician expounding the theorems of the platonic solids of regular polyhedra to his student. The suspended object top left is a rhombicuboctahedron, one of the 13 semi-regular solids, also called the Archimedean solids (Figure 2.29). The suspended object seems to be made of glass plates and it is half filled with water, capturing reflections and refractions of buildings through a window. An analysis of the painting suggests that the painter did not paint the object from real life.[109] Yet, filled with water, the crystalline form of the solid captures the humanist concern of the relationship between mathematical order, the natural world and the materiality of built space. The space over which this

Figure 2.29 *Portrait of Luca Pacioli (1445–1517) with a student,* via Wikimedia Commons

dialogue was superimposed was the Piazza San Marco and the Bacino with the two sides in the debate, city-craft and statecraft, interfacing *emporium* and *imperium*. In the next chapter this dialogue is transposed to literature, where Marco Polo, traveller and explorer from Venice, describes to Kublai Khan, the emperor of Mongolia, the cities of his empire.

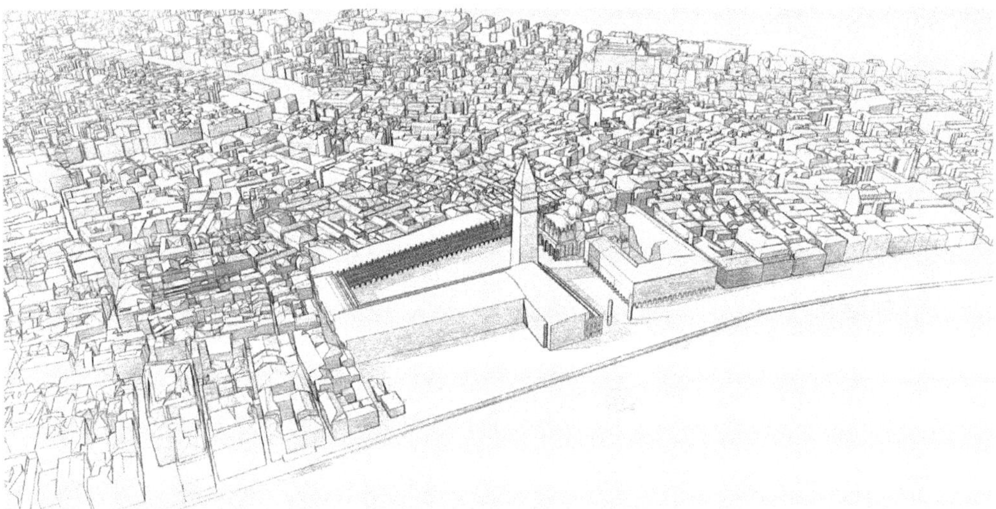

Figure 3.0 Venice. Drawing by Athina Lazaridou

3
Story-craft: The imagination as combinatorial machine in Italo Calvino's *Invisible Cities*

> No one, wise Kublai, knows better than you that the city must never be confused with the words that describe it.
>
> Italo Calvino, *Invisible Cities*

Introduction

If city-craft described the development of the city of Venice out of the everyday actions of people, and statecraft the attempts of the Republic to spatially exercise its visions, story-craft concerns a creative mind's use of Venice as a catalyst for invention. But what does Venice have to do with the imagination of an avant-garde writer? Not only were key parts of Venice the products of utopian fantasy, such as the Piazza San Marco, which was envisioned as a Roman forum; islands, *campi*, streets and works of art too had several authored and popular 'fantasies', variations on the Venice that exists (Figure 3.1).[1] From the Republic's rituals to carnival celebrations and from Canaletto's visions to Le Corbusier's Venice Hospital, Venice exemplifies the encounter of the physical city with the city of the imagination. It is not surprising, therefore, that it has provided the inspirational context for Italo Calvino's *Invisible Cities* (1972), his most acclaimed work of fiction, which has, for architects at least, attained legendary status.[2] Reminiscent in its visionary charge of the thirteenth-century travelogue *Il Milione* and More's *Utopia*, *Invisible Cities* is about the cities Marco Polo describes to Kublai Khan, the emperor of Mongolia.[3] These are fantastic places that the Venetian traveller invents in his mind. Soon the Khan realises that the cities Polo is speaking about have arisen

Figure 3.1 Canaletto. *Capriccio of Rialto with Palladian buildings.* Galleria Nazionale di Parma: su concessione del Ministero dei Beni e delle Attività Culturali e del Turismo - Complesso Monumentale della Pilotta

from the rearrangement of recognisable elements and that in speaking of other places Polo always says something about Venice. Leticia Modena explains that 'Polo is effectively an architect of invisible cities, and he models for the Khan and the work's readers how to become architects of their own invisible cities'.[4]

The title *Invisible Cities* implies the peculiar ability of the human imagination to 'see' the invisible. More importantly, the imagination is explicit in Polo's descriptions of multiform images, making fantastical faraway places 'visible' to the reader. The imagination is also central to the exchanges between the Venetian and the emperor, particularly at the end of the book, where they examine the Khan's atlas. Containing all past and future cities including those that were conceived in thought, the atlas expands the invisible cities to an imaginary universe of the possible. Various critics stress the work's relation to *ars combinatoria*, the art of uncovering combinatorial rules that govern the arrangement of information objects, such as words in language.[5] Calvino discussed the role of the imagination in *Invisible Cities*, explaining that readers can draw a number of paths and multiple intersecting routes through the fiction.[6] In this chapter I attempt to understand how he inspires the readers' imagination; by what mechanisms and rules he stimulates readers to envision their own alternatives; and what role the ever-present Venice plays in the fiction.

The idea of literature as a combinatorial machine was central to the Oulipo literary group that explored the possibilities of mathematics and science.[7] Calvino was a member of the group, absorbing many influences from them as well as from structuralist theorists. Roland Barthes's ideas about language-speech, mental visualisations and the figure of the author had a clear impact on the Italian novelist.[8] The Argentinian writer Jorge Luis Borges and the ancient Roman poet and philosopher Lucretius (c. AD 100) were his two other key sources of inspiration. Borges's story *The Garden of Forking Paths* was for Calvino a masterful expression of narrative possibility within a very short description. Lucretius attracted Calvino with his idea about atoms that deviate from their straight course, releasing a chain of events. Triggering possibility, Lucretius's universe granted freedom to atoms as well as to human beings.[9] Possibility was the central force also in Ovid's *Metamorphoses*, another key text for Calvino, in which 'everything can be transformed to everything else', opposing hierarchical values with freedom.[10]

Calvino was stimulated as much by these philosophical ideas as by a range of theories about the modern city. In Paris, where he wrote *Invisible Cities*, he became familiar with the utopian experimentations in architecture and urbanism in the sixties and seventies. Le Corbusier's project for the Venice Hospital and the visionary project of Richard Rogers and Renzo Piano for the Pompidou Centre (1969) were among the new design approaches that were emerging, searching for dynamic urban possibilities as opposed to the real-estate speculation that was changing cities in northern Europe. These were produced during the same period that Tafuri was debating the role of utopia, and the Italian radical architecture of Superstudio and Archizoom was questioning the undifferentiated expansion of cities under Modernism.[11] Architects such as Yona Friedman, Buckminster Fuller and the architectural group Archigram embraced fantasy and the maximum amount of freedom, playing with light-weight structures of mobility and combinability.[12]

The qualities of a work to be open-ended and indeterminate were explored in an array of other media, literature, music and art, as captured in Umberto Eco's *Open Work*.[13] Closely associated with these developments were contemporary debates on chaos theory and complexity, which aroused interest in networks, cybernetics, systems, ecology and cities as evolutionary organisms. Exerting influence on many fields, the combinatorial possibilities in networks were radically changing many kinds of processes. In his essay 'Cybernetics and Ghosts', Calvino addressed the future of literature in a digital world, referring to computers as electronic brains:

> even if they are still far from producing all the functions of the human brain, [they] are nonetheless capable of providing us with a convincing theoretical model for the most complex processes of our memory, our mental associations, our imagination, our conscience. Shannon, Weiner, von Neumann and Turing have radically altered our image of our mental processes.[14]

In the same essay, Calvino linked the Oulipo writers with cybernetics, referring to Queneau's poem *Cent Mille Milliards de Poèmes* as a 'rudimentary model of a machine for making sonnets, each one different from the last'.[15]

By the end of the twentieth century, *Invisible Cities* had become a key reference for architects and urban planners. However, the book had not been much noticed in architectural circles until interest began shifting away from cybernetics to post-modernism, with its emphasis on historicism, playfulness and the pursuit of complex imaginary meanings. Architects therefore may not have been aware of Calvino's relationship to the intellectual interactions that shaped architecture, urbanism, complexity theory and structuralism in the interdisciplinary climate of the sixties. Regardless of the repertory of formal variations available to architecture through new digital technologies, the combinatorial thinking of avant-garde writers like Calvino remains largely unexplored in architectural theory. If Calvino used architectural ideas in search of alternatives in literature, can the combinatorial dimensions in *Invisible Cities* contribute to the understanding of the architectural imagination? What can architecture and cities learn from his fiction?

Invisible Cities – in search of intelligibility

Calvino was fascinated by canonical and popular texts, which he appropriated in his own works. In *If on a Winter's Night a Traveller* he recycles the structure of *One Thousand and One Nights*.[16] In *The Castle of Crossed Destinies*, he reworks Ariosto's *Orlando Furioso* along with Western classics, while in *Invisible Cities* he borrows from Marco Polo's *Travels*.[17] Marco Polo was a Venetian merchant who opened Central and East Asia to the West with his journeys to the court of Kublai Khan, surpassing his predecessors in the reach and scale of his travels.[18] On his return he was imprisoned in Genoa, where he reportedly dictated his travels to Rustichello da Pisa, a romance writer. Entitled the *Description of the World*, or *Books of the Travels of the World*, or the *The Travels* in English editions, Polo's book was nicknamed *Il Milione* in reference to Polo's use of the word 'millions' to describe his revenues.[19]

Invisible Cities is structured as 55 short city descriptions and 18 dialogues between Kublai Khan and Marco Polo. As the emperor faces the potential destruction of his empire, he seeks in Polo's accounts 'the tracery of a pattern' that 'could escape the termites' gnawing'.[20] Polo feeds the emperor's quest for knowledge with pantomimes, games and dialogues that frame the narrative at the beginning and the end of each chapter. The short texts describe cities as fantastical constructions. There is a city suspended between two steep mountains, a city made of a forest of pipes, a microscopic city concentrically expanding over time. Some cities are heavy and monumental, while others are skeletal and dismountable. There are phantom cities reflected in lakes and cities that are subterranean. A few have a secret plan manifested in a carpet or a starry night. Others grow formless and uniform, a reference to the contemporary expansion of suburbs. Finally, there are cities where the roles of people and happenings are interconnected or repeat over time.

The range and sensory qualities of the places Polo describes compel Kublai to understand the invisible order of Polo's imagination. The dialogues, which are printed in italics, extend the ideas encountered in the city descriptions and move from the two characters' learning each other's language, to their establishing a conversation, thinking in silence, playing chess and examining the Khan's atlas. The novel is intended to provoke thought rather than develop a plot towards closure. However, as the last dialogue focuses on the question of utopia versus 'inferno', it advances a proposition: Polo's final utopia is a city that is 'discontinuous in space and time', consisting of interruptions.[21] His closing advice to the Khan is to learn to recognise 'who and what in the midst of the inferno is not inferno' and make them last, 'give them space'.[22] If the genre of utopia has been about idealised geometries, expressions of totality hierarchically applied, Calvino promotes a utopia that is constructed from the bottom up, recombinant and adaptive to change. Characterised in this way, Calvino's implicit proposition for the ideal city would seem to reflect many of the ideals of the resilient city, which are embodied in today's utopias.

The 55 city descriptions are organised in nine chapters and distributed under 11 thematic rubrics: 'Cities and Memory', 'Cities and

Desire', 'Cities and Signs', 'Thin Cities', 'Trading Cities', 'Cities and Eyes', 'Cities and Names', 'Cities and the Dead', 'Cities and Sky', 'Continuous Cities' and 'Hidden Cities'. Each chapter contains five city descriptions (with the exception of the first and last chapters, which consist of ten cities each), arranged so as to construct recursively descending sequences of numbers (from 5 to 1). In spite of this mathematical orchestration, to the average reader the fiction is a collection of loosely interrelated narratives that can be read in sequence from the first to the last page or at random. What complicates matters more, as Kublai suspects, is that cities seem to exchange their elements and come to resemble each other. When challenged by the emperor, Polo admits that Venice lies behind all his descriptions. The cities of *Esmeralda* and *Phyllis* that follow the dialogue on Venice branch out in 'tortuous optional routes on dry land or water'.[23] In this, Calvino alludes to the web of alleys and canals of Venice to express the ways in which the lack of unity in the fiction might create disorientation.

Losing oneself in a city or a book sharply contrasts with Kublai's search for a model from which all other cities derive. In the opening dialogue, Kublai is able to discern in Polo's descriptions a 'scaffolding' of abstract relations. In another dialogue he observes that 'a splendid hard diamond takes shape' and that the empire is made of the geometry of a crystal.[24] As the emperor plays chess with the merchant, he attempts to understand cities following the rules of the game. Yet, at the end of the game a bare square of wood remains, an emblem of nothingness. Polo advises Kublai to look at the pores of the wood to generate new stories. As the book advances to its end, the last two dialogues between Polo and the Khan focus on the Khan's atlas. These dialogues refer to cities in the Great Khan's empire and empires of the West, including all cities known and possible.

Invisible Cities juxtaposes images of lightness and coherence with images of entropy and decay, ruins, mazes filled by earth, dirt, refuse, and formless suburbs. Whether in narrative or dialectical mode, Polo systematically frustrates and excites the Khan – as Calvino does the reader – prompting him to think of the book as a labyrinth and speculate on an invisible order resembling the diaphanous 'tracery of a pattern'.[25] The city descriptions and the dialogues construct an echoing system that amplifies the challenge facing the Khan to reconstruct the labyrinth and dissolve its power. The emperor's search for intelligibility mirrors the question in readers' minds: what makes a book larger than the sum of the city descriptions, a novel out of these pieces, a story out of these fragments?

Two models of knowledge

Polo's refusal to speak of Venice is used as a mechanism to provoke the thought of Venice in the mind of the readers and help them visualise it. The Khan grasps Venice immediately as the ideal city, a Platonic model that might explain the variety of the cities Polo describes. Yet, aside from glimpses of green canals and a range of routes over water or land, Polo's cities tend to be increasingly homogeneous, sprawling through airports, expanding through suburbs or filled with garbage. The Khan searches for a proxy to understand the secret order in Polo's accounts that can make the 'formless ruin' of his empire cohere.[26] Confounding Kublai's interest in images that assert structural concepts of unity – the tracery of a pattern, a splendid hard diamond, a bridge, a chessboard, an atlas – Polo presents him with a multiplicity of treasures, ginger, cotton, pistachio nuts, silk, souks, tiled courts, whitewashed walls, rubbish bins, houses of zinc with water stored in barrels. The empire of the Khan, like every empire, thrives on order, classification, rules, labels, numbers, sets and systems on a grid where emblems, monuments, people and objects are logically arranged. Kublai seeks unity and coherence through the imposition of a bureaucracy of rituals and rules on a field of cities, vanquishing their variety. The merchant's interest, on the other hand, is in multiform things, summoned and exchanged one by one, a series of disparate memories, collections of stories and objects.[27] If the Khan yearns to possess his empire in abstract thought while seated in his garden, Polo takes pleasure in the visible surface of the world, exchanging wares, stories and tales through travelling.

Marco Polo and Kublai Khan represent two different modes of knowing. The Khan seeks an ideal order of things in his possession. Polo seeks not-yet-seen adventures, the variety of things that can be exchanged and collected. Soon, however, Polo's variety is also overcome by the endless homogeneity found in trading similar things in different places, as cities are 'everywhere the same, in all the bazaars inside and outside the Great Khan's empire, scattered at your feet on the same yellow mats'.[28] To the list of philosophical binaries and mirrors that permeate the text – author and reader, merchant and emperor, reason and intuition, ideal and real, rational and empirical, mind and matter, visible and invisible, material and immaterial – Calvino adds another opposition: between difference and homogeneity. There are cities that 'preserve their differences intact' and cities that merge over the surface of the earth into the same generic city with no beginning or end.[29] The interplay between variety and standardisation of places and wares infiltrates the dialogues and Polo's descriptions, drawing attention to the competing processes of innovation and reproduction in modern cities.

The strategy of opposition in poetry and literature often relies on symmetry, through which a particular problem is dramatised. Once a solution to the Khan's quest for intelligibility is expressed, through the idea of Venice or the tracery of a pattern, it is overturned. Embedded symbolisms in the text cause readers to oscillate between opposites, shifting and challenging meaning. As soon as they follow one direction, they discover that they have returned to the place in which they started. The role of symmetry raises the question of exploring the structure of the text in order to understand if there is an underlying order around which cities cohere.

'A splendid hard diamond takes shape' – the text as a digital file

Calvino's book opens with a list of contents outlining the structure of the fiction. Calvino gives each of the 55 cities a number and orders them from 5 to 1 in each of the nine chapters. The city descriptions have titles based on one of the 11 thematic classifications, each of which is periodically repeated in the book five times ('Cities and Memory', 'Cities and Desire', and so on). The sequence of numbers (from 5 to 1) remains invariant in all chapters. In contrast, the thematic classifications shift gradually, so that each time a new classification appears, another one is dropped. This pattern generates a gradual succession of repeating themes. By plotting the cities and aligning them according to their numerical indexes – or the forward-shifting numbers – critics have assembled the notation shown in Figure 3.2. This leads to a configuration which is reminiscent of Kublai's attempts to interpret his empire as a diamond-shaped structure.[30] Reading the diagram from left to right and from top to bottom corresponds with the linear sequence in which the cities are described in the text (Figure 3.3). We can cut the paper along the perimeter of the shape and bend it, joining the top with the bottom vertical lines to form a ribbon.[31] So, arriving at the end of the book we are led back to the start of the fiction. As we turn the pages of the book, the repeating numerical series (from 5 to 1) implies a cyclical pattern of time. The invisible matrix of cities and rubrics, on the other hand, is foreign to time, rendering the narrative armature transparent and motionless all at once in the mind.

The system of names and numbers provides a short list of exactly repeatable standardised signs. These signs lead to a notation which has an

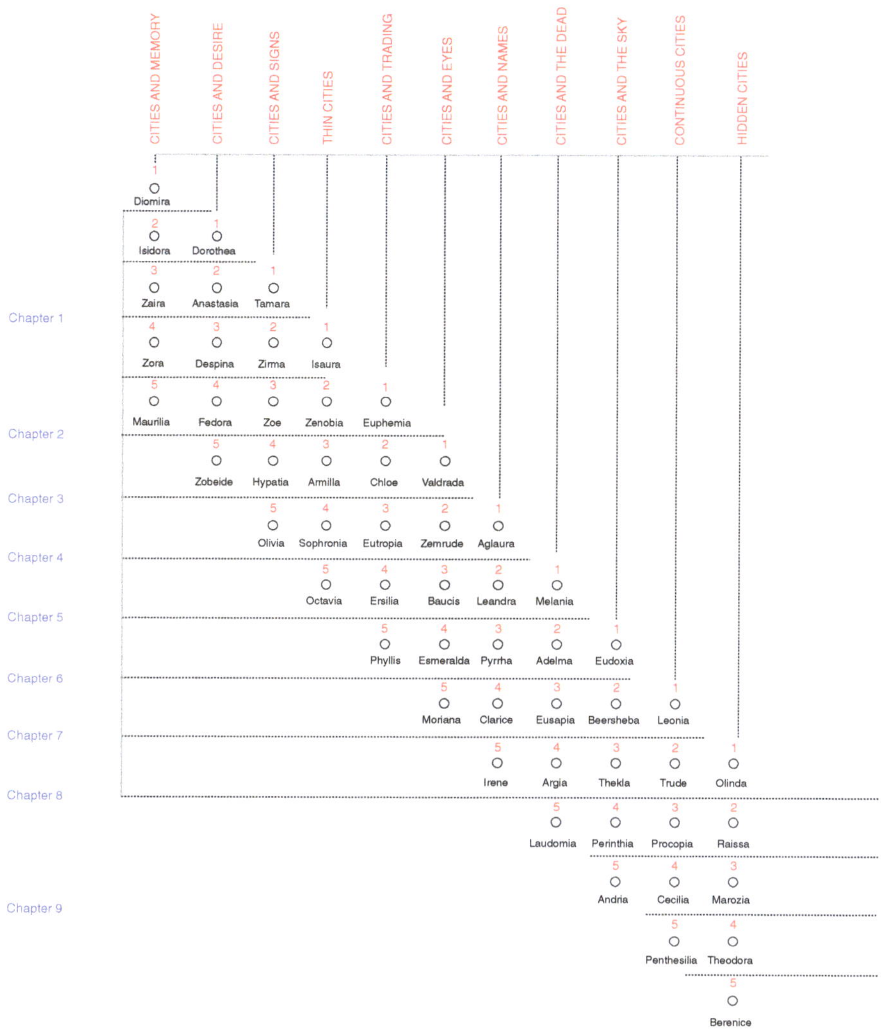

Figure 3.2 Italo Calvino. *Invisible Cities*. Notation of the narrative structure (based on names and numbers provided in the contents of the book). Drawing by the author

indexical relationship to the work, that is, it determines the precise position of cities in the text and thus the difference between each city and all others. Calvino 'digitises' the structure of the text, providing a list of coordinates, which are concepts and numbers. These can work as computational instructions, or as an algorithm converting the structure of the text into a digital file. Numerical consistency in the notation, based on

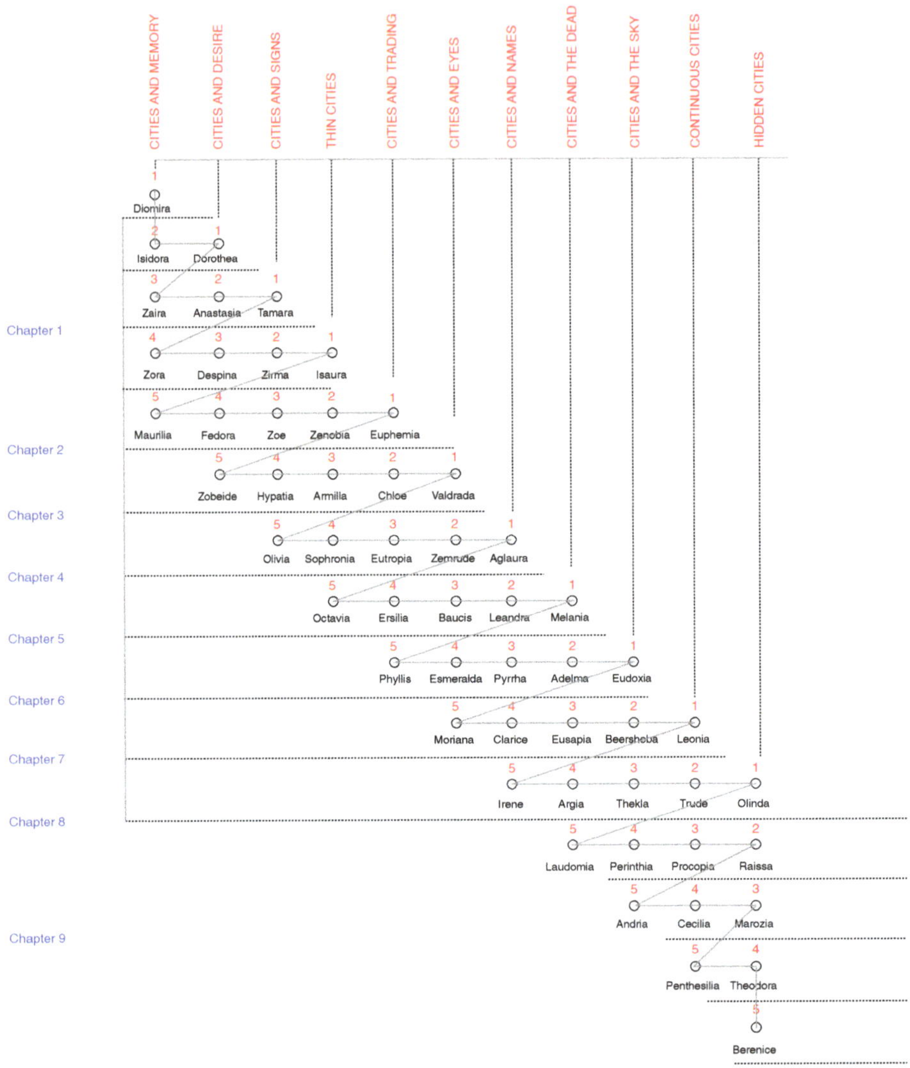

Figure 3.3 Italo Calvino. *Invisible Cities*. Notation of narrative structure and reading path sequence in which cities are presented in the fiction. Drawing by the author

the repetition of the identical series of numbers, allows it to be translated into a geometrically consistent pattern, which helps us visualise it and grasp it all at once as a single object.[32] Early in the twentieth century, Henri Poincaré had explained that 'the advantage of geometry lies precisely in the fact that the senses can come to the assistance of the intellect'.[33] We can understand the internal relations more easily by looking at Figure 3.3 than when reading the text, where conceptual ideas are in a state of flux, emerging step by step in the process of reading. The great advantage of the diamond shape is that it translates the sequences of ideas into numeric and geometric form, bringing geometry and the senses to the assistance of our thoughts in following the linear pathway of language.

This notation can be compared with a musical score, by which we can 'rehearse' the same 'piece', in this case following the sequence of cities from top-left to bottom-right. This is clearly implied in *Zora*, one of the cities, which, like a musical score, comprises notes that cannot be replaced or altered. We can also navigate through the diagram in many other ways if we join cities by horizontal and vertical lines (Figure 3.4). The resulting network captures various itineraries through the text, such as starting from any intermediary point, following chapters or thematic classifications, or ordering city descriptions into different sequences according to whether they are underground, geometrical, formless and so on. The diagram in Figure 3.4 is no longer a notation of the work's sequence, as we no longer adhere to the exact ordering of its elements. However, it is not entirely disengaged from the work, since the modular structure of Calvino's city-texts allow us to exercise choice, creating our own route through the pages.

This open-ended concordance between the notation and the text evokes Kublai's apprehension that cities exchange their elements and are perhaps similar to each other. It also alludes to the moment when the Khan attempts to reduce his knowledge of his vast territories to the various arrangements of pieces on the chessboard following the combinatorial laws of the game. We find here the roots of the structuralist understanding of language. If we think of the cities as linguistic units, the geometric notation provides the syntax that organises these units into a network of relationships. Like syntax and grammar in language, which translate a web of concepts into a string of words, the network can offer a code for generating possible strings of city descriptions as variations of the fiction. The notation expresses *Invisible Cities* as a particular expression of speech (*parole*) which remains part of the broader system of language (*langue*).[34]

These observations help us to accurately describe and distinguish three kinds of concordance in the work's structure. The first is the numeric concordance of the notation with the text, the thematic and numerical structure in the list of contents. The second is the geometric concordance encoding the work as a shape or figure. The third is a topological concordance based on relations of adjacency among cities in the order in which they are found in the novel (or any order in which they can be combined at will). While the topological concordance between the

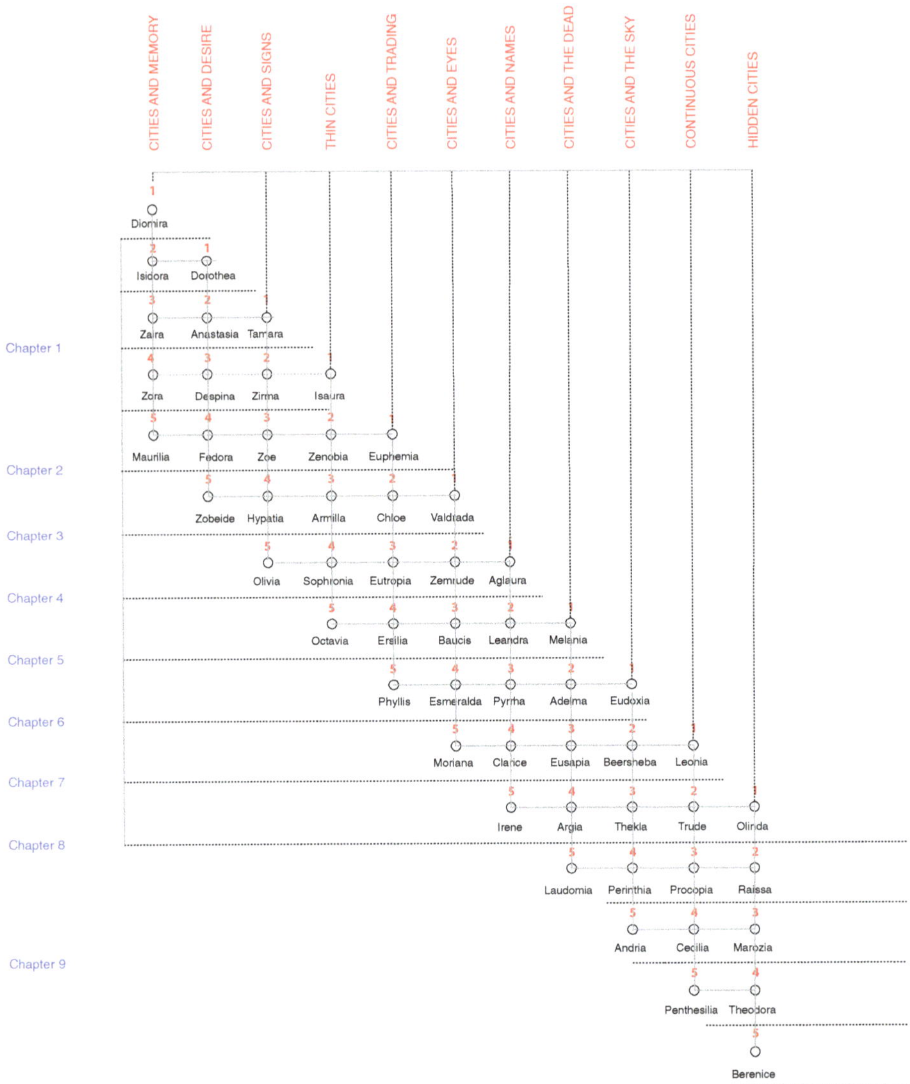

Figure 3.4 Italo Calvino. *Invisible Cities*. Notation of the grid structure of the fiction. Drawing by the author

diagram and the text provides the narrative sequence, the numeric and geometric concordances translate the sequence into a shape and a rhythmical pattern. By assigning names and numbers to cities (classifications), Calvino digitises and expresses geometrically the topology of the text, producing a stable image. Like a plan of a building or a city enmeshing the topological structure of spaces into a visual representation, the diagram maps a web of ideas into a geometric notation.

This representation can 'speak' notationally and geometrically, just as a plan does, adding conceptual relations to the fiction. In Peponis's view, the network exposes high-order symmetries with respect to 'Cities and Eyes', which are hidden between opposite concepts.[35] So, the past, which we process through memory, interacts with possibilities that are entailed in the future ('Cities and Memory' – 'Hidden Cities'); desires that give cities their form converse with formless cities that have been emptied of desire ('Cities and Desire' – 'Continuous Cities'); cities and their signs are mapped onto cities and their celestial patterns ('Cities and Signs' – 'Cities and the Sky'); cities of exchange that are in a state of unrest are paired with cities whose life is solidified by their name ('Cities and Desire' – 'Cities and Names'). Finally, cities that have a skeletal construction are paralleled with cities of the dead, expressing the idea of the skeleton as the common element between living and dead structures ('Thin Cities' – 'Cities and the Dead').[36] When thematic categories are mapped onto their diametric opposites along the axis of 'Cities and Eyes', the geometric symmetries intensify the relationship between the opaque surface of the text (*parole*) and the skeletal pattern (*langue*).[37] They help to unravel poetic relationships that are not made explicit, or are lost in the sequential motion of language.

However, achieving a visual and conceptual understanding of the work as a notation is other than *the work*, that is, other than Calvino's text and the experience of reading the fiction. This is not simply because a literary work is the text itself, but also because the diagram is a translation of the work, and not an instance of the work. As Nelson Goodman explains, 'a literary script is both a notation [the text] and is itself a work'. In contrast, in painting, 'the work is an individual object; and in etching, a class of objects. In music, the work is the class of performances compliant with a character.'[38] Thus, literature and painting are 'autographic', or handmade by their authors, while music and architecture are 'allographic', which means 'scripted by the authors in order to be executed by others'.[39] In a 1967 essay Calvino explains that in Borges's fictions 'the secret watermark of the universe always seems to be about to appear'.[40] Has Calvino then provided the notation as a 'watermark', implying that *Invisible Cities* becomes 'allographic', open to 'improvisation' by the work's readers? It is worth noting here that to Kublai's question whether on his return to the West Polo would repeat the stories he tells him, Polo answers that it is not the voice that commands the story, but the ear.

Arriving at the notation requires the procedure of plotting the numbers provided in the work's list of contents on paper. The process of producing the notation defines an analytic form of understanding, contrary to intuitive modes of perception emerging when reading the fiction. What matters is not only what the notation means, but also how the network 'gets into' the text; how the step-by-step experience of reading the fiction with its images, ideas, inversions, transpositions and pleasures enables us to grasp the notation as a particular mode of explaining the fiction. The task to undertake next is to describe how reading *Invisible Cities* leads from intuitive to conscious understanding. The question raised is thus two-fold: first, how the notation takes shape in our mind in the process of reading; and second, how 'improvising' – as readers often do, flipping through the text and choosing varied reading sequences – leads to grasping an emergent higher order, such as the previously mentioned symmetry between thematic classifications in the novel.

The world and its copies – emergent local symmetries

> The poet's mind, and at a few decisive moments the mind of the scientist, works according to a process of association of images that is the quickest way to link and to choose between the infinite forms of the possible and the impossible.
>
> Italo Calvino, *Six Memos for the Next Millennium*

Calvino was an Oulipian, fond of exactitude and mathematical patterns, and would have had a good grasp of the symmetries involved in his thematic and numerical structure. This structure has a close relation to a tessellation, created by repeating a triangle so as to cover a plane without gaps or overlaps. Group theory defines symmetry as an operation that leaves a configuration invariant. There are four types of symmetry in the tessellation: reflection, translation, glide-reflection and rotation (Figure 3.5). This means that bilateral symmetry articulates hierarchical relationships that distinguish 'Cities and Eyes' from the rest of the cities, but local-scale symmetries make all points in the diagram identical, confirming Kublai's idea that cities are interchangeable with each other. A closer look at the content of the city descriptions in the fiction makes one realise that it is often impossible to decide on the basis of a city's description what thematic classification it appears under. In addition, many concepts would be equally at home under some other city or rubric. In *Isidora*, for instance, desires become memories, blurring the thematic rubrics of 'Cities and Memory' with 'Cities and Desire'. In *Euphemia* memories are traded every solstice and every equinox, exchanging the theme of memory with that of trading. So, the semantic identity of either the discrete city descriptions or

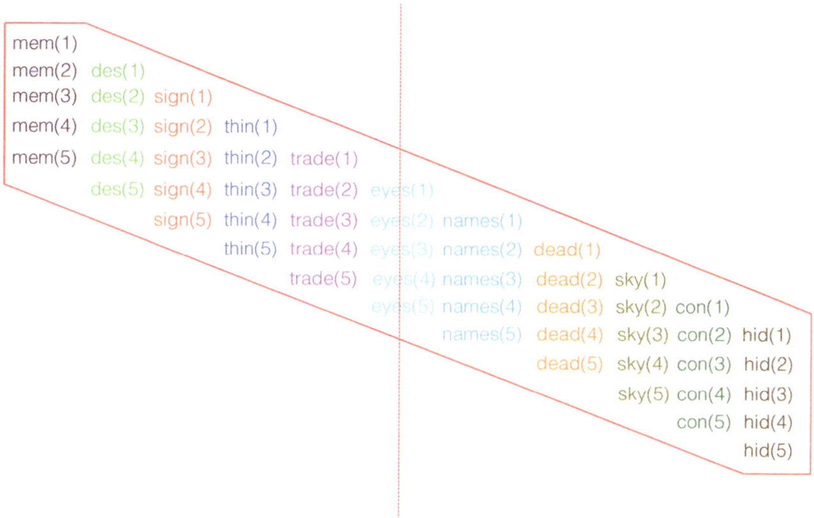

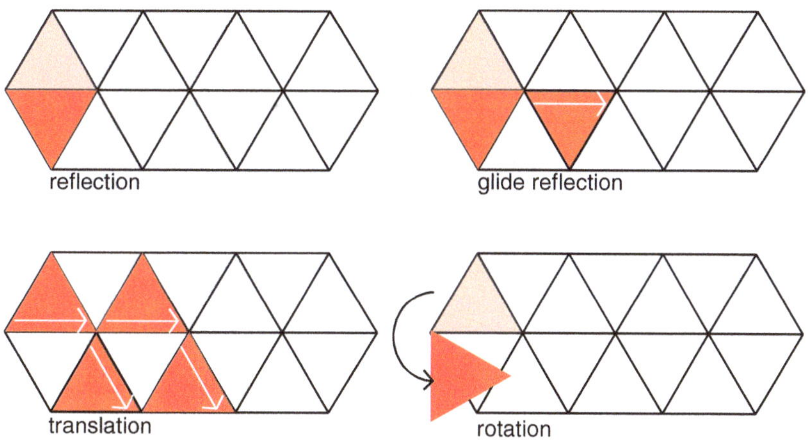

Figure 3.5 The four types of symmetry in a tessellation. Drawing by the author

the thematic categories is not unambiguously defined. Peponis's idea of symmetries notwithstanding, meaning in *Invisible Cities* is multi-scalar and multiform, fluid at the small scale of individual tales and more stable and fixed at the scale of the overall narrative structure.

The individual tales evoke conceptual relationships that express variations of the four symmetries in the tessellation. Reflection is systematically encountered throughout the fiction, as most cities have a mirror, an opposite or a double, such as *Valdrada*, which consists of twin cities, one erected above a lake, and the other reflected on water, or *Moriana*, which has a face and an obverse that cannot be separated or look at each other. Translation characterises those cities that are created and abandoned, this process being repeated in another location, such as *Eutropia*. Glide reflection occurs in cities which have a copy that influences the original. In *Eusapia*, for example, the inhabitants build an identical double of the city underground (reflection). As the city of the dead makes innovations that evolve over time (expressing a horizontal shift on the plane, or translation), the *Eusapia* of the living copies the novelties of its underground copy (denoting a reflection which together with translations provides glide reflection). Finally, rotation is expressed through cyclical patterns as in *Sophronia*, which consists of a permanent half and a temporary half. The former comprises a rollercoaster. The latter is made of stone and periodically shifts on trailers, returning to the original place after a certain time.

Invisible Cities is permeated with images and modalities that on the whole express two things: first, the four local-scale symmetries and their permutations, conveying the ideas of organic growth, transformation, evolution and adaptation; second, the idea of a combinatorial syntax between the physical city erect on the ground and the city in the mind as representation through language, signification, discourse, perception, nature, knowledge of the past, projections into the future, memory and desire; or a mathematics of combinations between signifier and signified. The four symmetries evoke the idea of tessellation, gradually constructing a representation of the narrative structure as a network in the reader's mind. At the same time, additional transformations are present in the text, such as rarefaction, bifurcation, scaling, indivisibility and *mise-en-abyme* (multiple reflections), working in a similar manner. Rarefaction characterises 'Thin Cities' like *Armilla*, consisting of a forest of pipes, or *Zenobia*, sitting on piles. These cities are disembodied and skeletal, devoid of the mass and weight we find in normal built structures. Bifurcation is found in cities in which travellers reflect on the multiplicity of routes during their journey, expressing the Borgesian theme of forking paths. Scaling and *mise-en-abyme* are encountered in cities like *Fedora*, in which small copies of the city are exhibited in a museum of metal, or in *Olinda*, which grows in circles, each circle blossoming inside the others. Finally, indivisibility is a characteristic of cities like *Zoe*, in which everything is exchangeable with everything else.

Plotting the transformations used in each city on the diamond shape provides a more detailed algorithm of symmetries in a tessellation than the original notation (Figure 3.6). If the network in the diagram provides the algorithm, the letters are the alphabet, expressing the interplay of mathematics and language in literary combinatorics. Combinatorics is the branch in mathematics that counts the number of ways objects can be combined or ordered. Given a number of different elements *n*, the number of arrangements that can be made of them in any order is expressed by their factorial n (n!), calculated as 1*2*3*4.......*n!. In the case of the four symmetries we have 24 combinations. Eco explains that such 'calculuses-algorithms' are employed in the solution of problems, but 'they can also serve as discovery procedures, that is, procedures for inventing a variety of possible scenarios'.[41] They work as expression systems, which can reveal possible content systems.

Invisible Cities is the most characteristic expression of what Calvino meant by the combinatorial imagination: 'a multi-faceted structure in which each brief-text, value or concept is close to the others in a series that does not imply a logical sequence or hierarchy, but a network in which one can follow multiple routes and draw multiple, ramified conclusions'.[42] This refers not only to the many ways in which it is possible to circulate through the fiction, but also to the relationship between the networks of images in the text and what they mean, or the signifiers and signifieds. In *Hypatia* the traveller realises: 'I had to free myself from the images which in the past had announced to me the things I sought.'[43] The power of *Invisible Cities* to stimulate the imagination lies in its capacity to convey a multiplicity of virtually embedded combinations leading to the generation of possibility, to meanings that are factual as well as potential and dynamic. Like the philosopher Raymond Lull (see Introduction, note 65), Calvino has created a combinatorial system where symmetries and thematic rubrics rotate on a wheel system, a type of computer, where meaning is encoded through the potential of the system rather than persistently expressed as a static representation.[44] This strategy exposes readers to a wealth of unexpected associations, and generates alternative worlds through a process of combinations, training their imagination.

If we return to the way in which the geometrical ideas are embedded in the semantic content of the text, we see that multiple references to 'cogwheels' and 'spider webs', 'interchangeable data',[45] 'symmetrical motifs in a carpet',[46] 'crystals',[47] 'carousels'[48] and 'kaleidoscopes'[49] express the idea of the network in readers' minds. More significant than these signifiers of symmetrical exchanges, though, are the mental operations constructing step by step the shuffling relationships among elements,

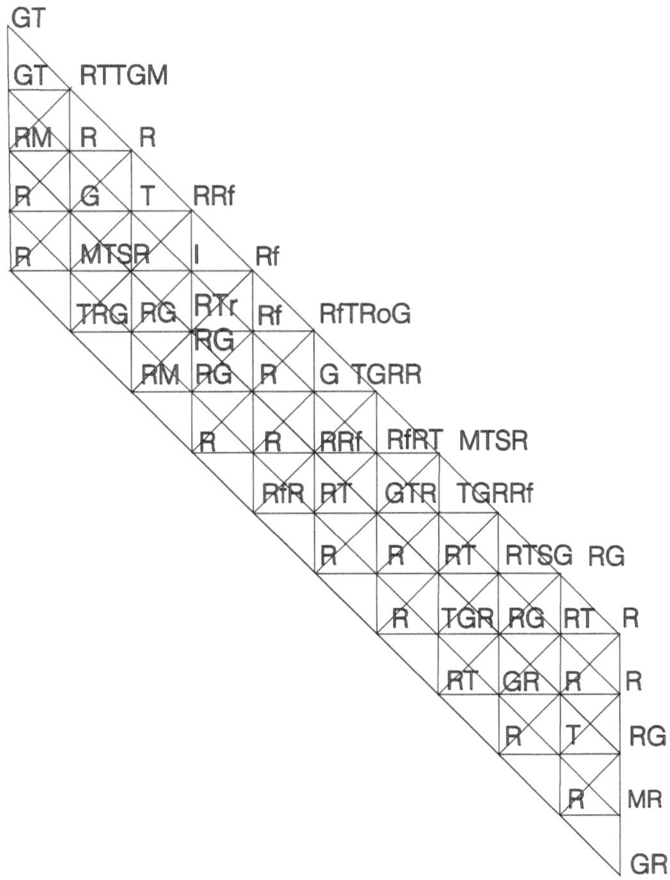

R e f l e c t i o n	inversion; duality; doubling; copying
T r a n s l a t i o n	repetition + displacement + shift
G l i d e t r a n s l a t i o n	inversion + repetition
R o t a t i o n	cycle
R a r e f a c t i o n (Rf)	decreasing density – Thin Cities
B i f u r c a t i o n	interconnectivity + synchronicity
S c a l i n g	reproducing; copying in smaller size
I n d i v i s i b i l i t y	identity; sameness
M i s e - e n - a b y m e	nesting

Figure 3.6 Italo Calvino. *Invisible Cities*. Notation of narrative structure and transformations embedded in the description of cities. Drawing by the author

actively invoking the tessellation in the reader's mind. This way of cognitively constructing the network is based on three main strategies: first, modularising the fiction through city descriptions, or discretising the representation of units in the narrative; second, doubling, splitting, copying and multiplying the narrative units in each text through symmetry operations, leading to many units – copies of the original – that are linked in a network-like structure; third, dissociating the signifier (the original unit) from the signified (the copies) through transformation over space and time. For example, the miniature models of *Fedora* in a museum inside *Fedora* exemplify the operations of mirroring, scaling, multiplying and mise-en-abyme. With time, these miniature models no longer resemble *Fedora*, which undergoes transformations that make it a different *Fedora* from the original and its copies. These strategies enable units to shift and express a variety of meanings. By repeating these microscopic rules in every city description, Calvino makes them accessible to intuition and visualisation, helping to assemble the idea of tessellation both as a single static shape and as an evolutionary network in the mind.

'This route was only one of the many that opened'

> [I]t would suffice to play a game according to the rules, and to consider each successive state of the board as one of the countless forms that the system of forms assembles and destroys.
>
> Italo Calvino, *Invisible Cities*

> [I]t is not sufficient to have the whole world at one's disposal – the very infinitude of possibilities cancels out possibilities, as it were, until limitations are discovered.
>
> Roger Sessions, quoted in Nelson Goodman, *Languages of Art*

Invisible Cities not only invokes the idea of the combinatorial novel through the symmetry operations in the text, but also allows multiple reading sequences and points of access. At the end of the fiction we encounter Polo and Kublai in their last dialogue on utopia. Polo advises the Khan 'to recognise and learn who and what, in the midst of the inferno, are not inferno, then make them endure, give them space'.[50] This final statement suggests that the fiction is potentially one of those things that can train us to 'to recognise and learn' through 'constant vigilance and apprehension' what is the 'inferno' and escape it.[51] Polo's advice and the folding of the diagram into a ribbon point to a second reading. Returning to the first pages, we encounter Kublai pondering about the diamond shape of his empire. The cities of *Diomira* and *Isidora* welcome us again, speaking of travellers that have passed through them, as we did. In *Dorothea*, which follows, we are reminded that the route that led travellers' caravans to it 'was only one of the many that opened', alluding to the many reading routes in the fiction.[52] We are at this point invited to consider possible pathways other than Calvino's route, which we have followed. With the directionality of the sequence we habitually follow suspended, we wonder which of the 55 cities best escapes the inferno, or what defines our escape from it, our own route and exit from the fiction. As Calvino writes:

> A book, I believe, is something with a beginning and an end (even if it is not a novel in the strict sense of the word); it is a space into which the reader must enter, roam around, maybe lose direction, but at a certain point will find a way out, or several ways out, or just the possibility of opening up a road to come out.[53]

The idea of endless choice at first seems liberating. Yet, the simple operation of freely circulating through the book entails key questions: what is the significance of open points of entry and exit? How many paths including all the cities in a sequence are there? We can use the formula from combinatorics we previously described: 1*2*3*4.......*n!, where 'n' is the number of entities to be combined, expressed as 'factorial n' or 'n!'. The 55 city descriptions and the 18 dialogues that make up the book lead to 73! distinct sequences. The value that this formula gives is: $4{,}470{,}115{,}462 \times 10^{105}$. If we assume that each of the possible sequences constitutes one book, we have $4{,}470{,}115{,}462 \times 10^{105}$ books, a number so vast that it is impossible to grasp or imagine.

To give an intuitive idea of the scale of possibilities we are dealing with, we can use William Bloch's computations and compare them with the size of the universe.[54] Current research approximates this size as being about 1.5×10^{26} metres. To simplify the calculations, Bloch supposes that the universe is shaped like a cube, each side of which measures 10^{26} metres and whose volume is therefore $10^{26} \times 10^{26} \times 10^{26} = 10^{78}$ cubic metres. If we can fit 1,000, that is, 10^3 books in one cubic metre, then our universe, if it consisted of nothing but books, would contain $10^{78} \times 10^3 = 10^{81}$ books. It would therefore take

$$\frac{4{,}470{,}115{,}462 \times 10^{105}}{10^{81}} = 4{,}470{,}115{,}462 \times 10^{24}$$

universes the size of ours to contain the variations of *Invisible Cities*.

We can reduce the vast number of books by devising sequences that keep the order of cities in each thematic classification constant, but combine the thematic categories in different ways to produce different sequences, each forming a different book. This gives a number of 39,916,800 sequences. We can reduce possibility further by combining the nine chapters, yielding 362,880 different ways to read the fiction. Finally, there are 120 possible sequences of combining cities within each chapter (5!). It is worth recalling that most descriptions of cities indicate an infinite process of subdivision into smaller units or multiplication. So, to the enormous potential of the book we could add the stories that could spring from the city descriptions to which these texts serve as a preface, summary or review. In *Chloe*, for example, 'in each encounter people imagine one thousand things about each other';[55] in *Zobeide* all men had a similar dream and built the city like the one in the dream; in *Zaira* old men tell the story that the city 'contains in its measurements of its space the events of the past'.[56]

Embedded as a potential in *Invisible Cities*, combinatorial explosion implies that the imagination is a revolving axis on which turn all the possibilities that have a place inside and outside the fiction, in the minds of the inhabitants of the cities Polo describes, and in the minds of the work's readers, their own imaginings, fears and dreams. As an exercise in theoretical possibility, combinatorial explosion leads to an unimaginable quantity beyond human conception. Even with the smaller number of sequences enumerated above, we need to extend beyond the bounds of life to read the fiction according to the number of possibilities it enfolds.[57] What is the significance of an enormous number of sequences beyond intuitive reach, and how can it be relevant to the reader? To answer this question, we need to return to the structure of the fiction.

'The answer it gives to a question of yours' – emergent global patterns

In *Invisible Cities* Calvino uses elements that are grouped in four main sets: narrative units (city descriptions), thematic categories, numbers for each city and chapters. If it is through the thematic categories, 'Cities and Memory', 'Cities and Desire' and so on, that the tension between the city and its representation is thematised, what is the logic that distributes cities into these categories and these categories into chapters? Answers to this question can be explored through a diagram based on connectivity relations among thematic classes (Figure 3.7). Each time a city belonging

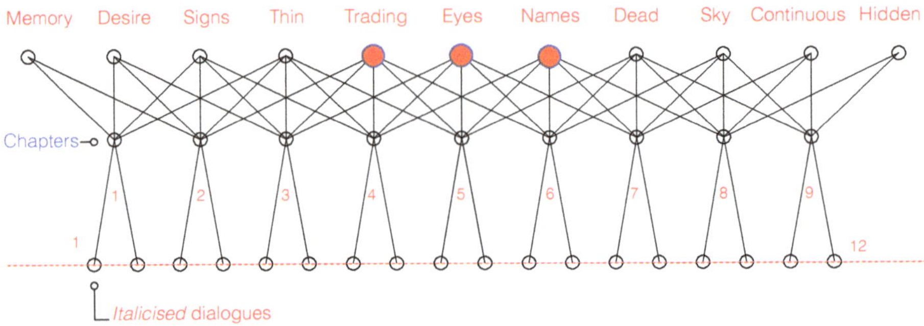

Figure 3.7 Italo Calvino. *Invisible Cities*. Network of adjacency relations among thematic classes. Drawing by the author

to a category is co-present with a city from another category in one or more chapters, we add a link between the thematic categories they are part of. The resulting representation is a graph in which thematic classes are the nodes and the connectivity links between them form edges, the lines connecting nodes. We can calculate the 'closeness centrality' and 'betweenness centrality' of each category, both being measures from network theory, which were used in the analysis of Venice. Closeness centrality captures the average number of 'steps' each class is 'away' from the others. Categories that are 'close' to every other category draw them all to themselves, whereas those that are 'distant' are less connected. It is worth explaining that closeness and distance is not metric but topological, in the sense of how many steps away in the graph is each element from the others. Betweenness centrality accounts for the shortest paths between all pairs of categories. If, for example, during reading, we move from a city description under the heading 'Cities and Trading' to one under the theme 'Cities and Names', this measure captures which thematic categories form the 'shortest' conceptual links between them.

All thematic groups have almost equally strong values, demonstrating the multi-focal nature of the network of thematic classes. This means that whichever page we are on in the fiction we are not far away from every other thematic class or from the shortest paths between them. However, 'Trading Cities', 'Cities and Eyes' and 'Cities and Names' have the highest values in the system. This means that, although the book can be read in different ways by skipping through the pages, the conceptual links that connect every thematic category to all others are formed through these three classes. The more readers explore *Invisible Cities*, rehearsing different routes, the more likely they are to discern that in most reading paths they encounter these three rubrics.

What is the significance of the conceptual symmetries based on Names, Eyes and Trading? In 'Cities and Names', cities do not match their descriptions, as they shift with the daily routines of people's lives. In 'Cities and Eyes', people either marvel at the visual qualities of their city, or, failing to engage with it, distance themselves from it, 'contemplating their own absence'.[58] In 'Cities and Trading', they trade memories or build new cities, resuming the roles they had in the previous city. The centrality of Eyes, Names and Trading highlights the importance of eyes in seeing and perceiving, names in identifying concepts in language, and trading in exchanging information in communication. For Calvino, Names, Eyes and Trading are at the juncture of thought with the visible world. Our knowledge begins with names or labels assigned to material things. The word 'bird', for example, is a universal term for both any particular bird and an unimaginable number of birds. Similarly, *Invisible Cities* is a particular sequence and an unimaginable number of sequences. The way in which the countless sequences are bound into the specific one (the one used in the fiction) is through the topological symmetries on the thematic categories of Names, Eyes and Trading. Calvino seems to suggest that the acts of seeing, naming and exchanging are what make entities identifiable, categorisable and transformable by human minds.

To Kublai's observation that 'his dreams are composed either by his mind or [by] chance', Polo responds that 'cities also believe they are the work of the mind or of chance but neither the one, nor the other suffices to hold up their walls. You take delight not in a city's seven or seventy wonders, but in the answer it gives to a question of yours.'[59] In *Invisible Cities*, Polo asks Kublai, and Calvino the reader, to recognise the centrality of eyes, names, and trading as the way of escaping their own 'inferno'. Escaping can range from defying dysfunctional cities to re-imagining our urban realities as a way to overcome their dysfunctionalities. Calvino provokes readers to 'learn and recognise' neither the diamond structure (the work of the mind) nor chance (the unimaginable number of random sequences), but their relationship. This relationship concerns the interplay between possibility and the rules that limit the number of variants to those permutations that organise the work, rendering it meaningful to oneself and to others.

So, our ability to grasp the rules in the fiction works in three, at least, interrelated ways: the first refers to operations which get into the text through geometric symmetry, defining microscopic conceptual relations; the second is related to topological symmetry, establishing relations of all-to-all thematic rubrics, or macroscopic patterns; the third concerns a visual kind of understanding, based on the diamond shape, a pattern we can grasp all at once. If local symmetries gradually assemble the network as a figurative structure in the mind, topological relationships lead to perception of large-scale centralities in this system. We may look at the notation and comprehend its visual structure, but it is through reading that we can gradually 'learn' and 'recognise' its invisible patterns. It is not argued that all these types of understanding are consciously absorbed by all readers. However, they are built into the text and are available to human intuition.

We encounter here the definition of imagination as *ars combinatoria*, the art of uncovering combinatorial rules and restrictions that govern the placement of information objects. In fact, all information systems can be reduced to combinatorial patterns in this way. It is from the restrictions in the combinatorial possibilities of letters that we can derive meaningful words, and it is the combinatorial rules inherent in the grammar and syntax of language which allow us to construct meaningful sentences. Pioneers of *ars combinatoria*, such as Lull, sought to understand the power of combinations to express and develop universal languages. Lull came up with a mechanism of three concentric circles of decreasing size inserted into each other. By turning the wheels, Lull could build statements consisting of 84 possible combinations.[60] Calvino was acquainted with the work of Lull, to which he referred in his essay 'Cybernetics and Ghosts' as one of the 'most arduous intellectual efforts of the Middle Ages that had become entirely real'.[61]

Il Milione – the work and its author(s)

> When you return to the West, will you repeat to your people the same tales you tell me?
>
> Calvino, *Invisible Cities*

The idea of literature as a combinatorial machine is hardly unique to Calvino. McCaffery explains that it was explored by Mallarmé and Valéry, and has been more systematically developed by structuralist critics such as Roland Barthes, Claude Brémond, A. J. Greimas, Vladimir Propp and Tzvetan Todorov. For these writers, a book expands beyond its own boundaries to wider adventures of knowledge in literature, music, poetry, scientific laws and open-ended systems in mathematics.[62] A work therefore is not simply an individual achievement, but also the result of collective formation. *Invisible Cities*, for example, invokes among other works Marco Polo's *Il Milione*. John Man writes that the original version of *Il Milione* was written in courtly French by Rustichello following Marco's dictation, and even incorporated Rustichello's own tales, but that it was eventually lost. One hundred and fifty copies of it are known to exist, some of which include extensive footnotes and annotations. The hand-made copies of Marco's book multiplied, 'many with glorious and utterly spurious illustrations'.[63] The copiers did not simply copy, but 'misread, shortened, omitted, corrected and translated, sometimes well, sometimes wrongly or badly, so that changes multiplied with every version, and no one could tell what was Marco's and what wasn't'.[64] The 150 surviving manuscripts are in many languages, while several are translations of translations. Sometimes translations are 'in a sixfold sequence: from French into Italian, into Latin, into Portuguese, into Latin again, and finally back into a French vastly different from the first French version'.[65] In its various editions *Il Milione* is, for instance, between 60,000 and 140,000 words. But even the (lost) original is itself a 'version' of Marco Polo's story, which was recounted to Rustichello, who interpreted it, converting Marco's memories into marvellous stories with paper and quill pen. As Man explains, 'still no one knows what Marco dictated, and what Rustichello wrote'.[66]

Il Milione was recognised as the most important account of the world outside Europe at that time and paved the way for the European voyages of exploration. Christopher Columbus had owned a copy printed in 1490, which contained his observations in the margins.[67] Marco's book also had an impact on the development of cartography. It informed Fra Mauro's *Mappa Mundi*, a portolan chart created by a monk from the island of Murano in the Venetian lagoon, with toponyms of Chinese cities familiar from *Il Milione*. For Man, 'Polo's memory in the book was vague, and he made mistakes and pretended, and exaggerated. But [...] Kublai Khan's China really was a land of millions.'[68] Laurence Breiner states that *Il Milione* is a 'haphazard recall of discrete bits of travel memory, lacking the chronological sequence of a travel diary, a prison rumination, told to an amanuensis'.[69] According to Henry Yule, Marco 'was the first traveller to trace a route across the whole longitude of Asia, naming and describing kingdom after kingdom'.[70] Accurately marking distances according to days of travel, Marco is considered as the precursor of the scientific geographer.

Calvino had a different view of Marco Polo's *Travels*:

> In all centuries there have been poets and writers that were inspired by *Milione* as a fantastic and esoteric scenography: Coleridge in his famous poetry, Kafka in the *Message to the Emperor*, Buzzati in the *Desert of the Tartars*. *One Thousand and One Nights* can pose a similar fate: books that become like imaginary continents in which

> other works of literature find their own space; continents of 'elsewhere', which today we can say do not exist anymore, as the whole world tends to be uniform.[71]

It is more the imaginary geography of Polo's travels and the imaginary 'library' of these books that attract Calvino to *Il Milione* than the accuracy of the original or the authenticity of the copies. Quoting Coleridge and appropriating *Il Milione*, he invites readers to *suspend disbelief*, and envision *Invisible Cities* in a larger network, a constellation of other books, maps and records of recounted legends and travels.[72]

Just as the 150 known copies of *Il Milione* are appropriations and variations on the original, which is itself an interpretation, when Kublai asks Marco whether, on his return, he would repeat his tales, Polo replies that these will be changed 'by a writer of adventure stories to whom he might dictate them at the end of his journey'.[73] Polo's anticipation projects from the mythical time of the novel, and the historical time of Marco's presence in Kublai Khan's court, to the time in which his travels 'would be written' by Rustichello (after Polo's return to the West), alluding to the copiers of the book, and the oral rehearsals of the stories, multiplying each time through a different listener and narrator. This forward leap in time makes readers conscious of their own historical time, introducing the possibility that *Invisible Cities* prefigures *Il Milione*, or that Calvino's fiction is the original source of Marco Polo's descriptions, or just one copy in the series of imperfect copies following Rustichello's version. An alternative possibility is that *Invisible Cities* is not Calvino's own but a pastiche narrative, the outcome of multiple appropriations by a plethora of authors. It is as though the stories Calvino recounts have been passed to us through generations since time immemorial.

Calvino's fiction is indivisible from the collective project of literature, history and geography, of recording, mapping and writing. *Invisible Cities* runs as mythic historicity based on *Il Milione*, a piece of literary history continuously adapted over time. It combines the order of the actual with the order of the possible, so that the historical provenance of Polo's travels can be appropriated by the mythical desires of the imagination. More importantly, it encourages readers to understand the work as a dynamic, extendable and variable fiction, part of a library of fantastic literature, a collective project of humanism, universal experience and world memory. We encounter here Barthes's ideas that the text depends not on its origin but on its destination. In his work *The Death of the Author*, Barthes proposed that the text consists of several writings, issuing from several cultures, and that the reader is someone who holds in a single text all the paths of which the text is constituted.[74] If the city is the analogue for literature and the text, it is Barthes's question of author and reader, origin and destination, that echoes throughout the novel, translating the dialogues between Polo and the Khan into a dialogue between Calvino and the reader in the reader's mind. The two characters and what they stand for are the force through which the key questions in the fiction become thematised: If cities inform Calvino's imagination, do architecture and cities as collective products of people also have an imagination of their own? How can they learn from this fiction? At the heart of these questions lies another one: Who produces cities and texts, and who owns them?

Variability of manuscripts was a common phenomenon in the Middle Ages. As Carpo explains, the modern technology of print ensured the production of exactly repeatable imprints, removing the possibility of errors in texts, which for many centuries had been 'mosaics of citations, interpolations, additional subtractions and plain copy errors'.[75] Calvino lived before the digital age of wiki-based interaction, which allows users to add, delete or revise content through a web browser, as in the pre-mechanical age of reproduction. However, like a contemporary Wikipedian, surrounded by the works of known and unknown authors, Calvino enfolds readers into the combinatorial adventures of the text and invites them to 'write' their own variations.[76] Seizing a narrative that is the amalgam of collective textual interaction with the work of a single author (Marco Polo), Calvino seizes an opportunity for *story-craft*. This concerns the intersection of multiple authorships: those that are virtually embedded in his own intellectual production and those that are virtually generated by the reader of his work. In a fiction based on an analogy between making stories and making cities, what the author says is that cities are neither the work of the mind nor the outcome of mindless assembly, but the interaction of individual authors with that which is collectively transmitted and imagined. Cities are produced by multiple, multiform, overlapping 'authorships'. Cities, like people, have imaginative minds.

'The great Khan owns an atlas' – the spatio-temporal imagination

> The Great Khan owns an atlas where all the cities of the empire and the neighbouring realms are drawn, building by building and street by street, with walls, rivers, bridges, harbours, cliffs.
>
> Calvino, *Invisible Cities*

In the last two dialogues between Polo and the Khan the interaction between single authorship and collective authorship becomes central to the discussion as the two characters examine the Khan's atlas. Each section of the text begins with the phrase 'The Great Khan owns an atlas', reminiscent of the repeating sequences of cities and their numbers. The atlas contains 'all cities of the empire and the neighbouring realms', gradually expanding to a catalogue of all possible places.[77] Polo recognises on the map cities he has visited, such as Constantinople and Jerusalem; cities he knows 'by word of mouth', such as Granada, Paris, Nefta; places that do not exist, such as Thomas More's Utopia; those that did exist but fell into ruins, such as Troy and Carthage; cities that will exist or might exist, and finally those that are as yet imagined.[78] From the fantastical places Polo describes, readers are suddenly catapulted into a description of cities of their own historical reality at the end of the book. Containing all cities, past and present, contemporary, fantastical and possible, the atlas must also contain Polo's imaginary cities. Through the atlas Calvino articulates a vision of *Invisible Cities* coincident with the world of the factual, the imaginary and the possible.

In contrast to this totalising vision of the geographer's eye and the writer's inner eye, which sees places mapped on the surface of the atlas all at once, the last section of the penultimate dialogue shifts back and forth in time. From a backward flash to Troy and Carthage, recalling Homer's and Virgil's epics, it moves forward to the seizure of Constantinople, finally dashing to San Francisco, New York, Los Angeles and Kyoto-Osaka. At the point where we recognise the current capitals founded by immigrants in the Pacific and the Atlantic, a millennium after the empire of the Khan, we become aware that not only the empirical universe, but also our own native system of reality, is enfolded in the fiction. Temporally dislocated and coexistent with Polo and the Khan, our 'eyes' follow the characters' 'eyes', scanning over the geography and the history of explorers, founders, conquerors, immigrants, travellers. Our empirical universe thus merges with the textual world and potential other worlds not present but implied in the fiction.

If the atlas represents both spatial and temporal knowledge, we can express the perspectives it enfolds in Figure 3.8. The x-axis shows cities mentioned in the text in narrative time, that is, the time it takes to move through the text expressed by the sequence of places it describes. The y-axis represents historical time, corresponding to when these cities were founded or encountered by Western explorers. The diagram reveals that Calvino describes an enormously dilated spread of historical time, in a condensed span of narrative time.[79] Of these centuries, of these cities

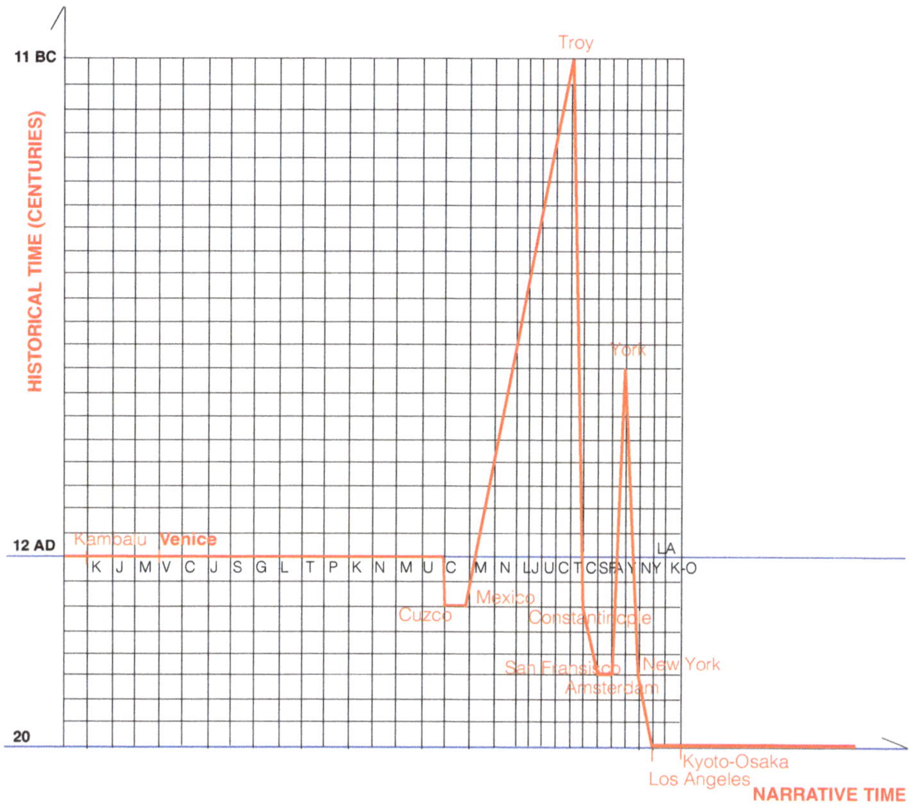

From left to right:

K: Kambalu; **J**: Java; **M**: Malabar; **V**: Venice; **C**: Constantinople; **J**: Jerusalem; **S**: Samarkand; **G**: Granada; **L**: Lubeck; **T**: Timbuktu; **P**: Paris; **N**: Nefta; **M**: Mont-Saint Michel; **U**: Urbino; **C**: Cuzco; **N**: Novgorod; **L**: Lhasa; **J**: Jericho; **U**: Ur; **C**: Carthage; **T**. Troy; **C**: Constantinople; **SF**: San Francisco; **A**. Amsterdam; **Y**; York; **NY**: New York; **LA**: Los Angeles; **K-O**: Kyoto-Osaka

Figure 3.8 Italo Calvino. *Invisible Cities*. Diagram of narrative space-time (x-axis) and historical time (y-axis) in the penultimate dialogue between Marco Polo and Kublai Khan. Drawing by the author

that were swallowed by the sands, only a few fragments, a few shards of memory can be retrieved and survive. The disproportional relationship between, on the one hand, the enormity of the atlas and the time of recollection (22 centuries) and, on the other, the time available to recollect (the narrative time, expressed through short dialogues) presents the tension between the totality of knowledge and the destructiveness of time. The imagination and the world's knowledge work with memory fragments from the past, which can never be possessed, but can be reconstructed and re-imagined. The reader's desire to imagine through

Invisible Cities becomes blurred with Kublai's desire to possess his empire and Polo's desire to continue interpreting the world through stories from his travels. Moreover, it is mixed up with the collective desire for remembering, preserving, transforming and aspiring, the factual and the imagined, through multiform cities, books, empires, conquests, discoveries, population shifts, immigrants' travels.

As readers access a world of possibility through Polo's cities and cities in our actual world, they are overcome by the desire to savour them and to transform them. They are thus made to consider the constraints that may prevent Polo's fantastic cities from materialising; and the limitations in shaping their reality or previous realities that no longer exist. Conversely, readers are asked to examine why their particular reality has evolved in this way, whether it could have taken a different course or what prevents it from being transformed in the future. If Polo's present, in Kublai's garden (in the fiction), defines our historical past and if his future is our present, what he could once change (his future) he can change no more. But this makes us aware that our present affords possibilities for transformation. We leap back to Polo's time and dash forward to current time not to change the possibility in the past that has materialised as the present, but to discover a third possibility that is not yet voiced but may exist. We can in this way look for the constraints that must be breached for it to be realised, in the combinatorial game of the possible.

Invisible Cities does not have a traditional closure like other narratives, advancing the action towards an end and a solution. Yet, by engulfing the reader in the fictional world at the end of the novel, Calvino offers a resolution to the dilemmas and dualities, the mirror-like oppositions and labyrinthine convolutions of images, arguments and thoughts contained in the description of cities and in the dialogues between the two actors. Instead of a relationship between Polo and the Khan (undisciplined imagination and analytical rationality), we are faced with a configurational interdependence between three parties. The two characters and their philosophical positions are at the end understood from a third perspective, the reader's, the third channel whose very presence externalises and synthesises the encounter between the two opposite channels of thought: on the one hand, the imagination as possibility, which is spontaneous, random, inexplicable, infinite, subjective and episodic; on the other, analytical rationality, which is ordered, reasoned, objective and subject to universal laws and constraints.

The imagination, Calvino wrote, is the union of the 'spontaneous generation of images and the intentionality of discursive thought, a plan carried out on the basis of a rational intention'.[80] We recognise here Polo's habit of generating images and the Khan's interest in knowledge and discourse. Together they constitute Calvino's imagination (and the reader's) as an empirical historical person with a consciousness and unconsciousness. The second definition Calvino gave to the imagination is as something outside the self, 'an electronic machine that takes account of all possible combinations and chooses the ones that are appropriate to a particular purpose'.[81] The imagination spans the 'repertory of what is potential, what is hypothetical, of what does not exist and has never existed, and perhaps will never exist but might have existed'.[82] This second definition concerns the countless combinations embedded in the text and the other works of fiction to which it relates, all seen as the collective project of society. Combining our empirical world with the textual world and the universal imagination, Calvino advances *Invisible Cities* as a model for creative invention.[83] His proposition is that the juxtaposition of Polo and the Khan presents the paradox of the imagination either as personal, random, obscure and subject to pure chance and flights of fancy, or as the outcome of universal laws that are pre-existing, passively received or waiting to be discovered. Introducing the reader (and writer), he advances the proposition: the imagination and its products, whether cities, buildings, poems or texts, are neither the outcome of individual minds nor the mindless creations of society, neither factual nor virtual. Cities are artefacts at the juncture where multiple authors meet individual empirical authors, and where empirical reality and its laws intersect with possible worlds.

Imperium and *emporium* – the role of Venice in *Invisible Cities*

What then is the significance of Venice in the fiction? Once Polo refuses to speak of Venice, Venice emerges as a secret watermark beneath the surge of changing images that the combinatorial game of opposites creates and distorts. Across the chessboard of the Khan and over his atlas, two empires, China and Venice, exchange domestic products and foreign treasures. The Khan is the instrument of *imperium*, of 'boundless extension of the territories he has conquered'.[84] Polo, instead, sails out from a unique bounded city that thrives because of people like him, the agents of *emporium*. Had the two characters met in Venice rather than in Kublai's court, Polo would have conducted his business from the Rialto.

The Khan instead would have presided from the room with maps and globes in the Doge's Palace at San Marco (Sala dello Scudo). Proponents of opposite models of thought, the two characters soon speculate about whether they are imagined by one another. Although different, they turn to two facing mirrors, multiplying and dissolving the diversity of the world into vast quantities of interchangeable data. Examining the atlas of real cities at the end of the fiction, Polo forewarns the Khan that 'where forms exhaust their variety and come apart, the end of cities begins'.[85] What is at stake, therefore, is something larger than the marvels of the cities readers linger over in the text. What attracts the reader's attention at the end of the work is the capacity of cities to give different forms to different desires. If sameness signals the end of cities, it is only through imaginative diversity that they can blossom and inspire.

Calvino considered Venice to be a model of complexity. He described it as a labyrinthine anti-Euclidian city, a net-like topography, which invokes the idea of infinity.[86] There are significant analogies between the structure of Venice's spatial networks and the conceptual structure in the fiction. Both consist of discrete, small-scale units that are aggregated into networks. The large number of divisible and combinable elements in Calvino's text can be compared to Venice's urban fabric, which consists of discrete islands, buildings and plots which are recursively linked, such as squares, churches, bell towers, wellheads, bridges and loading steps. Both *Invisible Cities* and Venice have a poly-focal structure and overlapping networks whose organising strength is almost equally distributed into multiple centres. Both have patterns that emerge out of the collective logic of elements, rather than a pre-conceived idea of a whole. Consisting of a street network and a canal network, Venice is made of 'one side and an obverse', the physical city and its reflection, like most cities in the fiction. Further, like *Invisible Cities*, it has a propensity for doubling and splitting into twin structures: the merchant city of wares and clocks, and the imperial city of rituals and conquests; the city pieced together by 'multiform treasures', and the bureaucratic city of ideal conceptions; the physical city of drainpipes and water, and the mythical city of celestial order or the geometrical design of carpets. These structures emphasise a dual process: making the physical city and constructing the city of invisible patterns. The latter is manifested in activities, beliefs, rituals, written records, legends, history and mythologies, through which we know society and recognise culture.

Hillier explains that almost every city is composed of small, local-scale elements. The aggregation of these elements into global structures emerges out of a dual process, one facilitating movement in order to support micro-economic activity, the other controlling movement that might undermine inherited customs.[87] This generic city-making process is one in which the city creates two kinds of network, one in the economic realm, the other in the socio-cultural domain. The former encourages the generation of unexpected events and information, informality, diversity and inclusiveness, marking differences of individuals rather than social categorisations.[88] The latter preserves socio-cultural and informational stability based on redundancy, formality, hierarchy, exclusiveness and sameness. The first side of the process is generative, privileging morphogenesis over stability; the second side is conservative, favouring the stability of structures over and above unpredictable events. In Chapter 1 (City-craft) I described how these two processes of the generic city gave rise to Venice, and how Venice's identity was formed by these two processes. In the early stage of its life Venice privileged the first side of the city-making process through open-ended networks of communication. In later stages, which I discussed in Chapter 2 (Statecraft), it shifted its emphasis towards the second side, privileging stability through institutional structures, rituals, political ideology and historiography, all of which found expression in the Myth of Venice as the Most Serene Republic. In the Khan's search for unities we can see the attempts of the Venetian state to expand the Piazza San Marco, integrate it with the city and re-invent it as the ancient Roman forum. In Kublai's anxieties regarding the formless ruin of his empire we can read Cristoforo Sabatino's and Marcantonio Sabellico's reassurances about Venetian political perfection and visual form.[89] Beside the dialogues between these two impulses, Calvino juxtaposes the practice of reading, the pleasure deriving from the text and from the experience of moving, viewing and living in cities. He trains readers, not in how to subjugate the variety of cities through excessive ideology, consumerism or bureaucracy, but in how to experience them in the three-dimensional world; how to generate potential other Venices from this experience, giving to different desires different forms.

I do not argue that Calvino wrote *Invisible Cities* as a literary model of Venice, as these attributes of Venice are generic characteristics of many cities, particularly when we think that Venice influenced Western ideas about cities and their governance. In addition, his fiction establishes movement towards other places and fictions that are present or absent from the text, training readers to think creatively and re-imagine cities in a combinatorial game across form, function and meaning. What is arguably more important than the structural analogy between Venice and the fiction, though, is Venice's explicit absence from the text, Calvino's poignant way of drawing attention to the fact that if today's Venice is present, tomorrow it may be present no more.[90] In his dialogue with the Khan over Venice, Polo admits his anxiety that, once fixed in words, memory's images are lost. This seems to allude to the diagrammatic structure of the fiction as a mnemonic device and to the classical art of memory. The art belonged to rhetoric as a technique by which the orator could improve his memory and give long speeches through an association of images with places and words. Frances Yates writes that 'the first thing was to imprint on the memory a series of loci or places [...] We have to think of the ancient narrator as moving in imagination, through his memory, building *whilst* he is making his speech, drawing from the memorialised places the images he has placed on them'.[91] Calvino articulates a vision for knowledge as the interplay of fixed image and combinatorial emergence (in the process of reading the fiction) rather than possessing it *a priori* as a memory palace, diagram, model or map.

Postscript

Calvino's text enables the exploration of the creative imagination in the medium of literature, a world in which in spite of its own laws and constraints the writer remains essentially free to innovate. The challenge for the creative imagination in the medium of architecture is to exercise innovation at the same time as confronting the physical and practical realities of the city. Yet it is through this resistance that architects can be inventive and that great architecture can come about. What might be seen as an obstacle to creativity in the end becomes an essential component of the creative process. The work of Palladio and Le Corbusier, two architectural minds engaging with Venice but centuries apart, will allow us to investigate this proposition in the following chapter.

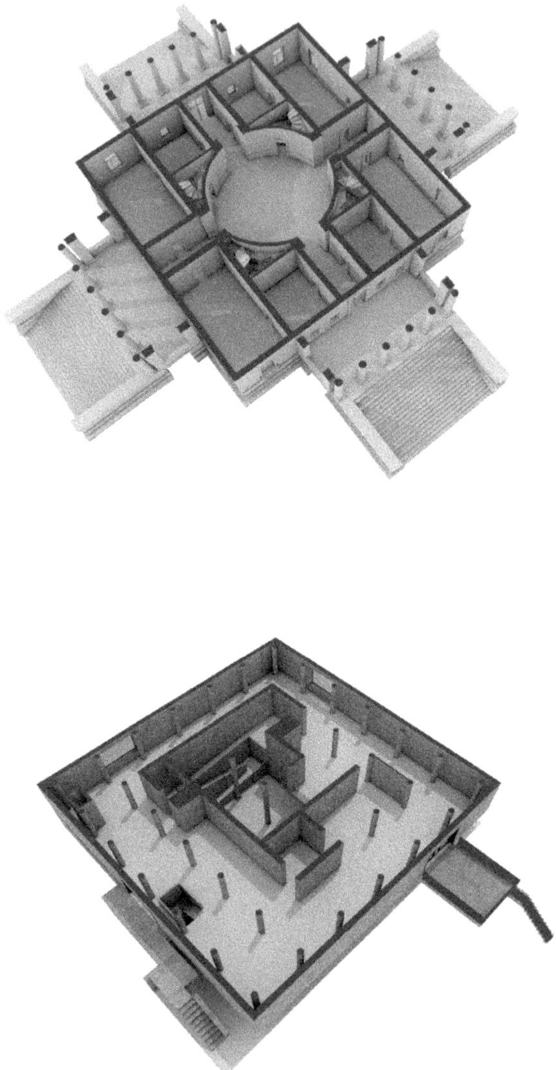

Figure 4.0 Palladio. Villa Rotonda (top). Le Corbusier. Tokyo Museum (bottom). Drawings by Athina Lazaridou

4
Crafting architectural space: Le Corbusier's Venice Hospital and the three paradigms

Introduction

Exploring Venice's urban networks and ceremonial spaces together with Calvino's authored work of fiction, I have described a range of versions of Venice inspired by the city. I looked at how it was gradually formed as the lived space of everyday practice by the physical linking and interconnecting of separated islands. Parallel to this physical manifestation of growth, there was the development of Venice as the imagined city, by artists, writers, cartographers and the Venetians themselves, who described it as an exemplary place in its own right. Architects in the sixteenth century saw it as the humanistic city, projecting the myth of Imperial Rome onto its spatial configuration. Calvino, a twentieth-century writer, saw Venice as the prototypical city, stimulating the imagination with its own particular form of utopia.[1] To this repertory of Venice's variations, I will add one more project: Le Corbusier's Venice Hospital (1964), which has also left a significant impression upon the architectural imagination (Figure 4.1). The Hospital is a unique project in Le Corbusier's *oeuvre*. Unlike his other architectural works, which were designed as simple volumes, it has an open-ended logic based on cell aggregation. In contrast to his urban visions, replacing dense urban areas with freestanding buildings in a park, it was designed to be embedded in Venice's age-old fabric. Yet, with an architectural language consisting of courtyards, classical proportions and the Modulor,[2] the Hospital project embodies key moments that informed the architectural practices of modernity, from the Renaissance to Le Corbusier's own body of work. This chapter has a two-fold purpose: first, to explore

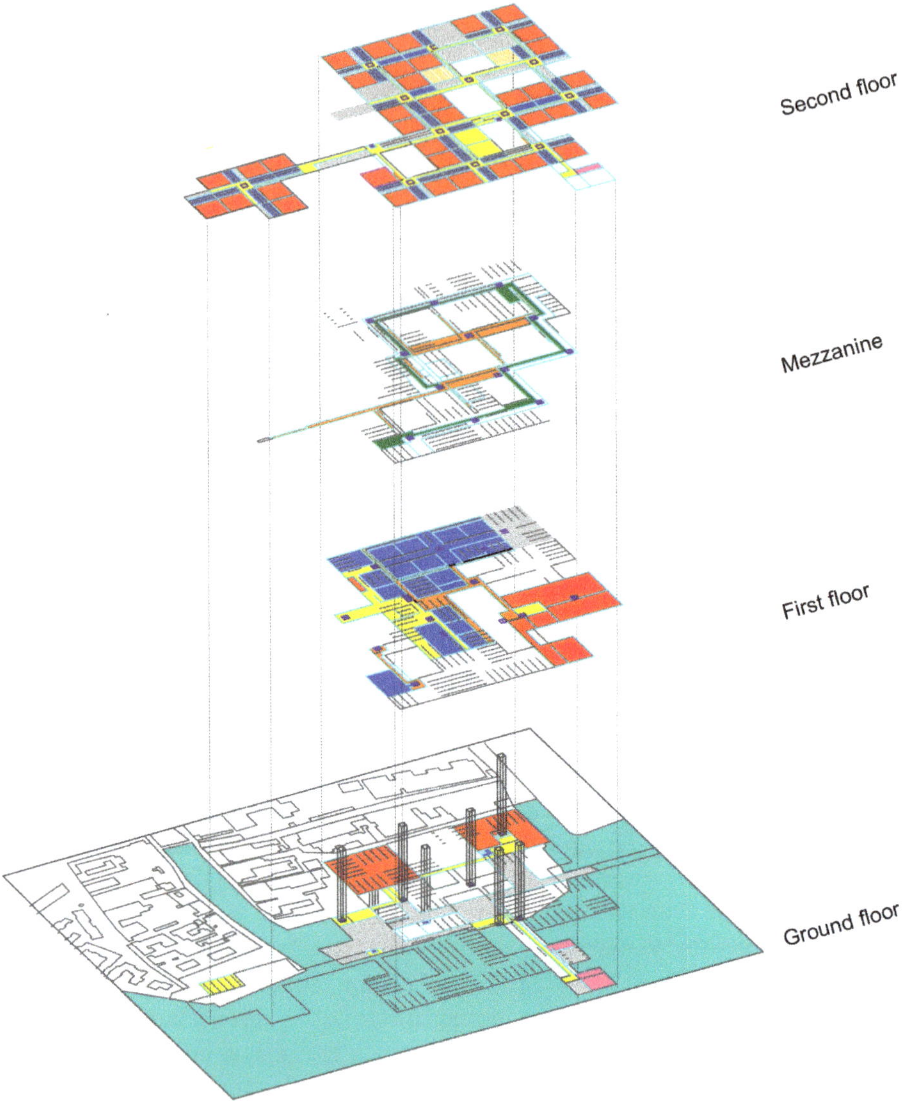

Figure 4.1 Le Corbusier. Venice Hospital. Drawing by the author

the influence Venice had on the Swiss architect and the design of the Hospital; and second, to trace a larger panorama of architectural ideas in the work of Palladio, Le Corbusier and some present-day architects, extending in this way the relevance of Venice into contemporary architecture.

Le Corbusier described Venice as a cardiac system, a testimony to functional precision, intersecting but also separating the waterways from the pedestrian routes.[3] He had a long-term fascination with organic architecture for its capacity to be appreciated on foot: 'it is by walking, by moving, that one sees the order of the architecture developing. It is a principle contrary to that of baroque architecture, which is conceived on paper, around a fixed theoretical point'.[4] When he accepted an invitation from Venice to design a new hospital in 1964, he had already generated some of the key tenets of Modernism, in various works from small houses to large urban projects, and experimented with the concept of the architectural promenade. As opposed to the clean-slate approach used in his early work, the Hospital was inspired by the *calli* (streets) and *campielli* (squares) of Venice. In the design of the project, these elements were translated into a series of pinwheel squares with radially arranged corridors, and were assembled into a matrix. The building was to be located in the run-down area of San Giobbe in the northwestern part of Cannaregio. It was intended to be spatially integrated with the city, serviced by both roads and pedestrian access. The purpose was to create an easily accessible system that could expand horizontally according to future changes in medical care and technological innovations. Systematically engaging constraints imposed by different kinds of demands, Le Corbusier articulated a response to one of the most complicated programmes and sensitive contexts of our time.

A site location map published in his *Oeuvre Complète* clearly demonstrates this point. The map shows the Hospital behind the train station of Santa Lucia, also identifying a number of other buildings in Venice (Figure 0.4). By choosing certain structures and omitting others, as illustrated through this map, Le Corbusier connected the Hospital at the 'backdoor' of Venice with Palladio's San Giorgio Maggiore at the celebrated front of the city. The link between the two places is through the Grand Canal, which he dotted by marking out patrician palazzi, the Rialto market, the Merceria, the Piazza San Marco and the Piazzetta. The Swiss architect had always aspired to design a public building in Venice comparable in scale and impact to Palladio's convent and church on the island of San Giorgio, the grand Piazza and the Ospedale Civile, an early Renaissance work by Mauro Codussi.[5] In his *Four Books of Architecture,* Palladio had described the convent as a monastery intended for the recreation of the 'houses of the ancients', a reference to classical antiquity.[6] The 'march' from the 'service yard' of Venice to San Giorgio Maggiore in this map expresses Le Corbusier's heroic entrance into Venice, claiming his part in the legacy that had begun with Roman architecture.

However, the link with Palladio's San Giorgio is not simply because Le Corbusier wanted to measure himself against the great classical architect. It is also because he was aware of the disciplinary roots of architecture. It is in Venice that the first translation of Vitruvius and Palladio's *Four Books of Architecture* (1570) were published.[7] More importantly, it is in Venice and the Veneto that Palladio had practised. Le Corbusier positions the Hospital not simply in the urban context, but also within the disciplinary tradition of structured architectural knowledge. With this map, he offers a synoptic notation of the history of architecture through three key canonical moments: Venice's evolutionary urban form; Classicism represented by San Giorgio, the Piazza and Codussi's Ospedale Civile; and finally, Modernism through his own project.

These three moments translate to the Organic, the Classical and the Modern paradigms in cities and architectural practice, respectively.[8] The Organic recognises the gradual evolution of cities like Venice as accumulations of buildings and spaces developing an emergent spatial logic over time (yet not entirely without control). The Classical, with its high point in the Renaissance, is based on designs and systems of thought rooted in classical antiquity and is very much the antithesis of the Organic. Finally, the Modern, originating in the early twentieth century, is based on a break with historical forms, heralding a new model for thinking about cities and buildings. The synthesis of these paradigms in Le Corbusier's map brings together the concept of the *tabula rasa* advanced by Modern architecture – of working afresh and innovating each time – with the idea that cities and buildings evolve over time, and with the transcendental values of Classicism across time. More specifically, as a synecdoche of the three periods, the map is a record of the trajectory of architecture, each type of structure expressing a paradigm that deviates at critical moments from a previously established model.

Had Le Corbusier's project been built, it would have given Venice a building that, while mindful of constraints imposed by the context, would be as radical in its form as his celebrated early Modern designs.[9] Like his avant-garde villas, it would have been rendered in white. It would have been supported on pillars reminiscent of previous designs, which rested on pilotis. A large number of these supports would have foundations in the water, analogous to the free-flowing parkland in his urban projects. It was envisioned that people would enter the building from underneath, as happens in Le Corbusier's Villa Savoie and the Tokyo Museum, which were designed without a main façade (Figure 4.2). The

Figure 4.2 Le Corbusier. Tokyo Museum. Front façade. © FLC/ ADAGP, Paris and DACS, London 2017

third floor of the Hospital was organised through the pinwheel pattern of movement, which had provided a standard for systematic variations on a theme in many of Le Corbusier's designs. Through the Hospital project, Le Corbusier would have demonstrated that building and innovating in Venice meant working with the medieval fabric, geometrical and spatial ideas from classical heritage, his own established language, and at the same time transcending all of these factors, including Venice as the immediate and present context.

Le Corbusier's dialogue with these paradigms shows that the Hospital is uniquely placed, contributing to the subject of the relationship between buildings and cities as collective products of society and as conscious designs by individual minds. It is a key project, raising issues about Venice and beyond Venice. By being responsive to many influences and design traditions, it advances the question of the multiplicity of the architectural imagination and the effect of cumulative comparative knowledge in architecture. The fact that the architect of the Hospital owed as much to Venice as to Palladio, as much to his own compositional devices as to classical architecture and the Organic tradition, raises the need to explore this building within the immediate context of Venice as well as the larger development of design ideas in their own right. Is Le Corbusier's design of the Hospital based on some superficial resemblance to the *calle* and *campiello*, or is it deeply rooted in the invisible structure of the city? How does it relate to the larger context of design practices of modernity that shaped cities and architecture? These questions structure the chapter in two parts: one concerned with the Hospital in the immediate context of Venice, the other with the broader context of architecture as spatial practice.

Part 1: The Venice Hospital

A shapeless hospital

In 1964, Guillermo Jullian de la Fuente, a young Chilean architect who was working for Le Corbusier, led the team that travelled to Venice for field research and for a presentation of the Venice Hospital project to the Venetian authorities. Earlier in 1962, Jullian had selected from a botanical treatise a picture that showed a cell splitting into four new nuclei and drew it over the plan of the Olivetti factory workshop.[10] Superimposed over the industrial building, the organic form was the nucleus of the idea to make a building expandable, liberating it from rigid boundaries. A year later, on his trip to Venice, Le Corbusier declared to Giuseppe Mazzariol that designing a hospital in Venice would be subject to height limitations, and that it would be paradoxically necessary 'to build without building'.[11] Le Corbusier presented the project on pilotis, like the Ducal Palace, and developed what many critics consider to be an example of a 'Mat-building', that is, a building without walls, overcoming the boundary between itself and the city. The Venetian authorities enthused over the horizontal arrangement of the volumes that left the silhouette of the city unchanged and generated the possibility for an extendable hospital.

In 1974, in her article 'How to Recognize and Read Mat-building: Mainstream Architecture as It Has Developed Towards the Mat-building', Alison Smithson defined this new typology as the epitome of the 'anonymous collective; where the functions come to enrich the fabric, and the individual gains new freedoms of action through a new and shuffled order, based on interconnection, close-knit patterns of association, and possibilities for growth diminution and change'.[12] Smithson used examples from vernacular and modern architecture to illustrate Mat-building, including Le Corbusier's and Jullian's Hospital in Venice. In the *Rapport Technique* – the technical document of the project – Le Corbusier associated the origin of the design idea with the urban form of the city, identifying the paths within the building that link the four care units as '*calli*', and the central spaces of communication between these units as '*campielli*'. Planned on the site of an abandoned slaughterhouse in San Giobbe, the hospital was intended mainly for the acutely and terminally ill. Poignantly, the hospital project was underway at the time of Le Corbusier's sudden death while swimming at Cap-Martin on 27 August 1965. The team continued working under Jullian's direction on a design that took more than nine years to develop and was never built. Le Corbusier and his team had designed a shapeless building without a single and clear overall form. For the following decades, it would attract renewed attention each time architects and critics became interested in methods of form aggregation, a design approach based on bottom-up processes of generation.[13]

The *Rapport Technique*

Le Corbusier organised the Hospital so as to emphasise its horizontal extension and layered it vertically, with the patients' area located on the top floor. This floor consists of a series of squares and pathways, arranged in a pinwheel pattern around a central space. The patient rooms form a matrix of building units with a square and a lift placed at each intersection (Figure 4.3). Each of the building units accommodates a different treatment, from gynaecology and paediatrics at the front to the neurological unit at the rear left of the complex. The patient rooms open to the outside only at the top, through a cave-like section, drawing light to the interior but blocking views to the outside. A service mezzanine floor facilitates sterilisation processes through special conduits of circulation, while a series of ramps enable communication between the top floor and the departments of surgery, radiotherapy, pharmacy and the doctors' offices on the first level (Figure 4.4). In addition to these facilities, the first floor housed emergencies, diagnostics, a free clinic, a maternity ward, laboratories, a theatre and a morgue. The ground floor accommodated the entrances, administrative offices and services. There were two means of access: by water and road (Figure 4.4). A chapel situated directly on the water on the north-west side of the hospital would act as a landmark reminiscent of the island cemetery of San Michele.

According to the *Rapport Technique*, the point of departure of the design is the *cellule*, or the room of the patient:

> This element gives rise to the 'care unit' [*Unité de soins*] of twenty-eight patients, which functions autonomously. This unit is organised around a central space of communication (*Campiello*) and four paths (*Calle*), which are intended for both inhabitation and circulation by

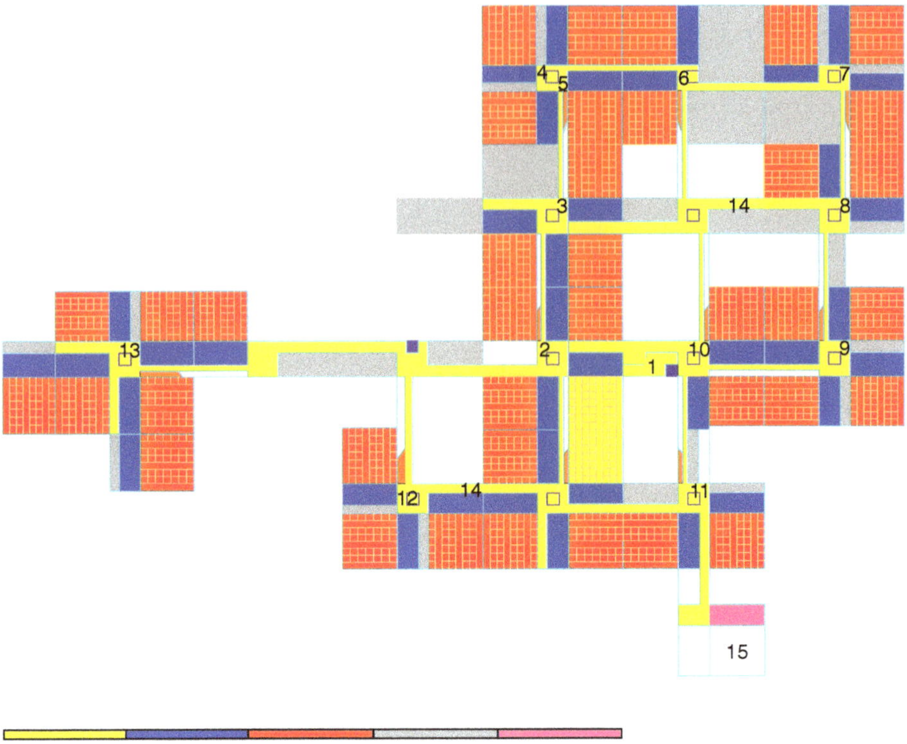

Circulation and surgeries | Treatment | Patient beds | Outside space | Church

1 Visitor's Entrance
2 General Medicine
3 General Surgery
4 Neurology
5 Neurosurgery
6 Thoracic Surgery
7 Urology
8 Dermopathy
9 Otology
10 Stomatology
11 Cancer Surgery
12 Obstetrics and Gynaecology
13 Paediatrics
14 Patients' Living Room
15 Church

Figure 4.3 Le Corbusier. Venice Hospital. Third floor. Drawing by the author

patients in convalescence. Four units of care form a 'building unit' [*Unité de batisse*]. Through the progressive juxtaposition of building units, this framework yields a horizontal hospital.[14]

The entire third floor was conceived to provide 'the same conditions of city life, upon entrance into the *Calle*, the *Campiello* and the hanging gardens'.[15] This system was claimed to have the flexibility to accommodate growth, presumably along the sides facing the lagoon and

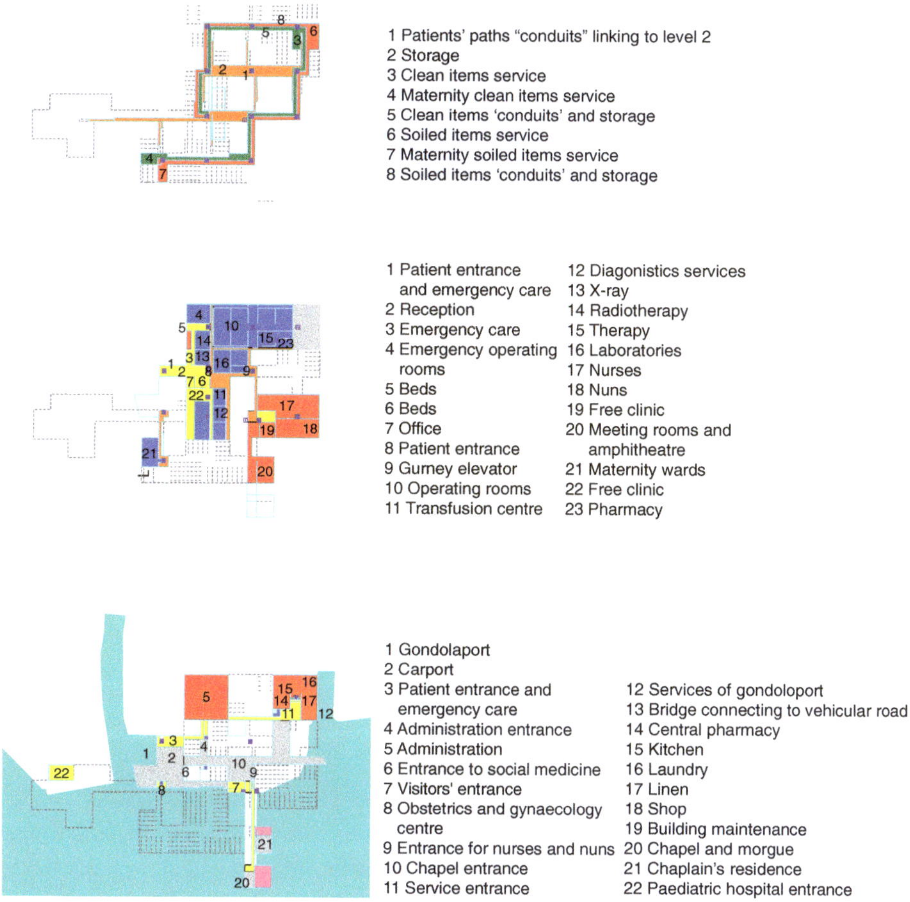

Figure 4.4 Le Corbusier. Venice Hospital. Ground floor (bottom); first floor (middle); mezzanine level (top). Drawings by the author

the Cannaregio Canal. It was also designed to adapt to future medical innovations and provide effective health care around the preventative capabilities of the hospital. 'By opening the ground floor directly onto the city, one allows for a city–hospital encounter and facilitates the visual transmission of medicine toward the outside.'[16] The technical document also stresses that it is

> above all man, rather than the patient, who is being considered. This is to say that the scale of construction had to be found at the level of humanity: the *cellule*, and everything that it comprises, is the primary element upon which the entire conception of the hospital is

articulated. The *Unité de soins*, the *Campiello* and the *Calle* serve to create relationships between the patient and the city.[17]

Signification

In the *Rapport Technique* the building is described as a successive agglutination of units derived from the patient cell, the minimum unit of the design. However, as Alan Colquhoun observes, the design is both 'additive' and 'geometric'. The additive logic is formed by the aggregation of cells into care units. The geometric logic is organised through a system of squares and golden-section rectangles.[18] The latter is made of a large square of 4 × 4 units, which is divided into an L shape and a smaller square, containing 3 × 3 units (Figure 4.5). The centre of the smaller square is the centre of the treatment department, also forming the main point of circulation for patients. It is open to the sky and directly linked through a cluster of voids with the ground floor. The 3 × 3 square is also shaped by the pinwheel pattern, consisting of a central core linked with four openings at the outer edges of the building through circulation corridors forming an off-set cruciform shape. By varying the closed and open elements in each care unit, the architects have provided a series of balconies, terraces or simply voids crossed by pathways.

Intertwining geometrical and spatial organisation with the city and the social programme, the *Rapport Technique* provides a description of the functional dimensions of the Hospital that is also a description of the compositional strategy and the ways it articulates meaning. By placing emphasis on the modular structure of the design, it conflates the idea of the evolutionary development of the city with the accumulative logic that produces the patient wards and the future expansion of the building. Le Corbusier placed the Modulor man on the hospital beds – which were raised on slabs – and made reference to Vittore Carpaccio's painting of the body of St Ursula raised over a crowd of pilgrims (1943) (Figure 4.6).[19] By defining the cell as the elementary unit, he expressed the patient as the universal man, and the Hospital as the realm of humanity. He thus dramatised the project as the interplay of the additive system of cells with the accumulative effect of human bodies raised in a cave-like interior over the water.[20] The emphasis on the Modulor and the universal man provides a link with humanist architecture rooted in Italy. The significance attributed to the direct encounter between the patients and the city suggests an egalitarian attitude, in accordance with the historic perception of Venice as an ideal society. Finally, by linking the *Unité de soins* with the *campielli* and *calli*,

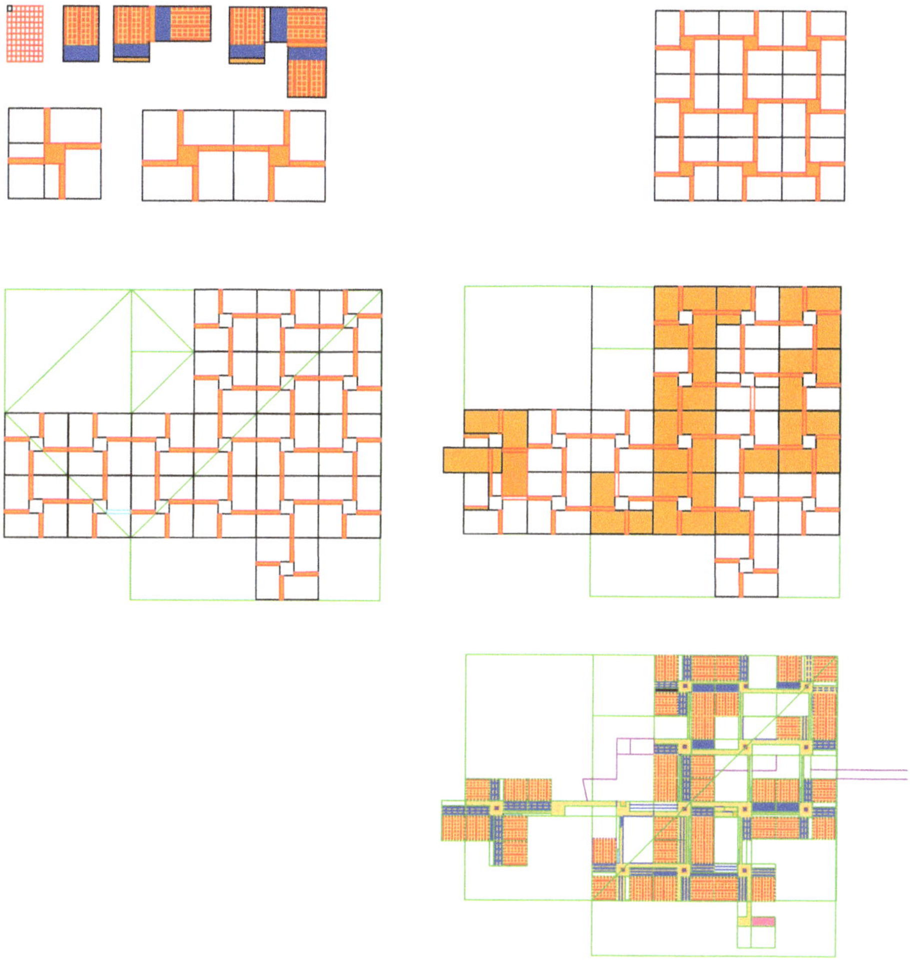

Figure 4.5 Le Corbusier. Venice Hospital. Diagrams of morphogenesis and geometrical analysis of the building. Drawing by the author

Le Corbusier guaranteed an unequivocal link between the Hospital and the floating city.

The *Rapport Technique* used the modularity of the design as the means to validate the functional efficiency of the Hospital and its expandable anti-institutional logic. At the same time, it established poetic affinities between the city, humanity and the building, universalising the project. If these are the means by which the project articulates *signification*, it is interesting to understand how it addresses *significance*, that is, the spatial relationship between the building and the city and the structural analogy between Venice's urban networks and the network of

Figure 4.6 Vittore Carpaccio. *Martyrdom of the Pingrims and the Funeral of Saint Ursula.* Museo Nazionale Gallerie dell'Accademia di Venezia

pathways and squares in the building.[21] Does the influence of Venice on the design extend beyond metaphoric association and the typologies of the *calle* and *campiello*?

The Hospital – the city–building encounter

We can represent each space in the Hospital with a line drawn tangentially to surfaces so as to capture the maximum linear extension of movement and sight. The resulting network (called the 'axial map' in space syntax terminology) is then analysed to measure closeness centrality (or integration), the measure previously used in the analysis of Venice, the Piazza and Calvino's network of themes in *Invisible Cities*.[22] The analysis of the building as a whole shows that it is well integrated in terms of both its internal organisation and its relationship with the exterior (Figure 4.7). This is evident in the large number of integrated lines which stretch from side to side, penetrating deeply from the ground to the deepest parts at the top level inside the building. The properties responsible for this pattern of integration are the large-scale connections along the vertical and horizontal axes. On the basis of previous research on hospitals and other building types, it is possible to suggest that the architectural intentions to create a strong city–Hospital encounter were likely to be met by the design.[23] On the basis of studies of large buildings resembling urban systems, one can also say that the Hospital would have the capacity to generate an emergent field of informal encounters between different categories of people.[24]

These characteristics explain the functionality and social performance of the design. However, a description of architecture that focuses on

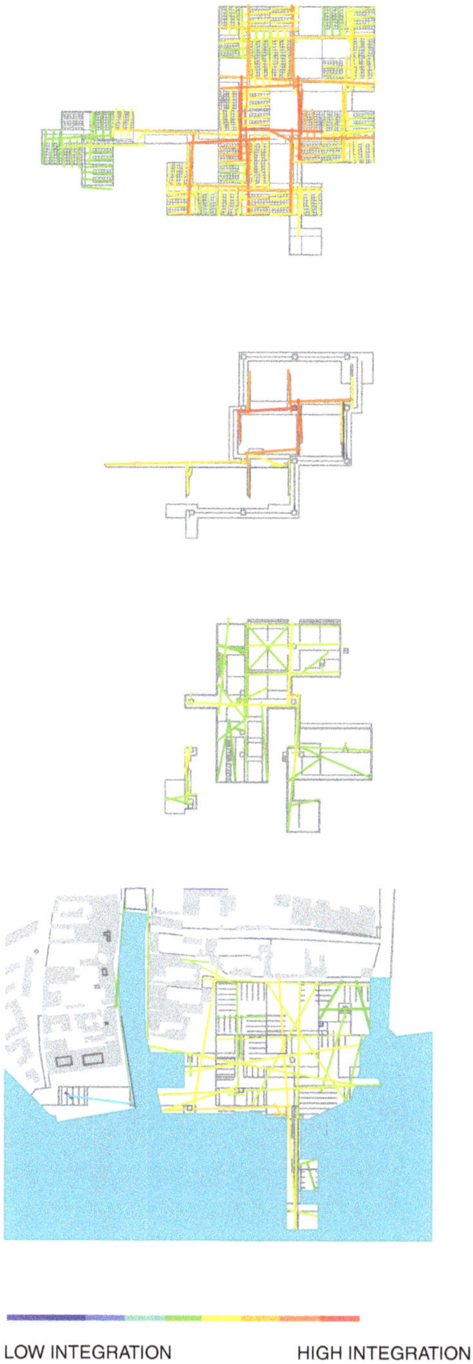

Figure 4.7 Le Corbusier. Venice Hospital. Axial integration analysis of the entire building. Drawing by the author

functional factors alone cannot account for the imaginative engagement of Le Corbusier with the city or the configurational analogy between the Hospital and Venice. Central to this question is whether the relationship of the Hospital to the urban fabric can be captured through the Mat-building typology, since it emulates the aggregate logic of organic processes of generation. Smithson's emphasis on Mat-buildings, Aldo van Eyck's concept of the 'organised casbah' and Candilis-Josic-Woods's principles of stems and webs might have had a direct influence on Le Corbusier and Guillermo Jullian de la Fuente.[25] Yet, a number of critics have stressed that the Hospital was not just another instance of Mat-building.[26] In contrast, the significance of the project was its 'poetic integration' into the essence of Venice. This essence was discovered 'not in the drawing board, but through [Le Corbusier's] eyes, his hands, and even his feet, that is, by observing and going throughout it for a long time'.[27] As for Le Corbusier, he explained he had invented nothing; inspiration for the Hospital was contained in the logic of the terrain on which it was to be founded.[28] It is thus essential to explore how the Hospital relates to the urban organisation of this terrain.

A hospital that is like Venice

> [...] because the eye, our only raw, fishlike internal organ, indeed swims here: it darts, flaps, oscillates, dives, rolls up. Its exposed jelly dwells with atavistic joy on reflected palazzi, spiky heels, gondolas, etc., recognising in the agency that brought them to the existential surfaces none other than itself.
>
> Joseph Brodsky, *Watermark: An Essay on Venice*

Looking at the diagram of distribution of betweenness centrality (or choice), capturing the shortest paths between all pairs of origins and destinations, a configurational analogy is revealed between the streets and squares of Venice and the pathways and square areas in the building (Figures 1.3, 4.8). This analogy becomes stronger if we focus on the visibility structure of the third floor in the Hospital, separately from the permeability structure (or the structure of movement). In order to let natural light into the inner core of the design, the architects have used a series of patios and courtyards that are traversed by pathways and bridges. These elements enable a large number of visual links partly coinciding with and partly diverging from the elements of circulation. The analysis of the visibility structure shows that integration develops along a set of orthogonal lines that cover the pathways and a few long lines that stretch diagonally on the plan from side to side (Figure 4.8a–b). The square-shaped areas (the centres of the *Unité de batisse*) are the points where the structure of

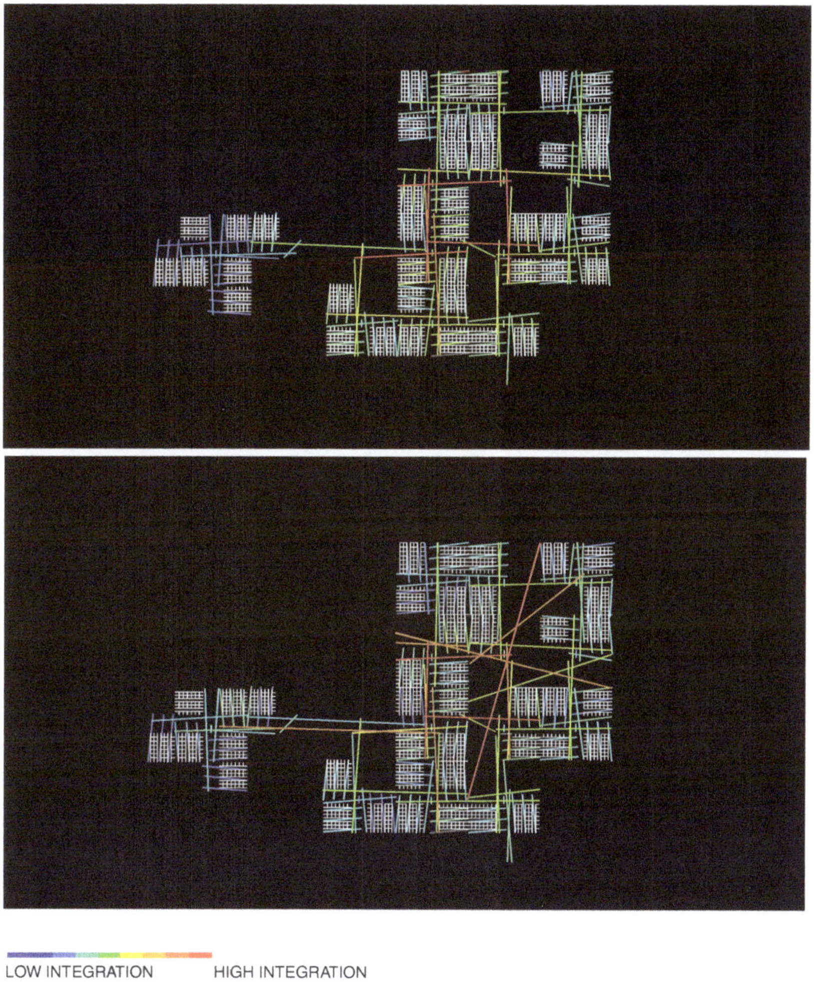

Figure 4.8 (a) Le Corbusier. Venice Hospital. Axial integration analysis of third floor without voids (top). Axial integration analysis through voids (bottom). Drawing by the author

visibility intersects with the structure of circulation. This is characteristically expressed by two geometrical systems: one follows the orthogonal geometry of the design; the other is rotated on a pivoting point found at the centre of a large rectangle that consists of 9 × 9 *Unités de batisse*. Like the dualistic system of water and land linking the urban squares of Venice, the square-shaped areas in the Hospital are connected by two network structures: one for visibility and the other for movement.

How is this characteristic configurationally possible? A closer look at the *campi* of Venice shows that they are adjacent as well as open to the

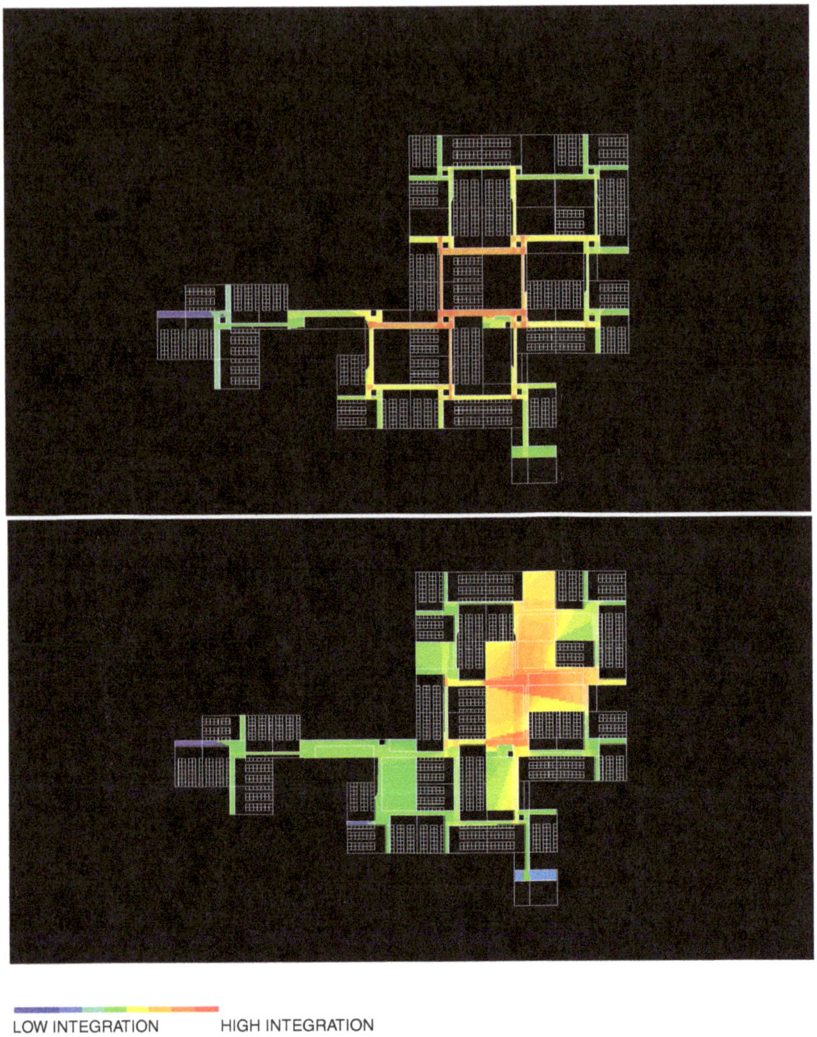

Figure 4.8 (b) Venice Hospital. Visual integration of third floor without voids (top). Visual integration through voids (bottom). Drawing by the author

canals at least on one side. This property has existed since Venice's early days, as can be seen in the map by de' Barbari (Figure 4.9a–c).[29] If we 'flood' the canals and all the squares with the same colour, we see that 65 per cent of the *campi* are not defensibly enclosed areas, but open on one side (Figure 4.9c). Similarly, 10 of the 15 square-shaped spaces in the Hospital are 'dematerialised', that is, not enclosed by physical boundaries on all four sides, but open to voids and gardens on at least two sides (Figure 4.10).

Figure 4.9 (a) Campo San Giovanni and Paolo. Photo by the author

Figure 4.9 (b) Campo San Giovanni and Paolo. Jacopo de' Barbari, *Venetie MD*. Bird's eye view of Venice, c. 1500. Museo Correr, Venice. The squares of Venice are adjacent to and open to the canals on at least one side. This can be seen in the map of de' Barbari and was a characteristic of squares from the city's early days

The *campi* in Venice and the square areas in the Hospital facilitate links between two frames of reference: on the one hand, local-scale properties we come across on our paths in Venice, articulating spatial connections between the pedestrian and water networks; on the other

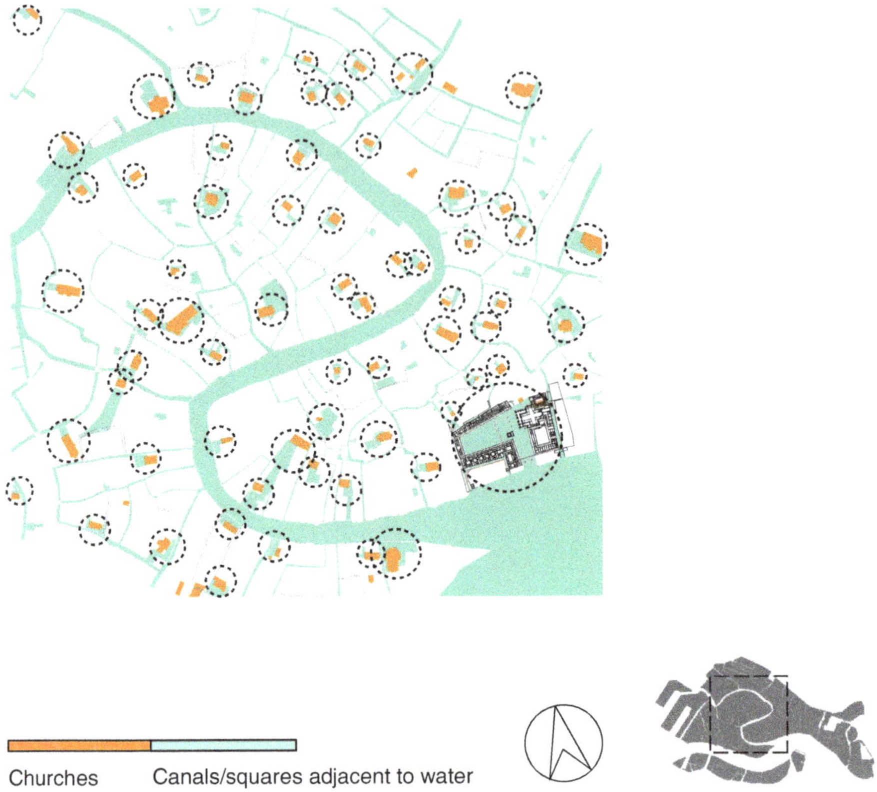

Figure 4.9 (c) Squares and canals are represented by the same colour (green), showing that a large number of them are next to the water (shown in circles) or a *rio terra*, a former canal. Drawing by the author

hand, large-scale properties describing the position of elements in the larger system. The former are immediately available to perception. In contrast, the latter cannot be observed through human recognition all at once. They can be grasped only through moving and living inside a city or a building over time. Venice, however, is different from other cities because its *campi* recurrently reveal, by opening to a canal and via bridges that connect them to neighbouring islands, their strategic position in the urban fabric. Conjoining local and global frameworks of reference, the squares of Venice and the square units in the Hospital are 'crossroads' where the invisible structure of the city and the building, respectively, meet their visible surface. The ability of Venice's squares to expose the visible and the invisible makes their strategic role available to human intuition. The power of urban elements to do this in other cities is not as strong, since they rarely recur with the same consistency, as we move

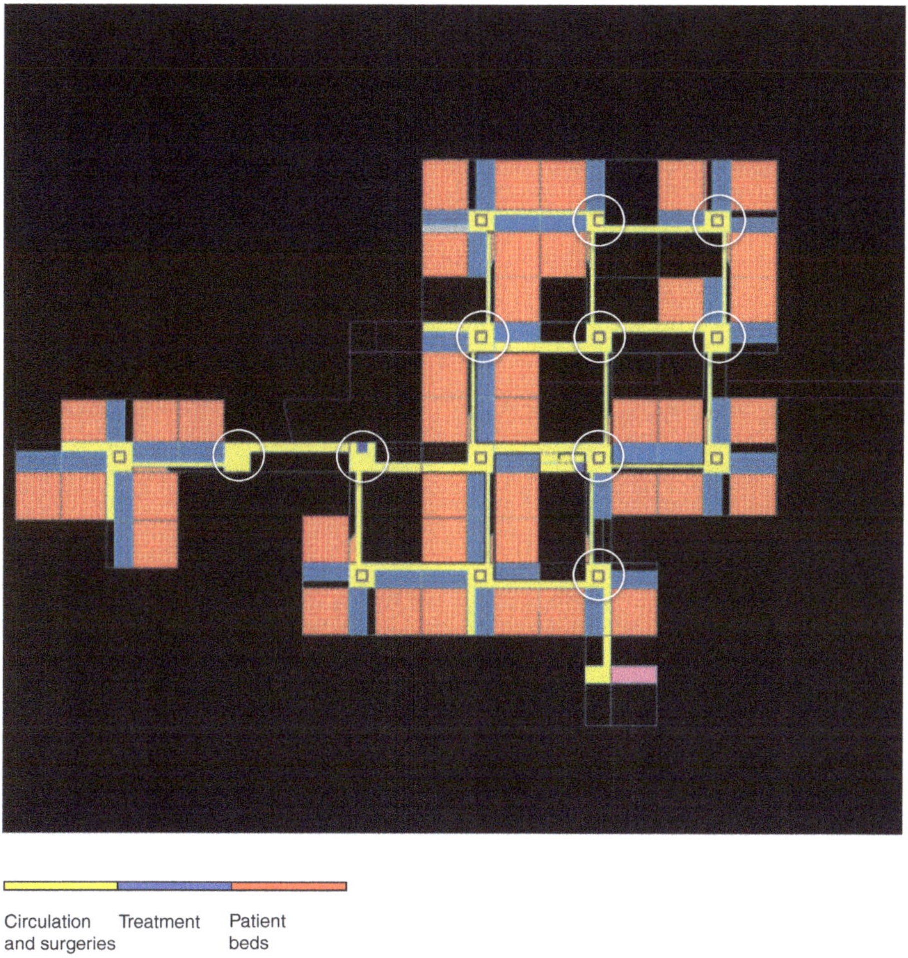

Figure 4.10 Le Corbusier. Venice Hospital. Dematerialised squares shown with circles. In a manner analogous to the squares in Venice which are adjacent to the water, the square-shaped areas in the Hospital are open to the exterior at least on one side. Drawing by the author

inside them, or consist of recursively repeated typological combinations. It is this capacity of the *campi* to interface two networks that enabled Le Corbusier to grasp their function in the city and use them imaginatively in a new project.

Venice is a city of 'lightness', both in metaphorical terms, in that it appears to float on water, and in literal terms, as functional demands since centuries past have led to waterfront *campi* that are open on one side. At the same time, structural demands for reducing building loads have resulted in filigree façades and buildings of pierced thickness. Water reaches these squares and penetrates the ground floor of buildings, which can be accessed by boat as well as on foot (Figure 4.11). One might say that what strikes the architectural imagination in the most architectural of cities is the balance of forces that enable weight and lightness to float on water. These forces do not have a mere visual effect, but enfold the body as it follows an up-and-down course over bridges, canals, steps and hanging landings (Figure 4.12). Whether the city is experienced through floating on a canal, walking on a bridge or dry land, or entering the loggia of a building, it heightens the

Figure 4.11 Doors in Venice connecting houses with the transportation system of the canals. Photos by the author

Figure 4.12 Venice. The sequence of bridges is analogous to the sequence of pathways crossing the voids in the Venice Hospital. Photo by the author

perception of weightless gravity through intersecting routes that dematerialise its mass, half liquid, half solid. To this we must add the pleasures of multiple forking itineraries, the endless variety in which the route segments can be combined in sequences, floating, elevated or at ground level.

The Hospital was also conceived as an aquatic realm in which the light would bounce on water, slabs, walls and the ever-extending sequences of pilotis, and water would penetrate the chapel and the patios, dissolving materiality and the physical limits of space.[30] The project dematerialises the patios and perforates the perimeter of the building at different levels. Reflections on the glass surfaces show that solid and transparent walls would merge so that it would be difficult to separate the enclosed spaces from the courtyards and the building from the city (Figure 4.13). What Le Corbusier captured in Venice through the *campielli*, the *calli*, the patios, the courtyards, the cat-walks and the hanging gardens were not simply

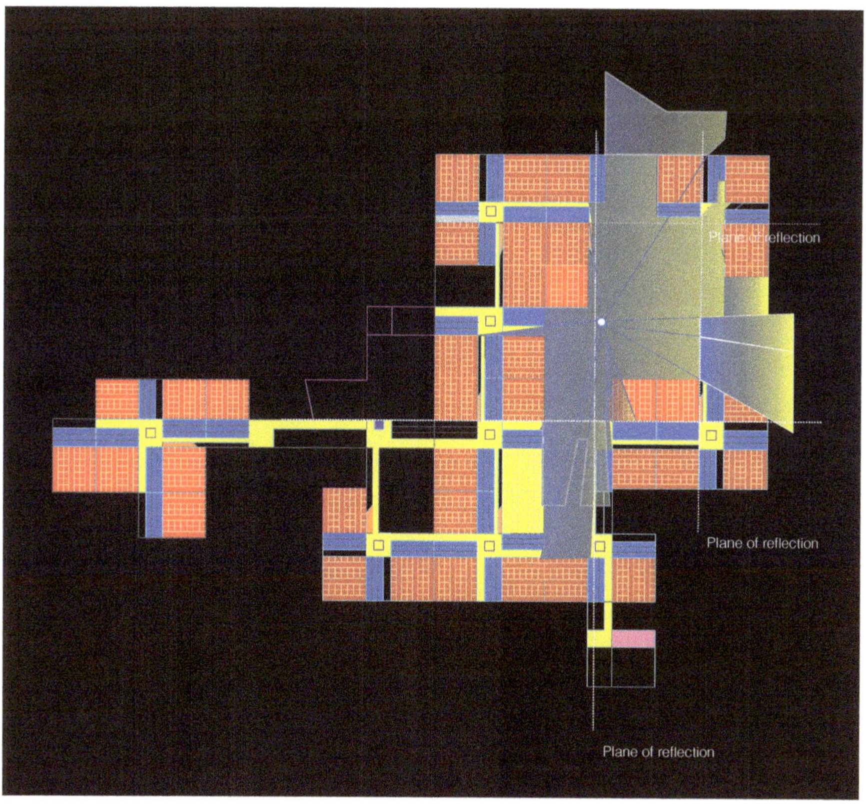

Figure 4.13 Le Corbusier. The Venice Hospital. View of accessible space and views of inaccessible spaces seen through reflections on glass surfaces. The view point is located at the central square area, which facilitates entrance by visitors to the third floor. Drawing by the author

individual urban types, fragments isolated from the urban fabric, but also integral parts of the visible city and its invisible substance.

Part 2: Geometry and space from Palladio to Le Corbusier

The Organic, Classical and Modern paradigms

As an example of conscious imaginative engagement with Venice, the Hospital has wider significance for Le Corbusier's work as well as in the history of ideas on architecture and urban planning. It contains in its form the interface of the city as a process of growth, which Venice exemplifies, with an architect's conscious understanding of the city and its urban structure. It also reflects the intellectual climate of the post-war period, during which architects were becoming aware of the difficulties of modern architecture to deliver its early-twentieth-century promises for the future. Faced with the complexity of cities as social realities, architects, planners and urban designers in the sixties considered that modern urban visions were socially rigid. Christopher Alexander began demonstrating the mathematical logic of networks, while Constantinos Doxiadis outlined the interaction of human habitation with all scales of human settlement.[31] Under the influence of Alexander and of Claude Lévi-Strauss, architects focused on ideas of evolutionary development in vernacular architecture, which in the case of Smithson found expression in Mat-buildings.[32] Generated through strategies of formal aggregation, Mat-buildings simulate urban growth characterised by formal variation. Consequently, they reflect no pre-existing knowledge of overall form in a design or preconceived ideas of formal organisation.[33]

Le Corbusier did not make explicit references to networked flexible cities, although it is possible that he was influenced by the visionary designs of the early sixties. More importantly, in the Hospital he went beyond the surface appearance of networks and Mats, translating the invisible substance of Venice into a new structure. Yet, as his location map indicates, the urban network of Venice was not the only influence in his design (Figure 0.4). Le Corbusier had always drawn inspiration from classical architecture and incorporated his explorations on mathematics and proportions in his buildings. I explained earlier that Palladio's churches were part of a coordinated theatrical scenography in the San Marco Basin, responding to geometrical alignments and an ideal image of Venice as classical theatre. To this integrative vision of the city Le Corbusier juxtaposed the late modern vision of the anti-ideal city, combined with the Classical idea of proportions in architecture and natural systems.

The Hospital is a unique project in Le Corbusier's work. None of his other buildings looks like it, yet the pinwheel theme he used on the third floor is frequently encountered in his other projects. This theme shows a preoccupation with two types of properties: first, classical centrality through the central square located at the intersection of two geometrical axes; and second, four offset pathways, splitting the classical axes of symmetry and movement into four elements and dislocating them away from the centre (Figure 4.5). The pinwheel arrangement is conceptually aligned with other dominant motifs in Le Corbusier's projects, such as the regulating lines and the architectural promenade, a twisting circulation path along stairs, balconies and ramps extending from the ground to the top level of a building in a flowing sweep. The pinwheel scheme shows a conscious engagement with the combinability of geometric rules and those of moving and seeing. Le Corbusier saw in the Hospital an opportunity to respond to the defining context of Venice, a body of work of humanist architecture, which had left a mark in the ceremonial parts of the city, and his own architectural repertory developed over time.

In parallel with the emerging interest in the Organic paradigm, which conceptualised buildings as evolutionary designs in the fifties and sixties, renewed engagement with Palladio's villas rose up through Rudolf Wittkower's publication *Architectural Principles in the Age of Humanism*, James Ackerman's *Palladio* and Colin Rowe's *The Mathematics of the Ideal Villa.*[34] Wittkower described Palladian villas as variations on a compositional logic, including universal laws of geometry and proportions. Rowe, on the other hand, through his audacious comparison of Palladio's Villa Malcontenta with Le Corbusier's Villa Stein, drew attention to the centripetal distribution of movement in Corbusier's building as opposed to the centrifugal classical composition of Palladio. Rowe's study developed readings of the two works that oscillated between the visual perceptions in the experience of the buildings and the conceptual organisation of their elevations, sections and plans. Pointing to the tensions between the visual and the mental, the ideal and the real in the work of the two architects, these historians revived interest in the classical principles of composition. More importantly, by emphasising Palladio's and Le Corbusier's critical understanding of architectural canons, they offered an approach to history over and above the limits of stylistic or historical periods, in support of comparative knowledge in architectural design. Rowe's unorthodox comparison between a classical and a modern building made an implicit yet significant contribution. His analysis showed a regard for buildings as open compositional systems, actively interacting with a universal repertory of structures that preceded and defined it.

This proposition and Le Corbusier's preoccupation with the Organic and Classical paradigms raise the need to explore the architectural imagination within a wider context. The question of how Venice inspires the imagination should expand to broader exploration, focusing on how the imagination can be compositionally defined. The intention is to place Venice and the Hospital within a repertory of design strategies underlying architectural thinking since early times. In what follows I explore the variable relationships of space and geometry through three canonical moments in architectural design. The first moment is when architecture emerges as a reformed discipline, coterminous with the invention of geometric notations. In these notations geometry served as the generator of design, guiding through symmetry and the axial organisation of plans, sections and elevations the distribution of rooms and the ways they were accessible from the outside. The second moment occurred with Modernism, disintegrating the classical correspondence between spatial organisation, movement and axial planning. Within this dismantling strategy, geometry played the role of the regulatory framework against free-flowing space, manifested in the work of Le Corbusier, Mies van der Rohe and other architects. The third moment brought an end to the geometric limitations imposed on design, a battle won by digital technology. Digital architecture dissolves the impact of geometric restrictions on the variability of form that, by and large, have conditioned design thinking for centuries. Nevertheless, the role of space and geometry in buildings and cities still remains largely unexplored. The following discussion extrapolates projects from their historical and physical context in order to understand them comparatively. Yet, it discusses them in chronological order, providing in this way a description of morphological relations which is evolutionary and synchronic. It is only within the combined sequential reading of history and the synchronic reading of morphology that innovative breaks in inherited norms are understood comparatively and as lineage.

Geometry, space and the invention of architectural notation

Alberti, Palladio and numerous architects saw Vitruvius as the source of rules for the correct arrangement and proportioning of plans, sections and elevations, on which architects and theorists over the centuries developed subtle variations.[35] Outstanding contributions by Wittkower, Rowe and Peter Eisenman extended the intellectual heritage of classical composition, defined as the logical organisation of parts into a whole, into the twentieth century. Yet it is primarily Robin Evans who focused on geometry as the *medium* through which buildings are produced and visualised, arguing that the architectural imagination resides in the gap between the building as three-dimensional world and its representation.[36] Studying the role of geometry in architectural drawing and architectural thinking, Evans outlined the imposition of laws from orthographic projection to spatial organisation.

Geometry was always present in architecture, but the conscious employment of it goes back to the Renaissance, where through intensive studies of ancient architecture and influential patronage, architects such as Alberti, Serlio and Palladio established architecture as a discipline separate from the artisanal inherited traditions. The purpose was to elevate it to an intellectual activity, conversing with learned men, poets, philosophers and literati. Alberti advises architects to conceive the design in the mind and revise it many times before building. Once revisions are finished, nothing should be altered, for better or worse.[37] Although Alberti produced the first architectural treatise of the Renaissance, it was not illustrated and was written in Latin. It was Serlio who pioneered the use of high-quality illustrations to supplement his text, which was written in Italian.[38] Illustrations and the discovery of the press spread the influence of these books in the Western world. While previously architects had had to travel in order to study ancient ruins, books brought to them the treasures of antiquity in illustrated volumes. Pocket-sized books in particular, like Palladio's guide book to the ancient sites of Rome, helped spread knowledge of classical architecture, paving the road for its revival.[39]

More importantly, it was orthographic projection, the use of techniques to survey existing fragments and generate plans, sections and elevations that facilitated the establishment of classical architecture. Orthographic projection has been since then – at least, up to the digital revolution in the late twentieth century – a method of representation, of collecting data about buildings and a process of design. In his Hospital project Le Corbusier employed the same method of drawing that had been in use for five hundred years. In his letter to Pope Leo X, Raphael describes this method of surveying and designing through scaled drawings:

> you should draw always measuring everything with the scale, and use a line that equals the width of the base of the entire building. From the central point along this line, draw another straight line that makes on either side two right angles; this will be the centre line of the building. From the two extremities of the width line draw two parallel lines, perpendicular with the base line; these two lines should be as tall as the building is to be. Between these two lines, which make the height, you should then measure off the columns,

> the pilasters, the windows and other ornaments drawn on the front part of the building. And do all this always drawing the lines from every single extremity point of the columns, pilasters, openings, or whatever else, such that these lines are parallel to the lines at the extremities.[40]

He goes on to describe how the elevation ('exterior wall') and the section ('interior wall') are derived from the plan. Corresponding parts are joined with parallel lines, which are the conservers of true measure. These lines are considered to be representations of light paths with the source set at infinite distance: 'the interior wall shows the inside of the building – half, that is, if cut down the middle [...] In short, with these three orders or styles, it is possible to consider in minute detail all the parts of any building, inside and out'.[41] This method of drawing was essential for the building to be constructed on true measures. But it was also the method that created space. As Evans explains,

> architectural space would remain, one way or another, limited by and bonded to the pictures that normally gave access to it [...] projection was an extra ingredient grasping more or less cautiously at the imaginary space behind the three drawings [...] if the side you see is the mirror image of the side you do not see – if, that is, the building is symmetrical about the sectional plane – you see it all through one cut [...] Vertical, bilateral symmetry is economical within the confines of the technique [...] A centre line projected through the cavity easily converts into a processional axis. Then the axial route will show up on the principal elevation as a principal entrance, thereby converting the simple, binary equality of left and right sides (a–a) into a tripartite, therefore hierarchical, centralised symmetry (a–b–a) [...] This is why in most classical architecture design and building are in a near perfect accord.[42]

Andrea Palladio – identity between design and building

Another way of saying this is that the building as three-dimensional physical space was an identical scaled copy of the design. Architects practised a method that constructed an isometric correspondence between the design and the building. The invention of geometrical notations provided – as an analogue algorithm – instructions for producing a design and experiencing a building as three-dimensional physical space. This can be illustrated by looking at Palladio's Villa Almerico

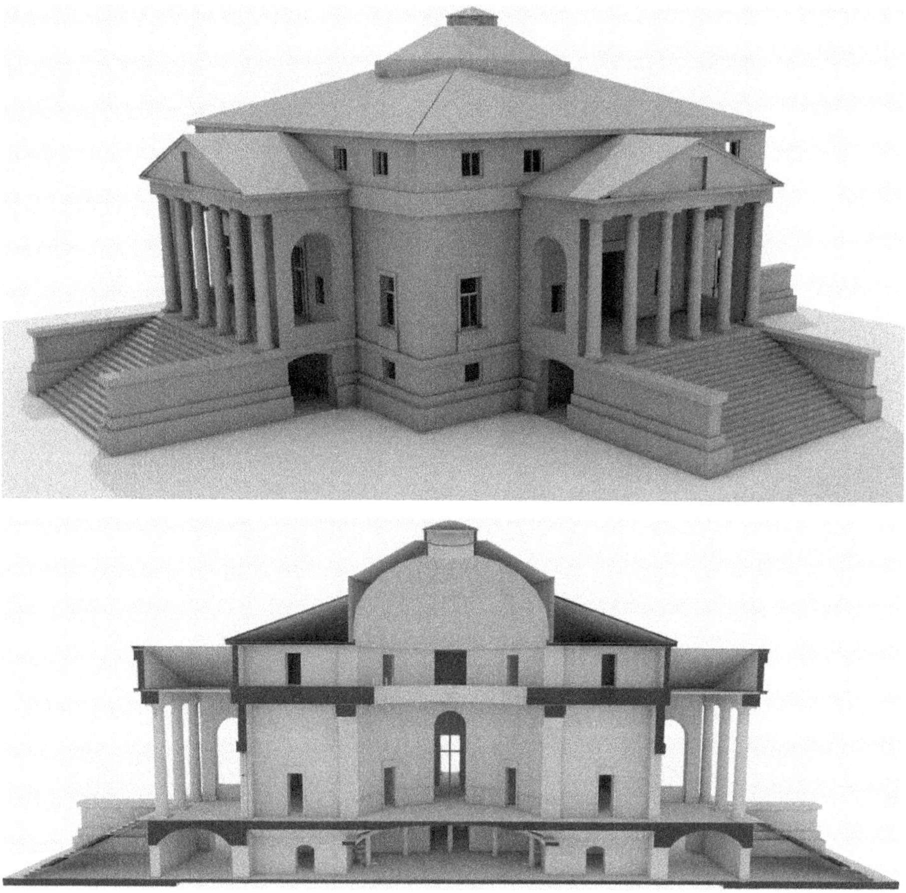

Figure 4.14 Palladio. Villa Rotonda. Drawings by Athina Lazaridou

Capra, known as the Rotonda, in Vicenza (1566), one of the most 'ideal' of Palladio's villas (Figure 4.0a, 4.14), which are often seen as exercises on the Roman ideal of the house in the countryside.[43] Following the conversion of the Venetian elite from mercantile nobles to landowners in Venice's mainland, the villas were a response to the practical demand for a new building type and a temporary defence against the decaying economy of the *Serenissima*.[44] Palladio's villas were generally adjoined by storage and gallery passages (the *barchesse*). In contrast, the Rotonda is a free-standing building on a hilltop outside Vicenza. Palladio included it in his *Four Books*, explaining that the site was

> one of the most pleasing and delightful that one could find [...] on one side it is bathed by the Bacchiglione, a navigable river, and on

> the other is surrounded by other pleasant hills which resemble a vast theatre [...]; so because it enjoys the most beautiful vistas on every side, some of which are restricted, others more extensive, and yet others which end at the horizon, loggias have been built on all four sides.[45]

The Rotonda features in the section about palaces in *The Four Books*. It resembles a temple-villa, closer to a suburban residence than a country house. Composed by two geometries, the perfect cube and the sphere, it offers views of the surrounding hills through four classical porticos which are geometrically aligned along the cardinal axes. The villa is traced to a number of ancient precedents that must have offered Palladio inspiration: the Pantheon, the mausoleum of Romulus and a drawing made by Palladio of the so-called Temple of Hercules at Tivoli, showing a porch with pediment repeated four times.[46]

Using the measure of integration, which was used in the analysis of the Hospital, we see that the most integrated positions in the Rotonda are situated in the circular hall, attracting all pathways and views from every space to every other space in the building (Figure 4.15). All systems of spatial relations, such as physical elements, lines of movement and lines of sight, obey the same laws of invariance. All systems of conceptual relations governing similarity and difference between elements, and all registers of symmetry, correspond with each other so that when viewers move in the villa, the geometric order of the design conditions their vision, movement and appreciation of the relationships between the parts and the whole. The transformations of visual fields, expressed by the way in which the angles and radials of visual polygons change, are symmetrical along the axes of movement. At the same time, views are symmetrical from symmetrical positions (Figure 4.16). Aligning the geometrical axes with the processional lines, as Raphael advised, has the effect of controlling the variability of visual information, so that the whole building can be experienced as a stable image.

Group theory is the branch of mathematics that describes symmetry as the properties that remain invariant under a transformation. In terms of geometry, the Rotonda has six symmetry transformations: reflection on two axes and rotation on 90, 180, 270 and 360 degrees (this is an approximation, as it is worth noting that passageways at the front and back are slightly wider than those located at the two sides). The spatial networks of movement and visibility can be represented by a graph, by assigning a circle to each space and joining circles through lines connecting adjacent spaces (Figure 4.15). The four porticos of the Rotonda in the graph are

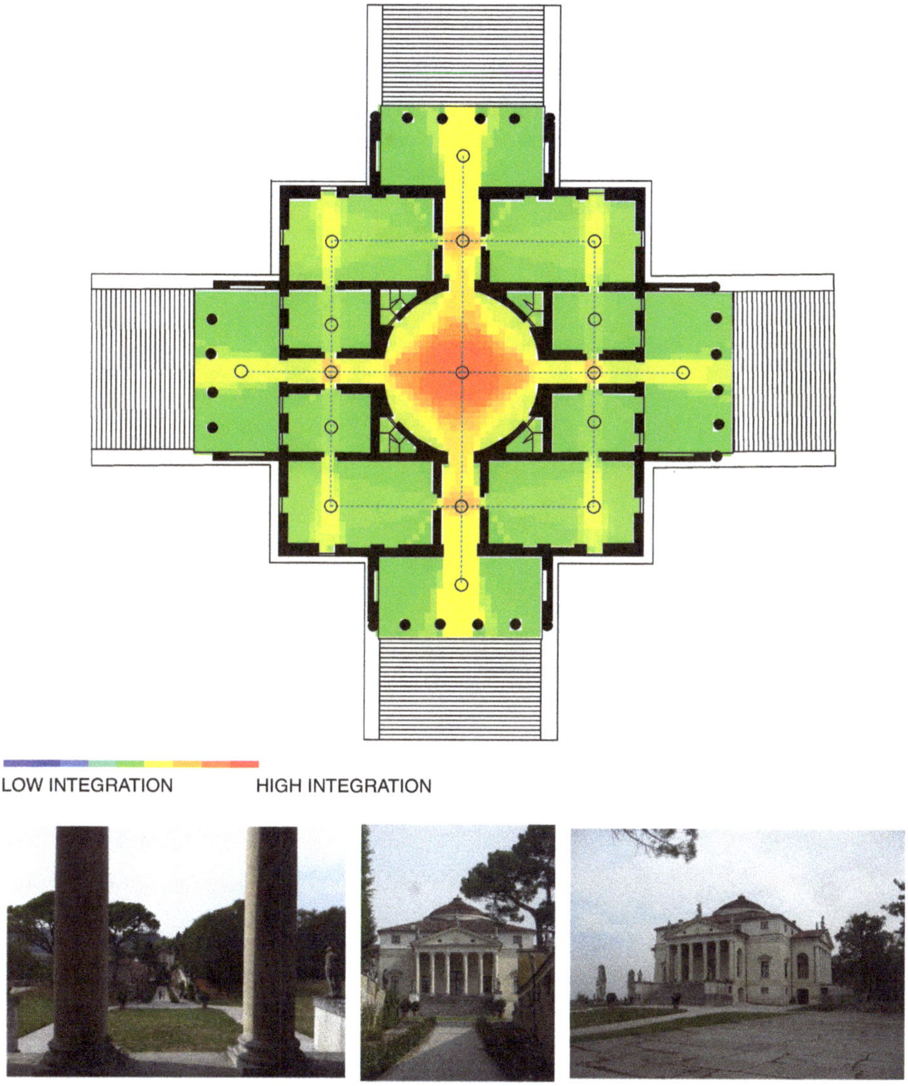

Figure 4.15 Palladio. Villa Rotonda. Visual integration and permeability graph (top). View to the outside from the front entrance (bottom left). Front view (bottom middle). Side view (bottom right). Drawing and photos by the author

symmetrical to each other with respect to the central hall and the outside. This is because they are directly connected with the outside and are situated at a distance of two 'steps' in the graph away from the central hall. The four passageways are symmetrical to each other with respect to each entrance, and so on. The conceptual ordering of porticos, passageways,

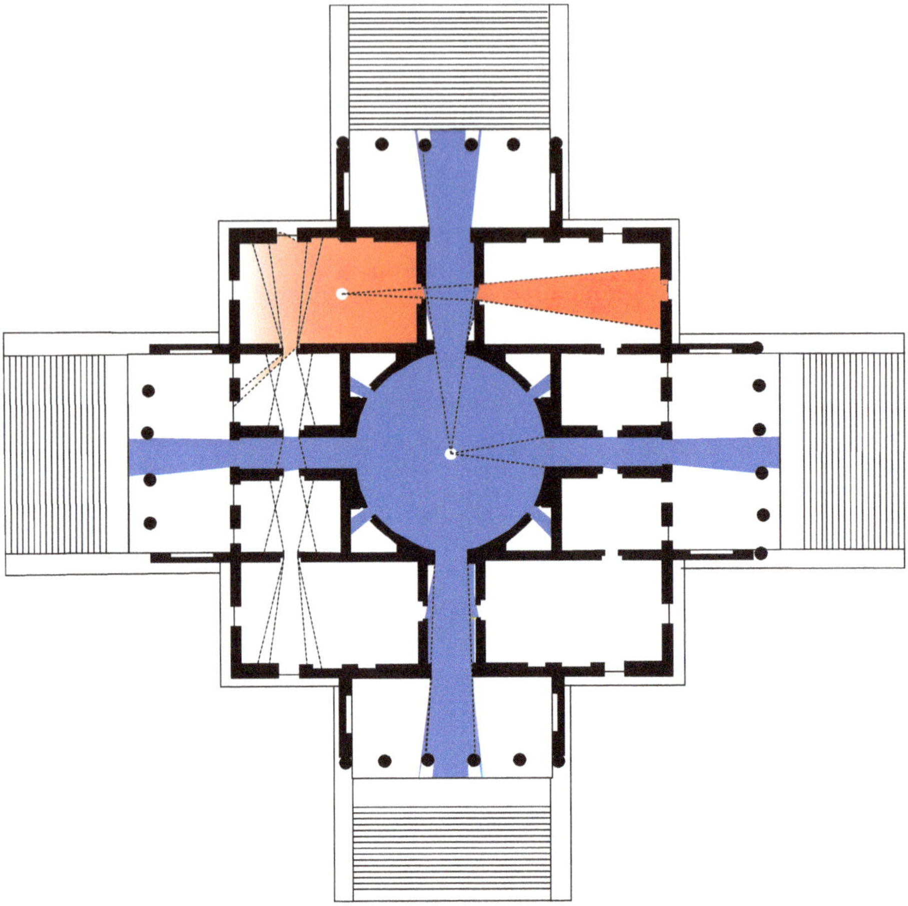

Figure 4.16 Palladio. Villa Rotonda. Visual polygons from the central hall and the space at the top left side. Drawing by the author

rooms and doorways into similarity classes is governed by geometrical symmetry. In addition, geometric symmetry and graph symmetry have the same registers of invariance. This means that conceptual rules, rules of geometry and the topological rules of adjacency and connectivity determining moving and seeing converge, following the same structure. As the eye is drawn along the enfilade axes, the body follows the course of these same axes. Coordinating all potential pathways and views, the central hall enables an understanding of the correspondence between compositional, spatial and geometrical structure, substituting dynamic spatial exploration for static appreciation.[47] Although the building can be experienced along infinite paths, the architectural composition foregrounds only a few of the possible ways of perceiving.

It is important to note that each room in the Rotonda is different from the other rooms due to the decoration, statues and frescos adorning the walls and ceilings and the views of the countryside offered through the windows. The villa absorbs viewers into different mythological scenes as they walk from room to room, drawing attention to the sensual pleasures of moving and seeing. Crowned by a dome that is reminiscent of the Pantheon, the circular hall was planned with an *oeil-de-boeuf*, which later was closed. Rainwater flew through the face of a perforated fawn, at the centre of the floor, to the lower level, where it was gathered in a container.[48] Axially linked with the spectacle of the surrounding hills and open to the sky, the hall would draw the landscape to the interior. Mindful of intellectual abstractions of space and geometry, the landscape and the weather, Palladio synthesised an abstract ideal with the changing evidence of the senses and the infinity of nature. He built this villa during the same period when he worked on the churches of San Giorgio Maggiore and the Redentore in Venice, the Valmarana and the Porto Barbaran palaces, the Capitano house at Vicenza and the little temple of Meser.[49] There is no evidence that he thought of the building as an abstract temple. There is a strong possibility, though, that he saw in it an opportunity to produce a *belvedere*, exploiting the theatrical qualities of the site, and a monument to the humanist principles he had engaged with throughout his life.

Palladio had a heightened understanding of the differences between an actual building and a design. Ackerman stresses his unique capacities to respond to practical functional problems and to specific sites using economical, elegant solutions.[50] This is evident when we compare his design for a palazzo in Venice with an ancient house in his *Four Books*, and his Teatro Olimpico in Vicenza with Vitruvius's Roman theatre.[51] Both projects were adjusted to the irregularity of the setting. Yet, in his book Palladio presented an idealised view of architecture in which all adjustments addressing the imperfections, misalignments and irregularities encountered in a physical site were eliminated. This marked difference between real and ideal was the outcome of the erudite climate of the period. Architects had to demonstrate to fellow architects and learned patrons that they practised architecture as liberal art and not as mechanical art, favouring design thinking over manual labour.

For Alberti, the design, essentially an informational model, was the product of the author, conceived in the mind. The building, on the other hand, was an identical copy of this product. In artisanal practices, it is the other way around.[52] Artisans and craftsmen 'inherit' 'designs' from existing building practices that survive the test of time by word of mouth. For Palladio, architecture resided in the tension, the gap or hinge, between the logical ordering of space and form, conditioned through drawings, and the empirical reality of the buildings themselves.

Notation became the medium of dissemination of architecture at large scale, gathering architectural orders, vocabularies and canons synoptically in one book or print and spreading them far away in space and time. Translating the three-dimensional world into a notation, geometry was until recently the tool through which relations of space and formal order were mapped onto simultaneous forms of knowledge. The mobility and transferability of notations meant that the visual and written language of geometry controlled the relationship between the built three-dimensional world we occupy with the body and the world of design. More importantly, it turned architectural drawings, including buildings and spaces, into 'objects' that were immutable, presentable, readable and combinable with one another. We saw in the discussion of the Bacino San Marco how age-old spatial relations rehearsed through movement and navigation were in the sixteenth century transcribed into a network of radial geometry, translating sequential to synchronic modes of understanding.

If the Renaissance artefact was designed as a microcosm of the universe, and the universe had mathematical origins, the architectural creation had to provide the union between mathematics and the world of the senses. Identity is a special property that defines a symmetry group in mathematics, where a thing can be superimposed upon its image through an isometric relationship of sameness. The classical system of notation established a relationship of identity – or sameness – between geometric notation and space, between the design and the building. This type of relationship caused the spatial to emerge from the flat surface. Once captured through geometry, the properties of space, beyond the reach of drawing and language, have since remained an *active* but *silent* partner.

Variably standard – geometric control and variable space

Palladio's ideas travelled to the West in the seventeenth century, engendering English Palladianism through Inigo Jones, who met Scamozzi, Palladio's student, in Italy. Jones's projects were based on antique building types, such as palaces, villas and baths. In the eighteenth and nineteenth centuries emerging modern social institutions

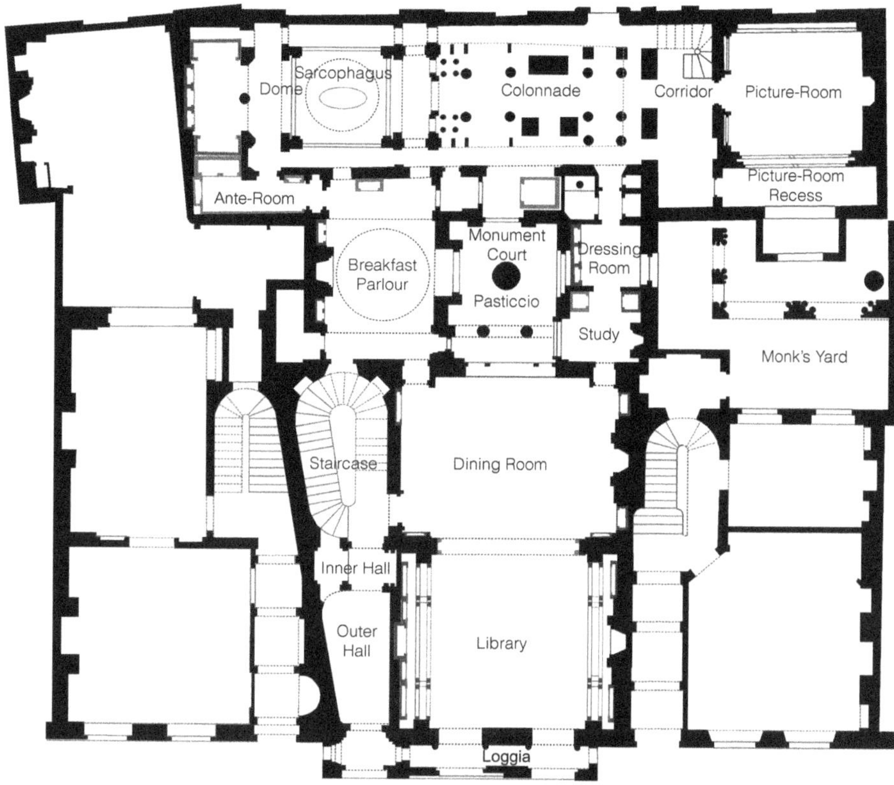

Figure 4.17 Plan of Soane's House, now Sir John Soane's Museum. Drawing by the author

required designs for new functional types. In his *Cours d'Architecture* Jean-Nicolas-Louis Durand (1760–1834) provided such types through a highly rationalised encyclopaedic survey, combining formal schemata that were literally empty of any specific content.[53] This approach was rejected by the twentieth-century avant-garde architects under the influence of organic evolutionary typology, inspired by studies such as D'Arcy Thomson's (1860–1948).

It is important to discuss a unique case of synthesis of classical ideal and empirical real (the Organic or Picturesque) before the arrival of Le Corbusier and modern architecture. Often considered as the first modern architect before the modern movement, John Soane built incrementally a house at 12–14 Lincoln's Inn Fields that challenged the classical isometric invariance between design and building (Figure 4.17). The distribution of visual integration on the ground floor captures the grid-like geometry of Durand's compositions, but the frontal axis of symmetry is fractured by the *pasticcio*, and the sequence of rooms, which in classical buildings are arranged in perspectival recession, is distorted. The doorways are aligned neither with the geometrical axes of rooms, nor with the lines of sight. In addition, there are multiple oblique views through courtyards, windows, tinted glass and mirrors (Figure 4.18a–b). Finally, compared with the visual fields in the Rotonda, the visual fields in Soane's house have greater variation in terms of shape, size, radial angles and direction, changing along with movement.[54]

It was Le Corbusier who intensively engaged, more than any other architect, with the complex relationship between space and geometry in modern and classical buildings. The origin of his pinwheel scheme goes right back to the Villa La Roche (1925), built for a wealthy client to house his collection of paintings.[55] This is also the project in which the architectural promenade was invented, guiding the visitor through changes of direction along ramps, stairs, balconies, vestibules, passages, suspended walkways and bridges. In contrast to the classical axial coordination, Le Corbusier used a twisting pattern of circulation covering heterogeneous elements. Rather than employing geometry to guide the body and the eye along the same course, he privileged human empirical movement.

Yet, the combination of a simple volume with a meandering path emerged in the project for the Villa Savoie (1928–1931) as the first instance of what would later become for him a persistent method of designing (Figure 4.19). While working on Savoie, Le Corbusier was also collaborating with Paul Otlet on the Mundaneum (1929) (Figure 4.20). Otlet was a significant figure in the history of information society and the networked knowledge of the future. His intentions for the Mundaneum were for a place that provided access to the world's knowledge. Otlet envisioned a 'city of knowledge' that would serve as a central repository for the world's information. The World City was a utopian vision, bringing together, like a universal exhibition, all the leading institutions of the world: a World Museum, a World University, a World Library and Documentation Centre, Offices for the International Associations, Offices or Embassies for the Nations, an Olympic Centre, a residential area and a park. Le Corbusier's design for the Mundaneum experimented with a giant circulation ramp forming a ziggurat shape. The two schemes, one domestic (Savoie), the other public (Mundaneum), were worked on in parallel, combining a simple solid with the twisting course of movement.

In his design for the Museum of Contemporary Art (1931) Le Corbusier shaped the whole building as an unfolding wall, defining

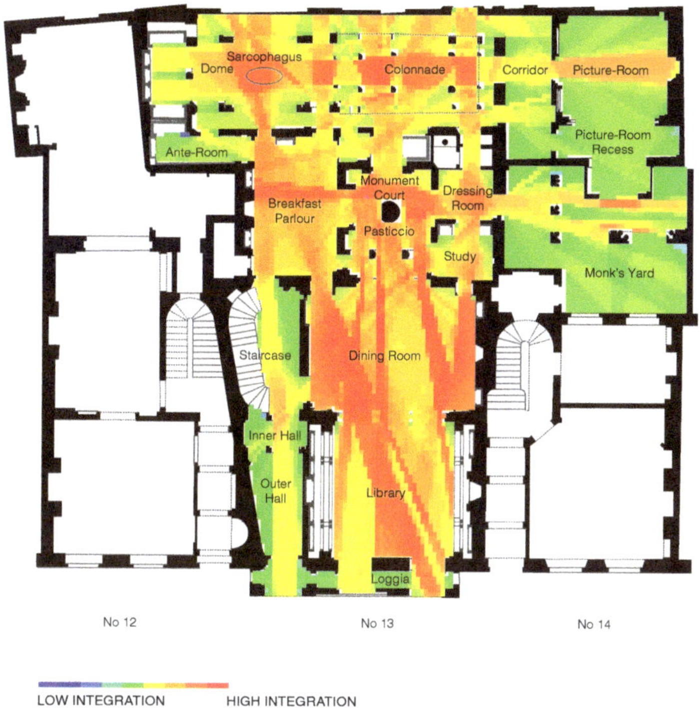

Figure 4.18 (a) Visual integration analysis of Sir John Soane's Museum. Drawing by the author

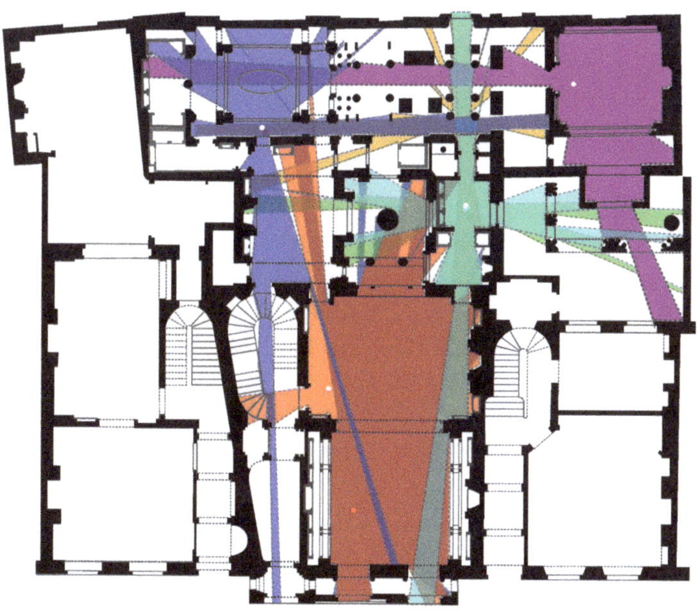

Figure 4.18 (b) Sir John Soane's Museum. Visual polygons representing views of accessible spaces, drawn from selected view-points (white circles). Drawing by the author

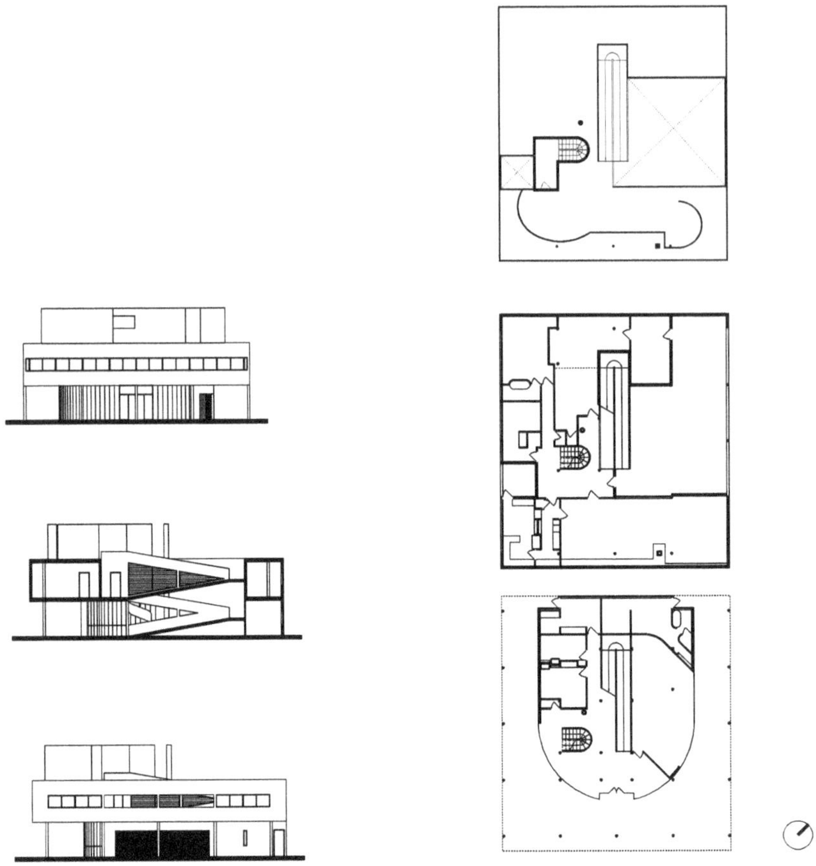

Figure 4.19 Le Corbusier. Villa Savoie. Plans, section and elevations. © Laurence King, FLC/ ADAGP, Paris and DACS, London 2017

continuous movement (Figure 4.21a–d). Lacking a façade, the museum is entered through an underground passage, absorbing the exterior into the interior. A few cuts made in its surface allow visitors to move outside the designated journey, circulating in different ways. Le Corbusier explained that the human eye requires rotation and change of scene, showing his concern that architectural space should stimulate the viewer's experience.[56] In 1936 he used the pinwheel pattern again in the Centre for Contemporary Aesthetics. In 1939 he employed this design theme in the French Pavilion in San Francisco and in the exposition in Liège. The same year marked the Museum of Unlimited Growth in Algeria, in which the future spiralling growth of its space is indicated on the ground around the simple box-like form of the building. In this project, the rotating

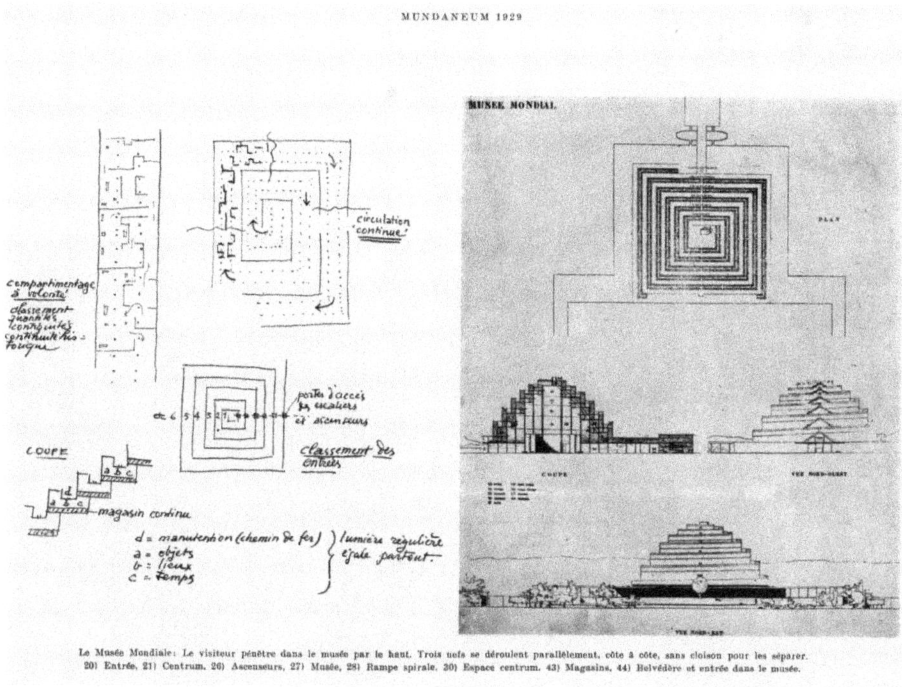

Figure 4.20 Le Corbusier. Design for the Mundaneum. Le Corbusier experimented with a large circulation ramp, spiralling upwards to form a ziggurat shape. © FLC/ADAGP, Paris and DACS, London 2017

pattern of movement is combined with a central void and four spaces, each located on a different side of the volume, defining the pinwheel schema of composition (Figure 4.21a–d). Le Corbusier used this schema in 23 designs of different sizes and different programmes, from museums and exhibition spaces to villas, including the monastery of La Tourette.[57] The persistence of this schema throughout his career and its development from a simple pattern of spiral movement to a prevailing structure suggests that it became a systematic structure or metalanguage. What was its significance, and why did it so preoccupy him?

We can find answers to these questions by analysing two of the projects constructed as variations of the endless museum and the pinwheel pattern: the Tokyo Museum (1959) and the Museum of the Cultural Centre in Ahmedabad (1951) (Figures 4.0b, 4.22, 4.23, 4.24, 4.25). Le Corbusier stated that in the Tokyo Museum 'every time a visitor, in the course of his wanderings, finds himself under the lowered ceiling [marked in the figure with the shaded areas], he will see, on one side, an exit to the garden, and on the opposite side, the way to the central hall'.[58]

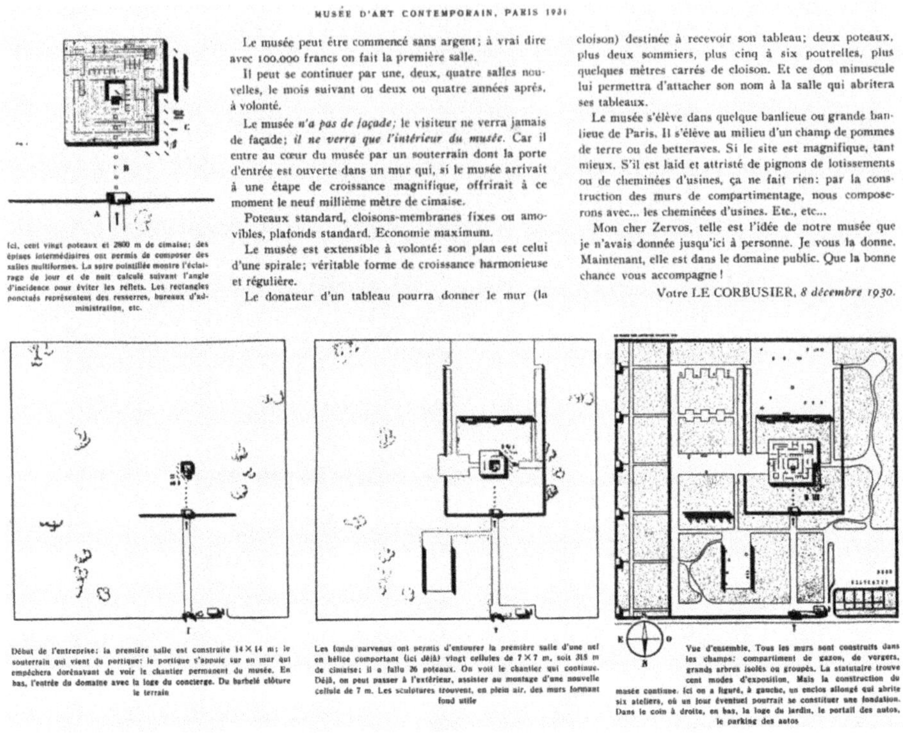

MUSÉE D'ART CONTEMPORAIN, PARIS 1931

Ici, cent vingt poteaux et 2800 m de cimaise; des épines intermédiaires ont permis de composer des salles multiformes. La spire pointillée montre l'éclairage de jour et de nuit calculé suivant l'angle d'incidence pour éviter les reflets. Les rectangles ponctués représentent des resserres, bureaux d'administration, etc.

Le musée peut être commencé sans argent; à vrai dire avec 100.000 francs on fait la première salle.

Il peut se continuer par une, deux, quatre salles nouvelles, le mois suivant ou deux ou quatre années après, à volonté.

Le musée *n'a pas de façade;* le visiteur ne verra jamais de façade; *il ne verra que l'intérieur du musée.* Car il entre au cœur du musée par un souterrain dont la porte d'entrée est ouverte dans un mur qui, si le musée arrivait à une étape de croissance magnifique, offrirait à ce moment le neuf millième mètre de cimaise.

Poteaux standard, cloisons-membranes fixes ou amovibles, plafonds standard. Economie maximum.

Le musée est extensible à volonté: son plan est celui d'une spirale; véritable forme de croissance harmonieuse et régulière.

Le donateur d'un tableau pourra donner le mur (la cloison) destinée à recevoir son tableau; deux poteaux, plus deux sommiers, plus cinq à six poutrelles, plus quelques mètres carrés de cloison. Et ce don minuscule lui permettra d'attacher son nom à la salle qui abritera ses tableaux.

Le musée s'élève dans quelque banlieue ou grande banlieue de Paris. Il s'élève au milieu d'un champ de pommes de terre ou de betteraves. Si le site est magnifique, tant mieux. S'il est laid et attristé de pignons de lotissements ou de cheminées d'usines, ça ne fait rien: par la construction des murs de compartimentage, nous composerons avec... les cheminées d'usines. Etc., etc...

Mon cher Zervos, telle est l'idée de notre musée que je n'avais donnée jusqu'ici à personne. Je vous la donne. Maintenant, elle est dans le domaine public. Que la bonne chance vous accompagne!

Votre LE CORBUSIER, *8 décembre 1930.*

Début de l'entreprise: la première salle est construite 14 × 14 m: le souterrain qui vient du portique: le portique s'appuie sur un mur qui empêchera dorénavant de voir le chantier permanent du musée. En bas, l'entrée du domaine avec la loge du concierge. Du barbelé clôture le terrain

Les fonds parvenus ont permis d'entourer la première salle d'une nef en hélice comportant (ici déjà) vingt cellules de 7 × 7 m, soit 315 m de cimaise: il a fallu 26 poteaux. On voit le chantier qui continue. Déjà, on peut passer à l'extérieur, assister au montage d'une nouvelle cellule de 7 m. Les sculptures trouvent, en plein air, des murs formant fond utile

Vue d'ensemble. Tous les murs sont construits dans les champs: compartiment de gazon, de vergers, grands arbres isolés ou groupés. La statutaire trouve cent modes d'exposition. Mais la construction du musée continue. Ici on a figuré, à gauche, un enclos allongé qui abrite six ateliers, où un jour éventuel pourrait se constituer une fondation. Dans le coin à droite, en bas, la loge du jardin, le portail des autos, le parking des autos

Figure 4.21 (a) Le Corbusier. Museum of Contemporary Art (1931). © FLC/ADAGP, Paris and DACS, London 2017

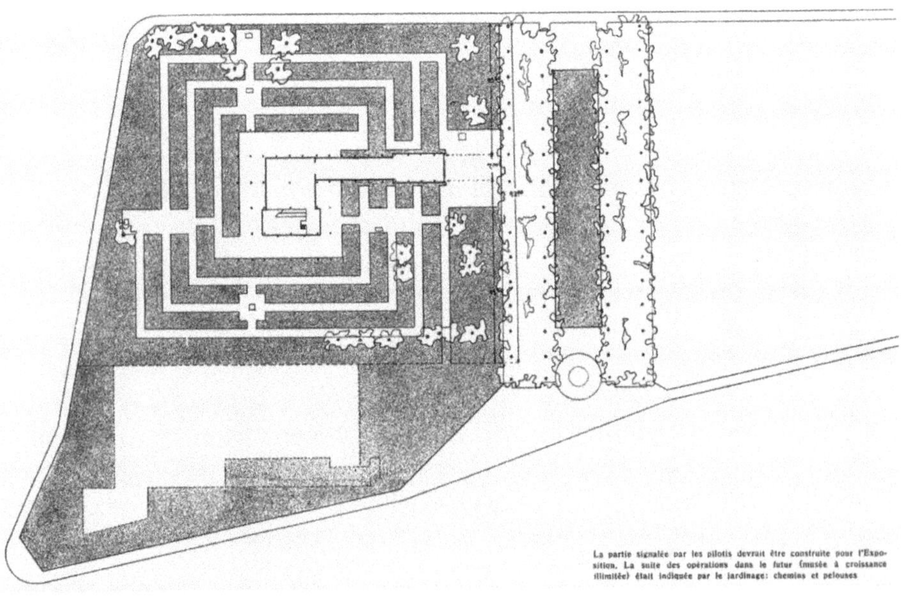

Figure 4.21 (b) Le Corbusier. Centre for Contemporary Aesthetics (1936). © FLC/ADAGP, Paris and DACS, London 2017

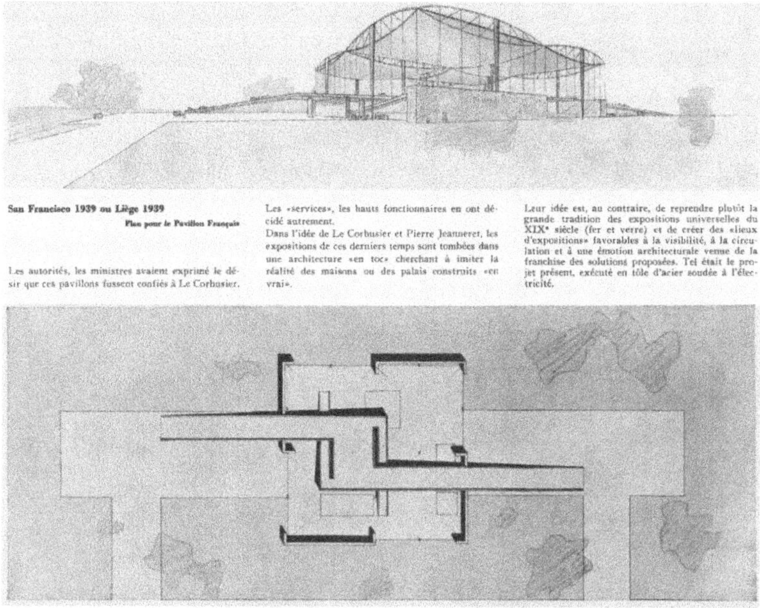

Figure 4.21 (c) Le Corbusier. French Pavilion in San Francisco (1939). © FLC/ADAGP, Paris and DACS, London 2017

Figure 4.21 (d) Le Corbusier. Museum of Unlimited Growth (1936). © FLC/ADAGP, Paris and DACS, London 2017

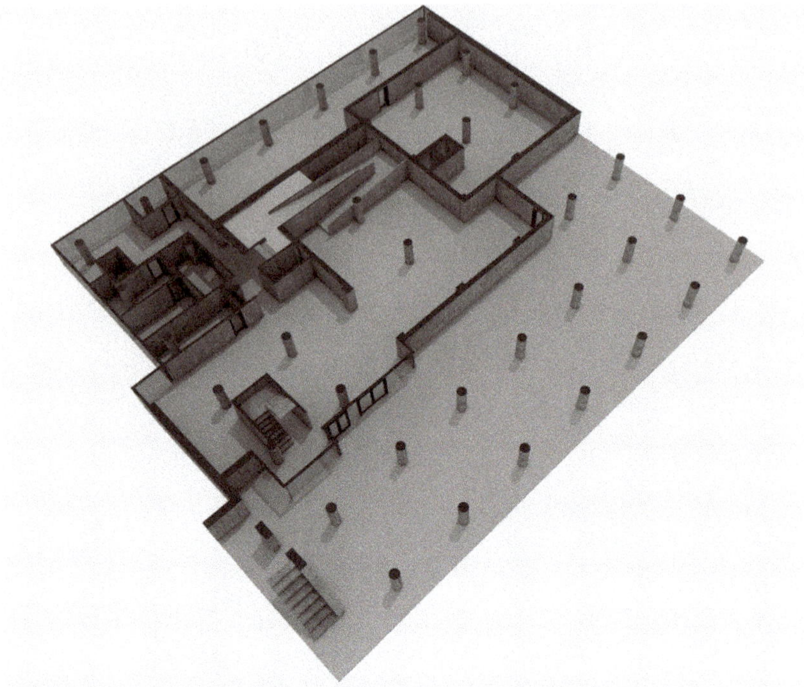

Figure 4.22 (a) Le Corbusier. Tokyo Museum (1959). Ground floor. Drawing by Athina Lazaridou

Figure 4.22 (b) Le Corbusier. Museum of the Cultural Centre in Ahmedabad (1951). © FLC/ADAGP, Paris and DACS, London 2017

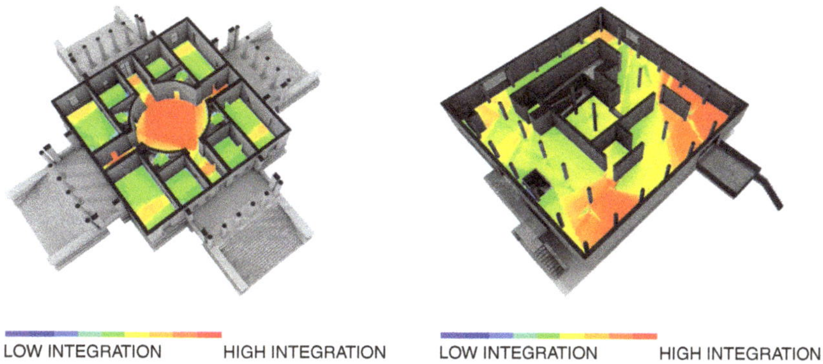

Figure 4.23 (Left) Palladio. Villa Rotonda. Visual integration analysis. (Right) Le Corbusier. Tokyo Museum. Visual integration analysis. Drawings by Athina Lazaridou

The views he refers to are those connecting the central space with the exterior. As with the Rotonda, there are four axial connections linking the central space with a large window or entry point (Figures 4.23). In contrast, these axial links travel along the perimeter of the central hall rather than traversing its centre. Looking at the graph of the main spaces, we see that graph symmetry operates only with respect to space 1 – at the end of the ramp – which is off the main axis. In the classical model, there are usually a higher number of elements bound in symmetrical relations. As a result, the distribution of integration in the Tokyo Museum follows a different logic from the one invested in its geometric ordering.

In addition, relationships between the central space and the peripheral galleries break the classical correspondence between seeing and moving. Analysing the building in terms of permeability and visibility structure, we see the clear impact of inserting an object at the centre of a layout and pushing integration values to the corners of the space.[59] More importantly, the central hall has the lowest values of integration, as opposed to the central hall in the Rotonda, which manifests the opposite property at the highest end of the integration spectrum (Figure 4.23). Particularly, the distribution of integration in terms of visibility emphasises the top- and bottom-left corners, in clear contrast with the processional axial element, which is off the main axis. A look at the Cultural Centre at Ahmedabad shows similar tensions. There is two-fold geometric symmetry on the horizontal and vertical axes; rotational symmetry in terms of permeability; and rotational symmetry and two-fold symmetry on the diagonal axes in terms of the visibility structure (Figure 4.25).

Looking at the Rotonda it is possible to intuit from the abstraction of the plan the distribution of integration, translating in our mind the

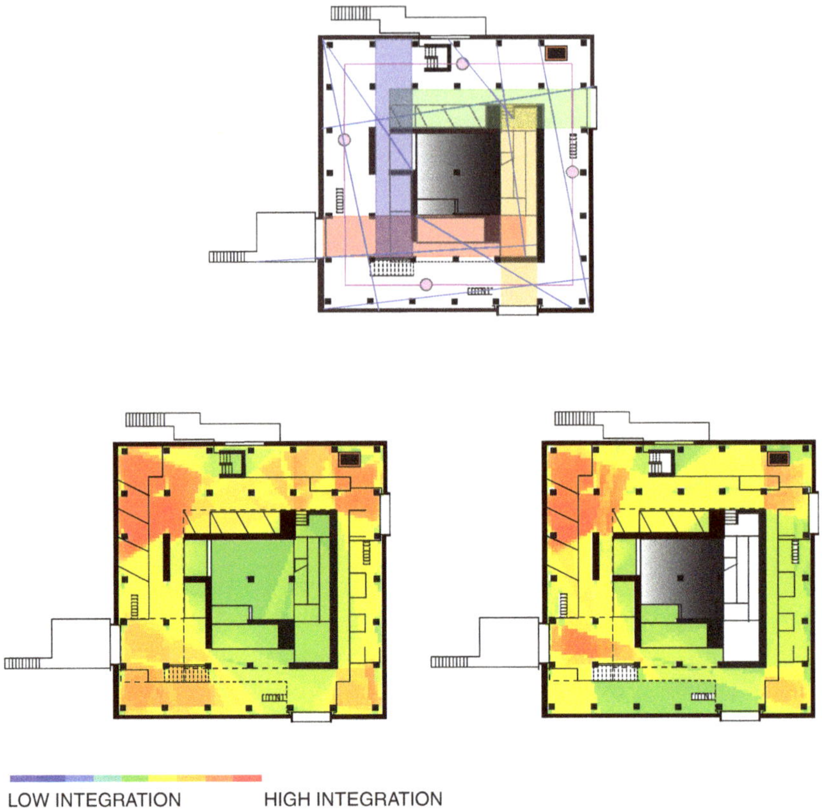

Figure 4.24 Le Corbusier. Tokyo Museum. (Top) Permeability graph and axial visual links. The four zones in different colours mark the pinwheel scheme. (Bottom left) Visual integration analysis (though central void and stairs). (Bottom right) Visual integration analysis (without central void and stairs). Drawings by the author

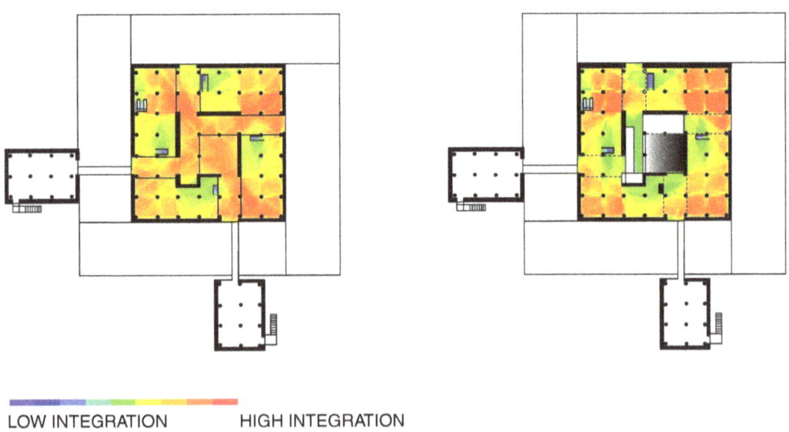

Figure 4.25 Le Corbusier. Cultural Centre at Ahmedabad. (Left) Visual integration analysis (though central void). (Right) Visual integration analysis (without central void). Drawings by the author

abstraction of the plan to empirical space. The correspondence between geometric order and the system of spatial interconnections, inherent in Raphael's method of design and notation, raises the structure of space to the level of perception and makes it understood in an instant. The effect is that the essential distance between the design and building in Palladio is removed, whereas in Le Corbusier's architecture it is accentuated. Palladio and Le Corbusier layered building and drawing (and writing), opening their work to tensions residing in between these modes of thinking and existence, with no mode taking precedence over another.

Developed over 30 years of architectural activity, the pinwheel plan became a standard formal type, producing different variations on a theme, based on invariance between conceptual ordering, visual perception and embodied experience.[60] There are three main mechanisms in Le Corbusier's approach: first, four-fold symmetry of the outer volume and the central space, the latter occupying the centre of the plan (sometimes slightly off axis); second, rotational symmetry governing the axial relationship between the central space-void and the adjoining galleries, exterior openings and pathways; third, selective screening of the central space-void from the galleries, dissociating the structure of seeing from that of moving. Le Corbusier dismissed the Beaux-Arts language of architecture, which is based on axial planning and symmetrical arrangements. Yet, he had a clear understanding of the classical strategy of correspondence between what is sensed by the body and what is accessed by the mind. He used axial principles to organise plans through variable rules, meaning that what is invariant in one set of rules differs from what is invariant in another. The spectator engendered by his architecture follows one course of movement while exploring vistas developing along a different direction. However, Le Corbusier's work cannot be fully understood by reference only to the building, the spectator's experience, or the invariant pattern of symmetries. Only by absorbing the tension between design and building, including their dialectic relationship with classical composition, does his architecture take on its full significance.

Modern practices

The strategy of breaking the isometric invariance between geometric order and spatial organisation was widely adopted by modern architects. In many modern buildings geometry simply works as a supporting armature rather than as the generator of the design. However, Le Corbusier and Mies van der Rohe were among the few architects attempting to establish through this persistent type of invariance a systematic

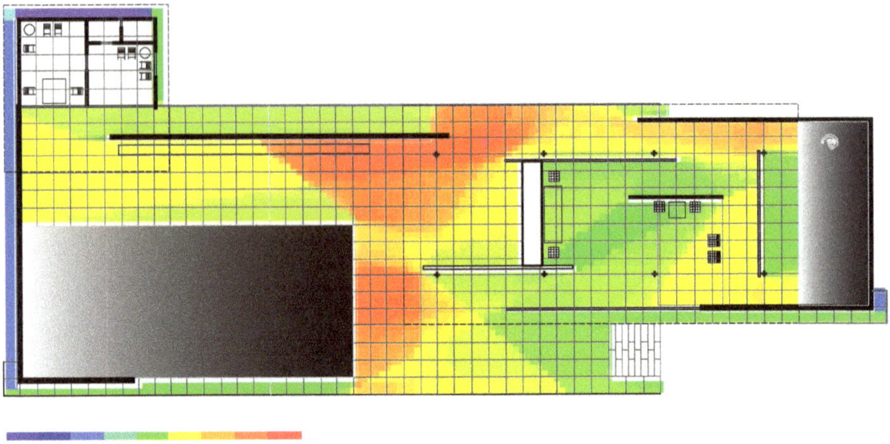

Figure 4.26 Mies van der Rohe. Barcelona Pavilion (1929). Visual integration analysis. Drawing by the author

language, critically positioned in relation to the Classical paradigm, responsive to the Modern paradigm and aware of the Organic paradigm.

During the same period that Le Corbusier was experimenting with his pinwheel schema of composition in architecture, Mies van der Rohe was opposing reductive functionalism through the idea of transcendental technology. Influenced by the Jesuit philosopher Romano Guarini, he used advanced construction technology to transcend functional material contingency, dematerialising light, glass and gleaming metal, a condition in architecture that Mies characterised as 'almost nothing'.[61] In Mies's Barcelona Pavilion there is almost inverse symmetrical distribution of integrated and segregated positions (Figure 4.26). More importantly, Mies aligned the end points of partitions by oblique lines of sight, obliterating the distance between the geometrical coordination of elements and optical experience (Figure 4.27).[62] The classical correspondence between building and design is still at work but through an oblique geometry, transferring importance from the geometry of space to visual interconnections among spaces.

Photographs of the Pavilion indicate that the geometrical-optical alignments were intentional. Mies found a block of onyx accidentally, and used its size to determine the height of the building.[63] Carefully calculating space, materials and dimensions, he must have worked with plan, section and interior perspectives to control the impact of reflections on the onyx wall, the inner dividing surface. The effect of this coordination is the illusion that the surface of the onyx wall is penetrated by vision (Figure 4.28). Similar effects were used by Mies in other projects,

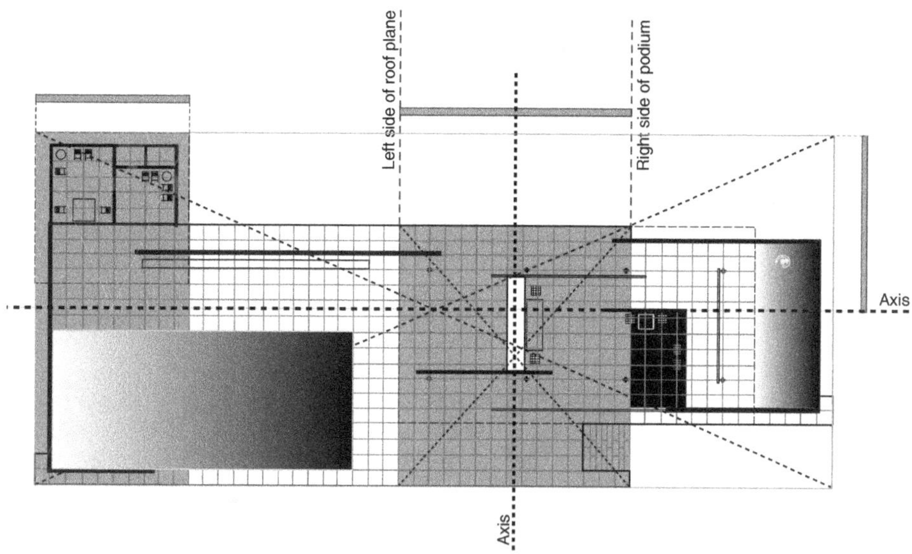

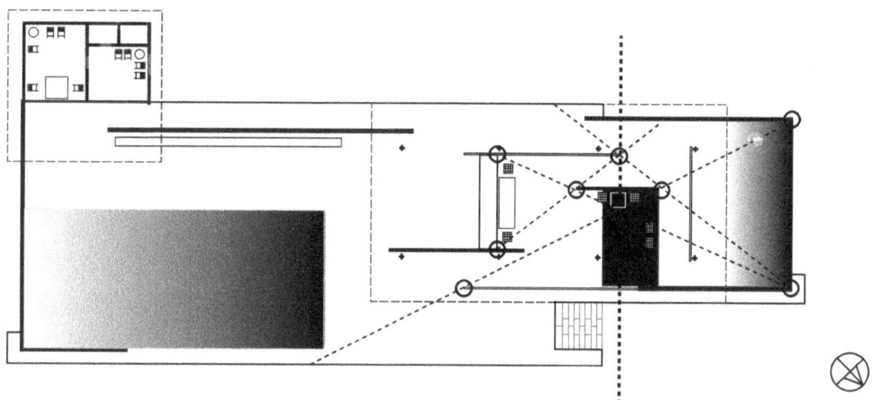

Figure 4.27 Mies van der Rohe. Barcelona Pavilion. (Top) The geometric analysis of the plan reveals local symmetries. The onyx wall and the luminous box are located at the centre of two rectangles. (Bottom) The edges of partitions in the Pavilion are aligned by lines of movement and sight. Drawings by the author

stretching erasure of optical obstruction to the point that the dividing plane did not exist to separate, but to heighten a unified perception of space.[64] Mies also made adjustments to the paving slabs of the Pavilion, working in a manner close to that of artisanal builders, that is, from the construction of the building to the design. In artisanal production, the design is a model that, once repeated often enough, becomes abstracted and transmitted to future generations. Unlike Alberti, who advised

Figure 4.28 Mies van der Rohe. Barcelona Pavilion. Reflections on the surface of the onyx wall create the illusion of surfaces that penetrate one another. Photo by the author

architects that the design is a conceptual model and the building its faithful copy, Mies designed the Pavilion taking into consideration the materials and process of construction. The design thus became a 'copy' of the building – not the other way around.

In the same way that Palladio influenced Le Corbusier and Mies, these modern architects affected contemporary architectural practice. An example of a return to classical traditions is the work of Mario Botta, using isometric invariance between space and geometry within the bounds of a Platonic solid, a clear distinction between front and back, and the principles of tripartite composition (Figure 4.29a–d). A contemporary case is Herzog and de Meuron's De Young Museum in San Francisco (Figure 4.30). The architects have used the corporeal geometry of the building to inform the incorporeal structure of moving and seeing. The museum seems to gather all the elements of a Beaux-Arts building – an open courtyard, a tower, a grand staircase, a portico – reassembling them in a new fashion. But the most striking reference to the Beaux-Arts method of design is made evident by the analysis. The pattern of integration picks up the lines defining the geometry of the building, replacing

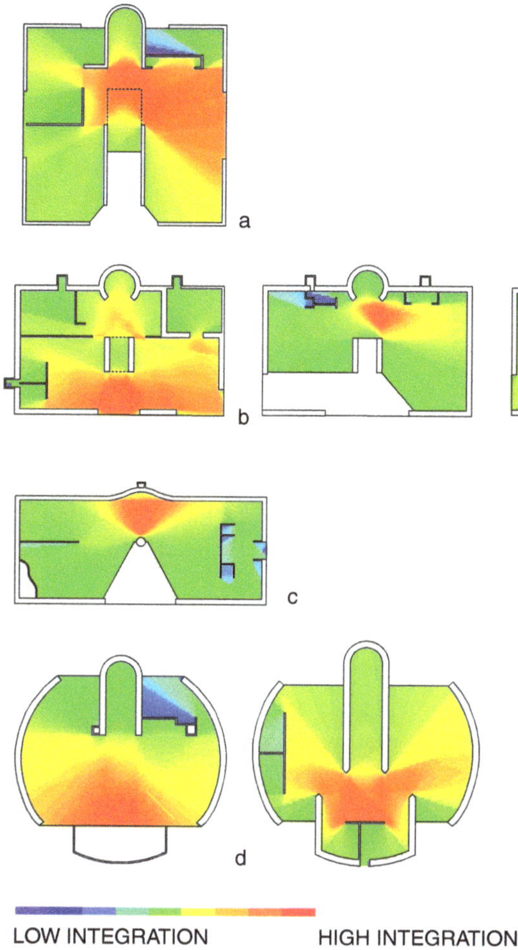

Figure 4.29 Mario Botta. Visual integration analysis of four houses. (Top) House at Pregassona (1979, 1980). (Second from top) House at Massagno (1980, 1981). (Third from top) House at Viganello (1980, 1981). (Bottom) House at Stabbio (1979, 1980). Drawings by the author

orthogonal geometry with oblique visual lines. Contemporary architecture thus is still choreographed by movement of the body and the eye.

Non-standard variation

Tracing morphological paradigms since early modernity, I have explored how geometrical notation influenced architecture. Traditional drawing was an additive process. The consistency and associative relations between plan, section and elevation, between one element and another, between geometry and space were managed by the designer. Raphael's

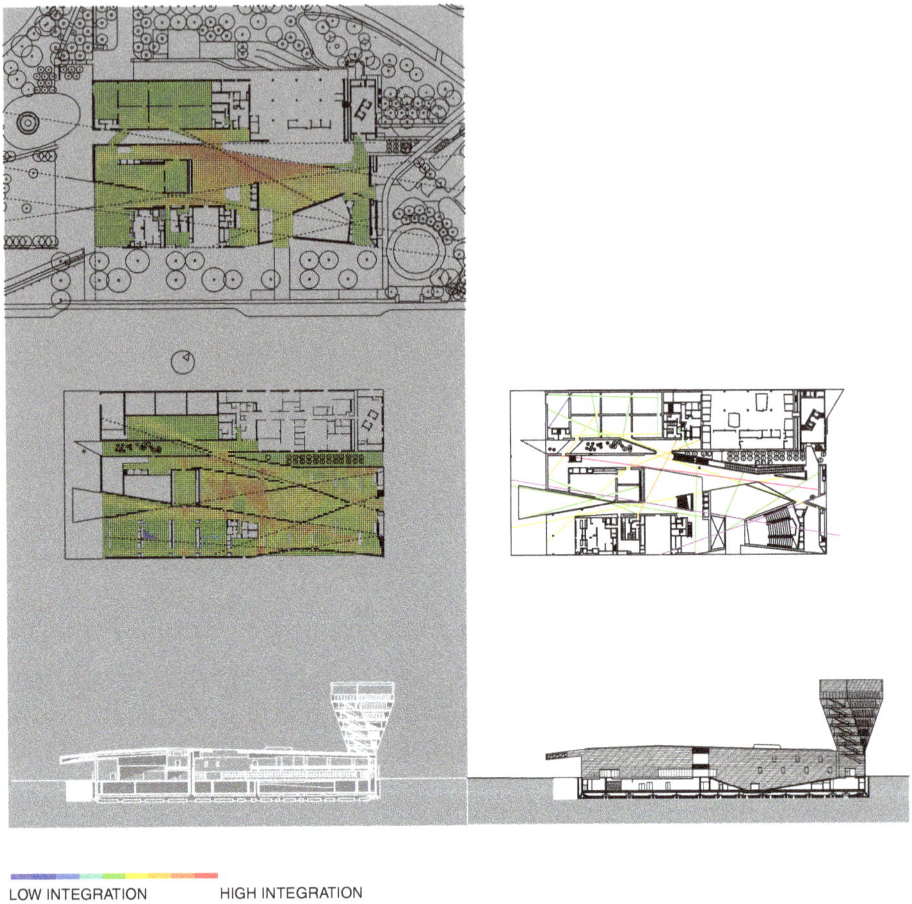

Figure 4.30 Herzog and de Meuron. De Young Museum (2005). (Top left) Visual Integration analysis of ground floor. (Middle left) Visual Integration analysis of first floor. (Top right) Axial integration analysis of first floor. (Bottom left, right) Sections. Laurence King Publishers, © FLC/ADAGP, DACS, London 2017

method of orthographic projection guaranteed exactly that. Geometry was not simply the scaffolding for designing buildings and holding them up, but also provided the conceptual and intellectual network of associations needed to establish internal coherence. By foregrounding a world of conceptually intelligible structures, geometric notation in classical architecture established an identity relationship between building and design, fastening temporally evolving spatial perceptions into a recognisable stable image.

By organising physical and conceptual relationships, geometry made symbolic messages more pronounced. It eventually articulated communication between built space and the symbolic realm of representations evident in both buildings and urban structures. The meaning of architectural space thus relied not only on what could be materially seen but also what should be symbolically evoked, the 'artist working as second Nature, so that an artefact is designed as a microcosm of the universe'.[65] A clear example was seen in Venice, in the scenographic order of the Venetian lagoon, which expressed a political and cosmological order at the service of the Venetian Republic. Being visible as well as abstract, geometry helped translate conceptual relations from one realm to the other, from abstract to physical, tangible to intangible, and from cities to architectural structures.

The power of geometry to bind design and building came to an end in the twentieth century. The technological invention of the structural grid lifted the constraints imposed by load-bearing partitions. Freed from geometrical limitations on the distribution of space and building loads, modern architecture established variability of moving and seeing, as manifested in the work of Le Corbusier. Yet, geometry and geometric notation remained the tools through which the associative relationships among various parts of the building were controlled and visualised. The invention of CAD software simply meant that this additive logic was continued in the digital realm. Even though geometry and space in modern architecture were decoupled, there were no changes in terms of notational tools (plans, elevations and sections) or the strict repertory of orthogonal geometrical forms until the rise of digital technology.

Over the last decades, digital architecture has led to interactive algorithmic models based on associative logic, responding to variations in the input by manipulating the entire system.

> Indeed, 3D printing, 3D scanning and reverse modeling have already made it possible to envisage a continuous design and production process where one or more designers may intervene, seamlessly, on a variety of two-dimensional visualisations and three-dimensional representations (or printouts) of the same object, and where all interventions or revisions can be incorporated into the same master file of the project.[66]

Further, Deleuze and Cache's description of the 'objectile' (originally the notation of a parametric function) defines design not as an object but as an algorithm, a parametric function which may determine an infinite variety of objects, all different yet all similar, as the underlying function is similar to all.[67]

The concept of the *objectile* is similar to Hillier and Hanson's idea of the genotype in the beady ring, an underlying structure of open spaces connected together like 'beads on a ring', producing endless phenotypical variations of the same model.[68] The objectile can be collaboratively manipulated to produce a series of non-identical elements. As Carpo explains, together with the demise of geometrical notation there is no longer the Albertian author of identical copies.[69]

The invention of the digital not only enabled design to operate directly on three-dimensional coordinates, but also provided a vast repertory of forms freed from the constraints imposed by buildable geometry. More importantly, it allowed the designing and building of 'digitally variable objects', whose geometric descriptions can vary within the same output, or in different outputs of a form.[70] However, although orthogonal geometric notations and the limitations they impose on formal variability have gone (not entirely of course), the essential link of geometry to space has not gone. Aided by computational tools, designers use geometry to generate complex variable forms and visualise what is experienced by seeing and moving in three dimensions. Even when a building is not intended to be aesthetically revealed by moving or to be geometrically consistent, it still embodies interrelations of geometry and movement. The spatial networks of cities also have geometrical relationships related to angle of incidence and alignments embedded in the urban grid and influencing their configuration and function. Whether conspicuous or hidden, regular or irregular, intentionally generating a building and urban plan or simply supporting their construction, geometry and movement arise from and translate back into the development of cities and architecture. Design software can produce different formal outputs through inputs that affect the geometry of objects, but the impact of the algorithm and geometry on space outputs is still in the blind spot, still in the shadows of these data and node diagrams of digital production.

Generic relations and the architectural imagination

So far, this chapter has introduced Palladio and Le Corbusier and the respective parts played in their work by geometry and topology. It now returns to the broader question of how these recombinant properties relate to the architectural imagination, or whether the imagination can be compositionally defined. Palladio's and Le Corbusier's work offers clues to answering these questions. Aware of the interplay between geometrical control and variable space brought about by the pinwheel scheme, Le Corbusier employed it in various public and private commissions, for different sites, programmes and cultural contexts. In *Une Maison – Un Palais*, published in 1928, he extended his ideas from the private house to the public building and to the city. For Beatrice Colomina, the use of the spiralling theme in villas and cultural projects indicates that domesticity may have been 'the real source of modernity in museums'.[71] A bourgeois house was not far away from being a treasury for a private collection. In museums and housing schemes, the houses became prototypes for a universal way of living, and the museum a prototype for the city. In effect, Le Corbusier's pinwheel plan and his translation of Venice's spatial structure into the design of the Hospital show investment over and above the functional performance of a house, a museum, a hospital or even an entire city. The persistence of the pinwheel layout beyond the specificity of site and programme in his work explains it as a generic framework for experimentation on the interplay between conceptual unity and perceptual variation. A museum of everything is in the end a museum of almost nothing, showing the modern architect's concern for abstract configurationality and universality.

If the preoccupation of modernity has been with generic properties, functions and terms, it is not a huge leap to suggest that the roots of modernity extend back into the classical villas of Palladio. While it is true that his villas satisfied particular social, economic and functional concerns, they reflect neither hierarchical social relations nor distinctions between servant and served spaces.[72] Decorated by statues and murals and hosting theatrical plays and concerts, the interconnected rooms of the Renaissance villas diffused boundaries between the house as space for private living and the house as art gallery, performance space or theatre. Influenced by Alberti, Palladio also claimed that a building is like a city.[73] His villas and churches were based on his studies of Roman baths, which suggested to him indoor miniaturised cities, theatrically framing space from the scale of the apse to the scale of the house and the landscape. Is the trans-nationality of these projects, the expansion from the room to the villa and museum, from the hospital to the city as a whole, and the fluid interpretation of functionally dissimilar programmes peculiar to Palladio, Le Corbusier and Mies, or does it suggest a framework for the imagination specific to the architecture discipline as a whole?

In a building that is like a house, a museum or a city, functional demands imposed by the site and social programme are just one filter among others. Without circumventing practical requirements, these architects had a conscious concern for crafting space and using geometric notation to establish coherence against different constraints and requirements. By interfacing generic relationships related to the empirical reality of moving and seeing as we encounter it in buildings and cities and the conscious crafting of architectural space, they operated over and above distinctions between functional types, architecture and urban contexts. The spatial networks of moving and seeing are shared between cities as multi-authored products of society and architecture as self-conscious product of design. However, these properties in architecture are consciously placed in relation to one another within a conceptual framework, using geometry to establish internal coherence. If cities (and, to a large extent, buildings) arise as collective products of micro-economic activity and reproducibility of culture, architecture is the result of conscious intentionality that recognises patterns common to all, permutes and transfers them to new structures through creative invention.

Architects may use different geometries and technologies of generation, but space, geometry and their relationship are generic properties of buildings and cities, defining the tools of architectural imagination. Yet, in contrast to proportions and geometry which were widely available through treatises and academic studies, the spatial properties of visibility and movement remained less pronounced. Unlike classical principles, which have been systematically articulated and visualised, embodied spatial relations of moving and seeing in architectural discourse have not been made thoroughly obvious; their logic has not been properly described.

In discussing ritual practices in Renaissance Venice, I explained that the activities of moving, seeing and interacting are intuitively performed rather than consciously recorded and transcribed. Spatial relationships and their capacity to stimulate the imagination lack a system through which they can become transmissible, not simply in a visual way, as geometry becomes evident through architectural drawing, but also operationally, mastering and aligning the representation of space with the distilled cognitive outcome of moving and seeing inside it.

Describing space as a configurational relational field, the analytic theory of Hillier and Hanson has in the last four decades studied space in buildings and cities in relation to human activity and function.[74] This theory explains that geometry gets into the topology of the urban network, affecting through the intersections of street lines and the angles of their incidence their spatial structure.[75] However, in spite of its extensive application in real projects, the social theory of configuration treats architecture and cities as entities that are already formed. It tends to regard them as 'found' environments, with little attention being paid to the conceptual processes which brought them about. In other words, it does not take into account how architecture is thought of and produced from without. If space has been a silent partner in architectural discourse, geometry has been a silent conductor in the theory of spatial configuration. The reason for this deficit is often explained by the fact that the relationship between design and use passes not through geometry or form but through the realm of space.[76] However, with a clear focus on how configurational ideas travel from cities to designs and vice versa, as revealed by this analysis, the picture is more complex than splitting architecture into analysis and design, aesthetic and social practice. It should be possible to explore buildings and cities as both the non-authored products of society and the authored products of design.

The examples discussed in this book help reveal a genealogy of ideas around which the concerns of architects converge and the architecture discipline is defined. Architecture concerns critical commitment to comparative architectural knowledge on the part of an empirical and historical architect, that is, a person endowed with historical consciousness (and an unconscious). Historical consciousness means understanding how architectural ideas and forms change with time, and that the fact that Palladio built before Le Corbusier, and Le Corbusier operated before Rem Koolhaas, is as significant as the exploration of their buildings. Comparative morphological knowledge and historical consciousness establish an architect's place in history in relation to the available knowledge of ideas and tools that shape the discipline up to one's present, together with the possibilities and limitations for the future one's historical position enables and withholds.

If architecture and innovation proceed from the intersection of possibility with constraint, the intersection of morphological knowledge and historical sequence brings us back to the question of the imagination. The architectural imagination transgresses functional restrictions, social programmes, and ontological and historical categories by transferring generic properties across different domains in ways which enable one to make innovations, and overcome constraints. The principles of space and geometry are not simply generic tools, but also the critical faculties in architects' work. Abstract comparative knowledge and historical consciousness can raise space and geometry from silent instruments to the level of abstract comparative thought, towards a unitary theory of generation and explanation in architecture and the architectural imagination. Developing intelligence on the ideas of space and geometry, including their history and theory, can transform contemporary architecture of non-standard variation from intuitive practice to principled understanding.

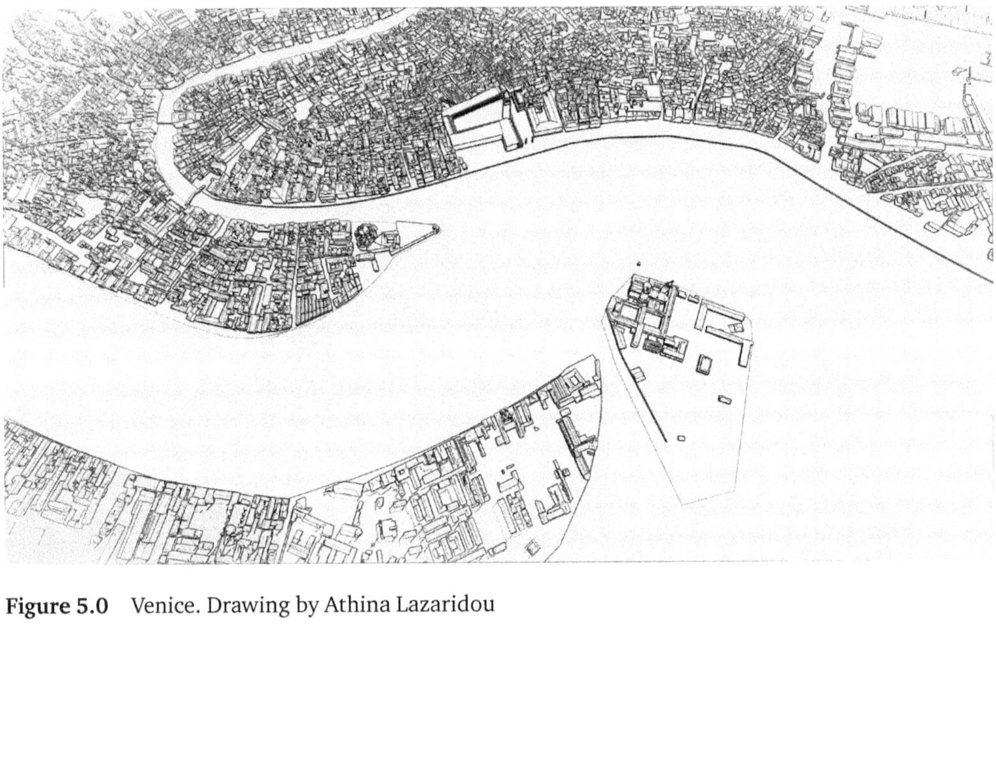

Figure 5.0 Venice. Drawing by Athina Lazaridou

5
The Venice Variations: Tracing the Architectural Imagination

> We had thought to use a universal category to authenticate a group of particulars, but the category has now been forced to cover such a heterogeneity that it is, itself, in danger of collapsing.
>
> Rosalind Krauss, 'Sculpture in the Expanded Field'

Venice outlived

For centuries Venice has been the locus of the imagination for architects, artists and writers, the living confirmation of the creativity of a society that, in the most inauspicious location, devised a city of unimaginable elegance and form. Nurturing creative inventiveness, Venice once managed to combine a collective talent for a spontaneous city-craft that could almost effortlessly adapt to unplanned improvisations with a keenly humanistic artistic intelligence that was consciously and precisely controlled. Although the driving forces behind the creativity of the floating city ebbed away centuries ago, it still represents a unique expression of human ingenuity and an enduring source of inspiration for the imagination. In exploring Venice's urban networks, I proposed that the city invites engagement as much through its audacious siting and outward appearance as through its capacity to embody in its form a memory of the processes through which it evolved over time. As Venice expanded, the requirement for a duality of access by water and over land led to a network of elements amplifying the intensity of its experience. I also suggested that certain properties inherent in Venice's urban form, such as modularity, combinability and interconnectedness, are analogically present in Calvino's *Invisible Cities* and Le Corbusier's Hospital project. In this final chapter, I return to the fundamental question posed at the outset: What is it, both in Venice and in these other works, that inspires imaginative invention?

As we progress through the twenty-first century subject to totally different forms, requirements and modes of production, are there transferable universal lessons to be learned about the architectural imagination from Venice and its relationships with these other two artefacts? Why does Venice still engage us, in spite of our historical distance from the dynamic processes that drove its cultural and economic life? How did it inspire Calvino and Le Corbusier, enabling a translation and transformation of meaning into very different media? How does Venice reveal itself to the observer so as to so insistently stimulate imaginative engagement?

The discussion addressing these questions is conducted in three parts. The first focuses on a comparative examination of Venice, Calvino's fiction and Le Corbusier's Hospital to identify how Venice is revealed to today's more or less contemporary observer, and how it was creatively interpreted through the other two artefacts. To explore these questions, I briefly revisit a key component emerging from the global analysis of Venice's layout: the urban squares and their connections with the adjoining islands. The analysis of the city revealed that the locations of maximum strength in terms of interconnectivity relations are concentrated on the squares and the associated canal-crossing points. While the earlier analysis looked at the position of the squares in relation to the entire urban landscape, this section explores how the city reveals itself to the pedestrian immersed in Venice from these specific points of intense spatial and functional interaction. This examination can establish the link between the conceptual logic of the city as a whole and the perceptual realm of situated movement, thus explaining the interplay between global spatial cognition, embodied human perception and the material structure of the city itself.

The second part of the chapter opens up a theoretical discussion about the origin of architectural ideas, using the example of Venice and the two artefacts to investigate a crucial question: where do design ideas come from – the built world or the individual imagination? This question is addressed in the context of some conceptual categories that have influenced thinking about authored objects and authorless cities, such as built environments and possible worlds, imaginary and actualised projects. By exploring the association between ideas and places, this discussion reveals an age-old binary relationship between the designer and their environment.

The third and final part suggests a possible resolution in terms of how to think of architecture and cities as engendering possible and actual worlds in an expanded interactive field, bringing them closer to the creative imagination.

The three artefacts

Venice

> I had plunged into a network of little alleys or *calli*... Packed tightly together, these *calli* divided in all directions with their furrows a small chunk of Venice carved out between a canal and the lagoon, as if it had crystallised in accordance with these innumerable tenuous and minute patterns. Suddenly at the end of one of the alleys, it seemed as though a distention had occurred in the crystallized matter. A vast and splendid *campo*, of which in this network of little streets, I should certainly never have guessed the scale, or even found room for it, spread out before me surrounded with charming palaces silvery in the moonlight. It was one of those architectural ensembles towards which, in any other town, the streets converge, lead you and point the way. Here it seemed to be deliberately concealed in an interlacement of alleys...
>
> Marcel Proust, *In Search of Lost Time*

As he explored how time affects memory, Marcel Proust engaged with the intersection between reality and recollection in each present moment. Memory for him was about elaborate fabrications, things that were ceaselessly changing, like his writing process, always being refined in the light of new knowledge. In his *Sojourn in Venice* he expressed this process through the discovery of a square he was led to through a series of alleys. This accidental encounter with the square triggered his imagination like the taste of the madeleine that set off the unfolding chain of associations at the start of the first novel.[1] What in Venice engenders this process of discovery, through which the city with its structure and its history, perception and imagination are continuously formed and re-formed?

Whether newly arrived in Venice or acquainted with the city from previous excursions, the visitor often has to rely on a map, at least for a part of the journey, to wend their way through the filigree of paths, canals and interlocking islands. Seeking from the multiplicity of possible routes a course to a specific destination, the eye relies on a synoptic view of the city as a whole before moving to topographical particulars, scanning the surface, moving from place to place. From close to, one encounters the interplay of three main constituents that combine in forming the topography of the city fabric: blocks, streets and islands.[2] Yet, to mentally draw a path on the map of Venice by scanning its fabric is an impossible task, often resulting in arriving at a private courtyard, a dead-end alley, the water's edge or a bridge leading to a private house. This is because the city challenges the typical pattern of a continuous pedestrian surface around blocks separated from vehicular traffic found in conventional urban environments.

Pathways in Venice traverse alleys, circumnavigate blocks, cross bridges and in a few cases trace the outline of islands. Venetian toponymy reflects the complexity and diversity of the urban tissue, often capturing its evolutionary logic: the *fondamenta* is a quayside, a strip of land between houses and canals; the *salizada* is an alley paved with cobblestones; the *calle* a lane, and the *ruga* and *rughetta* streets lined with shops; the *strada* is a wide street (like Strada Nova in Cannaregio); the *riva* is a promenade on the waterside, fronting an expanse of water (Riva dei Schiavoni in the Bacino); the *rio terrà* is a filled-in canal and the *piscina* a former pond. There are also pathway elements called *sottoportego* (a portico passing under houses) and *ramo* (a small branch). In addition to the *campi*, there are inner, more secluded, courtyards called *corte*, and there are of course the *Piazza*, the *Piazzetta* and the *Piazzalle.*[3]

These diverse elements are fused into a network penetrating some 123 islands and interspersed with waterways. The pathways and canals not only comprise a uniquely diverse urban geography, as the extensive list of street names reveals, but also form a complex topology. Venice appears different to the waterborne passenger than to the pedestrian. It is possible to navigate among the islands on water, which gives access to many large buildings and palaces. In contrast with Amsterdam's leafy canal banks, only two of Venice's islands have a walkable perimeter. Some islands lack any quaysides at all, while a large number of islands possess only intermittent quays on short stretches of their external façades. Finally, a few islands have quays extending the full length of one, two or three sides. Surrounded by canals, islands in Venice are discrete entities but are rarely recognisable as such by the pedestrian.

This complex topology means that canals and streets are knitted together so that walking routes seamlessly weave between islands and within islands, creating ambiguity and a multiplicity of borders. With time, and aided by a map, one might eventually realise that there are one or more squares on each island. Squares are located at the intersection between a canal and one or two primary *calli*, bisecting the island from one side to the other in two or more directions. They often appear suddenly, without warning or intimation; alternatively, the pedestrian discovers that a square manifesting its presence from a distance at the far end of a dark alley is on the other side of a waterway. Yet, as noted in Chapter 1, squares are pervasively connected through primary pathways into a network (the foreground, consisting of elements that have the highest values of betweenness centrality or choice) linking multiple islands. Pedestrians in Venice traverse squares joined like beads on a string as they unknowingly pass from island to island (Figure 1.14). The complexity of the city notwithstanding, mediating between water and land, local neighbourhoods and the city as a whole, the squares become significant aids to orientation and pedestrian navigation.

Furthermore, as seen in Chapter 4, squares are situated at the edges of islands, with one or more sides opening to a canal. They thus act as key connectors in the entire urban landscape as well as linking islands. If the urban structure as a whole captures the patterns of relations of all squares to all others, focusing on the local-scale connections among islands can explain the way the observer encounters transitions from island to island. Moreover, examining the role squares play in these transitions can reveal the link between Venice as an entire morphological construct and the perceptual field available to the viewer who moves through the city serially, encountering these elements in a sequence over time.

Starting with the patterns of local connections, we look for notional city blocks, as the smallest area forming a circuit and constructing linkages between neighbouring islands. There are six taxonomies of such notional blocks or island connectors (Figure 5.1a–f): a. *Two-block connectors*. These are paths adjacent to the sides of blocks each facing the interior of a different island (Figure 5.1a); b. *Block-quay connectors*, which border the interior side of a block on one island and run along a quay on the other or a square bordering the canal (Figure 5.1b); c. *Two-quay connectors*, which run parallel to two quaysides facing each other so that a walk covers the opposite banks of a canal (Figure 5.1c); d. *Extended block-quay connectors*, paths that stretch from the quayside of one island to the opposite quayside of another (Figure 5.1d); e. *Extended two-quay connectors*, which link two external quaysides (Figure 5.1e); f. *Hybrid connectors*, frequently joining several islands (Figure 5.1f).[4] If

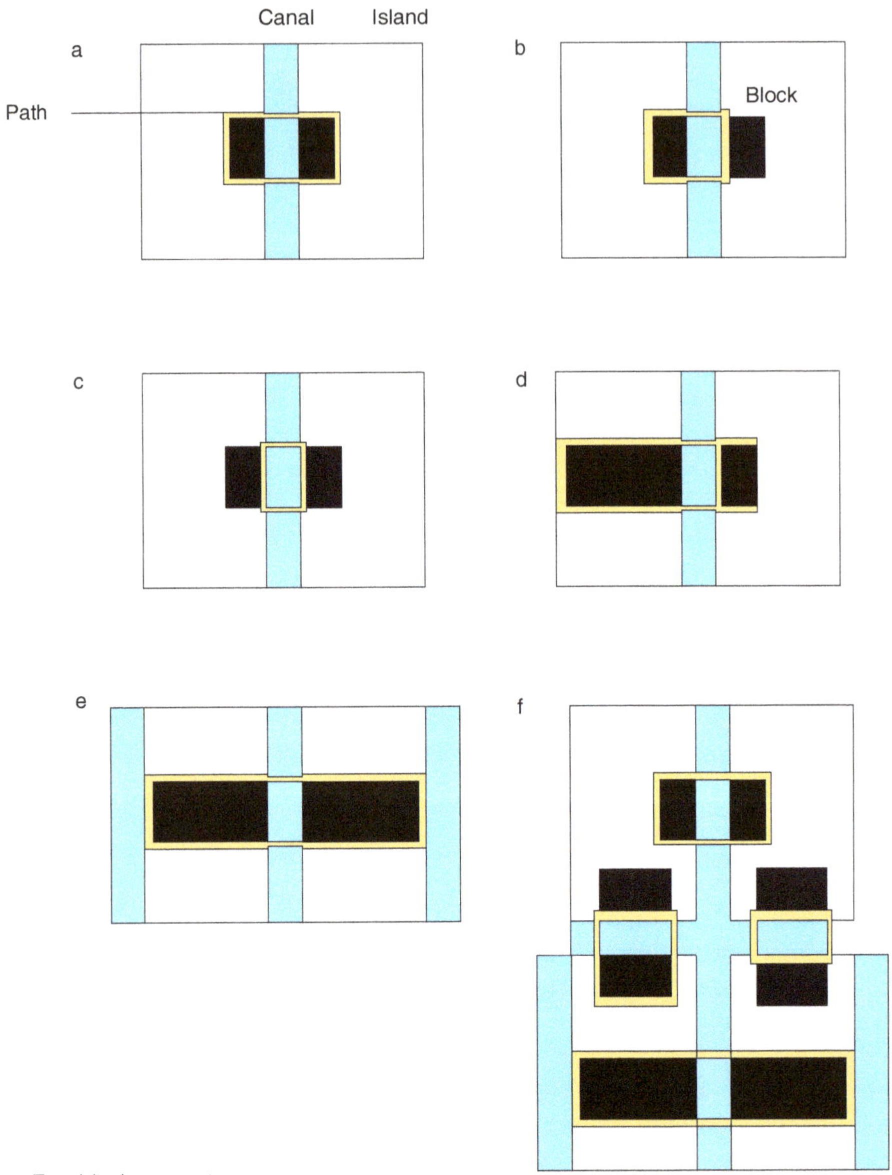

a. Two-block connector
b. Block-quay connector
c. Two-quay connector
d. Extended block-quay connector
e. Extended two-quay connector
f. A set of different path connectors linking adjoining islands.

Figure 5.1 Taxonomy of path connectors linking islands. Drawings by the author

in general cities have a generic topology of walkable space that is physically, topologically and typologically homogeneous (blocks, streets), Venice consists of overlapping topologies (canals, alleys, blocks) which are heterogeneously defined.

This classification of path connectors (Figure 5.1) uses dimensionless elements encompassing all types of connections. Looking at how squares relate to these connectors, we focus on some actual examples. Figure 5.2a–h zooms in on squares selected from those having a strong value of choice in the combined network of streets and canals in Figure 1.15c. Campo San Fantin (5.2a) and Campo San Polo (5.2b) are each joined to their respective opposite island through a two-block connector. Being a waterfront square, Campo San Toma (5.2c) is connected to a neighbouring island through a block-quay connector. While Figures 5.2a–b are examples of single squares, there are cases where more than one squares found on adjoining islands are linked together in sequence. Examples are Campo San Stin and Campo San Agostin (5.2d), joined by a block-quay connector. A more complex arrangement is seen in Campo Santa Maria Nova, Campo dei Miracoli and Campiello dei Miracoli (5.2e). These squares are linked in sequence by two two-quay connectors. Campo Santa Maria Zobenigo, Campiello dei Callengeri and Campo della Feltrina (5.2f) form a series of squares on three neighbouring islands joined by hybrid block-quay and two-quay connectors. Campo San Giacomo dall' Orio, Campo Nazario Sauro and Campo dei Tedeschi are located on two neighbouring islands joined by two-block connectors (5.2g). Finally, Campo San Barnava (5.2h) has two block-quay connectors, each linking to an island on the opposite side of the square.

It is no exaggeration to suggest that one might feel overwhelmed by the sheer variety of paths, squares, buildings and forms multiplying and diversifying perceptions in all directions. Winding between squares, quays and alleys and crossing canals, paths in Venice are variably defined by the back side of a block on one island, the front side of a different block and a canal on another island; or two front sides and a canal; two back sides and no canal, and so on. To this variable perceptual field of routes across islands, we should add variations in length and width of paths and squares, light, shade and sound, all richly communicated by the wide-ranging vocabulary of squares and pathways.

Yet, by virtue of their being integral parts of the global structure and path connectors stitching islands together, squares feature strongly in the perceptual field as people negotiate routes between islands. They can thus be recognised as both local- and global-scale connectors. They are irregular in form, variable in terms of shape, size and orientation, and heterogeneous in terms of the topology of elements joining them

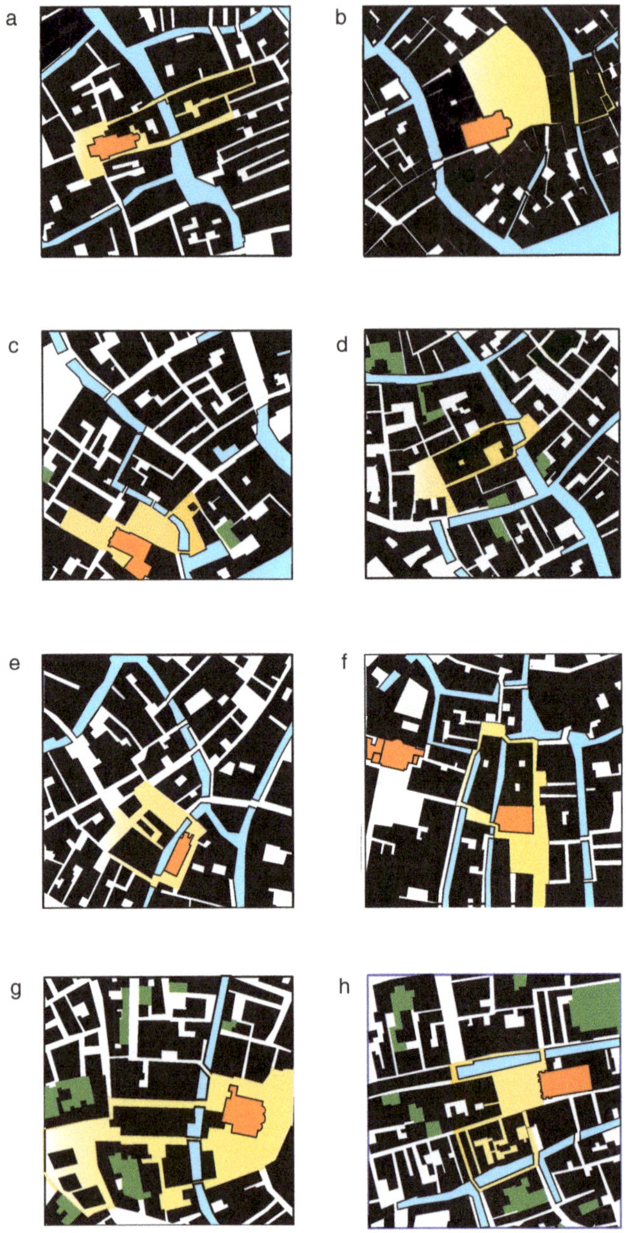

Figure 5.2 Examples of squares linked by different types of path connectors. Drawings by the author
(a) Campo San Fantin (b) Campo San Polo (c) Campo San Toma (d) Campo San Stin and Campo San Agostin (e) Campo Santa Maria Nova, Campo dei Miracoli and Campiello dei Miracoli (f) Campo Santa Maria Zobenigo, Campiello dei Callengeri and Campo della Feltrina (g) Campo San Giacomo dall' Orio, Campo Nazario Sauro and Campo dei Tedeschi (h) Campo San Barnava

Figure 5.3 Campo San Giacomo dall' Orio. Photo by the author

with the surrounding areas. They also form little communities in their own right. They penetrate the dense urban mass, scooping out a volumetric void next to a waterway. They are adorned by a church front and a tower, one or more wellheads centrally located in the square, one or two bridges on either side arching over the canal, and one or two flights of steps establishing the essential communication with the water. Scattered among these landmarks, lesser, more mundane, activities flourish: cafés, restaurants, shops, newsagents and benches for gossiping locals, children playing, tourists resting on the carved steps of the wellheads, and boats unloading building materials, delivering supplies or collecting garbage (Figure 5.3). From the impressively ceremonial space of the Piazza San Marco to the quietest square in Venice, this choreography of human activities, routines and element-types repeats itself throughout the lagoon city.

Punctuating the intersections of alleys and canals and establishing global-scale connections, the squares of Venice act as crossroads offering alternative ways of moving through the dense urban fabric. They provide rich spatial information and varying perceptual stimulation, as, moving from the inner side of a block, one crosses a *campo* opening to a canal before launching into the interior of another island and encountering another *campo*. Squares are also centres of sensual stimulation, contrasting the dark inner alleys with their bright waterfront space where boats slice through water lapping the walls of a palace, church bells chime, passers-by pause to peer over the parapet of the bridge and the sound of steps rebounds on the *campo*'s hard surface. They awaken a multiplicity of sensations and awaken associations, related to congregations, offerings, time cycles, histories, chronicles, festivals, sadnesses, celebrations and records.

More importantly, the squares are the points where the intersection of the canals and streets meets the same ensemble of immediately recognisable element-types (church-tower-wellhead-palace-canal-bridge-steps-alleys-quays) all linked into a continuous pathway lacing together adjacent islands. Working as spatial, sensual and semantic crossroads and consistently defined through a repeated coalescence of activities, types and forms, the *campi* perceptually register as a stock of *periodic composite structures*. In the *Art of Memory* Frances Yates explains that ancient orators would aid their memory by visualising a path through a particular space, such as a palace, relating parts of their speech to spatial features and stringing them together in sequence.[5] Venice's squares act like 'memory palaces', recited vocabularies of phrases, a stylised language of repeated beats like units of rhythmic sound. Marking the intersections of the canal and pedestrian networks, they are strategic, at the level of both the global and the local structure. On the other hand, due to restricted vistas, heterogeneous and proliferating connections with other squares and islands, they can be approached from different directions. The memory of how a specific *campo* can be reached again is thus always altering, poised between poles of orientation and disorientation.

The architectural heritage of Venice is primarily the result of pre-industrial craftsmanship, where urban types, built forms and their relationships were the outcome of rehearsed practices of building and making. These practices constituted the collective competence of craftsmen using proven inherited methods and 'designs', collectively producing, and transmitting, the form of the city over time. Unlike standardised industrial processes of production, hand-making practices have a limited range of inputs in terms of rules, but engender a large family of outputs, each form being different from the next, yet similar, as the 'genotype' is shared. The genotype of a *campo*, for example, specifies the same characteristics in terms of spatial networks and the same composite structures, but the results vary in outward appearance. Equally, the genotype of connecting pathways varies from island to island according to local context. Joined in non-identical but repetitive visual formations, canals, streets, buildings and open spaces in Venice provide variations on themes composed from a large range of observed types continually engaging and surprising observers. The Venetian builders did not primarily create their language in an effort to produce an effect; rather they were interested in meeting practical needs. But the resulting schematisation of space, paths and built forms, in all their subtle variations, reveals qualities of artistic creativity, arching over several centuries of collective effort.

Invisible Cities and the Venice Hospital

Calvino's *Invisible Cities* consists of city descriptions, in the form of discrete units linked into a network. The descriptions present cities as variable entities, each one having a different visual texture and appearance from the others. Cities are grouped into five classes based on numbers (from 5 to 1), eleven thematic rubrics ('Cities and Memory', 'Cities and

Desire' and so on) and nine chapters. However, individual cities are not limited to membership of a single category; for example, *Diomira* is part of the class of cities numbered 1, the thematic rubric 'Cities and Memory' and the first chapter. Furthermore, the thematic rubrics are interspersed among different chapters. 'Cities and Memory' for instance, is found in chapters 1 and 2, while 'Cities and Eyes' belongs to chapters 3–7. In addition to this pattern of overlapping memberships, thematic rubrics and city descriptions enter into multiple relations by virtue of containing conceptual symmetries, repeated elements, opposites or doubles. Enmeshed in thematic interconnections, the city descriptions evoke conceptual relationships, expressing variations of the four symmetry transformations in a tessellation. They thus activate cognitive operations in a lattice-like configuration, helping readers visualise the structure of the book as network.

By utilising discrete elements and the overlapping membership of elements among different classes, Calvino creates a large set of variable outputs, which, while not explicitly present, are indirectly embedded as possibilities in the system. The plotting of symmetry transformations on a diamond figure captures the construction of the text as a 'digital' algorithm, integrating combinatorial possibility with conscious intention (Figure 3.6). Readers of *Invisible Cities* can grasp the effect of preconceiving the overall structure of the work – available as geometric and numeric notation through the table of contents – but realising an enormous potential in the process of reading that guides and trains their imaginative processes.

Being mindful of limitations in analogic resemblance, we can suggest that, like the two networks in Venice (water and land), the 18 italic sections in *Invisible Cities* that form the dialogues between Polo and the Khan frame the narrative interspersed between chapters. At the numerical centre of the text – between chapters 5 and 6 – Polo describes a bridge stone by stone. This dialogue, and the one on Venice that follows, allude to Venice's islands, linked by bridges. If the reader encounters cities through immersive reading, as the pedestrian experiences Venice's islands, the interstitial material of the dialogues equates to Venice's canals. It thus provides a foreground network of discourse, framing Polo's descriptions of cities as expressions of human experience. I noted earlier that through these dialogues Calvino articulates the interaction between *emporium* and *imperium*, expressing Venice's dual personality as both maritime emporium and naval empire; a point at which the respective tenets of multiplicity (Polo) and intelligibility (Kublai) are finally expressed. Calvino's proposition is that, although the descriptions of cities have their own independent existence, the dialogues illuminate them. Discourse and language are thus integral parts of the ways cities and architecture are experienced and comprehended.

The city descriptions can be seen as the 'narrative blocks', the stones of Venice, which by virtue of overlapping memberships establish multiple connections with other city descriptions across the chapters. In the same way that the squares of Venice comprise recurring urban-types and pathway-types, Calvino's narrative consists of 'multiform treasures' (domes, stairs, springs, water clocks, precious metals) repeating across cities and chapters, and intermeshing connections (chapters, rubrics and numbers). When the reading path reaches Calvino's cities, it encounters multiple intersecting registers, numerical, conceptual, topological, semantic, sensual and imaginative. Calvino translated the conceptual logic of Venice based on a syntax of topological dualities (canals/streets – chapters/dialogues) that overlap at crossroads (squares – city descriptions) into a work of literature, allowing alternative reading pathways and multiple combinations.

The Venice Hospital also comprises two intersecting structures: voids and walkable surface. I noted in Chapter 4 that Le Corbusier severed the close association between the networks of moving and viewing in classical architecture, creating an effect similar to the interaction between Venice's pathways and the canals circumscribing the islands. This topological duality generates variable heterogeneous paths located either inside the care units or outside these units or both, like the connecting pathways joining Venice's islands (Figures 5.1 and 5.4). What this topological duality means is that by virtue of adjacency relations, paths in the Hospital straddle three different categories of elements: voids (canals), solids (blocks) and square-shaped areas (*campi*). In addition, the networks comprising patients' cells, square areas and pathways form the pinwheel scheme, a repeating standard configuration, like Venice's recurring composite structures. The project seems to have the potential to generate a series of variable forms derived from the same local rules that govern its morphogenetic structure, something confirmed by the different design versions produced by Le Corbusier and Guillermo Jullian de la Fuente.[6]

The three artefacts follow a similar generative logic based on dual networks, composite structures, overlapping memberships of elements in two or more classes and heterogeneous types of connections. Calvino and Le Corbusier extrapolated the conceptual structure of Venice and creatively transposed it into a different medium and new construction. What they grasped was not simply the abstract logic of networks

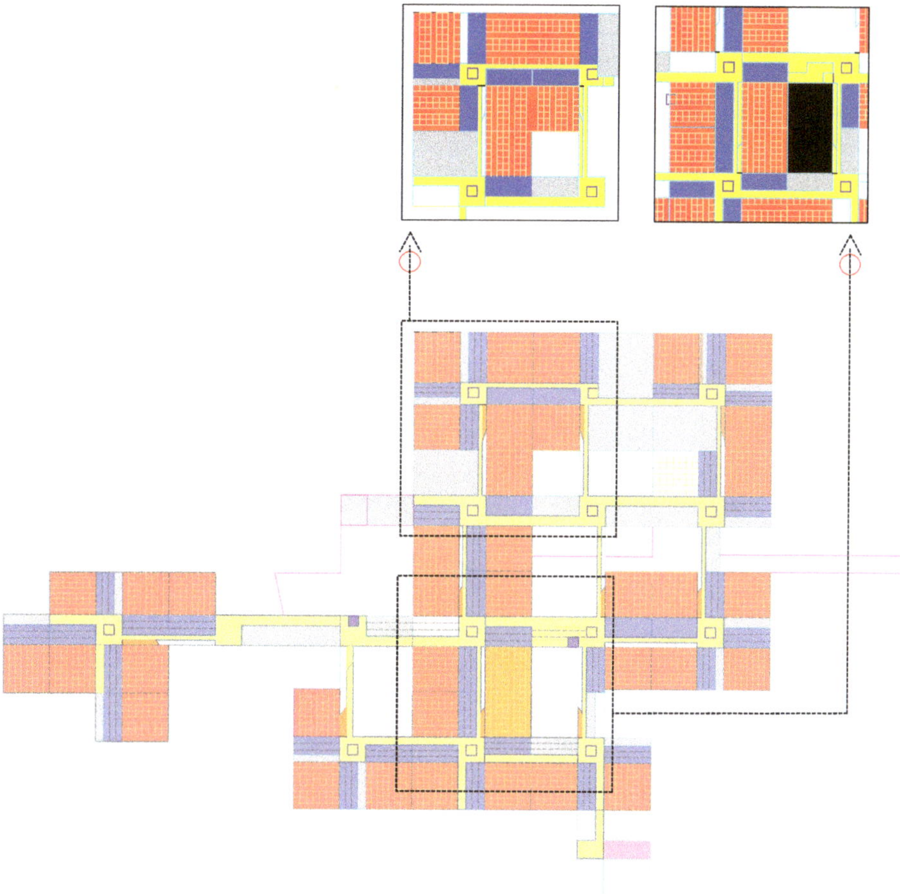

Figure 5.4 Le Corbusier. Venice Hospital. Examples of different path connectors. Drawing by the author

and these properties inherent in the lagoon city, but also an algorithmic generative model, activating potential motion towards new, unforeseen configurations. Yet, we should acknowledge that the comparison of these works has limitations, as one is a work of literature and the others an instance of architecture and a city, respectively. If Venice is the outcome of collective human intelligence, *Invisible Cities* and Le Corbusier's project are products of intentional, conscious activity by their authors.

Invisible Cities and the Hospital do not contain an intrinsic preconceived idea of the whole. This, however, does not mean that the whole is 'mindlessly' produced by the additive logic of local rules governing the joining of elements. Le Corbusier and Calvino conceive the morphogenetic rules of the work in such a way that the work is not fixed or static but open, encompassing a great deal of generative potential. The aim is not to create formal unity but a system of unanticipated generation. The analogies between the three artefacts bring into sharper focus aspects of each that might not be directly perceived if they were examined individually. However, the differences among them are also important, showing that design translation is not a replication of the original but a creative interpretation.[7]

Hillier and Hanson specify the rules governing the morphogenesis of real-world settlements, named 'beady rings', and compare them to computer-generated systems.[8] They explain that beady ring environments have a short description ('short models' or 'p-models'). Short descriptions comprise a few elements and relationships capable of producing a long list of phenotypical outputs. In contrast, long descriptions ('long models' or 'g-models') embody numerous relations, specifying the position of each element in relation to every other in the system. Short models are aggregative configurations, 'mindless' of overall shape and form. Long models, instead, have a strong figurative nature, as their rules tend to preserve the dominance of few elements, manifested through the visual effect of shape, figure or contour. Long models apply rules hierarchically, adding extra-semantic information to a configuration corresponding to conceptual, social or ideological superstructures. If short and long models are two extremes in a spectrum of forms, the Hospital and Calvino's fiction are situated midway between the two models. They combine the logic of self-generation with an overall framework, embedding bottom-up possibilities within the limits of a total structure. As for Venice, it is a clear case of an emergent logic found in short models, where rules satisfying local scale conditions produce over time variable local-scale configurations as well as global-scale effects.

Inspired by Venice, Calvino and Le Corbusier used the invisible structure of a city, a medium not conventionally considered as having similarities to literature or architecture. Venice for them was an abstract space providing abundant opportunity for heterogeneous categories – architecture, cities and literature – to be distilled into their essential characteristics; associated and translated into one another. Relying on these three artefacts, I discuss next how we can define the architectural imagination as a theoretical space, diversifying architectural knowledge; how to describe architecture, the city, and their relationship through multiple intersecting systems of authorships; finally, how to think of artefacts as having a real-world presence, such as Venice, and hypothetical projects, such as the Hospital, or even novels that can be appreciated only conceptually.

These questions impinge on the key issue as to where architectural ideas originate. What is the source of architectural form? Is form something that is generated in the imagination of the architect or is it embedded somewhere in the physical word? Is the generation of form a matter for the creative practitioner whose intellectual activity gives architectural products the status of authored objects, or is it the collective outcome of cultural processes and empirical contexts? Before exploring these questions, it is essential to discuss contemporary design discourse in relation to the ways it approaches the question of architectural form and its sources.

Objects and fields

In 1979 the art theorist and critic Rosalind Krauss wrote a seminal text entitled 'Sculpture in the Expanded Field'.[9] Published in *October*, the article was an attempt to interpret artistic practices, such as the work of Robert Irwin, Richard Serra, Richard Long and Donald Judd, that seemed to defy conventional categories. These artists, she claimed, expanded sculpture to being one among other structured possibilities available at the time, transcending differences between sculpture, architecture and landscape. Strongly reminiscent of Krauss's arguments and terms, Stan Allen's essay 'From Object to Field' promoted the conceptual, formal and material qualities found in aggregate configurations, which he named 'field conditions'.[10] In discussing phenomena ranging from flocks of birds to minimalist art, including a small number of building examples such as Le Corbusier's Venice Hospital, Allen juxtaposed field conditions with object-oriented hierarchical compositions.[11] Allen's essay was largely a response to contemporary design practices, which, since the nineties, have been reconfiguring the disciplinary boundaries between landscape, urbanism and architecture.[12]

I noted earlier that Le Corbusier's Hospital featured in Alison Smithson's essay on Mat-building.[13] Prompted by sources as diverse as Krauss, Smithson and Koolhaas, Allen also used the Hospital as a key reference point in his essay entitled 'Mat-urbanism', re-theorising the distinction between cities and buildings.[14] By bringing infrastructural concepts to design, such approaches have been expanding over the last two decades under the influence of complexity science and computer technology.[15] Metaphorically referencing the natural forces of form generation, these paradigms argue for the formless configurations that Corbusier's un-built project came to epitomise. From Smithson's concept of Mat-typology to Allen's idea of field conditions, the Hospital has been categorized as a design that is unmediated by material sensory engagement and geometrical figural composition.[16] Using the distinction between the long and short models discussed earlier, we can understand how these contemporary practices exhibit a clear preference for the generative logic of short models, often valorising their entrenched opposition to the figurative compositions resulting from long models.

These approaches to design were greatly influenced by Koolhaas's entry for the Parc de la Villette competition (1982–1983), which sought to avoid a definitive architectural-landscape proposition, proposing instead a project that works as an instrument for unintended results.[17] Thus the approach to architecture which emphasised the permanence of built forms and their cultural signification in the seventies has been superseded by design models that place primary importance on process rather than form, as a mode of evolutionary adaptation. This shift from the dominance of geometry to emergent patterns generated by local rules marks a turn away from the traditional idea of composition as the intellectual organisation of parts into a whole, to instrumentality, user activity, collective behaviour, interactive environments and the long-life performance of buildings and cities. It defines an instrumental turn, the foundations of which are implicit in Koolhaas's ideas of 'irrigating a site with potential', a design logic described by Jacques Lucan as 'architecture-through-process'.[18]

If these paradigms replace static configurations with process-based operations, a different wave of reactions emerges to question the Modernist approach to buildings and urban plans as authored products.[19] Prominent among the critics of Modernism, Jane Jacobs was the first to argue that, with their obsession with iconic buildings and mega-scale projects, architects and modern planners had failed to engage with the process of gentrification, the efforts of local communities to survive, the need for social diversity and the concept of the city as a dynamic field of interrelated forces.[20] Since then, increased pressures to respond to environmental demands and the advent of digital technology have undermined and enervated long-held positions about architecture and its role in society. The technological innovations that have emerged since the nineties have contributed to this deconstruction. In the late twentieth century we witnessed the decline of the mechanically produced drawing as the locus of information in design and its supplanting by digital models of communication, enabling the ubiquitous transmission of heterogeneous kinds of information. These digital technologies integrate makers and users into networks of co-production, termed 'bottom-up architecture'.[21] This is claimed to be an architecture not imposed on society by a group of experts, but rather emerging from multiple centres of enterprise.

In parallel with this conceptual sea change, a fundamental transformation in how designs are developed within a computational environment has brought the notion of emergence into the design process. Algorithmic geometries create evolutionary designs and generate forms of sophisticated complexity and variation.[22] In evolutionary design, architectural concepts are expressed as generative rules, and the rules are described in genetic language. Computer models are used to develop prototypical forms, which are then evaluated on the basis of their performance in a simulated environment: 'Very large numbers of evolutionary steps can be generated in a short space of time and the emergent forms are often unexpected'.[23] Since the design product is the result of an algorithm, if inputs into the algorithm are changed, the result is updated accordingly. As opposed to the traditional model of composition, presupposing knowledge of the design outcome based on parts–whole relationships, evolutionary design is bottom-up, 'clear in its intentions but "blind" to the eventual outcome of the design process'.[24] Overcoming the limitations of orthographic projection that had constrained and conditioned architecture since the Renaissance, architects have, theoretically at least, overcome the finality of the design object. With the exception of a small inventory of examples, never before has architectural imagination been freer to produce a theoretically unlimited range of forms and formal variations.[25]

A different kind of recognition of architecture which is collectively produced was evident in Koolhaas's Biennale in 2014 (*The Elements*), shifting away from the idea of authored buildings to a systemic view of market forces and technological transformations.[26] These forces 'mindlessly' operate beyond preconceived architectural intention. This view has been a hallmark of Koolhaas's approach ever since his book *Delirious New York*, where he interpreted Manhattan as a self-organising field maximising programmatic potential (Figure 5.5).[27] Yet, while *Delirious New York* celebrated the un-authored creativity of the city, *The Elements* in the Biennale focused on market-based generators of buildings and their morphology, bringing about an absolute loss of context. Koolhaas's proposition refashions architecture as an assemblage of elements. Such assemblages are evolutionary and 'blind' to the eventual outcome of design. In contrast, the model of design that has defined the profession since the Renaissance is strongly 'mindful', and in opposition to evolutionary process. Inspired by *Delirious New York*, Carol Willis termed the

Figure 5.5 Rem Koolhaas. *The City of the Captive Globe*. Image courtesy of the Office for Metropolitan Architecture (OMA)

skyscraper architecture of Manhattan 'capitalist vernacular'.[28] This characterisation might suggest describing Venice as 'mercantile vernacular', based on an early modern model of capitalism distributed across many centres and involving relatively small scales of action.

In its privileging of formal uncertainty, this approach to design, albeit facilitated by recent technological innovations, originally developed in the post-war period through proliferating experiments involving user empowerment, participation, interactivity, flexibility and adaptability as the main contributions of the architect. From Cedric Price's notion of the architect as provocateur in *Fun Palace*, produced in collaboration with the theatre director Joan Littlewood, to Bernard Rudofsky's romantic vision of 'non-pedigree architecture' (e.g. the pre-industrial vernacular), Christopher Alexander's *Notes on the Synthesis of Form* and *The Timeless Way of Building* and Smithson's notion of Mat-building typology, architects and theorists have been working to reconcile the idea of authorless architecture, existing for thousands of years, as a viable means to design with the idea of conscious architectural intention.[29]

If old ideas are resurfacing in the form of fresh provocations, the things that have really changed since the sixties are the social, economic, environmental and technological factors, affecting agency in architecture. The design paradigms originally developed five decades ago and those appearing in recent years are both attempts to radically transform the design thinking architects have inherited from the pre-industrial and industrial mechanical past, which no longer seems meaningful in a context of social restructuring, rapidly changing technologies and economies of production. Yet, as Koolhaas's Biennale has warned, in the absence of theories and tools, architecture becomes a practice without a theory, bereft of any capacity for critically influencing the decisions shaping social life. This is one example of how theoretical ideas seem to persist: on the one hand, there is a universe of spaces and forms without preconceived figurative order, contingent on algorithms and malleable through the participation of interactive users; on the other, there is an architecture of formal order and values. The former emerges over time, responding to an evolving set of parameters and functions. The latter is formed in the mind, shaping the environment from the inside out. One side in the debate sees design as falling within the influence of larger socio-economic or technological forces in an open-ended state of becoming. The opposition considers design to derive from its own unchanging autonomous operations. Since Vitruvius, the contrast between *contingent* and *autonomous* architecture has permeated practice and discourse alike, disguising the essential question of architectural form and its sources.

An age-old question

The discussion of the autonomous and the contingent problem falls into the category of existing binary philosophical problems. As Hillier explains,

> it is no surprise that philosophers have been fascinated by architecture, since architecture is an actual-world application of philosophy. But if architecture had an overarching theory that addresses these binaries it would be as though it had solved all problems in philosophy at once.[30]

It is suggested that the aim in architecture is to see them not as formulas or problems to be solved, but as research questions, opening up possibilities, whether we are in a theoretical or a design mode. The question of the autonomous object and contingent context took an intensified form in the Renaissance with the flowering of architecture as a liberal art, clearly demarcated from artisanal building traditions. Are architectural knowledge and authorship found outside conscious architecture or are they actively invented from within? This question translates to: What is the source of the architect's design ideas? What is the origin of the architect's knowledge? How does authorship work? I will explore these questions by looking at the logical paradoxes inherent in them. Using the three artefacts, I will discuss the logical structure of conscious architecture, as opposed to architecture untainted by conscious design intentions (characterised as 'found'). I will also address artefacts that are factual, part of our empirical world of experience, and those that are virtual, constructs that exist only virtually through unrealised designs, works of literature, art or the collective imagination.

If we support the autonomous object, we accept that ideas originate within the architect's mind and operations internal to design practice and discipline. If, on the other hand, we believe that architecture is solely contingent on external factors, such as socio-economic conditions, evolution, historical influences, socio-technical innovation or even chance, then it remains impervious to the discipline or designer. None of these positions alone seems sufficient to provide a convincing account of the source of architectural ideas. Mark Gelernter has asserted that 'if a theory can explain the role of the creative author in the generation of form, then it cannot explain how individuals seem to fall under the coercive influence of a prevailing style or a predominant ideology'.[31] Equally, if a theory accounts 'for how architects attend the idiosyncrasies of context, it does not explain why they often generate versions of familiar forms throughout history for many different functions and contexts'.[32] We can, of course, 'pick and choose', using one side or the other, or components from both arguments concerning the autonomous and the contingent object, but how can we avoid finding ourselves trapped in a narrow conception of design, particularly when the complexities of architecture demand rich rather than impoverished positions?

Gelernter argues that such problems originate in our philosophical heritage, and arise from a conceptual paradox deeply embedded in the Western system of knowledge. Known to philosophers as the 'subject–object' problem or the 'body–mind' problem, this dualism is responsible for similar confusions in many other fields, including psychology and the philosophy of science. The paradox has its origins in the innovations of the ancient Greeks, who devised a cosmological system to explain the workings of the universe that later evolved into a theory of how knowledge is possible, or, in other words, an epistemological system. This system suffered from a *dualistic* conception of the individual, allowing two simultaneous but mutually exclusive interpretations: on the one hand, the individual is a physical object in nature whose actions and behaviour are completely determined, as with all other physical objects, by universal laws. On the other hand, the individual is considered as a creative subject, acting and behaving from their own personal desires and motivations, free from external influence. For Gelernter, designers identify themselves with the creative side of this equation, epistemologists with the opposite. The underlying ambiguity of the subject–object problem has allowed the two sides to meld together in the Western production of knowledge, producing theories of creation resembling theories of knowledge, and vice versa.[33]

Authored and authorless

Having discussed the autonomous–contingent problem and how it ties in with theories of design and theories of knowledge, I now move to the humanistic idea of modern authorship that marked the beginning of modernity in the Renaissance. This idea introduces into architecture additional oppositions: first, the superior status of architectural design to that of building-craft and city-craft and, more generally, to inherited, collective, non-authored and tacit systems of spatial production; second, the superior status of the design original to that of variations, to which the original might otherwise be subjected. With Alberti, the design of the building became the original, and the building its identical copy.[34] Design might have a fluid state but for Alberti, when revisions stop, they should stop for good and forever. Yet, the Albertian model has deeper and wider repercussions than this. It confers the superior status of architectural design on buildings and cities as found, because they are mosaics of accidents, adaptations, adjustments, additions, subtractions, revisions and other errors, most significantly by lacking an identifiable author.

But we know, even if we do not know why or how, that architecture and found architectures, such as buildings, building assemblages, urban, sub-urban, peri-urban, landscape or infrastructural contexts, are not entirely separate from each other. In Hillier's view,

> we are bound up by the clear logic of various designs, but we also depend on exactly the absence of this. We delight in architecture produced by minds, but also in architectures, which are not produced by the ordering capacities of human minds, but emerge from the accumulation of unrelated acts of building spread over years.[35]

With the binaries of Koolhaas's Biennale in mind, the problem of designed and emergent architectures entails the danger of another duality. Koolhaas's exhibition drew attention to the gap between buildings that are architecturally conceived and those where authorship is diffused over multiple points of production. From planning codes and infrastructures to the absence of planning regulations in rapid urbanisation, there is a growing gap between the artistic aspirations of architects and the systemic operation of architecture as it happens on the ground. In the seventies, Tafuri claimed that capitalism had stripped architecture of its ideological purpose.[36] Today the schism between architecture, land values and profit has turned architecture into 'form without utopia'.[37] But if architecture is to have social agency, we need to address social significance in both authored buildings and authorless cities and architecture. To this purpose, we need to better understand the difficulties entailed in the gap between authored and authorless as two separate types of production.

Actual and virtual

The autonomous–contingent question is also the source of the gap between the imaginative processes of the designer, generally considered as products of the mind, and the built products of design that only by virtue of being realised belong to the physical environment. There is a similar division between design and the analytic processes of the architectural researcher. The idea of architecture as authored autonomous object concerns the imaginative processes of inventing. In contrast, the view of buildings and cities as evolutionary processes is frequently at the core of scientific or technological approaches, which analyse existing environments in order to detect patterns related to functional performance that can be evinced as evidence to support decisions in design. I referred in the Introduction to space syntax, a theory and a method that describes the physical patterns of built environments in relation to empirical data of movement and use. Architects generate designs using concepts, often assigning attributes to places and social operations which they might not intrinsically possess. Empirical physical analysis, on the other hand, enables a building of patterns from the bottom up. Yet, clearly set apart from design conceptions, space syntax treats the built environment as though it is devoid of processes characterising conception, such as thinking, memory, imagination, representation and desire.

This binary consideration splits the architectural imagination into two camps, considering it either as a mysterious possession of the creative individual or as an analysable property subject to the scientific process.[38] This paradox has led to opposing world-views in design and educational theory, where architecture falls into the divide between the arts and humanities on one hand, and the sciences on the other.[39] There is no obvious reason for conjoining the two approaches and fields into a single intellectual domain. As Philip Steadman explains, 'the prevalent notion that to apply scientific or rational thinking in design must in some sense involve making the design process itself "scientific" is nonsensical and ultimately highly dangerous.'[40] However, as he also suggests, rational thought in research applied to design can significantly contribute by subjecting the products of design to scientific study.[41] It is equally important to acknowledge that not all aspects of creativity are appropriate for scientific modes of inquiry. Yet, while design and scientific inquiry can remain intellectually and institutionally discrete, theoretically speaking, neither the autonomous imagination alone nor scientific knowledge is capable of explaining the architectural imagination as a particular kind of knowledge.

If the intention in analysis is to explain the world 'as it is', the purpose in architectural design is to explore a plurality of worlds, a complex system of different kinds of actuality, virtuality and presence. Whether situated in the actual world – the centre of our system of reality – or in hypothetical perspectives, design is a theoretical exercise that structures existing and alternative worlds as syntactic and semantic domains, each with their own modalities, combining many types of knowledge. First, there is direct *empirical knowledge* (Figure 5.6). If I happen to live in or have visited Venice, my knowledge of the city derives from direct experience of the empirical kind. Second, there is

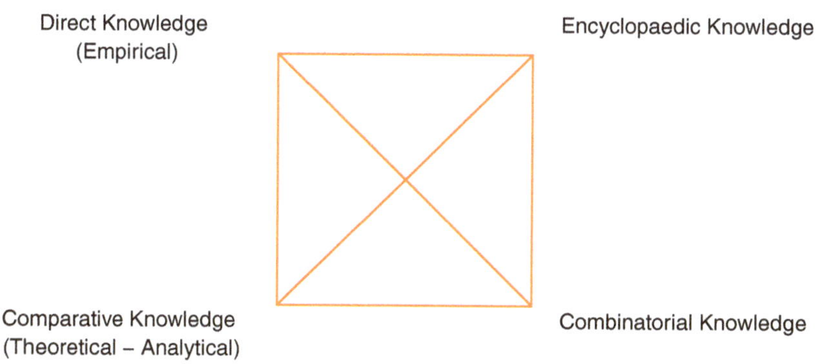

Figure 5.6 Four types of knowledge. Drawing by the author

encyclopaedic knowledge. I might have not been to Venice, but I know from the encyclopaedia that such a city exists, with such and such properties and qualities.[42] We trust the encyclopaedia for our factual knowledge to the extent of producing faithful reconstructions in our mind from what we have heard or read. The trust we place in it extends to including places, events and states of the past existing only as memory fragments or those yet to exist, but which will exist in the future – a weather forecast, a new town or building, a project at the design stage or under construction.

The third type of knowledge is *theoretical knowledge of the analytical kind*, such as knowledge generated through the processes used in the analysis of the three artefacts. Theoretical knowledge in design concerns three things: first, the configurational logic in such artefacts; second, the evolution of this logic through history: how ideas travel through generations and how innovations are affected by historical circumstances; third, how systems and artefacts are thought of, taking into account the modes in which architecture is conceptualised. Seen together, these levels describe how complexity is organised in space and in thought, as well as how it evolves over time.[43]

The fourth type of knowledge refers to the combinatorial world. This is knowledge of possibility, of variants consciously or unconsciously combined, expected or unexpected, realistic or imaginary combinations of elements, images and composite relationships, at multiple ranges, types and scales of magnitude.[44] It contains typologies, morphologies and projects, including places visited in thought but not yet discovered or realised, such as More's *Utopia*, Campanella's *City of the Sun*, Cedric Price's *Fun Palace*, Le Corbusier's Venice Hospital and Calvino's *Invisible Cities*.[45]

These branches of knowledge intersect with each other, informing the multiform, potential and conjectural nature of design. The designer navigates memories, direct experiences and facts, repertories and territories of possible and impossible worlds that may be actualised, discarded, concatenated or remain in a virtual state. Alternative possible worlds have the capacity to influence the world of our experience and factual knowledge. In contrast to the analytic understanding of how instrumentality and functional reasoning proceed, analytic theories know precious little in any formal or spatial sense of alternative possible worlds, or how to design buildings that are functional, imaginative and aesthetically intriguing.[46] Through the discussion of the three artefacts I will suggest that the diversification of knowledge is the most basic condition for understanding buildings and cities as products of analytical knowledge and imaginative design.

The imagination complex

In exploring the morphological affinities among the three works, I have disentangled two main ideas: one is the idea of *relatedness*, referring to architecture as being about elements simultaneously entering into relationships with other elements, which our minds read and creatively interpret; the second idea is that generic relatedness refers to generic properties operating across different kinds of artefacts and systems of knowledge. In the first chapter, for example, I argued that the typological composite structure of squares is interlaced with intersections between canals and alleys in Venice. Squares thus become intensified and amplified in our perception as relational systems. In the second chapter I argued that the structure of the Piazza San Marco and the semantic relations embedded in the architectural and iconographic programme of this space are mapped onto the topological structure of the urban network. In the case of de' Barbari's map, I suggested that the network centrality of the Rialto and the Piazza is translated into geometric and semantic centrality expressed by the mythological figures. In Calvino's *Invisible Cities*, the numerical structure and order of appearance of the thematic categories are mapped onto the linear series of city descriptions. When considering the Venice Hospital, we find that the network of squares and pathways is mapped onto Venice's spatial networks, which consist of island squares and the street and canal systems.

Relatedness enables generic properties to perform two kinds of operation: first, construct multiple memberships of elements into different classes of relationships, or frames of reference, bringing about densification and perceptual intensification; second, undergo transformations and traverse boundaries between categories (architecture and the city), discursive and non-discursive formations (architecture and literature), one type of structure and another (topology and geometry), actual sites and representational signs, signifiers and the signified. When a pattern is perceived in two self-consistent but different frames of reference, it registers simultaneously in two different classes of elements regulating different kinds of relationships. If the squares of Venice are parts of a conceptual class of elements, we can call the network properties relating the squares to a network the *syntax-of-a-class*. We can name the composite structure of elements constituting the squares (open space-churches-bridges-canals-steps etc.) as the *form-of-a-class* (Figure 1.14).[47] Registering simultaneously and repeatedly in these two types of relations, the squares become amplified in our perception as typological, morphological and syntactic structures. In *The Act of Creation*, Arthur Koestler describes this phenomenon as 'bisociation'.[48] We can then suggest that relatedness is generic enough to enable bisociations in which the same elements are simultaneously drafted into different class memberships, or categories, by virtue of being governed by different relations. Relatedness also enables bisociations through patterns that link two different associative contexts, such as the context of network properties of Venice (the syntax-of-a-class) and that of the abstract structure of language in Calvino's network of city descriptions. In the case of Venice and the Hospital, this structure is decoded in our perception onto a network where the perceiver can work backwards, fitting in the links between the associated classes of forms and spaces. In the case of Calvino's fiction, relatedness refers to the ways in which strings of words, text, paragraphs or chapters are translated into a web of thoughts, recovering the links between associated concepts in the form of a network.[49]

We may think we know what architecture and literature are about, but using relatedness within a particular medium, system or properties domain, and associative logic across media, writers and architects like Calvino and Le Corbusier expand the boundaries of their disciplines outside normative definitions of literature and architecture, respectively. The media, ontologies or categories I refer to are mapped in Figure 5.7, registering a set of binaries into a quartered field expressing the opposition between them while simultaneously opening it along the intersecting axes of *authored* and *authorless*, *factual* and *virtual* domains. Architecture, the city and literature thus become logically expanded structures, capturing alternative intersecting types of authorship and reality. The horizontal axis in the diagram plots the variance of artefacts based on whether they are built (factual) or un-built (virtual or imaginary). The vertical axis locates variations of artefacts along the designed and non-designed (or found). The three squares in the diagram capture differentiation of scale to include buildings, building complexes, cities and landscape.

Taking Venice as an example in this illustration, works by architects such as Palladio, Sansovino, Codussi and Scamozzi are found in the top right corner of the diagram, representing the production of built authored designs. Venice is at the bottom right corner of the smallest rectangle corresponding to cities, as the outcome of evolutionary collective authorship. The Venice Hospital is found at the top left of the figure by virtue of being a designed building complex that was not materialised. The places Polo describes in Calvino's *Invisible Cities* – complete by its own measures – and ideal cities such as Sforzinda by Filarete fall into the same quadrant as the Venice Hospital. They are

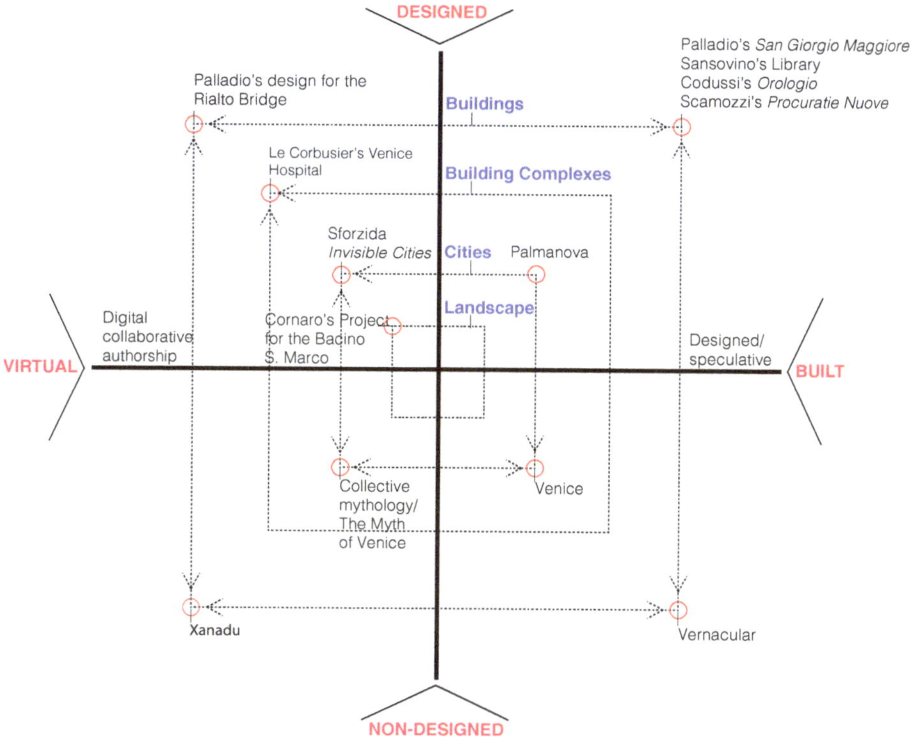

Figure 5.7 Diagram of architecture defined as expanded field. The horizontal axis plots the variance of artefacts based on whether they are built or un-built. The vertical axis marks variations from designed to non-designed artefacts. The four squares correspond to different scales of artefacts, buildings, building complexes, cities and landscape. The diagram should be seen as being analytical and generative, producing multiple hybrid forms of agency and authorship. The purpose is to challenge the opposition between individual and collective authorship, as well as between built structures which we can analyse and know objectively, and imaginative projection. Drawing by the author

characterised by 'design' intent but are only mentally accessible as creations. In contrast, cities like the ideal city of Palmanova occupy the opposite quadrant, having been built as a planned city for military purposes in the late Renaissance for the Venetian Republic. Products of collective mythology, such as Venice's collective myths, which were later formalised as The Myth of Venice, also have a place in this structure. This is found in the bottom left quadrant as legends, stories or beliefs held among people, which correspond to the collective and unconscious production of ideas in society. Finally, there are hybrid cases such as speculative architecture, which fall onto the right side of the x-axis, being consciously designed by architects but lacking intentionality of the architectural kind. Similarly, designs conceived as algorithmic models through collaborative authorship in a digital environment (and remaining virtual informational models) belong to the left side of this axis.

This diagram can feature as recombinant taxonomy, capable of generating hybrid versions. The various transformations of the Piazza San Marco are an instance of this possibility. What was combined in the Piazza was the authorless ubiquitous typology of the Venetian square evolving over an extended period with the authored interpretation of this square as the ancient typology of the Roman forum. Kublai Khan's palace and gardens in *Invisible Cities*, where Polo and Kublai have their italicised conversations, are historical and fictional places both in Calvino's novel and in Coleridge's poem (*Xanadu*). These spaces form another instance of recombinant transformation where ideas and forms are borrowed from history by virtue of the writer's imagination being informed by the collective imagination and vice versa. Even though this diagram constitutes a simplification, there is no reason for not imagining a term that would encompass both landscape and architecture. This term has in fact been imagined by Krauss in her concept of sculpture in the expanded field. Even when Krauss suggests that our culture has not been able to conceive of the expanded field, it can be argued that various architects and artists have thought of it in the past. Alberti, Palladio and Le Corbusier, for example, performed an imaginative analogical translation explaining that a building is a small city. Abstract, generic relatedness allows analogies and translations to be formed in the combinatorial expanded field. Like Lull's thinking machine, algorithmically combining principles in the pursuit of new knowledge, relatedness and combinatorial expansion of the field are demonstrations of the imaginative elasticity of media of expression.

Once we have the concepts of *multiple alternative authorships* and *relatedness*, we can begin to see how society and culture insert themselves into the form of the designed and the found, built and unbuilt architectures or objects. The example of the Hospital can help us understand how found architectures such as Venice infuse conscious architecture, and what the latter adds to them: abstract comparative knowledge of the designed and the found. Comparative knowledge is raised to the level of conscious reflective thought, and made the object of creative attention and innovation in a field of possibility expanded by this mode of thought.[50] The example of *Invisible Cities* shows the generative effect of preconceiving the general structure of the work (in the form of the diamond shape), but releasing a vast potential that trains the imagination of readers. The combinatorial aesthetics in the Hospital and Calvino's *Invisible Cities* is neither total nor local, but an amalgamation of intentional design with rules that are generative and systemic. The three examples demonstrate that ideas travel from the external world of artefacts to the mind and back to the world again through creative transformation. In response to the question of the source of architectural form, the Hospital and *Invisible Cities* originate neither inside nor outside the creative faculties of the author, but in the interaction with the world, whose logic the mind retrieves and translates into new patterns.

Possible worlds

> 'I have also thought of a model city from which I deduce all the others,' Marco answered. 'It is a city made only of exceptions, exclusions, incongruities, contradictions. If such a city is the most improbable, by reducing the number of abnormal elements, we increase the probability that the city really exists. So I have only to subtract exceptions from my model, and in whatever direction I proceed, I will arrive at one of the cities which, always as an exception, exists. But I cannot force my operation beyond a certain limit: I would achieve cities too probable to be real.'
>
> Italo Calvino, *Invisible Cities*

I have discussed the imagination as an abstract space of relations capable of associating matrixes of relations and translating them from one ontological category and medium to another. I will now return to the role of Venice in the creative imagination and the question posed at the beginning of the book. How does Venice stimulate imaginative reflection? A city like Venice appeals to the imagination for multiple reasons, and this book does not claim to exhaust them. However, the creative affinities between the three artefacts can explain the potency of the city of Venice itself and the two works to stimulate imaginative engagement. I argued that Venice, *Invisible Cities* and the Venice Hospital share the characteristics of a modular system based on discrete elements and recombinant network-like generative rules. These characteristics facilitate recognition of combinatorial universes and their embeddedness into networks of relationships.

In her study of narrative theory and possible worlds, Marie-Laure Ryan explains that 'the complexity of a plot depends on an underlying system of purely virtual embedded narratives [...] contained in dreams, fictions, fantasies and belief systems conceived or told by characters and any kind of representation concerning past and future states and events'. Among these embedded narratives, some reflect events from the factual domain, while others delineate un-actualised possibilities.[51] The aesthetic appeal of a plot is a function of the richness and variety of the network of virtual sequences, the narratives produced by speculative activity and promising plot lines. A plot is, therefore, not simply the textual world depicted in the narrative, but a larger and more complex universe containing possible worlds capable of being actualised or remaining virtual in readers' minds.

Like every multi-permeable urban system, Venice's spatial network affords many ways to connect points in space and time, as it can be expressed by a graph of interconnected nodes, encapsulating movement choices. What make Venice unique, though, are first, the networks of pedestrian and aquatic routes, which intersect and separate from each other; second, the combinatorial syntax of element-types; and third, the heterogeneous nature of its space, which consists of variable overlapping registers. As the canal network intersects with, and disrupts, the street pathways, any path from A to B contains interruptions, suspensions, sudden turns, and ups and downs, resulting in sequence networks produced by embodied activity and virtual networks produced by speculative activity in the mind. Arriving at a dead-end at the water's edge, one is forced to think of alternative routes to the one followed, linking the starting point with possible ways to move, actively intersecting actuality with possibility in the mind. The shortest and most frequently crossed paths intersect in the urban squares, revealing their nature as crossroads, as combinatorial universes of urban elements, actual and hypothetical routes over land or water.

Due to the tortuous network of short streets, squares in Venice materialise unannounced, enmeshed in the convolutions of canals and alleys dissecting the islands. Pedestrians anticipate another square emerging along their path, yet cannot determine whether or not it will be one previously experienced. This fleeting appearance and disappearance of *campi* assumes the character of a recollection, fluctuating and unstable, like a phantom. With time spent in Venice, the fleeting, newly discovered places and those remembered begin to mingle in perception. From Venice's squares, imagination and memory set forth, creating multiple Venices of pathways taken in actuality and in the mind, combining the explanatory function of intelligibility with the exploratory function of excursion, and the larger imaginative functions of prediction, projection, hypothesis, interpretation, correct and erroneous inferences, un-actualised plans, previous experiences, recollections, encyclopaedic knowledge and desires.[52] All of these universes inform our knowledge, calling into question the distinction between the actual and the possible and casting them all as forking paths on the actual map, thereby multiplying the size and diversity of territories travelled in the imagination.

In search of the irretrievable past, the hidden space in memory where time stops, Proust intuitively recognised the fictional nature of memory and imagination, which were inextricably related to some of Venice's most basic properties. Having 'plunged' into the network of little *calli*, he came across a 'vast and splendid *campo*'. Not able to find it again, he wondered whether he had visited it only in a dream.

> And as there is no great difference between the memory of a dream and the memory of a reality, I finally wondered whether it was during my sleep that there had occurred, in a dark patch of Venetian crystallisation, that strange mirage which offered a vast piazza [...] to the meditative eye of the moon.[53]

Proust seemed to have grasped in the complexity and plasticity of Venice's networks its capacity to affect the plasticity of memory and imagination. As studies in modern neuroscience have revealed, memories are malleable, continuously in the process of being modified: 'The novel and the life, the journalist and the fabulist, are really hopelessly blurred together'. Proust likes it this way because that is how memory actually is.[54] The potential of a city, building, landscape or novel to stimulate the imagination depends to a great extent on what is there, that is, its properties, perceptual qualities and associative logic. It is argued here that it also depends on the alternative pathways through which a place is accessed in our imagination. The memory of a particular place we have recently experienced is revised on the basis of the alternative routes we have approached it from, adapting it to what we know, and what is possible to know, each time.

This diversification of knowledge and possible combinatorial universes constitutes the most basic condition of dynamic generation of meaning. It also explains the intersection of analytic with generative knowledge. If generative knowledge concerns the production of variants and possible worlds, analytic knowledge restricts or limits the range of possible worlds conceivable in design. If we ascertain the impossibility of certain universes in relation to our past experience, or that they do not correspond to what encyclopaedic and analytical knowledge hold to be the laws of reason, we are, at this point, involving external criteria not only to discriminate against the results of the *ars combinatoria*, but also to introduce constraints within the art itself in order to control and limit the possibilities of the system.[55]

Analytic theories are based on the recognition that the generation of possibility is restricted by the laws of some generic functions, such as intelligibility, movement and occupation.[56] In this respect, Hillier and Hanson's theory, used to inform this analysis, is not specifically architectural, that is, relating to generative potential, but is an analytic theory of social performance and realisation.[57] However, the intersection of analytic and generative knowledge in design is the engine for producing un-actualised possibilities and evaluations according to the laws of reason. Even when the outcome of a work explicitly highlights one type of knowing rather than the other, as when the designer engages with generation, or the analyst with explanation, reflective activity always annexes both kinds of knowledge. Designers enable the possible to become the actual by surmounting limitations imposed by laws of necessity or reason. Theorists and scholars enumerate possibility and explain how we arrive at the actual by rational processes. The *reflective designer* and the *creative theorist*, on the other hand, identify both possibility and the laws needing to be contravened for design to engender new knowledge, thus locating the crucial creative space between necessity and freedom. Analytic and generative knowledge are central in design and theory, as each allows access to worlds whose centres of reality are not discrete, permanent and static but interacting and shifting dynamically with the processes of creative activity and time. In a nutshell: in addition to theories of explanation and generation, we need a combined theory of freedom and necessity in architecture and design.[58]

Voyage to *Venetia*

I have, in this book, described Venice as a story of urban form encapsulating the imagination in its spatial properties of growth and combinatorial worlds, containing a memory and an algorithm of existing and unforeseen generation. At the beginning of this work I explained that, present problems aside, Venice is like the ancient artefact of epic or myth, a tapestry of forms and fantasy folk tales where the theme of multiplicity develops its variations. In closing the book, I would like to return to this not so improbable analogy between Venice and epic narratives, which, like Venice, have survived through the ages and which we treasure, partly because we seem to have lost the ability to produce their contemporary successors.

It is no accident that, among the legends entertained by the Venetians about their origins, one lineage of stories traced their heritage from Trojan warriors, who had supposedly found refuge in 'Venetia' after the sack of their city by the Greeks.[59] The founding of Venice for the Venetians was attributed to a multitude of disparate fabled origins, partly touched upon in the second chapter and all, of course, unsubstantiated, but this is not the point. What is of significance here is the idea that the distant memory of the voyage of Ulysses or Aeneas marked the mythical founding of a city that developed through processes of artisanal craftsmanship similar to the way an improvised oral poem, recited from memory, incorporates fragments of narrative already sung by others. As Calvino explains, Ulysses' voyage to Ithaca or Aeneas' to Rome – or, I may add, to Venetia, as Venice was called in the era of its founding – is in essence a voyage to utopia, a past we have irrevocably lost but need to recite from memory as an aid to moving forward to a better future.[60]

This mythical voyage to utopia has other crucial characteristics: it is densely loaded with recognisable forms that multiply their own space at every turn; it is diverse, sung not by a single but by many 'bards', a fusion of different origins by many hands and minds; it is a merry-go-round of inventions of fun and freedom by 'gods', 'heroes' and ordinary people, their harsh experiences of pain, horror and anguish notwithstanding. For the bards of antiquity, who sang poems without a song sheet, the risk of forgetting must have made theirs the most precarious form of existence. The future we must strive to achieve is made possible by creating afresh at every occasion the memory of what has gone before, extemporising with whatever variations inspire on each occasion. This is what also inspires the imagination in Venice – from tourists, consuming what the city offers for them to see, to ordinary Venetians caught between modernity and ancient tradition; and from the visitors to international exhibitions to the pilgrims still paying annual visits to Santa Maria della Salute and the Redentore to give thanks for the ending of the plague.

Notes

Introduction: Between authored architecture and the non-authored city

1 Italo Calvino, *Invisible Cities*, trans. William Weaver (London: Vintage, 1997).
2 Letizia Modena, *Italo Calvino's Architecture of Lightness* (Oxford and New York: Routledge, 2011).
3 Italo Calvino, *Six Memos for the Next Millennium*, trans. Patrick Greagh (London: Penguin, 2002), 71.
4 Peter Hall, *Cities in Civilization* (London: Phoenix Giant, 1999).
5 John Julius Norwich, *The Great Cities in History* (London: Thames & Hudson, 2016), 152.
6 John Julius Norwich, *A History of Venice* (London and New York: Penguin, 2003), xxiv.
7 Mumford compares Venice with Amaurote, the capital in Thomas More's *Utopia*, which represents the *social city* of the future although consisting of the rigid forms of the late-medieval era. In contrast, Venice for Mumford prefigures the *physical city* of the future, particularly through its organisation of neighbourhoods, which could be recovered as the basic planning unit. See: Lewis Mumford, *The City in History. Its Origins, Its Transformations, and Its Prospects* (London: Secker & Warburg, 1961). See also: Thomas More, *Utopia*, trans. Paul Turner (Harmondsworth, England: Penguin, 1965).
8 Mahnaz Shah, *Le Corbusier's Venice Hospital Project: An Investigation into Its Structural Formulation* (Burlington, VT: Ashgate, 2013).
9 Kevin Lynch, *The Image of the City* (Cambridge, MA: The MIT Press, 1960).
10 Italo Calvino, 'Venezia: Archetypo E Utopia Della Città Aquatica', in *Saggi, 1945–1985*. Edited by M. Barenghi, 2 vols (Milan: Mondatori, 1995), 2688–92.
11 Jacob Burckhardt, *The Civilization of the Renaissance*, trans. S. G. Middlemore (New York, 1944).
12 Ingrid D. Rowland and Thomas Noble Howe, eds. *Vitruvius: The Ten Books on Architecture* (Cambridge: Cambridge University Press, 1999).
13 Deborah Howard, *The Architectural History of Venice* (New Haven; London: Yale University Press, 2002), 64.
14 Andrea Palladio, *I Quatro Libri Dell'Architettura* (Venice: Dominico de' Franceschi, 1570); *The Four Books on Architecture* (Cambridge, MA: The MIT Press, 2002); Sebastiano Serlio, *Regole Generali Di Architetura Sopra Le Cinque Maniere De Gli Edifici* (Venice, 1537).
15 Manfredo Tafuri, *Venice and the Renaissance*, trans. Jessica Levine (Cambridge, MA: The MIT Press, 1995).
16 Howard, *The Architectural History of Venice*.
17 Many cities include examples of traditional, classical and modern structures but, due to restrictions imposed for historical conservation purposes and its fixed outer boundary limits, Venice comprises the most intense and striking expression of these three periods.
18 For the role of geometry in ideal cities see: Ruth Eaton, *Ideal Cities: Utopianism and the (Un) Built Environment* (London: Thames & Hudson, 2001).
19 Jane Jacobs, *The Death and Life of Great American Cities: The Failure of Town Planning* (London: Pelican, 1965).
20 Calvino, *Six Memos for the Next Millennium*. See also: *The Literature Machine*, trans. Patrick Greagh (London: Vintage, 1997).
21 Calvino, *Six Memos for the Next Millennium*, 91.

22 Calvino, *Six Memos for the Next Millennium*.
23 James S. Grubb, 'When Myths Lose Power: Four Decades of Venetian Historiography', *The Journal of Modern History*, 58 (1986),43.
24 Confronted with the War of the League of Cambrai (1508–16) and the discovery of the New World, Venice in the sixteenth century shifted its interests from maritime enterprise in the east of the Mediterranean to land-based activities in the *terra firma*, engaging in a series of reclamation projects, cartographic mapping and hydrological control through the canalisation of rivers, which transformed the Veneto landscape to an Arcadian context for Palladio's countryside villas. See: Denis E. Cosgrove, *The Palladian Landscape: Geographical Change and Its Cultural Representations in Sixteenth-Century Italy* (Leicester; London: Leicester University Press, 1993). See also: Pier Vittorio Aureli, *The Possibility of an Absolute Architecture* (Cambridge, MA; London: MIT Press, 2011).
25 Howard, *The Architectural History of Venice*, 3.
26 Charles Dickens, *Pictures from Italy* (London: Robinson, 1973), 109.
27 Robert Harbison, *Eccentric Spaces* (London: Secker & Warburg, 1977).
28 Marcel Proust, *In Search of Lost Time*, trans. C. K. Scott Moncrieff and Terence Kilmartin, vol. V (New York; Toronto: Random House, 1992), 844.
29 Nietzsche dramatised the contrast between the ancient mythical figure of Apollo, the god of good form and intellectual restraint, and that of Dionysus, the god of sensual excess and passion. Friedrich Wilhelm Nietzsche, *The Birth of Tragedy*, trans. Shaun Whiteside (Oxford: Oxford University Press, 1991). See also: Thomas Mann, *Death in Venice and Other Stories* (London: Vintage, 1998).
30 Teresa Stoppani, *Paradigm Islands: Manhattan and Venice: Discourses on Architecture and the City* (Abingdon; New York: Routledge, 2010), 95.
31 Peter Lauritzen, *Venice: A Thousand Years of Culture and Civilization* (London: Weidenfeld and Nicolson, 1978), 220.
32 The Palazzo Leporelli is James's fictional equivalent of the Palazzo Barbaro-Curtis in Venice, where he stayed in 1892. Henry James, *The Wings of the Dove* (Ware: Wordsworth Classics, 2009), 266.
33 Edward Muir, *Civic Ritual in Renaissance Venice* (Princeton: Princeton University Press, 1981). See also: Denis Cosgrove, 'The Myth and the Stones of Venice: An Historical Geography of a Symbolic Landscape', *Journal of Historical Geography*, 8(2) (1982). The myth of Venice achieved its fullest expression in the writings of Gasparo Contarini, Marin Sanuto and Francesco Sansovino, the son of the architect Jacopo Sansovino. Gasparo Contarini, *The Commonwealth and Government of Venice*, trans. Lewes Lewkenor (London: Imprinted by John Windet for Edmund Mattes, 1599), https://www.bl.uk/collection-items/contarinis-commonwealth-and-government-of-venice-translated-by-lewkenor (accessed 4 September 2017); Marin Sanuto, *I Diarii*, 58 vols. (Venice, 1879–1903). See also: Francesco Sansovino, *Venetia Citta Nobilissima Et Singolare Descritta in Xiiii Libri*, vol. 13 (Venice: Venetia, 1581); Francesco Sansovino, edited and translated by Vaughan Hart and Peter Hicks, *Sansovino's Venice* (New Haven: Yale University Press, 2017).
34 Tafuri, *Venice and the Renaissance*, 15.
35 Tafuri, *Venice and the Renaissance*, 15.
36 Norwich, *A History of Venice*, xxii. The winning of an overwhelming majority at the general election by the Whigs in England (in 1715) engendered liberal politics and enlightenment spirits. The Whigs' political philosophy looked to the Myth of Venice and the achievements of the city-state, which combined middle-class commercialism and classical civic virtues. Rosie Razzall, Lucy Whitaker, *Canaletto: The Art of Venice* (London: Royal Collection Trust, 2017), 283.
37 Tony Tanner, *Venice Desired* (Oxford: Blackwell, 1992), 4.
38 Cosgrove, 'The Myth and the Stones of Venice'.
39 Cosgrove, 'The Myth and the Stones of Venice', 8.
40 Muir explains that 'studying the "Myth of Venice" in modern times has often meant attempting to sort out, from a puzzling set of beliefs that were not necessarily true and from an enigmatic series of events that are not historically verifiable, what was "reality"'. Muir, *Civic Ritual in Renaissance Venice*, 22. For an architectural perspective of the Myth of Venice, see: Tafuri, *Venice and the Renaissance*.
41 'No one, wise Kublai, knows better than you that the city must never be confused with the words that describe it.' Calvino, *Invisible Cities*, 53.

42 Elisabeth Crouzet-Pavan, 'Towards an Ecological Understanding of the Myth of Venice', in *Venice Reconsidered: The History and Civilization of an Italian City-State, 1297–1797*, ed. John Martin and Dennis Romano (Baltimore; London: Johns Hopkins University Press, 2000).

43 It is perhaps because he was aware of this danger rather than afraid that 'memory's images once fixed in words can become lost' that Marco Polo in Calvino's *Invisible Cities* never speaks of Venice. Instead, he approaches it through the description of other cities as imperfect reflections. Calvino, 78.

44 Tanner, *Venice Desired*, iv.

45 Henri Lefebvre, *The Production of Space* (Oxford: Blackwell, 1991).

46 The new style of building based on classical antiquity that arose through this process required a new way of disseminating knowledge. Unlike Gothic architecture, which was passed down from generation to generation by word of mouth, classical architecture required 'defining, argumentation, language and finally the written word'. The architects' treatises established a new level of communication between architects, clients and the public, mainly taking place in the princely court. Christof Thoenes, 'Introduction', in *Architectural Theory*, ed. Bernd Evers and Christof Thoenes (Cologne: Taschen, 2003), 10.

47 Aureli, *The Possibility of an Absolute Architecture*.

48 A disparate trend that loosely falls under the ambit of 'smart cities'.

49 Douglas Spencer, *The Architecture of Neoliberalism: How Contemporary Architecture Became an Instrument of Control and Compliance* (London: Bloomsbury Academic, 2016).

50 Rem Koolhaas, *Delirious New York* (New York: The Monacelli Press, 1994).

51 Spencer, *The Architecture of Neoliberalism*, 7.

52 Spencer, *The Architecture of Neoliberalism*, 4.

53 Rem Koolhaas, *Fundamentals: 14th International Architecture Exhibition – La Biennale Di Venezia* (Venice: Marsilio, 2014).

54 In response to the view of cities and buildings as assemblages of elements, it is important to note that in Venice – as in most cities – the whole is greater than the sum of the parts. As Norwich explained, 'however majestic the elements the ultimate masterpiece remains Venice itself'. Norwich, *A History of Venice*, xxi.

55 Jeremy Till, *Architecture Depends* (Cambridge, MA; London: MIT Press, 2009). See also: Jonathan Hill, *Immaterial Architecture* (London: Routledge, 2006).

56 Dennis Romano, *Patricians and Popolani: The Social Foundations of the Venetian Renaissance State* (Baltimore; London: Johns Hopkins University Press, 1987). See also: *Housecraft and Statecraft: Domestic Service in Renaissance Venice 1400–1600* (Baltimore; London: The Johns Hopkins University Press, 1996).

57 Space syntax is a theory and method developed at the Bartlett, UCL, by Bill Hillier, Julienne Hanson and their colleagues in the 1970s, and subsequently extended into a field of research by a worldwide community of researchers and academics. The fundamental consideration in this field of research is a space-first approach, where through the analysis of space combined with empirical data on human activity one can arrive at the underlying logic of social patterns. The purpose is to make the city 'speak', deriving description from its network-like properties, rather than speaking on behalf of the city through externally imposed characteristics. See: Bill Hillier and Julienne Hanson, *The Social Logic of Space* (Cambridge: Cambridge University Press, 1984). The second area of research, typo-morphology, also spans several decades of study describing urban forms based on detailed classifications of urban spaces and buildings by types. See: Anne Vernez Moudon, 'Getting to Know the Built Landscape: Typomorphology', in *Ordering Space: Types in Architecture and Design*, ed. K. A. Frankl and L. H. Schneecloth (New York: Van Nostrand Reinohld, 1994). For a more comprehensive description of approaches to morphology see: Anne Vernez Moudon, 'A Catholic Approach to Organizing What Urban Designers Should Know', *Journal of Planning Literature*, 6(4) (1992).

58 A clear exception is Phil Steadman's study of the biological analogy in the work of architects. Philip Steadman, *The Evolution of Designs: Biological Analogy in Architecture and the Applied Arts*, Revised ed. (Abingdon; New York: Routledge, 2008). Moreover, his more recent work on the elements of generic function across a large range of building types combines the history of built forms and their morphology as a way to explain the socio-technical factors affecting the emergence of new types or the disappearance of previous configurations. Phil Steadman, *Building Types and Built Forms* (Kibworth Beauchamp: Matador, 2014).

59 Muir, *Civic Ritual in Renaissance Venice*, 300.

60 Frances A. Yates, *The Art of Memory* (London: Pimlico, 2001).

61 The areas of building construction and geo-information have in recent years been working together towards a common language, integrating the geospatial disciplines with engineering, architecture and construction. This integration is being supported by software providers as well as policy-related initiatives. Bram Mommers, 'The Crossover Revolution', *Geospatial World* (2014), https://www.geospatialworld.net/article/the-crossover-revolution/ (accessed 4 September 2017).

62 The use of integrated digital technology means that the impact of design choices on a building and its environment can be communicated to the client and the user from an early stage in the process. Mommers, 'The Crossover Revolution'. In addition, integrated technology establishes continuity between digital design and fabrication, leading to a fully integrated design and production chain. See: Mario Carpo, *The Alphabet and the Algorithm* (Cambridge, MA: The MIT Press, 2007).

63 Simon Parker, *Cities, Politics and Power* (Oxford; New York: Routledge, 2011).

64 Steadman, *The Evolution of Designs*.

65 *Ars Combinatoria*, or the Art of Combinations, is attributed to Raymond Lull, a Catalan philosopher, who invented a method of understanding knowledge consisting of a complex combinatorial system of shapes, symbols, letters and concepts. It was meant to lead to a universal language, uniting various branches of knowledge at the time, and leading to peace between different religions. Lull invented a 'machine', which by combining elements of thinking, values and language led to new paths of insight and thought. Lull's ideas were developed in the sixteenth century by Giordano Bruno, who used the rotating discs of Lull as instruments for an artificial memory, and by Athanasius Kircher and Gottfried Leibniz in the seventeenth century. These philosophers dreamed of a thinking device in a search for combinations and permutations. Calvino, *Six Memos for the Next Millennium*. See also: Yates, *The Art of Memory*; Umberto Eco, *The Search for the Perfect Language*, trans. James Fentress (Oxford: Blackwell, 1995).

Chapter 1: City-craft: Assembling the city

1 Charles Dickens, *Pictures from Italy*.

2 Gustav Aschenbach is the main protagonist in Thomas Mann's *Death in Venice*. Overcome by the desire for spontaneous and exotic travel, Aschenbach visits Venice, where he is uplifted but increasingly obsessed by a beautiful youth. 'And as he contemplated it all he reflected that to arrive to Venice by land, at the station, was like entering a palace by the back door: that only as he was now doing, only by ship, over the high seas, should one come to this most extraordinary of cities.' Thomas Mann, *Death in Venice and Other Stories*, 213.

3 James S. Grubb, 'When Myths Lose Power: Four Decades of Venetian Historiography'.

4 Johann Wolfgang von Goethe, *Italian Journey 1786–1788*, trans. W.H. Auden and Elizabeth Mayer (London: Folio Society, 2010), 77.

5 Italo Calvino, 'Venezia: Archetypo E Utopia Della Città Aquatica'.

6 Elisabeth Crouzet-Pavan, *Venice Triumphant: The Horizons of a Myth*, trans. Lydia G. Cochrane (Baltimore; London: Johns Hopkins University Press, 2002), 10.

7 Richard J. Goy, *Venice: An Architectural Guide* (New Haven; London: Yale University Press, 2010), 7.

8 Crouzet-Pavan, *Venice Triumphant: The Horizons of a Myth*, 10.

9 Islands tended to grow 'saucer fashion around the edges, leaving depressions in the centre (*terre vacue*) that were sometimes even marshy or under water (*piscine*) and were only gradually reclaimed'. Juergen Schultz, 'The Printed Plans and Panoramic Views of Venice (1486–1797)', in *Saggi E Memorie Si Storia Dell'arte* (Florence: Leo S. Olschki Editore, 1970), 14.

10 MOSE (*Modulo Sperimentale Elettromeccanico*, Experimental Electromechanical Module) is a project intended to protect Venice from flooding: https://en.wikipedia.org/wiki/MOSE_Project, accessed 2 October 2016.

11 Bronwen Wilson, *The World in Venice: Print, the City and Early Modern Identity* (Toronto: University of Toronto Press, 2005).

12 Edward Muir, *Civic Ritual in Renaissance Venice*.

13 Dennis Romano, *Patricians and Popolani*.

14 Deborah Howard, *The Architectural History of Venice*, 4. See also: Elisabeth Crouzet-Pavan, 'Towards an Ecological Understanding of the Myth of Venice'.

15 Fra Paolino's map was the first hydrographic-urban record of the city, or the earliest representation of the city that survives. Although dating from the second half of the fourteenth century, it is based on an earlier prototype, representing the shape and extent of the city's development as it was in the twelfth century. See: Schultz, 'The Printed Plans and Panoramic Views of Venice (1486–1797)' (Florence: Leo S. Olschki Editore, 1970).

16 The analysis is conducted at different scales, which means that the measures of betweenness centrality, or choice, and closeness centrality, or integration, are calculated for each element at a metric distance or a radius, ranging from 250 and 500 metres to the scale of the city as a whole (in the case of Venice this is approximately 3,000 metres). Exploring the spatial properties of a city at different scales can show how local relationships are embedded in the global structure. Bill Hillier and Laura Vaughan, 'The City as One Thing,' *Progress in Planning*, 67, 3 (2007).

17 The measures of betweenness centrality, or choice, as it is known in space syntax terminology, refers to how many times a street lies on the simplest routes from all streets to all other streets, or how likely it is to be chosen on paths functioning as convenient through-routes. Streets that are often chosen as through-routes are indicated as having a high value. Bill Hillier and Shinichi Iida, 'Network and Psychological Effects in Urban Movement,' *Lecture Notes in Computer Science*, 3693 (2005).

18 Severio Muratori, *Studi Per Una Operante Storia Urbana Di Venezia* (Rome: Instituto Poligrafico dello Stato, 1959); see also: Giorgio Bellavitis and Giandomenico Romanelli, *Venezia* (Bari; Rome: Laterza, 1985); Howard, *The Architectural History of Venice*.

19 'A *campo* was literally a field, although by the time of de' Barbari's map most *campi* were paved'. Howard, *The Architectural History of Venice*, 50.

20 The saline and tidal waters of the lagoon meant that the city had no fresh water supply. Hundreds of wellheads still survive today, 'the oldest of them Byzantine survivors from the eleventh and twelfth centuries'. See: Goy, *Venice: An Architectural Guide*, 22.

21 Goy, *Venice: An Architectural Guide*, 8.

22 The northern and southern limits were not yet fully defined as the reclamations that formed the Zattere and the Fondamente Nove began in the sixteenth century. Goy, *Venice: An Architectural Guide*, 9.

23 Romano, *Patricians and Popolani*, 15.

24 In the twelfth century Venice became an international trade centre through the great profits made by the shipment of luxury items from the eastern Mediterranean. Diego Pugga and Daniel Trefler, 'International Trade and Institutional Change: Medieval Venice's Response to Globalisation,' *The Quarterly Journal of Economics* (2014); see also: Frederic C. Lane, *Venice: A Maritime Republic* (Baltimore; London: The Johns Hopkins University Press, 1973).

25 Howard, *The Architectural History of Venice*, 51.

26 Romano, *Patricians and Popolani*, 17.

27 Bill Hillier, 'What Are Cities For? And How Does This Relate to Their Spatial Form?', *The Journal of Space Syntax*, 6, 2 (2016).

28 A comparative analysis of a large number of cities by Hillier et al. reveals that the foreground network is captured by values ranging between 1.5 and 1.6. The background network controls movement, consisting of primary residential space where the foreground is embedded. It has universal as well as culturally determined spatial features, which play a strong role in both embodying and reproducing the underlying social order. Bill Hillier, Tao Young and Alasdair Turner, 'Normalising Least Angle Choice in Depthmap – and How It Opens up New Perspectives on the Global and Local Analysis of City Space,' *The Journal of Space Syntax*, 3, 2 (2012): 155–93.

29 Extended analysis reveals that cities as geometrically and culturally different as Denver in the USA and historical Shiraz have common generic relational properties. Bill Hillier, Tao Young and Alasdair Turner, 'Normalising Least Angle Choice in Depthmap'.

30 Peter Ackroyd, *Venice: Pure City* (London: Chatto & Windus, 2009), 254.

31 Muir, *Civic Ritual in Renaissance Venice*, 146.

32 Muir, *Civic Ritual in Renaissance Venice*, 148.

33 The layout of the major canals was the outcome of the lagoon's natural channels. Canals were constantly being remodelled through drainage and filling, while new ones were being dug in

newly reclaimed zones. On the whole, it was essential not 'to impede the natural flow of the tides, which was vital for the removal of sewage and debris'. Howard, *The Architectural History of Venice*, 50. Tides penetrate the barrier islands (known as *lidi*), flowing through the channels of the lagoon to the canals, renewing and purifying the waters. The two systems of communication served different functions. The former was used by heavy ships 'from the port to the market, from the Arsenal to the basin of San Marco, or from one warehouse to another'. The latter allowed people to use the *calle*, 'unless a waterway without a bridge obliged them to use a gondola *traghetto*'. See: Crouzet-Pavan, *Venice Triumphant*, 13.

34 *Traghetti* are the passenger boats that cross the canals at seven locations between the rail station and the Basin of San Marco.

35 The origin of Venice is located in *Rivo Alto* (high bank) or Rialto, the narrowest point of the Grand Canal, providing a natural site for a bridgehead. See: Richard J. Goy, *Building Renaissance Venice: Patrons, Architects and Builders, c. 1430–1500* (New Haven; London: Yale University Press, 2006). 'Situated in two zones east and west of the *flumen*, the first settlements gave definition to the Canal's U-shaped bends, with ten parishes between San Bartolomeo and San Marco defining the left side, and ten parishes shaping the Canal's right side'. See: Romano, *Patricians and Popolani*, 14. According to the extensive studies of Muratori, the gradual process of settlement continued during the eleventh century, giving Venice almost all of its island-parishes and the geographic contours it has today. See: Muratori, *Studi Per Una Operante Storia Urbana Di Venezia*.

36 The values of the other major canals express their global position in navigation routes between Venice's islands and between the city and the Adriatic, specially the Cannaregio Canal, which linked the north-westward area with the mainland, and the Grand Canal, where large vessels would arrive from the Adriatic.

37 Historians observe that Venice has 'few straight streets of any length, recalling the dense layouts of Islamic cities'. Howard, *The Architectural History of Venice*, 50. Travelling on water is faster and simpler than travelling on foot, which is confirmed through the organisation of large-scale water-based transportation till today.

38 'Wealthy households owned private gondolas for their own transportation and small flat-bottomed boats for carrying supplies. Among the watercraft serving the lagoon was the small, wooden fishing vessel named *sanpierota* [and] the larger, sailed *topo sandalo da s'ciopo*, used in shallow waters to hunt duck and other game. While only the wealthy could afford private *gondolas* with rowers, the city did provide public transportation by *traghetto*, a gondola propelled by two oarsmen that normally crossed the Grand Canal or taxied merchants to and from the mainland'. Joanne Marrie Ferraro, *Venice: History of the Floating City* (New York: Cambridge University Press, 2012), 8.

39 The combined network is studied by joining the water and land networks through the various points where they intersect. These are the points at which footpaths and *campi* are linked with water access steps.

40 Each change of direction along these pathways corresponds to a 'topological step' or a single 'step depth'. The morphology of the route is revealed by calculating the topological steps (topological distance) from the canals.

41 Crouzet-Pavan, *Venice Triumphant*.

42 Crouzet-Pavan, *Venice Triumphant*, 139.

43 These were communities of 'spiritually oriented laymen and laywomen who through spiritual exercises hoped to approach the holy … and promote a sense of community amongst the living'. They drew their members from wide sectors of the Venetian society and were known as *Scuole Grandi* and *Scuole Piccole*. See: Romano, *Patricians and Popolani*, 106.

44 This was the German trading centre built for the convenience of the German merchants on the north bank at the Rialto. The Fondaco dei Tedeschi was at once a warehouse and a residence.

45 This is because in tests performed in 50 cities the maximum choice value is in the region of 1.5–1.6. In Venice the maximum choice value is 1.4 and so the maximum values are set above 1.3. Hillier, Young and Turner, 'Normalising Least Angle Choice in Depthmap'.

46 Hillier and Hanson, *The Social Logic of Space*.

47 Hillier and Hanson, *The Social Logic of Space*.

48 The location of the Rialto, 'in the precise centre of the archipelago, ensured its permanent role as a meeting place of routes, and a natural location for a market. These market functions grew to embrace almost every aspect and level of human commercial exchange, from the purchase

of a day's domestic provisions of bread, fruit and wine to international banking, from shipping insurance to brothels, from goldsmith to fish-gutting. Most of these activities (if not quite all) still take place here today.' Goy, *Building Renaissance Venice*, 11–12.

49 The Piazza and the Piazzetta, the space in front of the Ducal Palace, formed the formal entrance to the city and a regular place of celebrations with marching processions.

50 For a definition of the measure of integration see Hillier and Hanson, *The Social Logic of Space*. Choice and integration capture different relationships between parts and whole. Integration measures the relationship of every element to every other element, or all-to-all relations in a system. The latter accounts for area-to-area interconnections. In Venice, the two measures together expose the association between the *campi* and the twin hubs of the Piazza San Marco and the Rialto.

51 Hillier and Iida, 'Network and Psychological Effects in Urban Movement'.

52 Muir, *Civic Ritual in Renaissance Venice*.

53 Muir, *Civic Ritual in Renaissance Venice*, 305.

54 The first group formed the nobility based on membership of the Major Council. Until 1297 membership was, theoretically at least, open to all members of Venetian society, while after the closing of the Council it was based on hereditary rights. The *popolano grande* consisted of officials and merchants, including those Venetians who owned property and employed several workers. The *popolano minuto* included the city's artisans, craftsmen, day labourers, servants and the poor. See: Romano, *Patricians and Popolani*.

55 The Greeks, Slavs, Milanese, Florentines and the Jews. See: Romano, *Patricians and Popolani*. For an account of the Jews and their life in the Venice ghetto see Richard Sennett, *Building and Dwelling: Ethics for the City* (Milton Keynes: Penguin Random House, 2018) and Richard Sennett, *Flesh and Stone: The Body and the City in Western Civilization* (New York: Faber, 2002).

56 For patricians the familial networks were an affirmation of political domination and their place in society. For the *popolano grande*, on the other hand, they were a vehicle for upward mobility and association with political powers. All actions undertaken by the kin group 'were seen within the familial context and were designed to enhance the prestige and honor of the house'. Romano, *Patricians and Popolani*, 63.

57 At the end of the thirteenth century, though, the city's oligarchs erected barriers in the political and economic markets. Nevertheless, the commercial character of the city required flexible social ties. Pugga and Trefler, 'International Trade and Institutional Change'.

58 Romano, *Patricians and Popolani*.

59 Places of cultural homogeneity were the parish of San Nicolò, the quarter of the Arsenale, and the areas where the ethnic communities lived. A street of market shops and workshops at Rialto (*ruga*) would sometimes be a place 'where guildsmen would concentrate, exchange wares and keep an eye on competitors ... In some trades, artisans did live and work in the same place; in others they did not.' Romano, *Patricians and Popolani*, 78–79.

60 The clergy formed an integral element of the life of parishes, providing religious as well as legal services, such as delivering sanctions and sermons, and providing investments and loans. Romano, *Patricians and Popolani*.

61 The *arte* was a trade guild and worked as an association of those practising the same profession.

62 Artisans in Venice normally consisted 'of persons who practiced the same trade or craft, and of a *scuola* – a corporation consisting of members of a given arte, who, meeting on the premises of a particular monastery, placed themselves under the protection of a chosen saint, and undertook to perform certain services for their own poor, sick and dead'. Brian Pullan, *Rich and Poor in Renaissance Venice* (Cambridge, MA: Harvard University Press, 1971), 33. In the early centuries of the Republic these charitable institutions had only male members but in the seventeenth and eighteenth centuries they included large numbers of women.

63 Richard Mackenney, *Tradesmen and Traders: The World of the Guilds in Venice and Europe c.1250 – c.1650* (New Jersey: Barnes and Noble, 1987).

64 Mackenney, *Tradesmen and Traders*, 69.

65 Romano, *Patricians and Popolani*.

66 Romano, *Patricians and Popolani*, 81.

67 Romano, *Patricians and Popolani*.

68 Romano, *Patricians and Popolani*.

69 Goy, *Building Renaissance Venice*.

70 At the front of the *piano nobile* was the *portego* with long windows that let light into a longitudinal space behind it. The typology developed from a post-Romanesque style to Gothic and Venetian Gothic, while the later fifteenth century saw the first Renaissance façades by Codussi, Sanmicheli and Sansovino. Finally, the Baroque was also adopted. Goy, *Building Renaissance Venice*.

71 A scaled-down version of the impressive palazzo, the *palazzetto* was the house of middle-class families. Goy, *Building Renaissance Venice*.

72 Howard, *The Architectural History of Venice*, 49.

73 The general structure of governance in Venice formed a pyramid with the General Assembly at its base and the Doge at its apex. In between these layers were the Major Council, the Forty and Senate, and the Ducal Council. 'Distrust of individual power made the Venetians depend on committees and councils'. Lane, *Venice: A Maritime Republic*, 95. This system was later modified to a more complex structure. For a detailed diagram of the structure of government, see Lane, *Venice: A Maritime Republic*, 429.

74 'The banks of the Grand Canal are lined with palaces from all periods and styles, from the earliest Venetian-Byzantine survivors (Ca' Farsetti) to the Gothic (Ca' Giustinian) and the early Renaissance (Palazzo Corner Spinelli) and the High Renaissance (Ca' Corner)'. Goy, *Building Renaissance Venice*, 193.

75 'While the home was the symbol of the family kin, its spatial location did not have the same strength in expressing the patrilineal patrician or *popolano* family. Residential and kinship worlds gradually shifted away from defensive enclaves and arms to wide dispersion throughout the city'. Romano, *Patricians and Popolani*, 49.

76 Romano, *Patricians and Popolani*.

77 Romano, *Patricians and Popolani*, 135.

78 Romano, *Housecraft and Statecraft*.

79 The *Scuole Grandi* were distinguished buildings with their own impressive halls, decorated walls and painted ceilings.

80 This was projected through furnishings, books, shields, altars, paintings and works of art, banners and objects held in urban processions.

81 Previous research into the spatial form of cities and their live centres, namely the uses of retail, catering outlets and markets, suggests that as movement-rich locations attract land uses that benefit from movement, such as shops, the migration of retail to these places attracts more and more movement. This cycle sets up a multiplier effect, bringing more diverse uses to that location. Bill Hillier, 'Centrality as a Process: Accounting for Attraction Inequalities in Deformed Grids,' *Urban Design International*, 4, 3–4 (1999).

82 Hillier, 'What Are Cities For?', 200.

83 Hillier, 'What Are Cities For?'.

84 Hillier, 'What Are Cities For?'.

85 Stanley Chojnacki, 'In Search of the Venetian Patriciate: Families and Factions in the Fourteenth Century', in *Renaissance Venice*, ed. J. R. Hale (London: Faber and Faber, 1974), 60. Chojnacki explains that, although living in different parts of the town, the families had strong ties. However, 14 families dominated the government structure. They had the highest number of family members and the largest amount of immovable wealth of all the patrician families in Venice. This group of patricians did not represent a single set of political principles, 'but they did represent a numerically unshakable bulwark of the Venetian political tradition whose leading products they were.' Chojnacki, 71.

86 Chojnacki, 'In Search of the Venetian Patriciate', 60.

87 The writings of Gasparo Contarini and other humanists had elaborated the Myth of Venice, which already existed unofficially, 'portraying the Venetian constitution as the classic modern instance of a "mixed constitution" miraculously resistant to change and decay'. Romano, *Patricians and Popolani*, 4. See also: Pullan, *Rich and Poor in Renaissance Venice*.

88 Conflict went through political, economic and familial relations, including the city's parishes, guilds and religious confraternities. See: Romano, *Patricians and Popolani*.

89 Romano, *Patricians and Popolani*, 18.

90 Muir, *Civic Ritual in Renaissance Venice*, 301.

91 Equally important to the Myth has been what Romano calls the 'antimyth'. This term describes Venice not as the exemplary Republic but as decadence, especially during the

eighteenth century, when Enlightenment ideas did not affect the lifestyle policies and ideologies of the aristocracy. John Martin and Dennis Romano, 'Reconsidering Venice', in *Venice Reconsidered: The History and Civilisation of an Italian City-State 1297–1797* (Baltimore; London: The Johns Hopkins University Press, 2000), 6.

92 John Martin and Dennis Romano, eds. *Venice Reconsidered*.

93 Romano, *Patricians and Popolani*.

94 Romano, *Patricians and Popolani*, 152.

95 Romano, *Patricians and Popolani*.

96 Romano, *Patricians and Popolani*, 152.

97 Muir, *Civic Ritual in Renaissance Venice*.

98 Mackenney, *Tradesmen and Traders*.

99 Romano, *Patricians and Popolani*.

100 Martin and Romano, *Venice Reconsidered*. A characteristic example of this view is Muir's study of civic ritual, which argues that ritual in Venice was one of the main vehicles that celebrated, reproduced and helped restructure Venetian society and culture. Muir, *Civic Ritual in Renaissance Venice*.

101 For Hillier and Hanson, configurational space has syntactic meaning and can influence – not deterministically, but probabilistically – movement and interaction. It is through syntactic analysis that these configurational properties can be extracted, and then interpreted as containing social meaning. Hillier and Hanson, *The Social Logic of Space*.

102 'In its early phases, expansion was the work of the major property owners, some of whom were laymen, but more typically the entrepreneurs were ecclesiastics or religious institutions embarked on land-reclamation projects on the scale of an entire quarter.' Crouzet-Pavan, *Venice Triumphant*, 11.

103 Hillier, Young, and Turner, 'Normalising Least Angle Choice in Depthmap'.

104 Hillier, Young, and Turner, 'Normalising Least Angle Choice in Depthmap'.

105 The values are based on standard scores varying about 0, with the negative minimum at the centre and the positive maximum at the edge.

106 Hillier, Young, and Turner, 'Normalising Least Angle Choice in Depthmap'. See also: Hillier, 'What Are Cities For?'.

107 Romano, *Patricians and Popolani*, 22.

108 Romano writes that 'the rulings of the *guidici del piovego* and the laws passed by the Major Council show that by the fourteenth century the government had a clear sense of Venice as a civic community – a place in which the common good was paramount'. The *piovego* used the term *publicam utilitatem* with 'clear resonances of Roman law and the classical *res publica*'. Romano, *Patricians and Popolani*, 26.

109 Crouzet-Pavan, *Venice Triumphant*, 29.

110 Crouzet-Pavan, *Venice Triumphant*.

111 Colin Rowe and Leon Satkowski, *Italian Architecture of the 16th Century* (New York: Princenton Architectural Press, 2002), 166.

112 Crouzet-Pavan, *Venice Triumphant*.

113 Crouzet-Pavan, *Venice Triumphant*. See also footnotes 33, 65.

114 Crouzet-Pavan, *Venice Triumphant*.

115 Wilson, *The World in Venice*, 34.

116 Anthony Black, *Guilds and Civil Society in European Political Thought from the Twelfth Century to the Present* (Ithaca, NY: Cornell University Press, 1984). See also: Simon Parker, *Cities, Politics and Power* (Oxford; New York: Routledge, 2011).

117 Stoppani, *Paradigm Islands*.

118 Hillier, Young and Turner, 'Normalising Least Angle Choice in Depthmap'.

119 Muir, *Civic Ritual in Renaissance Venice*, 25.

120 Muir, *Civic Ritual in Renaissance Venice*.

121 The map of 1829 follows the time of pedestrian reform brought about by the Napoleonic occupation, which opened new roads as a result of shifts in the governance of the city. Other transformations were the inauguration of Venice as a free port, the construction of warehouses, housing and the enclosed dock guarded by two light houses designed by Mezzani-Venturelli. The map of 1859 is one year before the construction of the railway, begun in Venice, capturing urban form before the major impact of industrialisation. Finally, the map of 1910 is a few years after the first Biennale (1895) and before the film festival began, capturing the early impact of international exhibitions in the city.

Chapter 2: Statecraft: A remarkably well-ordered society

1 Statecraft concerns the origins and fundamentals for state management.

2 Additional operations were hydraulic improvements, modification of the shores, diversion of rivers and currents, protection of beaches, changes in the depth of the lagoon and its silted beds, sand bars and deposited sediment, reshaping of bays and the boundary between flowing and stagnant water, and combating waves with sea walls. Crouzet-Pavan, 'Towards an Ecological Understanding of the Myth of Venice'.

3 Edward Muir, *Civic Ritual in Renaissance Venice*. See also: Iain Fenlon, *Piazza San Marco*. London: Profile Books, 2010.

4 Alessandro Marzo Magno, *Bound in Venice: The Serene Republic and the Dawn of the Book* (New York: Europa Editions, 2013).

5 As Norwich remarks, 'at this time Venice had become the intellectual centre of Italy. Barely thirty years after Doge Cristoforo Moro had issued the first printer's licence in 1469, more books had been published in the city than in Rome, Milan, Florence and Naples combined.' John Julius Norwich, *A History of Venice*, 412.

6 Denis E. Cosgrove, *The Palladian Landscape*.

7 Juergen Schultz, 'Jacopo de' Barbari's View of Venice: Map Making, City Views and Moralised Geography before the Year 1500'. *The Art Bulletin*, 60, 3: 425.

8 Wilson, *The World in Venice*.

9 Pier Vittorio Aureli, *The Possibility of an Absolute Architecture*.

10 Richard J. Goy, *Building Renaissance Venice*.

11 'The transformation of the open area in front of the church into what was effectively a new and imposing civic space was one of the three major projects carried out by the Venetian authorities during this period; the other two were the development of the area around the Rialto bridge as the principal trading centre of the city, and the reconstruction of the naval dockyard (the Arsenal), which was destined to become the largest industrial complex of medieval Europe. Taken as a whole, these three ambitious initiatives signalled a determination to embellish the principal sites of the military, commercial and politico-ecclesiastical life of Venice.' Fenlon, *Piazza San Marco*, 52.

12 A long series of interventions reduced congestion and improved the appearance of the dense quarter of Rialto. As Richard Goy writes, 'the Rialto was even more vital to the prosperity of the Serenissima than was San Marco'. Goy, *Building Renaissance Venice*, 40. A new triumphal arch was designed for the Arsenale, the walled naval base and largest industrial-military complex in Europe, paralleled to hell in the *Divine Comedy* by Dante. Dante (Alighieri), *The Divine Comedy*, trans. James Romanes Sibbalb (Edinburgh: D. Douglas, 1984).

13 Venice's reputation as a literary centre was such that the Roman printer and humanist Teobaldo Pio Manuzio – better known as Aldus Manutius – made it his home, 'and, setting up his presses in the Campo S. Agostino, embarked on the task which was to occupy him for the next twenty-five years: the editing, printing and publication of the whole canon of Greek classical literature'. Norwich, *A History of Venice*, 412. Manutius was a refined intellectual, the first modern publisher, inventor of italics, punctuation, the octavo and of reading for pleasure, who brought 'cultural heritage, technical skills, and an intuition for market demand, so much so, that the history of publishing is divided into before Manutius and after'. Magno, *Bound in Venice*, 44.

14 Thanks to Manutius the books were sold cheaply and in large quantities, reaching many sectors of the population both in Venice and abroad in northern Europe, to which they were exported by the northern European merchants of the Fondaco dei Tedeschi. See: Norwich, *A History of Venice*. Manutius had published what is considered the most beautiful book ever printed, the *Hypnerotomachia Poliphili*, a pagan work of love and journeying written by a Venetian monk and illustrated by Benedetto Bordone with Renaissance figures, architectural monuments, landscapes and gardens. See: Magno, *Bound in Venice*. See also: Vaughan Hart with Peter Hicks, eds. *Paper Palaces: The Rise of the Renaissance Architectural Treatise* (New Haven; London: Yale University Press, 1998).

15 It was Fra Giovanni Giocondo's first edition of Vitruvius, printed as a large-folio book by Giovanni Tacuino in Venice, that made an impact among architects. Ingrid D. Rowland, 'Vitruvius in Print and in Vernacular Translation: Fra Giocondo, Bramante, Raphael and

Cesare Cesariano', in *Paper Palaces: The Rise of the Renaissance Architectural Treatise*, eds Vaughan Hart with Peter Hicks (New Haven; London: Yale Architectural Press).

16 Goy, *Building Renaissance Venice*.

17 Ingrid D. Rowland and Thomas Noble Howe, eds, *Vitruvius*. Robert Tavernor, 'Introduction', in *Andrea Palladio: The Four Books of Architecture* (Cambridge, MA: The MIT Press, 2002).

18 Manfredo Tafuri, *Venice and the Renaissance*.

19 Deborah Howard, *Jacopo Sansovino: Architecture and Patronage in Renaissance Venice* (New Haven; London: Yale University Press, 1975).

20 Norwich, *A History of Venice*. See also: Dennis Romano, *Patricians and Popolani*.

21 'The one home today of liberty, peace and justice, the one refuge of honourable men, the one port to which can repair the storm-tossed, tyrant-hounded craft of men who seek the good life.' Petrarch, *Letters from Petrarch*, trans. Morris Bishop (Bloomington: Indiana University Press, 1966), 146.

22 The Basilica was rebuilt in the second half of the eleventh century after the church of the Holy Apostles in Constantinople (the *Apostoleion*), indicating the historic link between Venice and Byzantium. See: Fenlon, *Piazza San Marco*.

23 Ziani enlarged the Piazza to its present 160 metres by reclaiming land from the canal at the western end of the space. See: Giulia Foscari Widmann Rezzonico and Rem Koolhaas, *Elements of Venice* (Zurich: Lars Müller Publishers, 2014).

24 As with the Basilica, the source of inspiration for the Procuratie was 'Constantinople with its sequence of forum-like squares, surrounded by meeting halls, public baths, shops, churches and palaces all linked by porticos'. Fenlon, *Piazza San Marco*, 54. On the opposite side of the Procuratie were the Ospizio Orseolo, a hostel for pilgrims, and the Campanile, with buildings on two sides.

25 By 1420 the Basilica was essentially completed as we see it today, while the rebuilding of the palace continued, after the completion of the Molo wing, with the wing facing the Piazzetta. The third wing of the palace forms the eastern side of its inner courtyard, and was begun after the fire that destroyed the Doge's residence in 1483. Fenlon, *Piazza San Marco*.

26 Built by Giovanni and Bartolomeo Bon. See: Goy, *Building Renaissance Venice*.

27 The Orologio is considered to be the work of Mauro Codussi. See: Deborah Howard, *The Architectural History of Venice*.

28 Sansovino came to Venice in 1527 from Rome. Having gained the friendship of Doge Gritti and the trust of the Procurators (after the death of Bartolomeo Bon in 1529), he became the master architect of all buildings and works in the Piazza and the Piazzetta with the exception of the Ducal Palace. Howard, *Jacopo Sansovino*.

29 In 1580, after Sansovino's death in 1570, a series of events led to the completion of the Library and the Procuratie Nuove. In 1579 a number of operations refurbished the Arsenale. In 1587–1590 the construction of Rialto Bridge in stone and the Fondamente Nove were begun. Connected to these transformations was the project for the city-fortress of Palmanova (1592–1593). For Tafuri these works were interconnected, showing a deliberate process of urban renewal. They came out of a precise political and economic project, focusing on the sites of institutions, the productive capacities of the Arsenal, the economic revitalisation of the Rialto and the northern section of the city. See: Tafuri, *Venice and the Renaissance*.

30 Three of Palladio's churches had their façades completed after his death: first, the Redentore (1592), next San Pietro di Castello (1595–1596), and finally San Giorgio Maggiore (1607–1611). The completion of the façades was based on drawings, contract descriptions, models and details that Palladio had left. See: Tracy E. Cooper, *Palladio's Venice: Architecture and Society in a Renaissance Republic* (London: Yale University Press, 2005).

31 Each panel measured approximately 66 × 99 cm, twice the width of the paper used for imperial folios. See: Deborah Howard, 'Venice as a Dolphin: Further Investigations into Jacopo de' Barbari's View', *Artibus e Historiae*, 38, 35 (1997).

32 Wilson, *The World in Venice*.

33 Mercury, god of commerce, is encircled by the legend 'I Mercury shine favourably on this above all other emporia'. Neptune, god of the sea, carries the legend 'I Neptune reside here, smoothing the waters at this port'. Schultz, 'Jacopo de' Barbari's View of Venice', 468.

34 Petitioning the Venetian government for sole publication rights to the print, the publisher Anton Kolb described it as showing 'the city of Venice just as it lies and is situated'. Schultz, 'Jacopo de' Barbari's View of Venice', 472.

35 In the earliest record of an impression of the print, from 1627, it is listed as part of a princely collection together with other city views, maps and works of art. See: Schultz, 'Jacopo de' Barbari's View of Venice'. Intended for an international market but also appealing to Venetians, the print was rather a luxury item for collectors, to be displayed on a wall and viewed from some distance. See: Howard, 'Venice as a Dolphin'.

36 *Mappae Mundi* provided a synoptic image, or a syncretic view of the world, teaching geographical and non-geographical facts. They consisted of rational information – by fifteenth-century standards – overlaid on historical and classical events, biblical lands and mythical monsters. Medieval and early Renaissance artists used such city views for conceptual illustration and as emblems of ideas. A *Mappa Mundi* decorated the public loggia at the Rialto market in Venice and wall maps of the world were made for the audience chamber in the Ducal Palace under Doge Francesco Dandolo (1329–1339). See: Schultz, 'Jacopo de' Barbari's View of Venice'.

37 Schultz, 'Jacopo de' Barbari's View of Venice', 468.

38 Wilson, *The World in Venice*.

39 Jacopo's unimaginable viewing position and the technical accuracy of the image has attracted a large amount of scholarship, speculating that it might have been produced from a plan and that Jacopo would have used elevations to complete the perspective. See: Schultz. This idea presupposes an urban survey or at least a series of reference points probably positioned in bell towers, and surveyed using polar coordinates or triangulation. See: Caterina Balletti, 'Analytical and Quantitative Methods for the Analysis of the Geometrical Content of Historical Cartography', *International Archives of Photogrametry and Remote Sensing*, XXXIII, B5 (2000). A number of inaccuracies and distortions in the perspective used in the print indicate that it was not based on an accurate survey. In the light of the surveying data that were technologically possible at Jacopo's time, as well as studies by Imhof and Bellavitis, Schultz concludes that Jacopo's view resulted from the montage of separate drawings made from different view-points. See: Schultz, 'Jacopo de' Barbari's View of Venice'; Giorgio Bellavitis and Giandomenico Romanelli, *Venezia* (Bari; Rome: Laterza, 1985). Using projective transformations that return the print to a correct central projection, Balleti has confirmed that the view is not an exact planimetric or altimetric perspective in terms of projection and metric geometry. This proposition reinforces Schultz's idea that it must have been assembled in the studio from a large number of small views drawn from towers. A general conception of Venice's plan must have been used as a model, informed by unsystematic plans of the city drawn over 300 years by the offices of the Republic, and adjusted to the direction from which the city may be seen from San Giorgio. Corrections may have been incorporated into the model from the actual view from San Giorgio and from the information acquired by the individual drawings. Built upon a vision of the imagination, Jacopo's woodcut is the work of a single highly gifted person in its synthesis of perspectival views derived from different empirical observations and assembled as a single perspective. Schultz writes: 'We of the twentieth century who have had the experience of air travel and see aerial photographs every day in the press are able only with difficulty to realize what an imaginative feat this view ... represented in an age without the gift of flight. ... The view of Venice is the creation of an artist from beginning to end ... the work of a single, highly gifted draftsman: Jacopo.' See: Schultz, 'Jacopo de' Barbari's View of Venice', 441.

40 Schultz, 'Jacopo de' Barbari's View of Venice', 439.

41 It combined two ways of mapping: from the heights of towers and from the ground, expressing them as the imaginative transposition of embodied vision. It recognised streets, places and their relationships as seen from the the earth's surface, as well as a totalising view of the metropolis. These two ways of perceiving Venice encompassed the tension between experiencing the city as a pedestrian and grasping the unbroken unity of the urban body. They also expressed the dialogue between the mosaic of parish centres and the entire urban landscape. In the analysis of Venice's urban networks, I noted that these spatial and social tensions had driven the development of the floating city. Jacopo's map therefore reveals a fair amount of knowledge about the urban form and the social organisation of the city based on parish centres. Yet, through its homogeneous detail and geometrical symmetry, the image calls viewers to marvel, against all diversity, at the unparalleled urbanity and unity of the whole.

42 Crouzet-Pavan explains that the city's location in the lagoon had a profound influence on the development of the Most Serene Republic as an idealised picture. The lagoon was seen as a tranquil sanctuary protecting and separating the city from 'the vagaries of Continental affairs'.

Over the years it was reduced to a pacified element of décor against the city's spectacular theatricality. Elisabeth Crouzet-Pavan, 'Towards an Ecological Understanding of the Myth of Venice', 42.

43 Bill Hillier and Julienne Hanson, *The Social Logic of Space*.

44 Howard, *Jacopo Sansovino*.

45 Leon Battista Alberti, *On the Art of Building in Ten Books*, trans. Neil Leach, Robert Tavernor and Joseph Rykvert (Cambridge, MA: The MIT Press, 1988).

46 Andrea Palladio, *The Four Books on Architecture*, xxi.

47 Howard, *Jacopo Sansovino*, 175.

48 Howard, *Jacopo Sansovino*.

49 Foscari Widmann Rezzonico and Koolhaas, *Elements of Venice*.

50 Wilson, *The World of Venice*, 25.

51 Howard, *Jacopo Sansovino*, 3.

52 Tafuri, *Venice and the Renaissance*.

53 As with Palladio's churches, the Salute has a bright white surface built with Istrian stone. Unlike these churches, it addresses San Marco's large dome with its own vast dome over a central plan. Howard, *The Architectural History of Venice*. See also: Rudolf Wittkower, 'S. Maria Della Salute', *Saggi e Memorie di Storia dell'Arte*, 3 (1963).

54 Palladio, *The Four Books on Architecture*, 213.

55 Palladio, *The Four Books on Architecture*.

56 Cooper, *Palladio's Venice*. See also: Daniel Savoy, 'Palladio and the Water-Oriented Scenography of Venice', *Journal of the Society of Architectural Historians*, 71, 2.

57 Wittkower, 'S. Maria Della Salute'.

58 'A Portolan chart, also called harbour-finding chart, compass chart or rhumb chart, was a navigational chart of the European Middle Ages (1300–1500). The earliest dated navigational chart extant was produced at Genoa by Petrus Vesconte in 1311 and is said to mark the beginning of professional cartography. The portolan charts were characterized by rhumb lines, lines that radiate from the centre in the direction of the wind or compass points and that were used by pilots to lay courses from one harbor to another. The charts were usually drawn on vellum and embellished with a frame and other decorations. Of the roughly 130 portolans surviving, most were made in Italy or Catalonia and a few in Portugal. The Italian portolans tend to encompass only Western Europe and the Mediterranean basin, but some Catalan charts can be considered world maps.' *Encyclopedia Britannica*, last updated 6.2.2009, https://www.britannica.com/technology/portolan-chart, accessed 24 February 2017.

59 Muir, *Civic Ritual in Renaissance Venice*, 211.

60 Louis Marin, *Utopics: Spatial Play*, trans. Robert A. Vollrath (Atlantic Highlands, NJ: Humanities Press, 1983).

61 Howard, *Jacopo Sansovino*. See also: Fenlon, *Piazza San Marco*.

62 Fenlon, *Piazza San Marco*, xx–xxi.

63 Howard, *The Architectural History of Venice*, 11.

64 Evelyn S. Welch, *Shopping in the Renaissance: Consumer Cultures in Italy 1400–1600* (New Haven; London: Yale University Press, 2005).

65 Alberti, *On the Art of Building in Ten Books*, 118.

66 Welch, *Shopping in the Renaissance*, 103.

67 See: Fenlon, *Piazza San Marco*; Savoy, 'Palladio and the Water-Oriented Scenography of Venice'. See also: Cosgrove, *The Palladian Landscape*; Alberto Perez-Gomez and Louise Pelletier, *Architectural Representation and the Perspective Hinge* (Cambridge, MA; London: The MIT Press, 2000).

68 Ellen Rosand, *Opera in Seventeenth-Century Venice: The Creation of a Genre* (Berkeley; Oxford: University of California Press, 1991); See also: Savoy, 'Palladio and the Water-Oriented Scenography of Venice'.

69 Anthony Vidler, *The Scenes of the Street and Other Essays* (New York: Monacelli Press, 2011).

70 Contarini here placed the *cittadini* and *popolani* together. Muir, *Civic Ritual in Renaissance Venice*, 41. See also: Gasparo Contarini, *The Commonwealth and Government of Venice*.

71 Tafuri, *Venice and the Renaissance*.

72 Howard, *Jacopo Sansovino*.

73 Muir, *Civic Ritual in Renaissance Venice*.

74 'According to legend, the city was founded on March 25 (421AD), mystically conjoined with the founding of Rome, the beginning of the Christian era, the annual rebirth of nature, and the

first day of the calendar year.' Muir, *Civic Ritual in Renaissance Venice*, 71. Its origin was due to a divine revelation, an apparition St Mark the Evangelist had at *Rivo Alto* (the island of Rialto), which foretold that refugees would on someday build on that spot a glorious city and honour his relics. The translation (*translatio*) of the body of St Mark to Venice was as a gift to the Doge (*Particiaco*). If the myth of the apparition explained the foundation of the city, the *translatio* and the *Particiaco* secured the saint's patronage and the spiritual union between politics and religion. Muir, *Civic Ritual in Renaissance Venice*.

75 The Doge had a central role in the annual ritual of St Mark's feast day (25 April) and the cult of St Mark, as well as over the trade institutions of Venice. Muir, *Civic Ritual in Renaissance Venice*, 91.

76 Muir, *Civic Ritual in Renaissance Venice*, 101. See also: Cosgrove: 'the islands around the Rialto were located at the centre of the world, the meeting point of commerce and the mediating pivot between Rome and the Byzantium, Empire and Papacy. The legend that St Mark himself had introduced Christianity to the lagoons ... served to give Venice an apostolic status equal to that of Rome. The enshrinement of the evangelist's body in the Doge's church reinforced the idea of Venice as a sacred centre, an axis mundi ... Venice ... could be imagined as a second eternal city. Eternal and perfect, these characteristics spoke to a stasis which denied historical change and legitimated the promise of future permanence.' *The Palladian Landscape*, 147.

77 *La Senza* was the annual marriage of the Doge to the sea, on Ascension Day, at the Lido, where a breach opened the lagoon to the Adriatic. Muir, *Civic Ritual in Renaissance Venice*.

78 Victor W. Turner, *The Ritual Process: Structure and Anti-Structure* (London: Routledge & Kegan Paul, 1969).

79 Muir, *Civic Ritual in Renaissance Venice*, 13. Muir explains that the ruling system combined 'monarchy in the person of the Doge, aristocracy in the 300 senators and popular republican rule in the broad membership of the 2,000-strong Great Council'. *Civic Ritual in Renaissance Venice*, 147.

80 Muir, *Civic Ritual in Renaissance Venice*.

81 William J. Bouwsma, *Venice and the Defence of Republican Liberty: Renaissance Values in the Age of the Counter Reformation* (Berkeley; London: University of California Press, 1984).

82 Muir, *Civic Ritual in Renaissance Venice*.

83 Romano, *Patricians and Popolani*.

84 Muir, *Civic Ritual in Renaissance Venice*.

85 Muir, *Civic Ritual in Renaissance Venice*,148.

86 Muir, *Civic Ritual in Renaissance Venice*, 302.

87 Tafuri, *Venice and the Renaissance*, 19.

88 Tafuri, *Venice and the Renaissance*, 25.

89 Tafuri, *Venice and the Renaissance*. See also: Savoy, 'Palladio and the Water-Oriented Scenography of Venice'.

90 Howard, *Jacopo Sansovino*, 129, 91.

91 Cooper, *Palladio's Venice*, ix.

92 Savoy, 'Palladio and the Water-Oriented Scenography of Venice'.

93 Tafuri, *Venice and the Renaissance*.

94 Savoy, 'Palladio and the Water-Oriented Scenography of Venice'. See also: Cooper, *Palladio's Venice*.

95 'Proposals by Fra Giocondo and Palladio to reorganize the market area according to an absolute geometry of classical space contravened the medieval morphology and were rejected in favour of a piecemeal programme better attuned to the wisdom of commerce than to the humanism which dominated at San Marco'. Denis Cosgrove, 'The Myth and The Stones of Venice: An Historical Geography of a Symbolic Landscape', *Journal of Historical Geography*, 8, 2 (1982).

96 Savoy, 'Palladio and the Water-Oriented Scenography of Venice', 219.

97 Cosgrove, 'The Myth and The Stones of Venice,' 242.

98 Howard, *The Architectural History of Venice*, 214.

99 James S. Ackerman, *Palladio* (Harmondsworth: Penguin, 1966).

100 Cosgrove, 'The Myth and The Stones of Venice', 242.

101 Denis Cosgrove, 'New Worlds: Culture and Cartography in Sixteenth-Century Venice', *Imago Mundi*, 44 (1992): 69.

102 Bruno Latour, 'Visualisation and Cognition: Drawing Things Together', *Knowledge and Society: Studies in the Sociology of Culture Past and Present*, 6 (1986).

103 Wilson, *The World in Venice*.

104 Latour, 'Visualisation and Cognition'.
105 Guido Beltramini, Davide Gasparotto and Giulio Menieri Elia, 'Aldo Manuzio: Renaissance in Venice' (Venice: Marsilio, 2016).
106 Joan Zimmerman, 'The City as Practice: Urban Topography, Pictorial Construction and Liminality in Venetian Renaissance Painting, 1495–1595' (PhD thesis, The University of Texas at Austin, 1999).
107 Zimmerman, 'The City as Practice'.
108 Mario Carpo, *The Alphabet and the Algorithm* (Cambridge, MA: The MIT Press, 2007), 12.
109 Séquin Reymond Shiau, Carlo H. Sequin, 'Rendering Pacioli's Rhombicuboctahedron', *Journal of Mathematics and the Arts*, 9 (2015): 103–110.

Chapter 3: Story-craft: The imagination as combinatorial machine in Italo Calvino's *Invisible Cities*

1 Canaletto painted a series of *Capricci* depictions of Venice, combining his accurate topographical views of the city with imaginary and real architecture. His paintings and drawings often mixed existing structures, elements or settings with fictive ones placed in imaginary compositions or transported from their original setting to a different place. His work 'had always involved an element of manipulation and imagination and his *capricci* paintings explored these artistic possibilities further'. Rosie Razzall and Lucy Whitaker, *Canaletto: The Art of Venice* (London: Royal Collection Trust, 2017), 259. Canaletto also painted 13 overdoor paintings celebrating Palladio's architecture (although only five paintings depicted Palladio's buildings); all referred to Palladio's plates in *Quattro Libri* and were accurately represented in fanciful settings. Rosie Razzall and Lucy Whitaker, *Canaletto: The Art of Venice*.
2 Italo Calvino, *Invisible Cities*.
3 Marco Polo, *The Travels of Marco Polo: The Venetian*, trans. Colin Thubron (London: Everyman, 2008). See also: Thomas More, *Utopia*.
4 Letizia Modena, *Italo Calvino's Architecture of Lightness,* 2.
5 Laurence A. Breiner, 'Italo Calvino: The Place of the Emperor in Invisible Cities,' *Modern Fiction Studies* Volume 34, 4 Winter (1988).
6 Italo Calvino, *Six Memos for the Next Millennium*.
7 Oulipo members, such as Raymond Queneau, George Perec and Francis Ponge, used mathematical constraints and combinatorial exercises to generate new forms of poems and writing. See: Alastair Brotchie, Harry Mathews, eds., *Oulipo Compendium* (London: Atlas Press, 1998). Calvino's encounters with these experimental writers led to numerical and mathematical patterns in fictions such as *Mr Palomar* and *The Castle of Crossed Destinies*. Italo Calvino, *Mr Palomar*, trans. William Weaver (London: Vintage, 1999). Italo Calvino, *The Castle of Crossed Destinies*, trans William Weaver (London: Vintage, 1997). In the latter Calvino brings together a group of travellers that tell their stories with the aid of tarot cards. The cards are presented in the margin of the text, while the characters construct their stories with cards played by other characters. The stories can be read from left to right, top to bottom or the reverse, as they contain multiple possibilities for narrative combinations.
8 Roland Barthes, *Image, Music, Text*, trans. Stephen Heath (London: Flamingo, 1977).
9 Calvino, *Six Memos for the Next Millennium*, 9; Jorge Luis Borges, *Fictions*, trans. Andrew Hurley (London: Penguin, 2000, 1998); Titus Lucretius Carus, *On the Nature of Things*, trans. Frank O. Copley (New York: W.W. Norton & Co., 2011).
10 Calvino, *Six Memos for the Next Millennium*, 9; Ovid, *The Essential Metamorphoses*, trans. Stanley Lombardo (Indianapolis: Hackett Pub. Co., 2011).
11 Manfredo Tafuri, *Architecture and Utopia: Design and Capitalist Development*, trans. Barbara Luigia La Penta (Cambridge, MA; London: MIT Press, 1976).
12 Modena, *Italo Calvino's Architecture of Lightness*, 144.
13 Umberto Eco, *The Open Work*, trans. Anna Cancogni (Cambridge, MA: Harvard University Press, 1989).
14 Italo Calvino, *The Literature Machine*, trans. Patrick Greagh (London: Vintage, 1997), 8.
15 Calvino, *The Literature Machine*, 12.
16 Italo Calvino, *If on a Winter's Night a Traveller*, trans. William Weaver (London: Everyman's Library, 1993); Hanan Shaykh, *One Thousand and One Nights* (London: Bloomsbury, 2013).

17 Martin McLaughlin, *Italo Calvino* (Edinburgh: Edinburgh University Press, 1998).
18 During his explorations Marco Polo became a confidant to the Khan, who, frustrated by the inadequacies of his officials' reports, entrusted him to go on research trips across the empire. John Man, *Xanadu: Marco Polo and Europe's Discovery of the East* (London: Transworld Publishers, 2009).
19 Man, *Xanadu*.
20 Calvino, *Invisible Cities*, 5.
21 Calvino, *Invisible Cities*, 147.
22 Calvino, *Invisible Cities*, 148.
23 Calvino, *Invisible Cities*, 79.
24 Calvino, *Invisible Cities*.
25 Calvino, *Invisible Cities*, 5.
26 Calvino, *Invisible Cities*.
27 Breiner, 'Italo Calvino', 569.
28 Calvino, *Invisible Cities*, 31.
29 Calvino, *Invisible Cities*, 125.
30 Many texts have been written about *Invisible Cities*, mainly by literary critics, based on the organisation of the text through the numbering of cities and headings in the table of contents. The diamond shape in Figure 3.2 corresponds to the shape included in Calvino's notes. McLaughlin, *Italo Calvino*. See also: Bruno Ferraro, 'Italo Calvino's "Le Città Invisibili" and "La Sfida Al Labirinto"', *The Italianist*, 8, 1 (1988); John Peponis, *Chorographies* (Athens: Alexandria Press, 1997).
31 Peponis, *Chorographies*.
32 A similar argument is put forward by Bill Hillier in the context of geometrical and topological relationships among elements in a graph representing streets in an urban grid. Bill Hillier, 'The Hidden Geometry of Deformed Grids: Or Why Space Syntax Works When It Looks as Though It Shouldn't', *Environment and Planning B: Planning and Design*, 26, (2 March 1999).
33 Henri Poincaré, *Science and Method* (New York: Dover Publications, 2003), 42.
34 Roland Barthes, *Writing Degree Zero*, trans. Annette Lavers and Colin Smith (London: Jonathan Cape, 1967).
35 Peponis, *Chorographies*.
36 Peponis, *Chorographies*.
37 Peponis, *Chorographies*.
38 Nelson Goodman, *Languages of Art* (London: Oxford University Press, 1969), 209.
39 Mario Carpo, *The Alphabet and the Algorithm* 16.
40 McLaughlin, *Italo Calvino*, 102.
41 Umberto Eco, *The Search for the Perfect Language*, trans. James Fentress (Oxford: Blackwell, 1995), 55.
42 Calvino, *Six Memos for the Next Millennium*, 71.
43 Calvino, *Invisible Cities*, 40–41.
44 See Chapter 1, note 61.
45 Calvino, *Invisible Cities*, 19.
46 Calvino, *Invisible Cities*, 86.
47 Calvino, *Invisible Cities*, 52.
48 Calvino, *Invisible Cities*, 44, 68.
49 Calvino, *Invisible Cities*, 84.
50 Calvino, *Invisible Cities*, 148.
51 Calvino, *Invisible Cities*. Looking at the atlas with Polo, Kublai observes that Polo's strategy for an imaginative way of constructing his ideal city or utopia 'is all useless, if the last landing place can only be the infernal city, and it is there that, in ever-narrowing circles, the current is drawing us'. Calvino, *Invisible Cities*, 147. There is an obvious reference to Dante's Inferno here, which was depicted as comprising concentric circles. Dante (Alighieri), *The Divine Comedy of Dante Alighieri*.
52 Calvino, *Invisible Cities*, 8.
53 Calvino, *Six Memos for the Next Millennium*, 61.
54 Inspired by Borges's *Library of Babel*, Bloch calculated the number of books in Borges's Library and explored other instances of mathematics embedded in this fiction. William Goldbloom Bloch, *The Unimaginable Mathematics of Borges' Library of Babel* (Oxford: Oxford University Press, 2008).

55 Calvino, *Invisible Cities*, 44.
56 Calvino, *Invisible Cities*, 9.
57 In particular, Borges's *The Garden of Forking Paths* was much admired by Calvino for condensing infinite contemporary universes in which all possibilities are realised in all possible combinations in a short fiction, 'the structure of which is accumulative, modular and combinatory'. Jorge Luis Borges, *Fictions*; see: Calvino, *Six Memos for the Next Millennium*, 120. Calvino absorbed multiple other influences, from the urbanists Lewis Mumford, Jane Jacobs and Kevin Lynch to the utopian thinker Charles Fourier, the literary critic Northrop Frey, the structuralist theorist Roland Barthes, the computer scientist Alan Turing and the experimental writers of the Oulipo group. These influences show his diverse interests in architecture, urbanism, complexity theory, structural semiotics, post-structuralism and generative literature. Lewis Mumford, *The City in History*; Jane Jacobs, *The Death and Life of Great American Cities*; Kevin Lynch, *The Image of the City*; Charles Fourier, Gareth Stedman Jones, and Ian Patterson, *The Theory of the Four Movements* (Cambridge: Cambridge University Press, 1996); Northrop Frye, *Anatomy of Criticism: Four Essays* (Harmondsworth: Penguin, 1990, 1957); Barthes, *Writing Degree Zero*.
58 Calvino, *Invisible Cities*, 69.
59 Calvino, *Invisible Cities*, 38.
60 Eco, *The Search for the Perfect Language.*
61 Calvino, *The Literature Machine*, 9.
62 Larry McCaffery, 'Form, Formula and Fantasy: Generative Structures in Contemporary Fiction', in *Bridges to Fantasy*, eds. Eric S. Rabkin, George E. Slusser, Robert Scholes (Carbondale III: Southern Illinois University Press, 1882).
63 Man, *Xanadu*, 274.
64 Man, *Xanadu*, 268.
65 Man, *Xanadu*, 268–69.
66 Man, *Xanadu*, 269. Man explains that the book and its copies soon sparked interest in the overland journey to China by missionaries and merchants. However, the Ming dynasty that replaced the Mongols and the Yuan emperors made the memory of the links between East and West fade away, turning Marco's *Travels* into a book of unbelievable marvels, until its resurrection in print form in Germany in 1477.
67 Man, *Xanadu*.
68 Man, *Xanadu*, 2.
69 Breiner, *Italo Calvino*, 560.
70 Henry Yule and Henri Cordier, *The Travels of Marco Polo: The Complete Yule-Cordier Edition*, 2 vols (New York: Dover, 1993), 291.
71 Introduction by Calvino, see: Italo Calvino, *Le Città Invisibili* (Milano: Oscar Mondadori), viii.
72 Calvino refers to Coleridge's famous poem:

    In Xanadu did Kubla Khan
    A Stately pleasure-dome decree
    Where Alf, the sacred river, ran
    Through caverns measureless to man
    Down to a sunless sea.

    This was an image that came to Coleridge in an opium-tinged dream and has been associated with the imagination and the creative impulse. See: Arthur Koestler, *The Act of Creation* (New York: Macmillan, 1964).
73 Calvino, *Invisible Cities*, 123.
74 Barthes, *Writing Degree Zero.*
75 Carpo, *The Alphabet and the Algorithm*, 24.
76 Calvino often stressed the role of 'hidden ghosts' and Italian folk tales or works emerging out of virtual literary interactions. See: Calvino, *The Literature Machine*.
77 The Khan's atlas includes a range of cities such as Kambalu and Malabar in Kublai's empire; Constantinople and Granada, both imperial cities of the middle ages; Mexico and Cuzco, cities of the Americas discovered by the West and named as the 'new world' in the fifteenth and sixteenth centuries; cities of the Hanseatic League, all of which can be reached from other places. Calvino, *Invisible Cities*, 123.
78 The cities that are as yet to be imagined form the focus of the closing discussion between Polo and the Khan, bringing about the question of utopia, and works such as Thomas Bacon's *New*

Atlantis, Thomas More's *Utopia*, Campanella's *City of the Sun*, James Harrington's *Oceana*, Marquis De Sade's *Tamoé,* Robert Owen's *New Harmony* and *New Lanark* and Etiennne Cabet's *Icaria*. Calvino, *Invisible Cities*.

79 The enormous size of possibility the short penultimate dialogue between Polo and the Khan refers to invokes Calvino's values of multiplicity and lightness, poignantly condensing space, knowledge and the literary epics of the past into a short narrative. Calvino, *Six Memos for the Next Millennium*.

80 Calvino, *Six Memos for the Next Millennium*, 91.

81 Calvino, *Six Memos for the Next Millennium.*

82 Calvino, *Six Memos for the Next Millennium.*

83 Calvino regarded *Invisible Cities* as the work where he was best able to express his idea of the imagination. Calvino, *Six Memos for the Next Millennium.*

84 Calvino, *Invisible Cities*, 5.

85 Calvino, *Invisible Cities*, 126.

86 'Si tratta di un particolare clima mentalle che Venezia determina intorno a noi, una geometria speciale [...] non euclidea che scatena la nostra immaginazione per vie inconsuete' ('This is a particular mental climate Venice engulfs us with, a special non-Euclidean geometry that stimulates our imagination in unusual ways' – author's translation). See: 'Venezia: Archetypo E Utopia Della Città Aquatica', 2689–90. See also: Kerstin Pilz, *Mapping Complexity: Literature and Science in the Works of Italo Calvino* (Leicester: Troubador Publishing, 2005).

87 Bill Hillier, 'What Are Cities For?'.

88 Hillier, 'What Are Cities For?'.

89 Edward Muir, *Civic Ritual in Renaissance Venice*.

90 The verbal absence of Venice from the text recalls the idea that, accustomed to seeing their city, people might fail to re-imagine it. Following the italicised dialogue on Venice, the city of *Esmeralda* 'spares its inhabitants the boredom of taking the same streets every day'. Calvino, *Invisible Cities*, 79.

91 Frances A. Yates, *The Art of Memory*, 18.

Chapter 4: Crafting architectural space: Le Corbusier's Venice Hospital and the three paradigms

1 Italo Calvino, 'Venezia: Archetypo e Utopia Della Città Aquatica', in *Saggi*.

2 The Modulor was a system of proportions based on the height of a man with his arm raised.

3 Le Corbusier, *La Ville Radieuse* (1933).

4 Le Corbusier, *Oeuvre*, vol. 2 1929–1934 (Basel: Birkhäuser, 1995), 24.

5 The Ospedale was finished by Codussi. Deborah Howard, *The Architectural History of Venice*.

6 Andrea Palladio, *The Four Books on Architecture*.

7 Andrea Palladio, *I Quatro Libri Dell'Architettura*.

8 Kenneth Frampton has recently argued that there were three conflicting paradigms shaping Modernism: the Technological, the Classical, and the Vernacular. The first was the impulse to use the technological methods of the period. The second was a normative standard embodying a rational, and international, design culture. The Vernacular derived its strength from the morphology of organically grown environments and regional building culture. Kenneth Frampton, *A Genealogy of Modern Architecture: Comparative Analysis of Built Form* (Zurich: Lars Muller Publishers, 2015). Le Corbusier's interest in the Vernacular, or the Organic, was articulated through his attention to vernacular architecture, which is experienced on foot 'and the direct transformation of a functional organism into appropriate form'. Alan Colquhoun, *Essays in Architectural Criticism: Modern Architecture and Historical Change* (London: The MIT Press, 1981), 31. In the Venice Hospital this paradigm found expression through a design that provided not simply a metaphor or an image, but an analogic translation of the city into a functional type and a building complex.

9 Robert Maxwell in a foreword to Mahnaz Shah's book. Mahnaz Shah, *Le Corbusier's Venice Hospital Project* (Burlington: Ashgate, 2013).

10 Hashim Sarkis, *Le Corbusier's Venice Hospital and the Mat Building Revival* (Munich; London; New York: Prestel, 2001), 22.

11 Giuseppe Mazzariol, 'Le Corbusier in Venice: His Project for a New Hospital', *Zodiac* 16 (1966): 241.
12 Alison Smithson, 'How to Recognise and Read Mat-Building: Mainstream Architecture as It Has Developed Towards the Mat-Building', *Architectural Design*, September (1974): 573.
13 Stan Allen, 'From Object to Field,' *Architectural Design*, 67, 5/6 (1997).
14 Le Corbusier, 'Rapport Technique', in *Le Corbusier's Venice Hospital*, ed. Hashim Sarkis (Munich; London; New York: Prestel Verlag, 2001), 42.
15 Le Corbusier, 'Rapport Technique'.
16 Le Corbusier, 'Rapport Technique'.
17 Le Corbusier, 'Rapport Technique'.
18 Colquhoun, *Essays in Architectural Criticism*, 38.
19 Vittore Carpaccio, *Martyrdom of the Pilgrims and the Funeral of Saint Ursula.*
20 Colquhoun, *Essays in Architectural Criticism.*
21 Hillier uses the notions of 'significance' and 'signification' to explain the difference of meaning, referring first and foremost to the intrinsic nature of buildings as architecture, as instances of the field of ordering possibilities that we call architecture, and those that develop through cultural association (signification), respectively. Bill Hillier, 'Quite Unlike the Pleasures of Scratching: Theory and Meaning in Architectural Form', *9H*, 7 (1985).
22 Hillier and Hanson, *The Social Logic of Space.*
23 Hillier and Hanson, *The Social Logic of Space.*
24 Bil Hillier, *Space Is the Machine: A Configurational Theory of Architecture* (Cambridge: Cambridge University Press, 1996). See also: Alan Penn, Dessylas Jake and Vaughan Laura, 'The Space of Innovation: Interaction and Communication in the Work Environment', *Environment and Planning B: Planning and Design*, 26, 2 (1999); Jake Desyllas, 'Domestic Asylum: A Study of Eleven Local Authority Hostels for Mentally Handicapped People', Proceedings of the Space Syntax Symposium II, University of Brasilia (1999).
25 Eric Mumford, 'The Emergence of Mat or Field Buildings', in *Le Corbusier's Venice Hospital*, ed. Hashim Sarkis (Munich; London; New York: Prestel Verlag, 2001), 48–65, 58.
26 Pablo Allard, 'Bridge over Venice: Speculations on Cross-Fertilization of Ideas between Team 10 and Le Corbusier (after a Conversation with Guillermo Jullian De La Fuente)', in *Le Corbusier's Venice Hospital*, ed. Hashim Sarkis (Munich; London; New York: Prestel Verlag, 2001), 18–37.
27 Guillermo Jullian de la Fuente, quoted by Pablo Allard, 'Bridge over Venice', 30.
28 Eric Mumford explains that Le Corbusier described the city as a 'witness' to the possibilities of urbanism conceptualised as a dense interconnected structure of pedestrian ways, canals and built fabric. He said of the Hospital design, 'The city of Venice is there and I have followed. I have invented nothing.' Mumford, 'The Emergence of Mat or Field Buildings', 58.
29 Howard, *The Architectural History of Venice*, 48.
30 Allard, 'Bridge over Venice'.
31 Konstantinos Doxiades, *Ekistics: An Introduction to the Science of Human Settlement* (London: Hutchinson, 1966).
32 Mumford, 'The Emergence of Mat or Field Buildings'.
33 This is similar to Hillier and Hanson's 'beady ring' settlement. Hillier and Hanson, *The Social Logic of Space*, 57–58.
34 Rudolf Wittkower, *Architectural Principles in the Age of Humanism*; Colin Rowe, *The Mathematics of the Ideal Villa and Other Essays* (Cambridge, MA; London: The MIT Press, 1976).
35 Christof Thoenes, 'Introduction', in *Architectural Theory*, eds. Bernd Evers and Christof Thoenes (Cologne: Taschen, 2003).
36 Robin Evans, *The Projective Cast: Architecture and Its Three Geometries* (Cambridge, MA: The MIT Press, 1995).
37 Leon Battista Alberti, *On the Art of Building in Ten Books.*
38 Sebastiano Serlio, *Tutte L'opere D'Architettura E Prospettiva* (Venice 1611).
39 Andrea Palladio, *Palladio's Rome: A Translation of Andrea Palladio's Two Guidebooks to Rome*, trans. Vaughan Hart with Peter Hicks (New Haven; London: Yale University Press, 2006).
40 Palladio, *Palladio's Rome*, 188.
41 Palladio, *Palladio's Rome.*
42 Evans, *The Projective Cast*, 109.
43 The Villa was designed for Canon Paolo Almerico, who came to Vicenza after leaving his career at the papal court. It took 40 years to complete and was finished by Scamozzi after both Palladio and the client had passed away.

44 The changes in Venice's economy concerned a shift from maritime economy to agricultural production, through vast projects of land reclamation, irrigation and canalisation as well as distribution of private and public lands among investors. Both the *Renovatio Urbis* and the agricultural investment required skills in the arts of building, hydraulic engineering, surveying and cartography in order to meet functional ends, as well as to express the fundamental continuity and values of the Republic. Ackerman, *Palladio.*

45 Palladio, *The Four Books on Architecture*, 2.3.

46 Michelle Furnari, *Formal Design in Renaissance Architecture* (New York: Rizzoli, 1995). See also: Peter Eisenman with Matt Roman, *Palladio Virtuel* (New Haven and London: Yale University Press, 2015). Eisenman and Roman explain that the villa is organised by two different strategies: the spatial layering of the interior across the major front-to-back axis and the spatial grain parallel to the cross axis. The authors also suggest that there are inconsistencies in compositional organisation in the villa and more generally in Palladio's work, such as misalignments. They conclude that attempting to provide any homogeneous reading of Palladio's work is an impossible task.

47 In 'Figures, Doors and Passages', Evans compares the interconnected matrix of rooms in classical villas with the English corridor plan and their effects in relation to social organisation. In contrast to the English corridor, which disconnected the owners from the servants, villas in Italy facilitated accidental encounters by embedding in their spatial structure the opportunity for crossed pathways potentially leading to interaction. Evans drew a direct connection between the layout of villas and paintings of the period, arguing that by joining public with private spaces, villas manifest the tenets of sensuality in the society that created them. In contrast, the English country houses set a precedent where daily pathways and routines are separate from each other. Robin Evans, *Translations from Drawing to Building and Other Essays* (Cambridge, MA: The MIT Press, 1997).

48 This was an idea that Scamozzi used in the Rocca Pisana. Camillo Semenzato, *The Rotonda* (Venice: Edizioni Gino Rosato, 2013).

49 Ackerman, *Palladio*.

50 Ackerman, *Palladio*.

51 Palladio, *The Four Books on Architecture*.

52 Carpo, *The Alphabet and the Algorithm*.

53 Jean-Nicolas-Louis Durand, *Précis Des Leçons d'Architecture Données À l'École Polytechnique* (Paris: Firmin Didot, 1805).

54 Sophia Psarra, *Architecture and Narrative: The Formation of Space and Cultural Meaning* (London and New York: Routledge, 2009).

55 Beatrice Colomina, 'The Endless Museum: Le Corbusier and Mies Van Der Rohe', *Log*, 15 (2009). See also: Antony Mulis, 'Forms and Techniques: Le Corbusier, the Spiral Plan and Diagram Architecture', *Architectural Research Quarterly*, 14, 4 (2011).

56 Le Corbusier, *Towards a New Architecture* (London: The Architectural Press, 1987).

57 With the exception of the period of the Second World War, there is no more than a three-year gap between successive projects involving the pinwheel pattern. Mulis, 'Forms and Techniques'. The projects were: Villa La Roche-Jeanneret (1923); Villa Meyer (1925); The Mundaneum (1928); Museum of Contemporary Art (1931); Bata Boutique (1935); University Campus Rio de Janeiro (1936); Centre of Contemporary Aesthetics (1936); Pavilion des Temps Nouveaux (1937); Museum of Unlimited Growth (1939); French Pavilion in San Francisco (1939); Exposition Habitat 45 (1945); Urban Development, Saint-Die (1946); Exposition Synthèse Des Arts, Porte Maillot (1949); Cultural Centre Ahmedabad (1951); Tokyo Museum (1959); Étude d'Urbanisation, Meaux (1950); Le Couvent de la Tourette (1950); Museum at Chandigarh (1959); Cultural Centre, Chad (1960); Museum of the Twentieth Century, Eisenbach (1963); Museum of the Twentieth Century, Nanterre (1965); Musée de Lotissement (undated); Venice Hospital, Venice (1965).

58 Le Corbusier, *Oeuvre Complète 1938–1946* (Basel: Birkhäuser, 1995), 16.

59 Bill Hillier, 'The Architectures of Seeing and Going. Or, Are Cities Shaped by Bodies or Minds? And Is there a Syntax of Spatial Cognition?' Proceedings of the Space Syntax Symposium IV, University College London, 2003): 06.1–06.34.

60 The pinwheel scheme finds realisation even in Le Corbusier's religious architecture, such as the raised pathways in La Tourette, and the three entrances in Ronchamp, each placed on a different side of the plan, suggesting a rotating pattern of movement.

61 Frampton, *A Genealogy of Modern Architecture*, 11.

62 Psarra, *Architecture and Narrative*; see also: Sophia Psarra, 'Self-Organisation and Theoretical Reflection: the (Im)material architecture of Venice and Venice Hospital', in *Materiality and Architecture*, ed. Sandra Karina Löschke (Abingdon; New York: Routledge, 2016), 162–181.
63 Evans, *Translations from Drawing to Building and Other Essays*.
64 Psarra, *Architecture and Narrative*.
65 Lionel March, *Architectonics of Humanism: Essays on Number in Architecture* (London: Academy Editions, 1998), ix.
66 Carpo, *The Alphabet and the Algorithm*, 33.
67 Carpo, *The Alphabet and the Algorithm*.
68 Hillier and Hanson, *The Social Logic of Space*.
69 Carpo, *The Alphabet and the Algorithm*.
70 Carpo, *The Alphabet and the Algorithm*, 39.
71 Colomina, *The Endless Museum*, 55.
72 Evans, *Translations from Drawing to Building and Other Essays*.
73 Alberti, *On the Art of Building in Ten Books*. See also: Palladio, *The Four Books on Architecture*.
74 Hillier and Hanson, *The Social Logic of Space*.
75 Bill Hillier, 'The Hidden Geometry of Deformed Grids: Or Why Space Syntax Works When It Looks as Though It Shouldn't', *Environment and Planning B: Planning and Design*, 26 (2 March 1999).
76 Hillier, 'The Hidden Geometry of Deformed Grids'.

Chapter 5: *The Venice Variations: Tracing the Architectural Imagination*

1 Proust, *In Search of Lost Time*.
2 Green spaces are also indicated on the map, as apparently Venice possesses a great number of parks, public and private gardens. These, however, are either located at the periphery of the city or cloistered into privacy by high walls.
3 G. Paolo Nadali and Renzo Vianello, eds, *Calli, Campielli e Canali: Guida di Venezia e Delle Sue Isole (A Guide to Venice and Its Islands)*, Sixth Edition (Spinea: Helvetia Editrice, 2013).
4 There are five types of street network: the first one (comb-shaped) consists of a primary quayside street running longitudinally parallel to a canal (*fondamenta*), intersecting at right angles with short alleys traversing the island in the other direction. This is the most regular geometrical network typology, primarily found in the back areas of Cannaregio. The second network typology (fishbone-shaped) comprises a primary (and sometimes a secondary) street traversing the island, either bordering a canal or through the centre of the island or both, intersecting with shorter streets. The third typology (U-shaped) consists of a street that covers a substantial part of the perimeter of an island, giving access to the inner areas through secondary alleys. The fourth type of network (pinwheel-shaped) forms a primary street (sometimes alongside a secondary) linking the centre of the island with its periphery in opposite directions. The fifth network typology (T-shaped) has two primary streets almost at right angles to each other, one covering the longitudinal and the other the lateral extension of the island. Finally, there are hybrid types of network consisting of more than one of the above typologies. Further studies could explore the taxonomy of street networks in the islands, the impact of the shape of islands on the type of network formed inside an island and the connectors with neighbouring islands.
5 Yates, *The Art of Memory*.
6 Allard, 'Bridge over Venice', 18–37.
7 Aarati Kanekar, *Architecture's Pretexts: Spaces of Translation* (Abingdon; New York: Routledge, 2015).
8 Bill Hillier and Julienne Hanson, *The Social Logic of Space* (Cambridge: Cambridge University Press, 1984).
9 Rosalind Krauss, 'Sculpture in the Expanded Field', *October*, 8 (1979).
10 In the article 'From Object to Field', Stan Allen describes 'field conditions' as bottom-up phenomena ranging from architecture, city planning and landscape, to graphic effects and natural processes, and from the flocking behaviour of birds to artistic practices and institutions. Allen, 'From Object to Field'.

11 While Krauss pursues the concept of sculpture in the expanded field, opening up original binaries between what is architecture and what is landscape, Allen endorses the opposition between objects and fields. Any potential communication between the two categories is thus inevitably suspended.

12 The earliest examples of these approaches are Bernard Tschumi's and Rem Koolhaas's entries for the Parc de la Villette competition of 1982–1983, which were conceived so as to work as instruments of unintended functional results. Caroline Constant, *Modern Architectural Landscape* (Minneapolis, MN: University of Minnesota Press, 2012). See also: Jacques Lucan, *Composition, Non-Composition: Architecture and Theory in the Nineteenth and Twentieth Centuries* (Lausanne: EPFL Press, 2012). In the past two decades, influences from biology, ecology, advanced computer technology and complexity science have found their way into architecture, metaphorically modelling the natural forces of form generation. Stan Allen, 'Landscape Infrastructures', in *Infrastructure as Architecture: Designing Composite Networks*, ed. Scott Lloyd Katrina Stoll (Berlin: Jovis, 2010). Examples of these approaches are those of Geoffrey Thun and Kathy Velikov, and Lateral Office. Scott Lloyd and Katrina Stoll, eds., *Infrastructure as Architecture: Designing Composite Networks* (Berlin: Jovis, 2010).

13 Smithson, 'How to Recognise and Read Mat-Building'.

14 Allen's article largely provides theoretical support to 'Landscape Urbanism', a sub-discipline synthesising expertise from the areas of architecture, infrastructure, urbanism, ecology, hydrology, horticulture and civil engineering. The design practices of Landscape Urbanism operate 'of necessity on a long-term horizon of implementation'. Allen Stan, 'The Future That Is Now'. http://placesjournal.org/article/the-future-that-is-now/, accessed 29 September 2014.

15 According to Peter Corning, '[e]mergence is a term in evolutionary theory describing what self-organising processes produce. It has been used by physicists to explain Bénard (convection) cells, by psychologists to explain consciousness, by economists and investment advisors to explain stock market behavior, and by organization theorists to explain informal "networks" in large companies. Indeed, a number of recent books view the evolutionary process itself as a self-organizing, emergent phenomenon.' Peter Corning, 'The Re-Emergence of Emergence: A Vulnerable Concept in Search of a Theory', *Complexity*, 7, 6 (2002): 2.

16 Jane Burry, 'Philosophy of Mathematics for Computational Design: Spatial Intuition Versus Logic', in *Computational Design Thinking*, ed. Sean Ahlquist Achim Menges (Oxford: Wiley and Sons, 2011).

17 Constant, *Modern Architectural Landscape*. See also: Lucan, *Composition, Non-Composition*.

18 Lucan, *Composition, Non-Composition*.

19 Keller Easterling, *Extrastatecraft: The Power of Infrastructure Space* (London; New York: Verso, 2014); see also: Carlo Ratti with Matthew Claudel, *Open Source Architecture* (London: Thames & Hudson, 2015).

20 Jacobs, *The Death and Life of Great American Cities*. Jonathan Hill, *Immaterial Architecture*.

21 Ratti with Claudel, *Open Source Architecture*.

22 There is a variety of terms describing evolutionary design, such as computational design, automated design, autopoiesis, genetic coding, replication and selection (in an analogy with natural evolution), morphogenetic design, generative algorithms, and parametric modelling. John Fraser, *An Evolutionary Architecture* (London: John Fraser and the Architectural Association, 1995).

23 Fraser, *An Evolutionary Architecture*, 9.

24 Fraser, *An Evolutionary Architecture*, 12.

25 Carpo, *The Alphabet and the Algorithm*.

26 Rem Koolhaas, 'Fundamentals'.

27 Rem Koolhaas, *Delirious New York* (New York: The Monacelli Press, 1994).

28 Carol Willis, *Form Follows Finance* (New York: Princeton Architectural Press, 1995).

29 Bernard Rudofsky, 'Architecture without Architects: A Short Introduction to Non-Pedigreed Architecture', ed. New York The Museum of Modern Art (Albuquerque: University of New Mexico Press, 1964); Christopher Alexander, *The Timeless Way of Building* (New York: Oxford University Press, 1979); Christopher Alexander, *Notes on the Synthesis of Form* (Cambridge: Harvard University Press, 1966).

30 Bill Hillier, 'Specifically Architectural Theory', unpublished lecture, MSc Spatial Design: Architecture, Cities, Bartlett School of Architecture, UCL, 2016. See also: Bill Hillier, 'Specifically Architectural Theory: A Partial Account of the Ascent from Building as Cultural

Transmission to Architecture as Theoretical Concretion', *Harvard Architectural Review*, 9 (1993): 8–27.

31 Mark Gelernter, *Sources of Architectural Form: A Critical History of Western Design Theory* (Manchester: Manchester University Press, 1994), 18.

32 Gelernter, *Sources of Architectural Form*, 20.

33 Gelernter, *Sources of Architectural Form*, 29.

34 Carpo, *The Alphabet and the Algorithm*.

35 Hillier, 'Specifically Architectural Theory'.

36 Tafuri, *Architecture and Utopia*.

37 Justin McGuirk, *Radical Cities: Across Latin America in Search of New Architecture* (London: Verso, 2014), 14.

38 For many designers and researchers, the activities of design and research are not separate but interact, informing one another. Designers often derive ideas from analytic understanding of existing phenomena and use examples of tested performance as evidence for their propositions. Researchers in turn explain larger phenomena through intuitive leaps described as hypotheses, much like the ways designers propose a form as a response to a design brief or programme. There are undeniably strong differences between modes of design thinking which are associative and integrative in nature and those of researchers, which are logical and analytical. The paradox in considering them as generating different kinds of knowledge, though, is in regarding the imagination as the source for design knowledge, and the empirical world as the only source of knowledge of how buildings and cities work, while they are both the source of design ideas and reasoning.

39 Various approaches have recently emerged, considering design as research with an inter-disciplinary emphasis, such as the Design PhD programme at the Bartlett School of Architecture, UCL, which serves as a model for the establishment of other similar programmes in other universities. However, the dichotomy between humanities-based design research and sciences-based analysis still compartmentalises architecture and education in many educational programmes around the world, each seen as being intrinsically different from the other.

40 Steadman, *The Evolution of Designs*, 2.

41 Steadman, *The Evolution of Designs*.

42 Umberto Eco, *Six Walks in the Fictional Woods* (Cambridge, MA; London: Harvard University Press, 1995).

43 Psarra, *Architecture and Narrative*; 'The Ghost of Conceived Space', *The Journal of Space Syntax*, 1, 17–29 (2010).

44 Sophia Psarra, 'Beyond Analytical Knowledge: The Need for a Combined Theory of Generation and Explanation', *ITU A|Z*, 11, 2 (2014).

45 More, *Utopia*. See also: Calvino, *Invisible Cities*.

46 A similar assertion was recently made by Sonit Bafna in an attempt to define the 'imaginative function' of architecture. Bafna approaches the imagination through the notion of 'imaginative seeing', defined through perception. I approach the imagination as the intersection of diverse forms of knowledge including combinatorial knowledge of possibility and not simply perceptual knowledge. Sonit Bafna, 'The Imaginative Function of Architecture: A Classification of Some Conceptual Issues', proceedings of the International Space Syntax Symposium VIII Santiago, Chile (2012). The most notable attempt to describe and enumerate possibility in built form is Phil Steadman's approach in his book *Building Types and Built Forms*. In it, Steadman provides a description of building types based on processes by which they can be derived from an archetypal building satisfying generic elements of function. Steadman, *Building Types and Built Forms*.

47 The syntax-of-a-class captures network relationships. The form-of-a-class captures relationships of visual form and visual types.

48 Koestler, *The Act of Creation*.

49 Steven Pinker, *The Sense of Style: The Thinking Person's Guide to Writing in the 21st Century* (London: Penguin Group, 2014).

50 Hillier, *Space Is the Machine*.

51 Marie-Laure Ryan, *Possible Worlds, Artificial Intelligence and Narrative Theory* (Indianapolis: Indiana University Press, 1991), 156.

52 In their study of the British Museum, Penn, Martinez and Lemlij refer to Ryan's notion of a 'tellable story', suggesting that viewers 'make active choices about where to move next which are at least in part informed by their imagination of the possibilities embodied in any particular

choice'. Alan Penn, Maximo Martinez and Maia Lemlij, 'Structure, Agency and Space in the Emergence of Organisational Culture', proceedings of International Space Syntax Symposium VI, Istanbul, 2007, 73.1–12.

53 'The next day I set out in quest of my beautiful nocturnal piazza, following *calle* after *calle* which were exactly like one another and refused to give me the smallest piece of information, except such as would lead me further astray. Sometimes a vague landmark which I seemed to recognise led me to suppose that I was about to see appear, in its seclusion, solitude and silence, the beautiful exiled piazza. At that moment, some evil genie which had assumed the form of a new *calle* made me unwittingly retrace my steps, and I found myself suddenly brought back to the Grand Canal.' Proust, V, 882–83. It is worth explaining that Proust's intuitions with the workings of memory, and the fictional nature of remembering, have been confirmed by neuroscience, revealing that memory 'is a ceaseless process, not a repository of inert information'. See: Jonah Lehrer, *Proust Was a Neuroscientist* (Boston; New York: Houghton Mifflin Company, 2007), 85.

54 Lehrer, *Proust Was a Neuroscientist*, 89.

55 Umberto Eco, *The Search for the Perfect Language*, trans. James Fentress (Oxford: Blackwell, 1995).

56 Steadman, *Building Types and Built Forms*. See also: Hillier, *Space is the Machine*.

57 Hillier explains that 'combinatoric possibility is the framework within which architectural actuality exists, and the proper form of a theory is one that describes how possibility becomes actuality'. So, although we need to 'eliminate combinatorics as a theory of architecture, we must re-admit it as meta-theory'. Hillier, *Space is the Machine*, 258.

58 Psarra, 'Beyond Analytical Knowledge'.

59 Lane, *Venice: A Maritime Republic*. See also: Edward Muir, *Civic Ritual in Renaissance Venice*.

60 Italo Calvino, *Why Read the Classics?*, trans. Martin McLaughlin (London: Jonathan Cape, 1999).

Bibliography

Ackerman, James S. *Palladio*. Harmondsworth: Penguin, 1966.

Ackroyd, Peter. *Venice: Pure City*. London: Chatto & Windus, 2009.

Alberti, Leon Battista. *On the Art of Building in Ten Books*. Translated by Joseph Rykvert, Neil Leach, Robert Tavernor. Cambridge, MA: The MIT Press, 1988.

Alexander, Christopher. *Notes on the Synthesis of Form*. Cambridge: Harvard University Press, 1966.

Alexander, Christopher. *The Timeless Way of Building*. New York: Oxford University Press, 1979.

Allard, Pablo. 'Bridge over Venice: Speculations on Cross-Fertilization of Ideas between Team 10 and Le Corbusier (after a Conversation with Guillermo Jullian De La Fuente)'. In *Le Corbusier's Venice Hospital*, 18–35. Munich; London; New York: Prestel Verlag, 2001.

Allen, Stan. 'From Object to Field'. *Architectural Design* 67 (5/6 May–June 1997): 24–32.

Allen, Stan. 'Landscape Infrastructures'. In *Infrastructure as Architecture: Designing Composite Networks*, edited by Scott Lloyd Katrina Stoll, 36–45. Berlin: Jovis, 2010.

Allen, Stan. 'The Future That Is Now'. *Places Journal* (March 2012). https://placesjournal.org/article/the-future-that-is-now/, accessed 4 September 2017.

Aureli, Pier Vittorio. *The Possibility of an Absolute Architecture*. Cambridge, MA; London: MIT Press, 2011.

Bafna, Sonit. 'The Imaginative Function of Architecture: A Classification of Some Conceptual Issues'. Proceedings of the International Space Syntax Symposium VIII Santiago, Chile, 2012.

Balletti, Caterina. 'Analytical and Quantitative Methods for the Analysis of the Geometrical Content of Historical Cartography'. *International Archives of Photogrametry and Remote Sensing* XXXIII, B5 (2000): 30–37.

Barthes, Roland. *Writing Degree Zero*. Translated by Annette Lavers, Colin Smith. London: Jonathan Cape, 1967.

Barthes, Roland. *Image, Music, Text*. Translated by Stephen Heath. London: Fontana, 1977.

Bellavitis, Giorgio, Giandomenico Romanelli. *Venezia*. Bari; Rome: Laterza, 1985.

Beltramini Guido, Davide Gasparotto, Giulio Elia Menieri. *Aldo Manuzio: Renaissance in Venice*. Edited by Gallerie Dell' Academia. Venice: Marsilio Editori, 2016.

Black, Anthony. *Guilds and Civil Society in European Political Thought from the Twelfth Century to the Present*. Ithaca, New York: Cornell University Press, 1984.

Bloch, William Goldbloom. *The Unimaginable Mathematics of Borges' Library of Babel*. Oxford: Oxford University Press, 2008.

Borges, Jorge Luis. *Fictions*. Translated by Andrew Hurley. London: Penguin, 2000, 1998.

Bouwsma, William J. *Venice and the Defence of Republican Liberty: Renaissance Values in the Age of the Counter Reformation*. Berkeley; London: University of California Press, 1984.

Breiner, Laurence A. 'Italo Calvino: The Place of the Emperor in Invisible Cities'. *Modern Fiction Studies* 34, 4 (Winter 1988): 559–73.

Brodsky, Joseph. *Watermark: An Essay on Venice*. London: Penguin, 1992.

Brotchie, Alastair, Harry Mathews, eds. *Oulipo Compendium*. London: Atlas Press, 1998.

Burckhardt, Jacob. *The Civilization of the Renaissance*. Translated by S.G. Middlemore. London: Phaedon, 1944.

Burry, Jane. 'Philosophy of Mathematics for Computational Design: Spatial Intuition Versus Logic'. In *Computational Design Thinking*, edited by Sean Ahlquist, Achim Menges. West Sussex: Wiley and Sons, 2011.

Calvino, Italo. 'Venezia: Archetypo E Utopia Della Città Aquatica.' In *Saggi*, 2688–92, 1974.

Calvino, Italo. *If on a Winter's Night a Traveller*. Translated by William Weaver. London: Everyman's Library, 1993.

Calvino, Italo. *Mr Palomar*. Translated by William Weaver. London: Minerva, 1994.

Calvino, Italo. *Saggi 1945–1985*, edited by M. Barenghi. 2 vols. Milan: Mondatori, 1995.

Calvino, Italo. *The Literature Machine*. Translated by Patrick Greagh. London: Vintage, 1997.

Calvino, Italo. *The Castle of Crossed Destinies*. Translated by William Weaver. London: Vintage, 1997.

Calvino, Italo. *Invisible Cities*. Translated by William Weaver. London: Vintage, 1997.

Calvino, Italo. *Why Read the Classics?* Translated by Martin McLaughlin. London: Jonathan Cape, 1999.

Calvino, Italo. *Six Memos for the Next Millennium*. Translated by Patrick Greagh. London: Penguin, 2002.

Calvino, Italo. *Le Città Invisibili*. Milano: Oscar Mondadori, 2010.

Carpo, Mario. 'The Making of the Typographical Architect'. In *Paper Palaces: The Rise of the Renaissance Architectural Treatise*, edited by Vaughan Hart, Peter Hicks, 158–69. New Haven; London: Yale University Press, 1998.

Carpo, Mario. *The Alphabet and the Algorithm*. Cambridge, MA: The MIT Press, 2007.

Carpo, Mario, Francesco Furlan, eds. *Leon Batista Alberti's Delineation of the City of Rome*. Arizona: Arizona State University, 2007.

Chojnacki, Stanley. 'In Search of the Venetian Patriciate: Families and Factions in the Fourteenth Century'. In *Renaissance Venice*, edited by J.R. Hale, 47–90. London: Faber and Faber, 1974.

Colomina, Beatrice. 'The Endless Museum: Le Corbusier and Mies van der Rohe'. *Log*, 15 (Winter 2009): 55–68.

Colquhoun, Alan. *Essays in Architectural Criticism: Modern Architecture and Historical Change*. London: The MIT Press, 1981.

Constant, Caroline. *Modern Architectural Landscape*. Minneapolis, MN: University of Minnesota Press, 2012.

Contarini, Gasparo Cardinal Bishop of Belluno. *The Commonwealth and Government of Venice*. Translated by Lewes Lewkenor. Imprinted by John Windet for Edmund Mattes, 1599. https://www.bl.uk/collection-items/contarinis-commonwealth-and-government-of-venice-translated-by-lewkeno, accessed 4 September 2017.

Cooper, Tracy E. *Palladio's Venice: Architecture and Society in a Renaissance Republic*. London: Yale University Press, 2005.

Corning, Peter. 'The Re-Emergence of Emergence: A Vulnerable Concept in Search of a Theory'. *Complexity* 7, 6 (2002): 18–30.

Cosgrove, Denis. 'The Myth and The Stones of Venice: An Historical Geography of a Symbolic Landscape'. *Journal of Historical Geography* 8, 2 (1982): 145–69.

Cosgrove, Denis. 'New Worlds: Culture and Cartography in Sixteenth-Century Venice'. *Imago Mundi* 44 (1992): 65–89.

Cosgrove, Denis E. *The Palladian Landscape: Geographical Change and Its Cultural Representations in Sixteenth-Century Italy*. Leicester; London: Leicester University Press, 1993.

Crouzet-Pavan, Elisabeth. 'Towards an Ecological Understanding of the Myth of Venice'. In *Venice Reconsidered: The History and Civilization of an Italian City-State, 1297–1797*, edited by John Martin, Dennis Romano, 39–64. Baltimore; London: Johns Hopkins University Press, 2000.

Crouzet-Pavan, Elisabeth. *Venice Triumphant: The Horizons of a Myth*. Translated by Lydia G. Cochrane. Baltimore; London: Johns Hopkins University Press, 2002.

Dante Alighieri. *The Divine Comedy*. Translated by James Romanes Sibbalb. Edinburgh: D. Douglas, 1984.

Deleuze, Gilles, Felix Guattari. *A Thousand Plateaus*. London: Continuum, 2004.

Desyllas, Jake. 'Domestic Asylum: A Study of Eleven Local Authority Hostels for Mentally Handicapped People'. Proceedings of the Space Syntax Symposium II, University of Brasilia, 1999.

Dickens, Charles. *Pictures from Italy*. London: Robinson, 1989, 1973.

Doxiades, Konstantinos Apostolou. *Ekistics: An Introduction to the Science of Human Settlements*. London: Hutchinson, 1968.

Durand, Jean-Nicolas-Louis. *Précis des Leçons D'architecture Données à l'École Polytechnique*. Paris: Firmin Didot, 1805, 87–93.

Easterling, Keller. *Extrastatecraft: The Power of Infrastructure Space*. London, New York: Verso, 2014.

Eaton, Ruth. *Ideal Cities: Utopianism and the (Un)Built Environment*. London: Thames & Hudson, 2002, 2001.

Eco, Umberto. *The Open Work*. Translated by Anna Cancogni. Cambridge, MA: Harvard University Press, 1989.

Eco, Umberto. *The Search for the Perfect Language*. Translated by James Fentress. Oxford: Blackwell, 1995.

Eco, Umberto. *Six Walks in the Fictional Woods*. Cambridge, MA; London: Harvard University Press, 1995.

Eisenman, Peter, Matt Roman. *Palladio Virtuel*. New Haven; London: Yale University Press, 2015.

Evans, Robin. *The Projective Cast: Architecture and Its Three Geometries*. Cambridge, MA: The MIT Press, 1995.

Evans, Robin. *Translations from Drawing to Building and Other Essays*. Cambridge, MA: The MIT Press, 1997.

Fenlon, Iain. *Piazza San Marco*. London: Profile Books, 2010.

Ferraro, Bruno. 'Italo Calvino's "Le Città Invisibil" and "La Sfida Al Labirinto"'. *The Italianist* 8, 1 (1988): 56–65.

Ferraro, Joanne Marrie. *Venice: History of the Floating City*. New York: Cambridge University Press, 2012.

Foscari Widmann Rezzonico, Giulia, Rem Koolhaas. *Elements of Venice*. Lars Müller Publishers, 2014.

Fourier, Charles, Gareth Stedman Jones, and Ian Patterson, *The Theory of the Four Movements*. Cambridge: Cambridge University Press, 1996.

Frampton, Kenneth. *A Genealogy of Modern Architecture: Comparative Analysis of Built Form*. Zurich: Lars Müller Publishers, 2015.

Fraser, John. *An Evolutionary Architecture*. London: John Fraser and the Architectural Association, 1995.

Frye, Northrop. *Anatomy of Criticism: Four Essays*. Harmondsworth: Penguin, 1990, 1957.

Furnari, Michelle. *Formal Design in Renaissance Architecture*. New York: Rizzoli, 1995.

Gelernter, Mark. *Sources of Architectural Form: A Critical History of Western Design Theory*. Manchester: Manchester University Press, 1994.

Goethe, Johann Wolfgang von. Translated by W.H. Auden, Elizabeth Mayer. *Italian Journey 1786–1788*. London: Folio Society, 2010.

Goodman, Nelson. *Languages of Art*. London: Oxford University Press, 1969.

Goy, Richard J. *Building Renaissance Venice: Patrons, Architects and Builders, c. 1430–1500*. New Haven; London: Yale University Press, 2006.

Goy, Richard J. *Venice: An Architectural Guide*. New Haven; London: Yale University Press, 2010.

Gregory, Rob. *Key Contemporary Buildings: Plans, Sections and Elevations*. London: Laurence King Publishing, 2008.

Grubb, James S. 'When Myths Lose Power: Four Decades of Venetian Historiography'. *The Journal of Modern History* 58 (1986): 43–94.

Hall, Peter. *Cities in Civilization*. London: Phoenix Giant, 1999.

Harbison, Robert. *Eccentric Spaces*. London: Secker & Warburg, 1989, 1977.

Hart, Vaughan, Peter Hicks, eds. *Paper Palaces: The Rise of the Renaissance Architectural Treatise*. New Haven; London: Yale University Press, 1998.

Hays, K. Michael, ed. *Architecture Theory since 1968*. London: The MIT Press, 1988.

Hensel, Michael, Christopher Hight, Achim Menges, eds. *Space Reader: Heterogeneous Space in Architecture*. Oxford: John Wiley, 2009.

Hill, Jonathan. *Immaterial Architecture*. London: Routledge, 2006.

Hillier, Bill. 'Quite Unlike the Pleasures of Scratching: Theory and Meaning in Architectural Form'. *9H*, 7 (1985): 66–72.

Hillier, Bill. 'Specifically Architectural Theory: A Partial Account of the Ascent from Building as Cultural Transmission to Architecture as Theoretical Concretion'. *The Harvard Architectural Review*, 9 (1993): 8–27.

Hillier, Bill. *Space is the Machine: A Configurational Theory of Architecture*. Cambridge: Cambridge University Press, 1996.

Hillier, Bill. 'Centrality as a Process: Accounting for attraction inequalities in deformed grids'. *Urban Design International*, 4, 3–4 (1999): 107–27.

Hillier, Bill. 'The Hidden Geometry of Deformed Grids: Or Why Space Syntax Works When It Looks As Though It Shouldn't'. *Environment and Planning B: Planning and Design* 26, 2 (1999).

Hillier, Bill. 'The Architectures of Seeing and Going. Or, Are Cities Shaped by Bodies or Minds? And Is there a Syntax of Spatial Cognition'. Proceedings of the Space Syntax Symposium IV, University College London (2003): 06.1–06.34.

Hillier, Bill. 'What Are Cities for? And How Does It Relate to Their Spatial Form?' *The Journal of Space Syntax* 6, 2 (2016): 199–212.

Hillier, Bill. 'Specifically Architectural Theory'. Unpublished lecture, MSc Spatial Design: Architecture, Cities, Bartlett School of Architecture, UCL, 2016.

Hillier, Bill, Julienne Hanson. *The Social Logic of Space*. Cambridge: Cambridge University Press, 1984.

Hillier, Bill, Shinichi Iida. 'Network and Psychological Effects in Urban Movement'. *Lecture Notes in Computer Science* 3693 (2005): 475–90.

Hillier, Bill, Laura Vaughan. 'The City as One Thing'. *Progress in Planning* 67, 3 (2007): 205–30.

Hillier, Bill, Tao Young, Alasdair Turner. 'Normalising Least Angle Choice in Depthmap – and How It Opens up New Perspectives on the Global and Local Analysis of City Space'. *The Journal of Space Syntax* 3, 2 (2012): 155–93.

Howard, Deborah. *Jacopo Sansovino: Architecture and Patronage in Renaissance Venice*. New Haven; London: Yale University Press, 1975.

Howard, Deborah. 'Venice as a Dolphin: Further Investigations into Jacopo de' Barbari's View'. *Artibus e Historiae* 38, 35 (1997): 101–11.

Howard, Deborah. *The Architectural History of Venice*. New Haven; London: Yale University Press, 2002.

Jacobs, Jane. *The Death and Life of Great American Cities: The Failure of Town Planning*. London: Pelican, 1965.

Koestler, Arthur. *The Act of Creation*. New York: Macmillan, 1964.

Koolhaas, Rem. *Delirious New York*. New York: The Monacelli Press, 1994.

Koolhaas, Rem. 'Fundamentals: 14th International Architecture Exhibition – La Biennale Di Venezia'. Venice: Marsilio, 2014.

Krauss, Rosalind. 'Sculpture in the Expanded Field'. *October* 8 (1979): 30–44.

Lane, Frederic C. *Venice: A Maritime Republic*. Baltimore; London: The Johns Hopkins University Press, 1973.

Latour, Bruno. 'Visualisation and Cognition: Drawing Things Together'. *Knowledge and Society: Studies in the Sociology of Culture Past and Present* 6 (1986): 1–40.

Le Corbusier. *Oeuvre Complète 1929–34*. 8 vols. Vol. 2. 1929–34. Basel: Birkhäuser, 1995.

Le Corbusier. *Oeuvre Complète 1929–34*. Vol. 3. 1934–38. Basel: Birkhäuser, 1995.

Le Corbusier. *Oeuvre Complète 1929–34*. Vol. 4. 1938–46. Basel: Birkhäuser, 1995.

Le Corbusier. *Towards a New Architecture*. London: The Architectural Press, 1987.

Le Corbusier. 'Rapport Technique'. Translated by Lucia Allais. In *Le Corbusier's Venice Hospital*, edited by Hashim Sarkis, 38–47. Munich; London; New York: Prestel Verlag, 2001.

Lefebvre, Henri. *The Production of Space*. Oxford: Blackwell, 1991.

Lucan, Jacques. *Composition, Non-Composition: Architecture and Theory in the Nineteenth and Twentieth Centuries*. Lausanne: Lausanne: EPFL Press, 2012.

Lucretius Carus, Titus. *On the Nature of Things*. Translated by Frank O. Copley. New York: W.W. Norton & Co., 2011.

Lynch, Kevin. *The Image of the City*. Cambridge, MA: The MIT Press, 1960.

McCaffery, Larry. 'Form, Formula and Fantasy: Generative Structures in Contemporary Fiction'. In *Bridges to Fantasy*, edited by Eric S. Rabkin, George E. Slusser, Robert Scholes. Carbondale: Southern Illinois University Press, 1982.

McGuirk, Justin. *Radical Cities: Across Latin America in Search of New Architecture*. London: Verso, 2014.

McLaughlin, Martin. *Italo Calvino*. Edinburgh: Edinburgh University Press, 1998.

Mackenney, Richard. *Tradesmen and Traders: The World of the Guilds in Venice and Europe c.1250 – c.1650*. New Jersey: Barnes and Noble, 1987.

Magno, Alessandro Marzo. *Bound in Venice: The Serene Republic and the Dawn of the Book*. New York: Europa Editions, 2013.

Man, John. *Xanadu: Marco Polo and Europe's Discovery of the East*. London: Transworld Publishers, 2009.

Mann, Thomas. *Death in Venice and Other Stories*. Translated by David Luke. London: Vintage, 1998.

Mancuso, Franco. *Venezia è una città: Come è esta construira e come vive*. Venezia: Corte del Fontego, 2009.

Marin, Louis. *Utopics: Spatial Play*. Translated by Robert A. Vollrath. New Jersey: Humanities Press, 1984.

Mazzariol, Giuseppe. 'Le Corbusier in Venice: His Project for a New Hospital'. *Zodiac* 16 (1966).

Modena, Letizia. *Italo Calvino's Architecture of Lightness*. Oxford; New York: Routledge, 2011.

More, Thomas. *Utopia*. Translated by Paul Turner. Harmondsworth: Penguin, 1965.

Morris, Jan. *Venice*. London: Faber and Faber, 1993.

Moudon, Anne Vernez. 'A Catholic Approach to Organizing What Urban Designers Should Know'. *Journal of Planning Literature* 6, 4 (1992): 331–49.

Moudon, Anne Vernez. 'Getting to Know the Built Landscape: Typomorphology'. In *Ordering Space: Types in Architecture and Design*, edited by K.A. Frankl, L. H. Schneecloth. New York: Van Nostrand Reinhold 1994: 289–311.

Muir, Edward. *Civic Ritual in Renaissance Venice*. Princeton: Princeton University Press, 1981.

Mulis, Antony. 'Forms and Techniques: Le Corbusier, the Spiral Plan and Diagram Architecture'. *Architectural Research Quarterly* 14, 4 (2011): 137–326.

Mumford, Eric. 'The Emergence of Mat or Field Buildings'. In *Le Corbusier's Venice Hospital*, edited by Hashim Sarkis, 48–65. Munich; London; New York: Prestel Verlag, 2001.

Mumford, Lewis. *The City in History. Its Origins, Its Transformations, and Its Prospects*. London: Secker & Warburg, 1961.

Muratori, Severio. *Studi Per Una Operante Storia Urbana Di Venezia* Rome: Instituto Poligrafico dello Stato, 1959.

Nadali, G.P., R. Vianello. *Calli, Campielli, Canali*. Venice: Helvetia Editrice, 2013.

Nietzsche, Friedrich Wilhelm. *Daybreak: Thoughts on the Prejudices of Morality*. Translated by R.J. Hollingdale, edited by Maudemarie Clark, Brian Leiter. Cambridge: Cambridge University Press, 1997.

Nietzsche, Friedrich Wilhelm. *The Birth of Tragedy*. Translated by Douglas Smith. Oxford: Oxford University Press, 2000.

Norwich, John Julius. *A History of Venice*. London; New York: Penguin, 2003.

Norwich, John Julius. *The Great Cities in History*. London: Thames & Hudson, 2016.

Ovid. *The Essential Metamorphoses*. Translated by Stanley Lombardo. Indianapolis: Hackett Pub. Co., 2011.

Palladio, Andrea. *I Quattro Libri Dell' Architettura*. Venice: Dominico de' Franceschi, 1570.

Palladio, Andrea. *Andrea Palladio: The Four Books of Architecture*. Translated by R. Tavernor, R. Schofield. Cambridge, MA: The MIT Press, 1997.

Palladio, Andrea. *Palladio's Rome: A Translation of Andrea Palladio's Two Guidebooks to Rome*. Edited and translated by Vaughan Hart, Peter Hicks. New Haven; London: Yale University Press, 2006.

Parker, Simon. *Cities, Politics and Power*. Oxford; New York: Routledge, 2011.

Perez-Gomez, Alberto, Louise Pelletier. *Architectural Representation and the Perspective Hinge*. Cambridge, MA; London: The MIT Press, 2000.

Penn, Allan, Jake Dessylas, Laura Vaughan. 'The Space of Innovation: Interaction and Communication in the Work Environment'. *Environment and Planning B: Planning and Design* 26, 2 (1999): 193–218.

Penn, Allan, Maximo Martinez, Maia Lemlij. 'Structure, Agency and Space in the Emergence of Organisational Culture'. Proceedings of International Space Syntax Symposium VI, Istanbul (2007): 073.01–16

Peponis, John. *Chorographies* [in Greek]. Athens: Alexandria Press, 1997.

Petrarch. *Letters from Petrarch*. Translated by Morris Bishop. Bloomington, IN: Indiana University Press, 1966.

Pilz, Kerstin. *Mapping Complexity: Literature and Science in the Works of Italo Calvino*. Leicester: Troubador Publishing, 2005.

Pinker, Steven. *The Sense of Style: The Thinking Person's Guide to Writing in the 21st Century*. London: Penguin Group, 2014.

Poincaré, Henri. *Science and Method*. New York: Dover Publications, 2003.

Polo, Marco. *The Travels of Marco Polo: The Venetian*, edited by Peter Harris. Translated by Colin Thubron. London: Everyman, 2008.

Psarra, Sophia. *Architecture and Narrative: The Formation of Space and Cultural Meaning*. Abingdon; New York: Routledge, 2009.

Psarra, Sophia. 'The Ghost of Conceived Space'. *The Journal of Space Syntax* 1, 1 (2010): 17–29.

Psarra, Sophia. 'Beyond Analytical Knowledge: The Need for a Combined Theory of Generation and Explanation'. *ITU A|Z* 11, 2 (2014): 47–68.

Psarra, Sophia. 'Self-Organisation and Theoretical Reflection: The (Im) material Architecture of Venice and Venice Hospital'. In *Materiality and Architecture*, edited by Sandra Karina Löschke, 162–81, Abingdon; New York: Routledge, 2016.

Puga, Diego, Daniel Trefler. 'International Trade and Institutional Change: Medieval Venice's Response to Globalisation'. *The Quarterly Journal of Economics* 129, 2 (2014): 753–821.

Pullan, Brian. *Rich and Poor in Renaissance Venice*. Cambridge, MA: Harvard University Press, 1971.

Ratti, Carlo, Matthew Claudel. *Open Source Architecture*. London: Thames & Hudson, 2015.

Romano, Dennis. *Patricians and Popolani: The Social Foundations of the Venetian Renaissance State*. Baltimore; London: Johns Hopkins University Press, 1987.

Romano, Dennis. *Housecraft and Statecraft: Domestic Service in Renaissance Venice 1400–1600*. Baltimore; London: The Johns Hopkins University Press, 1996.

Romano, Dennis, John Martin, eds. *Venice Reconsidered: The History and Civilization of an Italian City-State, 1297–1797*. Baltimore; London: Johns Hopkins University Press, 2000.

Romano, Dennis, John Martin, eds. 'Reconsidering Venice'. In *Venice Reconsidered: The History and Civilisation of an Italian City-State 1297–1797*. Baltimore: The Johns Hopkins University Press, 2000.

Rosand, Ellen. *Opera in Seventeenth-Century Venice: The Creation of a Genre*. Berkeley; Oxford: University of California Press, 1991.

Rowe, Colin. *The Mathematics of the Ideal Villa, and Other Essays*. Cambridge, MA; London: The MIT Press, 1976.

Rowland, Ingrid D. 'Vitruvius in Print and in Vernacular Translation: Fra Giocondo, Bramante, Raphael and Cesare Cesariano'. In *Paper Palaces: The Rise of the Renaissance Architectural Treatise*, edited by Vaughan Hart, Peter Hicks, 105–21. New Haven; London: Yale Architectural Press, 1998.

Rowland, Ingrid D., Thomas Noble Howe, eds. *Vitruvius: The Ten Books on Architecture*. Cambridge: Cambridge University Press, 1999.

Rudofsky, Bernard. 'Architecture without Architects: A Short Introduction to Non-Pedigreed Architecture'. New York: The Museum of Modern Art; Albuquerque: University of New Mexico Press, 1964.

Ryan, Marie-Laure. *Possible Worlds, Artificial Intelligence and Narrative Theory*. Indianapolis: Indiana University Press, 1991.

Sansovino, Francesco. *Venetia Citta Nobilissima Et Singolare Descritta in Xiiii Libri*. Vol. 13, Venice: Appresso Steffano Curti, 1581.

Sanudo, Marin. *I Nei Diarii Di Marin Sanudo*. Translated by Biancamaria Scarcia Amoretti. Roma: Istituto per l'Oriente, 1979.

Sarkis, Hashim. *Le Corbusier's Venice Hospital and the Mat Building Revival*. Munich; London; New York: Prestel, 2001.

Satkowski, Leon, Colin Rowe. *Italian Architecture of the 16th Century*. New York: Princeton Architectural Press, 2002.

Savoy, Daniel. 'Palladio and the Water-Oriented Scenography of Venice'. *Journal of the Society of Architectural Historians* 71 (2 June 2012): 203–25.

Schultz, Juergen. 'The Printed Plans and Panoramic Views of Venice (1486–1797)'. In *Saggi e Memorie Di Storia Dell'arte*. Florence: Leo S. Olschki Editore, 1970.

Schultz, Juergen. 'Jacopo de' Barbari's View of Venice: Map Making, City Views and Moralised Geography before the Year 1500'. *The Art Bulletin* 60 (3 September 1978): 425–74.

Semenzato, Camillo. *The Rotonda*. Venezia: Edizioni Gino Rosato, 2013.

Sennett, Richard. *Flesh & Stone: The Body and the City in Western Civilization*. London: Penguin, 2002.

Sennett, Richard. *Building and Dwelling: Ethics for the City*. Milton Keynes: Penguin Random House, 2018.

Serlio, Sebastiano. *Regole Generali Di Architettura Sopra Le Cinque Maniere De Gli Edifici [Being the Fourth Book of the Architecture of S. Serlio]*. Venice, 1537.

Serlio, Sebastiano. *Tutte L'opere D'Architettura E Prospettiva*. Venice, 1611.

Shah, Mahnaz. *Le Corbusier's Venice Hospital Project: An Investigation into Its Structural Formulation*. Farnham; Burlington: Ashgate Publishing Company, 2013.

Shaykh, Hanan. *One Thousand and One Nights*. London: Bloomsbury, 2013.

Shiau, Raymond, Carlo H. Séquin. 'Rendering Issues in Pacioli's Rhombicuboctahedron'. 2015. Technical Report UCB/EECS-2015–169, 24 June. https://www2.eecs.berkeley.edu/Pubs/TechRpts/2015/EECS-2015–169.pdf, accessed 4 September 2017.

Smithson, Alison. 'How to Recognise and Read Mat-Building: Mainstream Architecture as It Has Developed Towards the Mat-Building'. *Architectural Design* (September 1974): 573–90.

Spencer, Douglas. *The Architecture of Neoliberalism: How Contemporary Architecture Became an Instrument of Control and Compliance*. London: Bloomsbury, 2016.

Steadman, Philip. *The Evolution of Designs: Biological Analogy in Architecture and the Applied Arts*. Revised ed. London; New York: Routledge, 2008.

Steadman, Philip. *Building Types and Built Forms*. Leicester: Matador, 2014.

Stoll, Katrina, Scott Lloyd, eds. *Infrastructure as Architecture: Designing Composite Networks*. Berlin: Jovis Verlag, 2010.

Stoppani, Teresa. *Paradigm Islands: Manhattan and Venice: Discourses on Architecture and the City*. Abingdon; New York: Routledge, 2010.

Tafuri, Manfredo. *Architecture and Utopia: Design and Capitalist Development*. Translated by Barbara Luigia La Penta. Cambridge, MA; London: The MIT Press, 1976.

Tafuri, Manfredo. *Venice and the Renaissance*. Translated by Jessica Levine. Cambridge, MA: The MIT Press, 1995.

Tanner, Tony. *Venice Desired*. Oxford: Blackwell, 1992.

Tavernor, Robert. 'Introduction'. In *Andrea Palladio: The Four Books of Architecture*, vii–xiv. Translated by Robert Tavernor, Richard Schofield. Cambridge, MA: The MIT Press, 2002.

Thoenes, Christof. 'Introduction'. In *Architectural Theory*, edited by Bernd Evers, Christof Thoenes. Cologne: Taschen, 2003.

Thucydides. *History of the Peloponnesian War*. Translated by Richard Crowley. Dover Books on History, Political and Social Science. Y. Mineola, NY: Dover Publications, 2004.

Till, Jeremy. *Architecture Depends*. Cambridge, MA; London: The MIT Press, 2009.

Vidler, Anthony. *The Scenes of the Street and Other Essays*. New York: Monacelli, 2011.

Welch, Evelyn S. *Shopping in the Renaissance: Consumer Cultures in Italy 1400–1600*. New Haven; London: Yale University Press, 2005.

Weston, Richard. *Key Buildings of the 20th Century: Plans, Sections & Elevations*. London: Laurence King Publishing, 2004.

Willis, Carol. *Form Follows Finance*. New York: Princeton Architectural Press, 1995.

Wilson, Bronwen. *The World of Venice: Print, the City and Early Modern Identity*. Toronto: University of Toronto Press, 2005.

Wittkower, Rudolf. *Architectural Principles in the Age of Humanism*. London: Warburg Institute, 1949.

Wittkower, Rudolf. 'S. Maria Della Salute'. *Saggi e Memorie di Storia dell'Arte* 3 (1963): 33–54, 147–70.

Yates, Frances A. *The Art of Memory*. London: Pimlico, 2001.

Yule, Henry, Henri Cordier. *The Travels of Marco Polo: The Complete Yule-Cordier Edition*. 2 vols. New York: Dover, 1993.

Zimmerman, Joan. 'The City as Practice: Urban Topography, Pictorial Construction and Liminality in Venetian Renaissance Painting, 1495–1595.' PhD Thesis, The University of Texas at Austin, 1999.

Zimring, Saif Haq. 'Just Down the Road a Piece: The Development of Topological Knowledge of Building Layouts'. Proceedings of the International Space Syntax Symposium III, Georgia Institute of Technology, Atlanta, 2001.

Index

Page references to figures are shown in *italics*.

www.ingramcontent.com/pod-product-compliance
Lightning Source LLC
LaVergne TN
LVHW052016300826
846742LV00020B/73
9781787352407